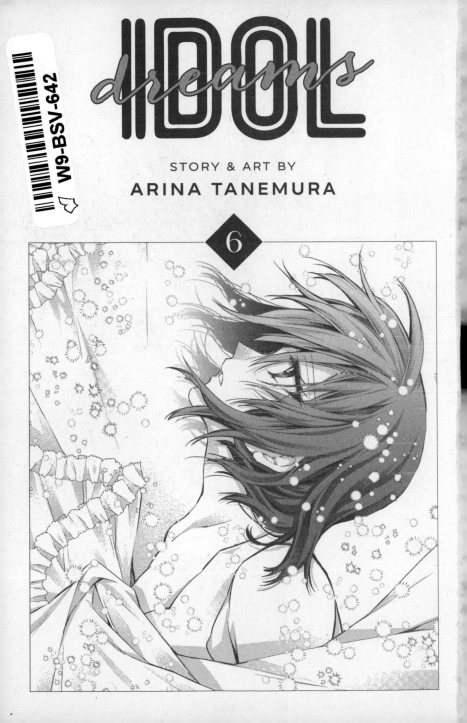

IDOL dreams

STORY & ART BY

ARINA TANEMURA

6

IDOL *dreams* ◆ 6

CONTENTS

Chapter 26

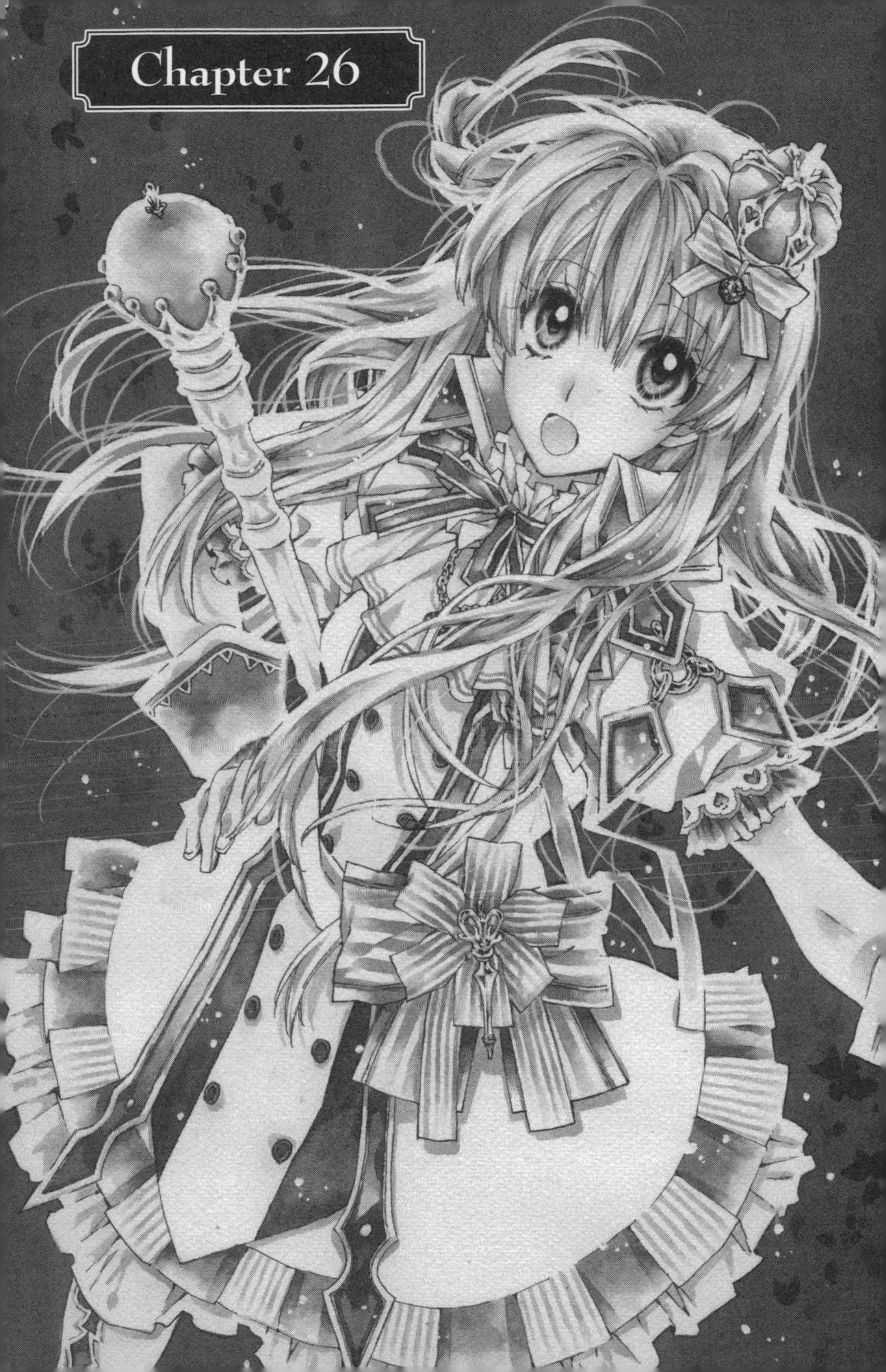

IDOL *dreams*

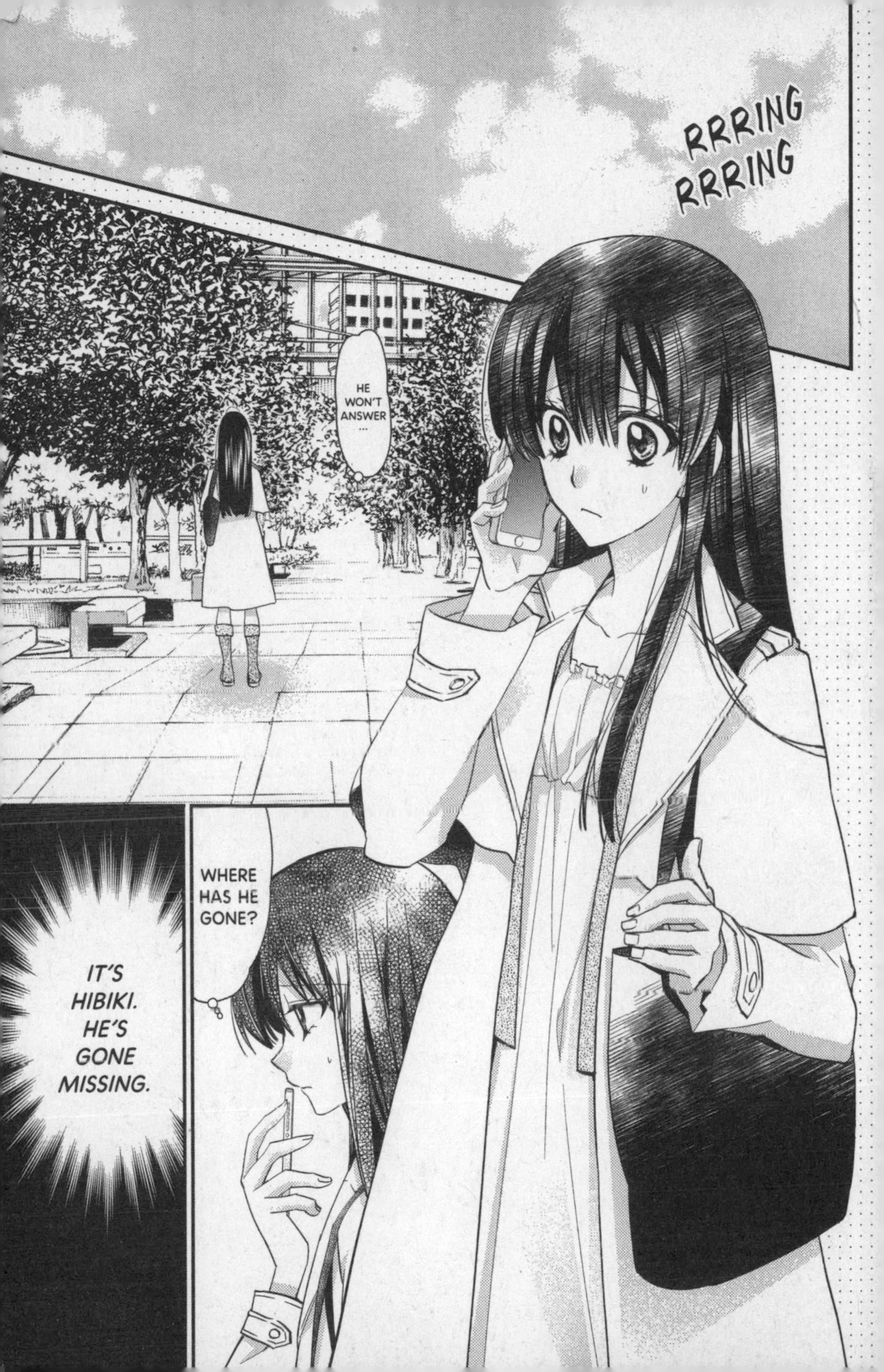
RRRING RRRING
HE WON'T ANSWER ...
WHERE HAS HE GONE?
IT'S HIBIKI. HE'S GONE MISSING.

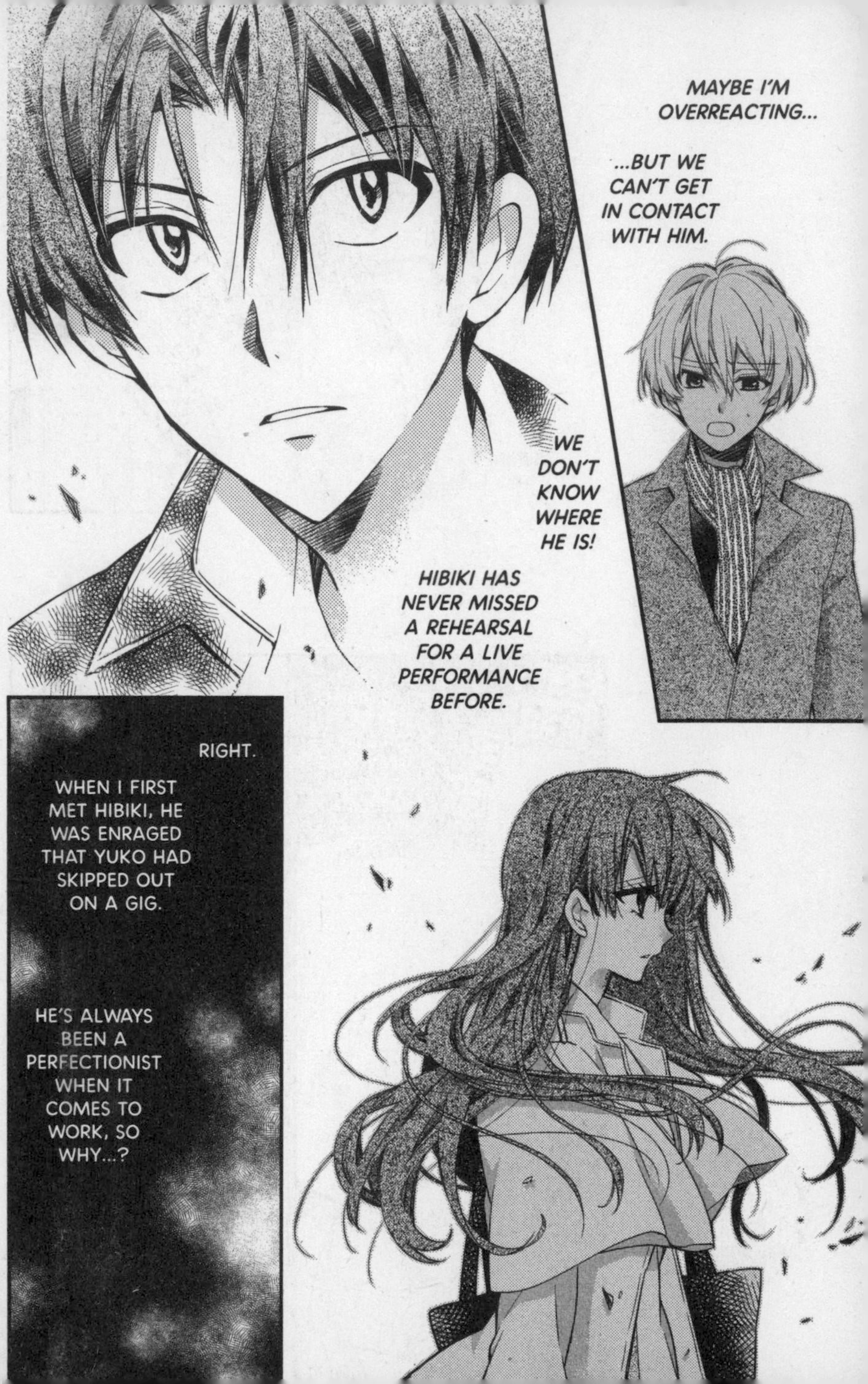
MAYBE I'M OVERREACTING...
...BUT WE CAN'T GET IN CONTACT WITH HIM.
WE DON'T KNOW WHERE HE IS!
HIBIKI HAS NEVER MISSED A REHEARSAL FOR A LIVE PERFORMANCE BEFORE.
RIGHT.
WHEN I FIRST MET HIBIKI, HE WAS ENRAGED THAT YUKO HAD SKIPPED OUT ON A GIG.
HE'S ALWAYS BEEN A PERFECTIONIST WHEN IT COMES TO WORK, SO WHY...?

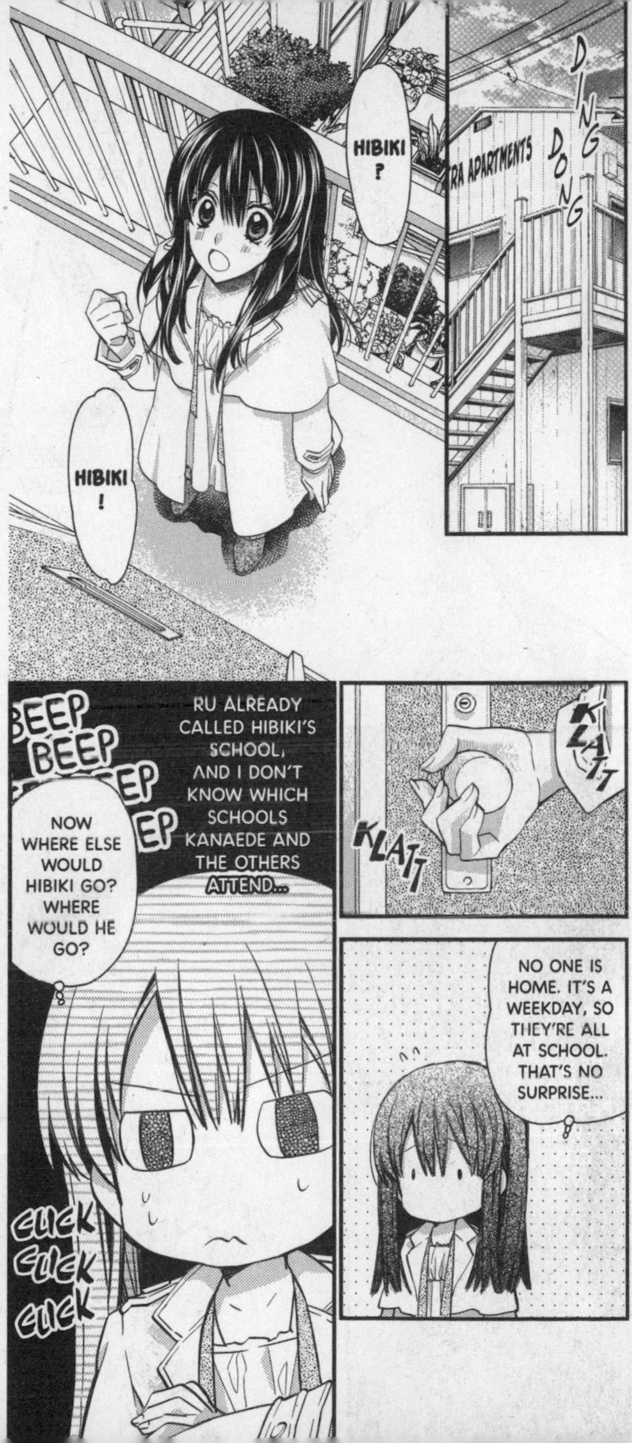
RA APARTMENTS
DING
DONG
HIBIKI?
HIBIKI!
KLATT
KLATT
NO ONE IS HOME. IT'S A WEEKDAY, SO THEY'RE ALL AT SCHOOL. THAT'S NO SURPRISE...
RU ALREADY CALLED HIBIKI'S SCHOOL, AND I DON'T KNOW WHICH SCHOOLS KANAEDE AND THE OTHERS ATTEND...
BEEP
BEEP
NOW WHERE ELSE WOULD HIBIKI GO? WHERE WOULD HE GO?
CLICK
CLICK
CLICK

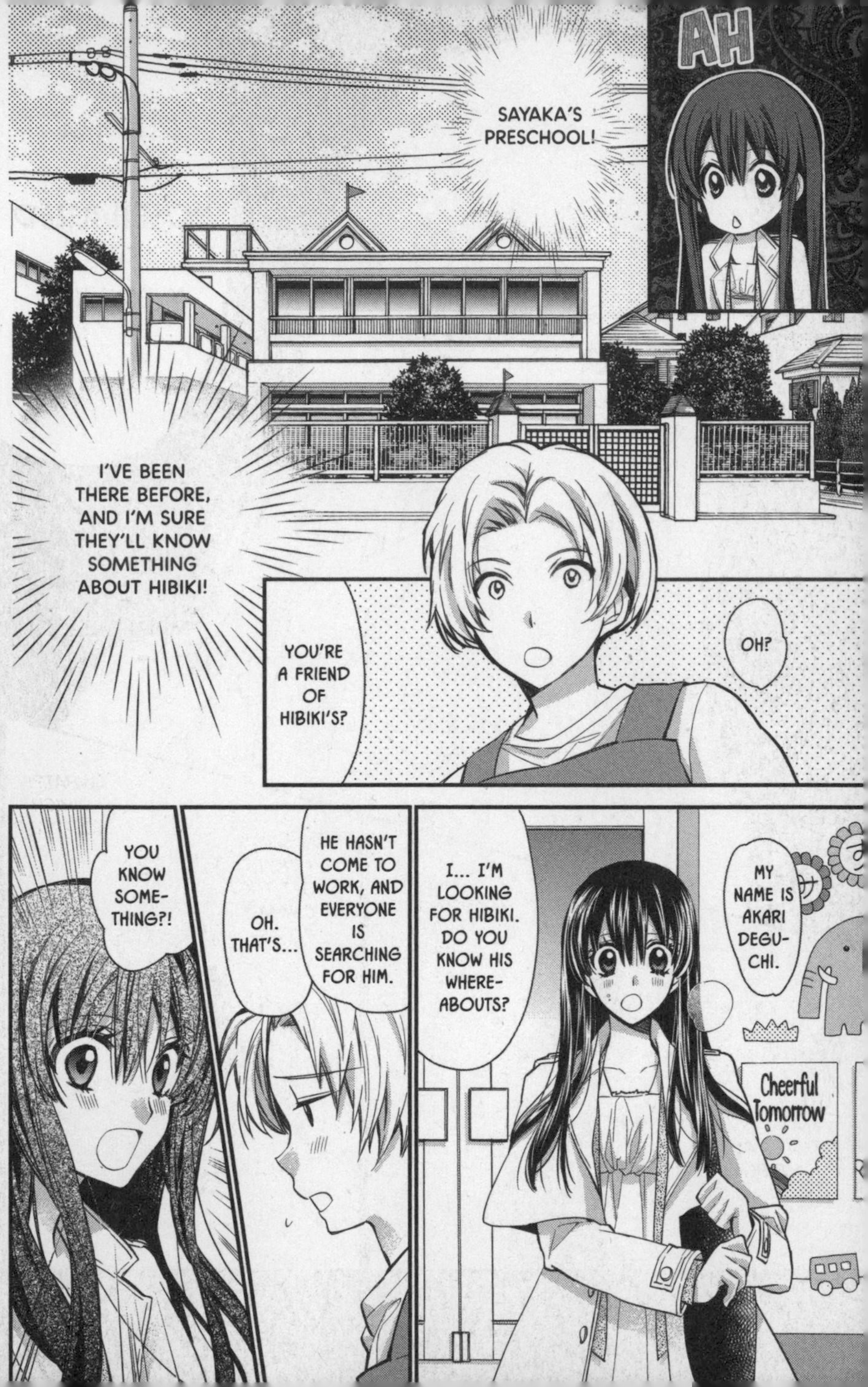
AH
SAYAKA'S PRESCHOOL!
I'VE BEEN THERE BEFORE, AND I'M SURE THEY'LL KNOW SOMETHING ABOUT HIBIKI!
OH?
YOU'RE A FRIEND OF HIBIKI'S?
MY NAME IS AKARI DEGUCHI.
Cheerful Tomorrow
I... I'M LOOKING FOR HIBIKI. DO YOU KNOW HIS WHEREABOUTS?
HE HASN'T COME TO WORK, AND EVERYONE IS SEARCHING FOR HIM.
OH. THAT'S...
YOU KNOW SOMETHING?!

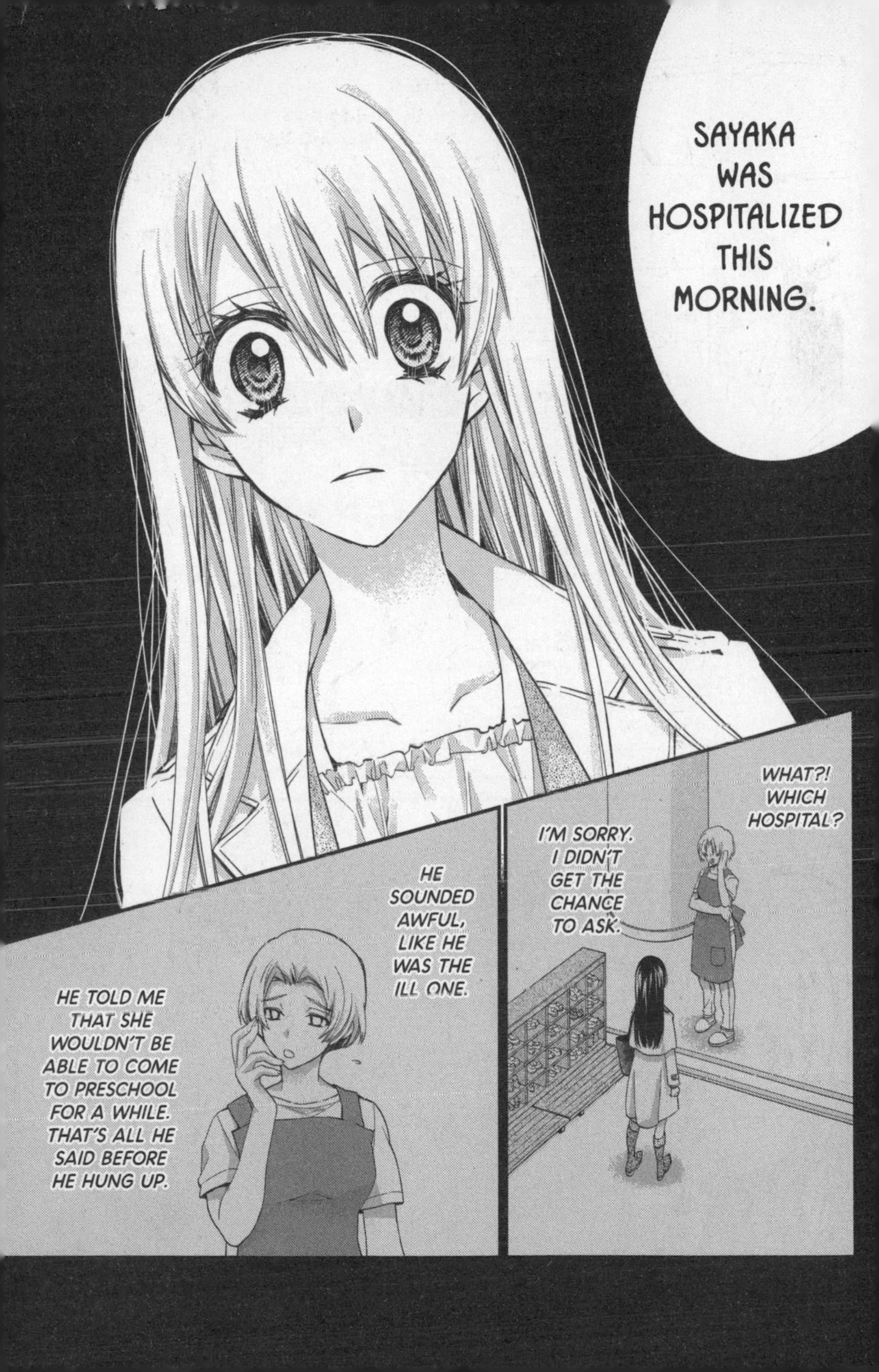
SAYAKA WAS HOSPITALIZED THIS MORNING.
WHAT?! WHICH HOSPITAL?
I'M SORRY. I DIDN'T GET THE CHANCE TO ASK.
HE SOUNDED AWFUL, LIKE HE WAS THE ILL ONE.
HE TOLD ME THAT SHE WOULDN'T BE ABLE TO COME TO PRESCHOOL FOR A WHILE. THAT'S ALL HE SAID BEFORE HE HUNG UP.

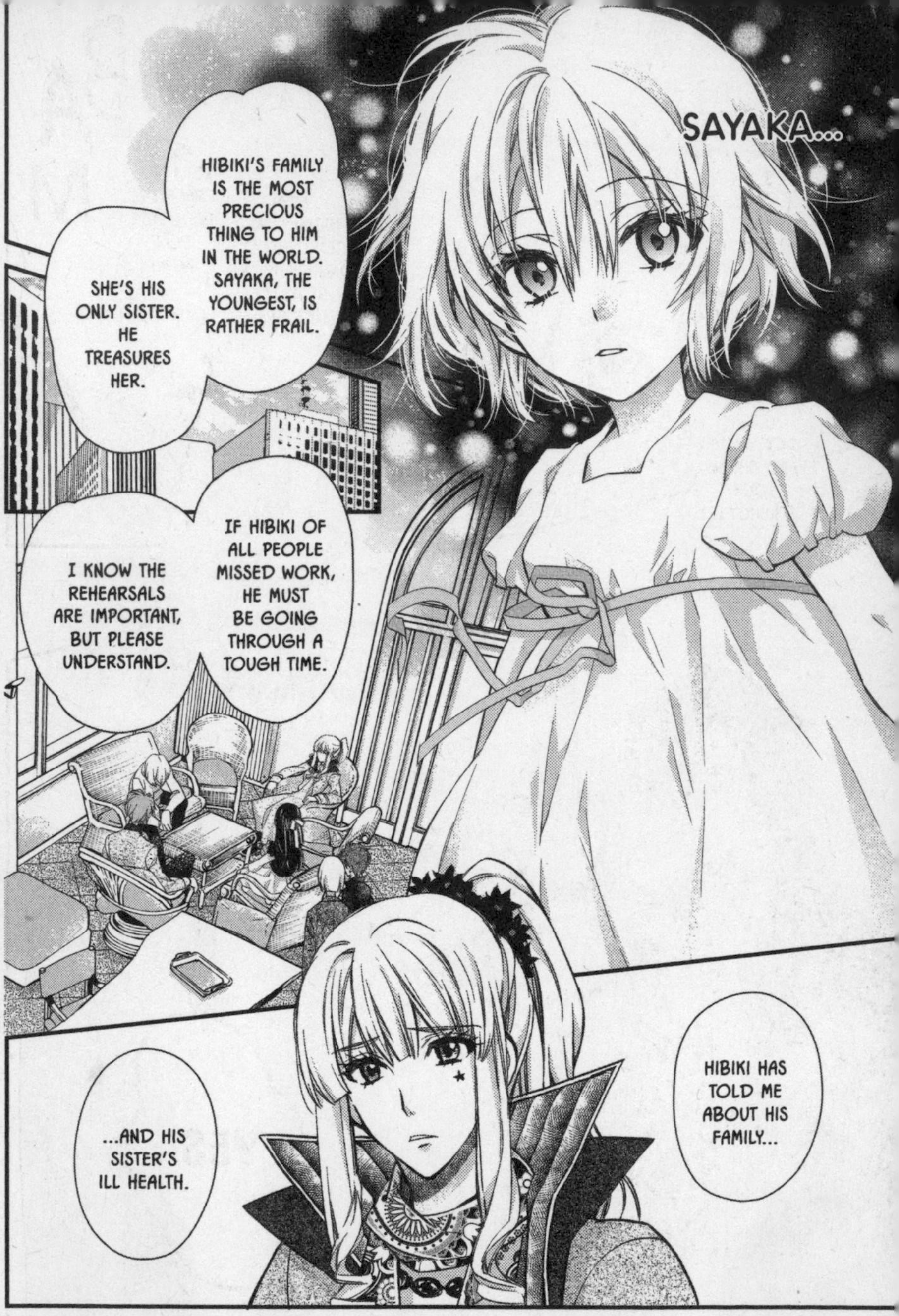
SAYAKA...
HIBIKI'S FAMILY IS THE MOST PRECIOUS THING TO HIM IN THE WORLD. SAYAKA, THE YOUNGEST, IS RATHER FRAIL.
SHE'S HIS ONLY SISTER. HE TREASURES HER.
IF HIBIKI OF ALL PEOPLE MISSED WORK, HE MUST BE GOING THROUGH A TOUGH TIME.
I KNOW THE REHEARSALS ARE IMPORTANT, BUT PLEASE UNDERSTAND.
HIBIKI HAS TOLD ME ABOUT HIS FAMILY...
...AND HIS SISTER'S ILL HEALTH.

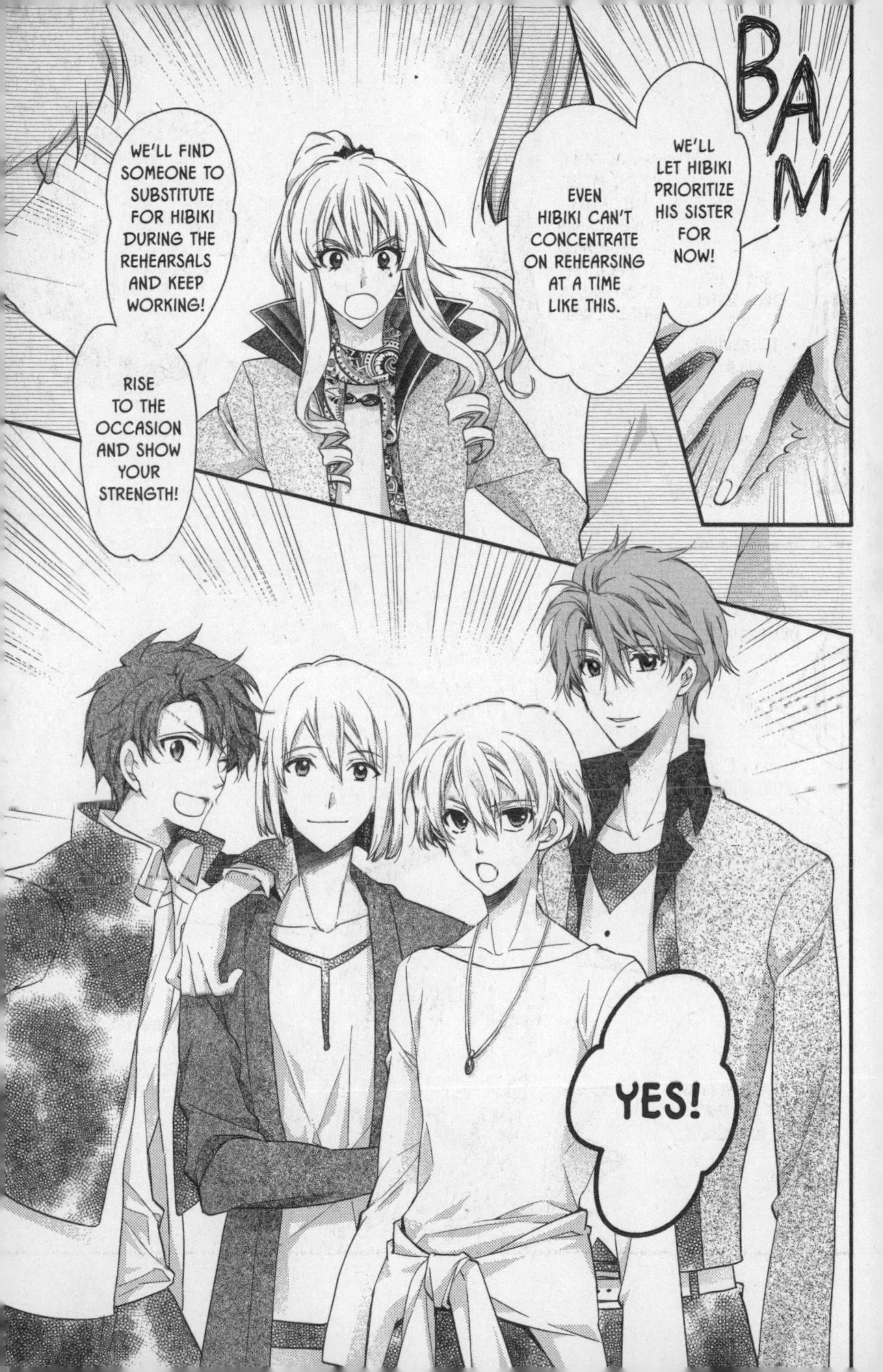
BAM
WE'LL LET HIBIKI PRIORITIZE HIS SISTER FOR NOW!
EVEN HIBIKI CAN'T CONCENTRATE ON REHEARSING AT A TIME LIKE THIS.
WE'LL FIND SOMEONE TO SUBSTITUTE FOR HIBIKI DURING THE REHEARSALS AND KEEP WORKING!
RISE TO THE OCCASION AND SHOW YOUR STRENGTH!
YES!

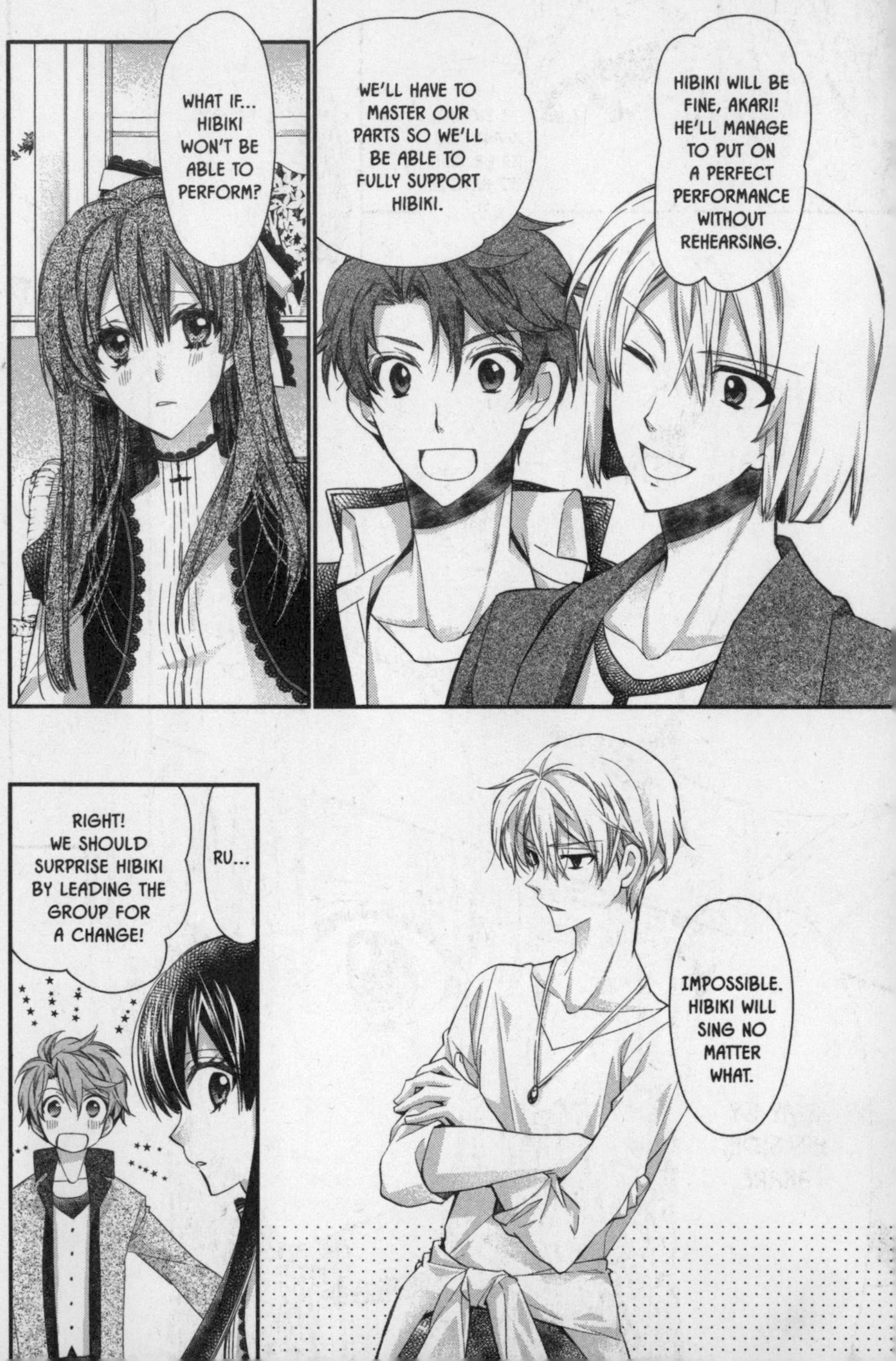
HIBIKI WILL BE FINE, AKARI! HE'LL MANAGE TO PUT ON A PERFECT PERFORMANCE WITHOUT REHEARSING.
WE'LL HAVE TO MASTER OUR PARTS SO WE'LL BE ABLE TO FULLY SUPPORT HIBIKI.
WHAT IF... HIBIKI WON'T BE ABLE TO PERFORM?
IMPOSSIBLE. HIBIKI WILL SING NO MATTER WHAT.
RU...
RIGHT! WE SHOULD SURPRISE HIBIKI BY LEADING THE GROUP FOR A CHANGE!

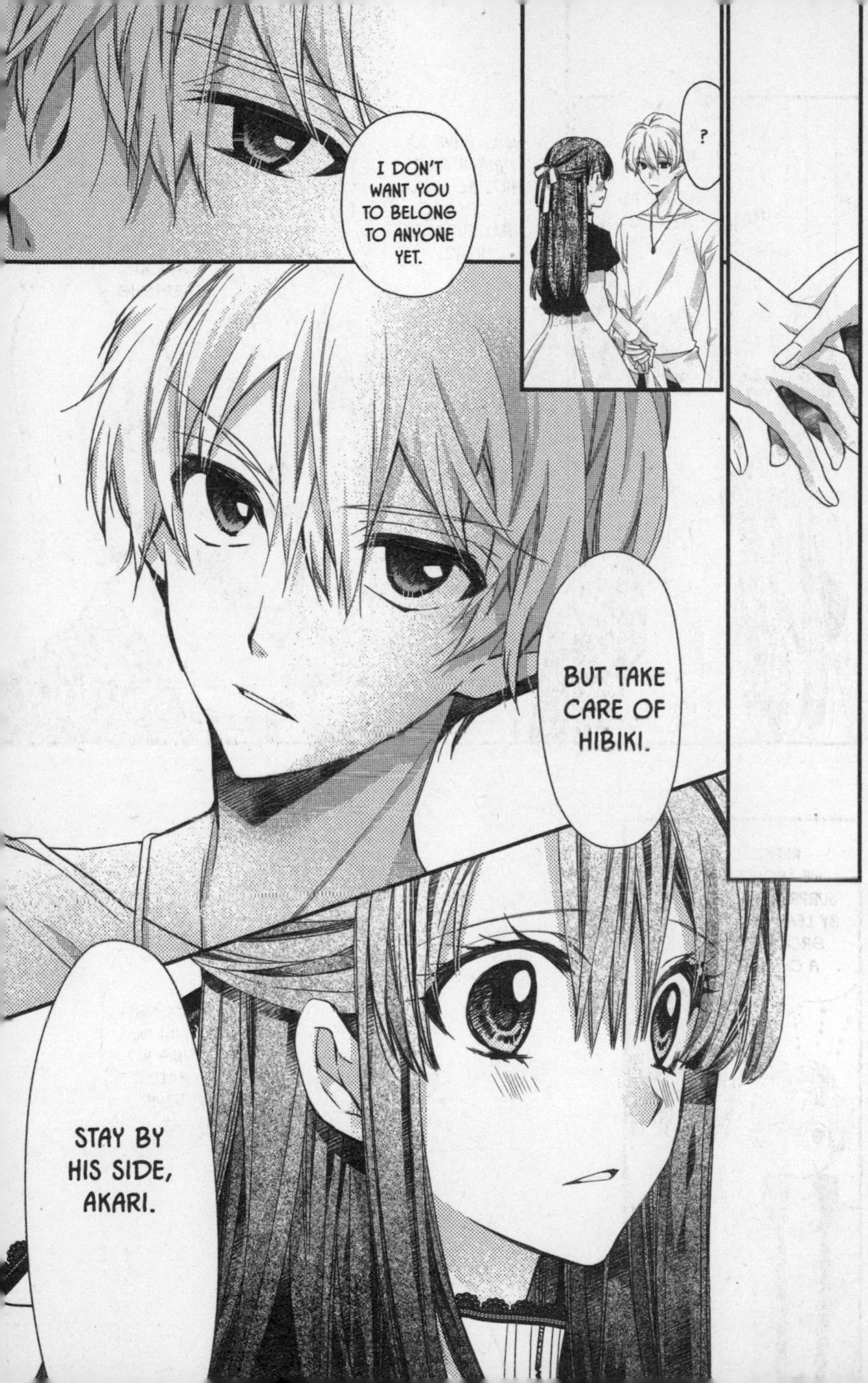
?
I DON'T WANT YOU TO BELONG TO ANYONE YET.
BUT TAKE CARE OF HIBIKI.
STAY BY HIS SIDE, AKARI.

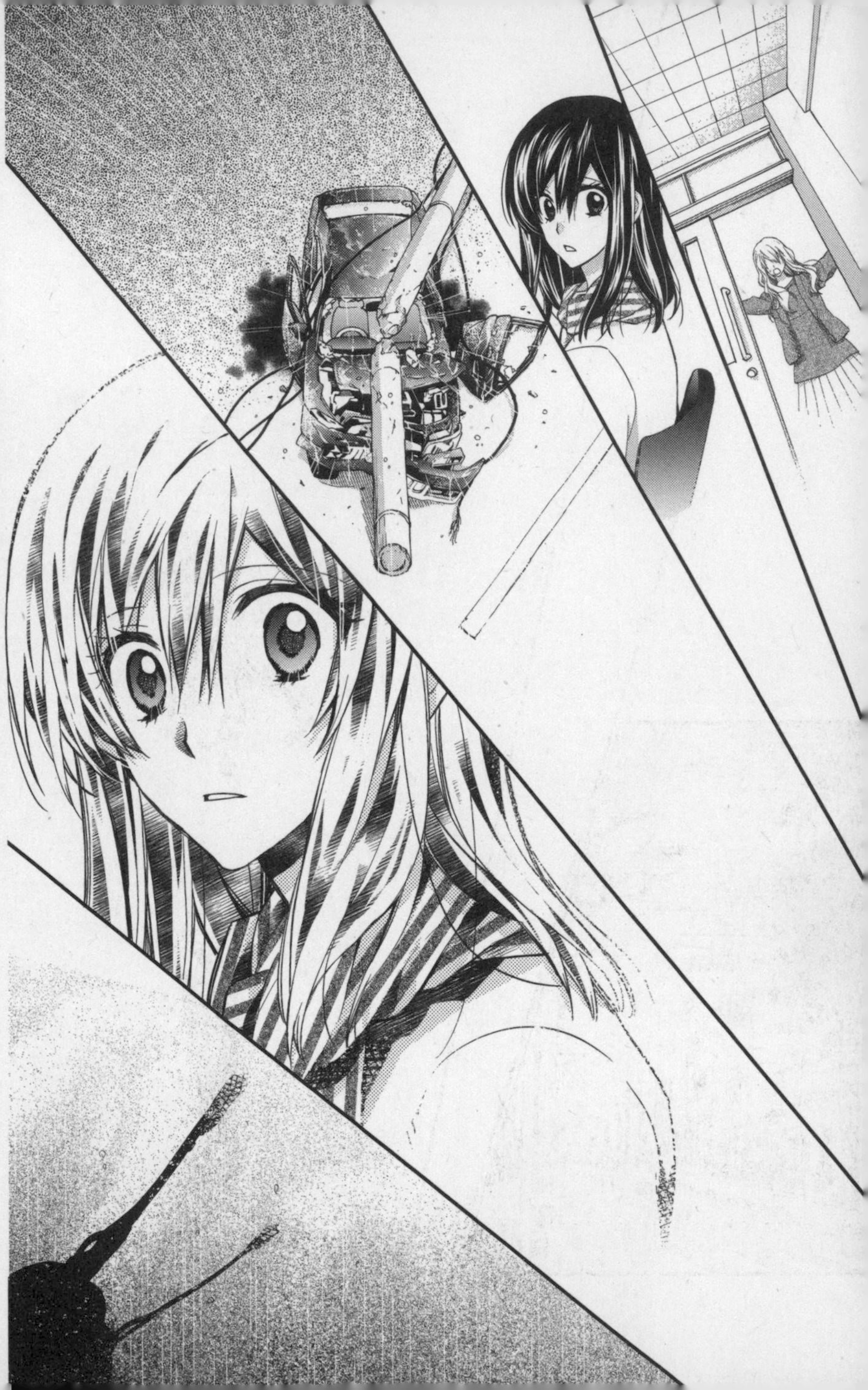

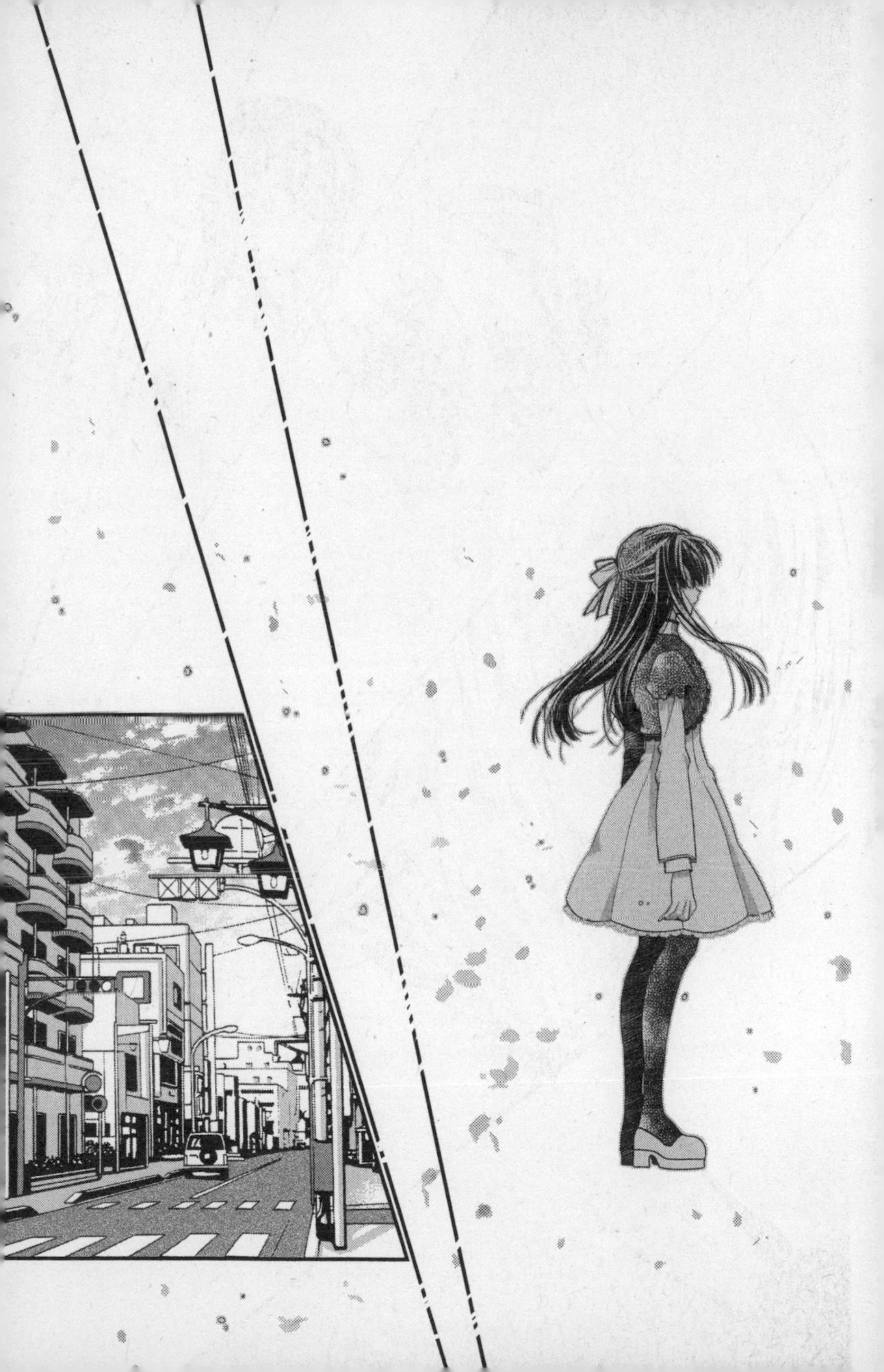

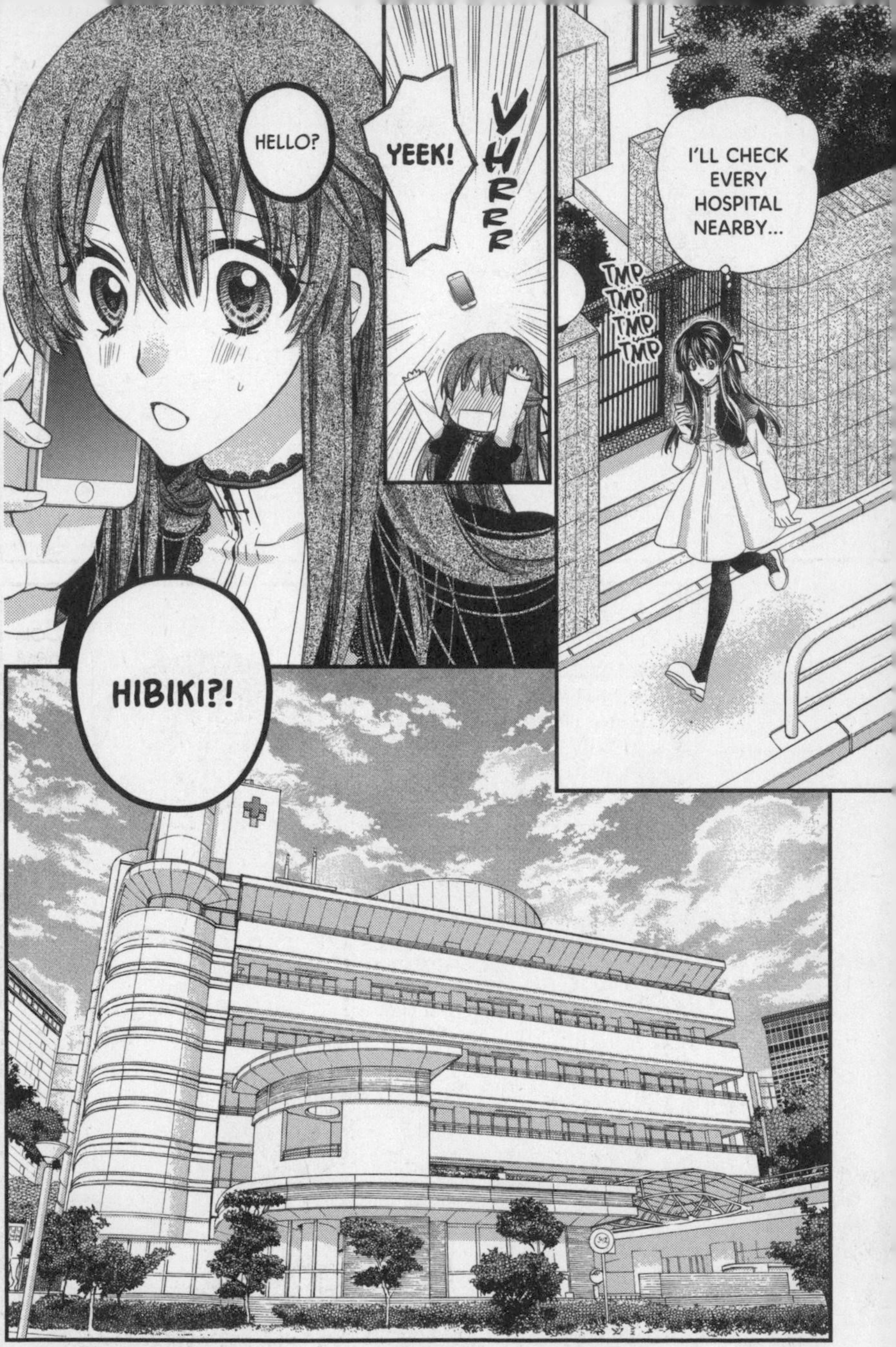
I'LL CHECK EVERY HOSPITAL NEARBY...
TMP TMP TMP TMP
VHRRR
YEEK!
HELLO?
HIBIKI?!

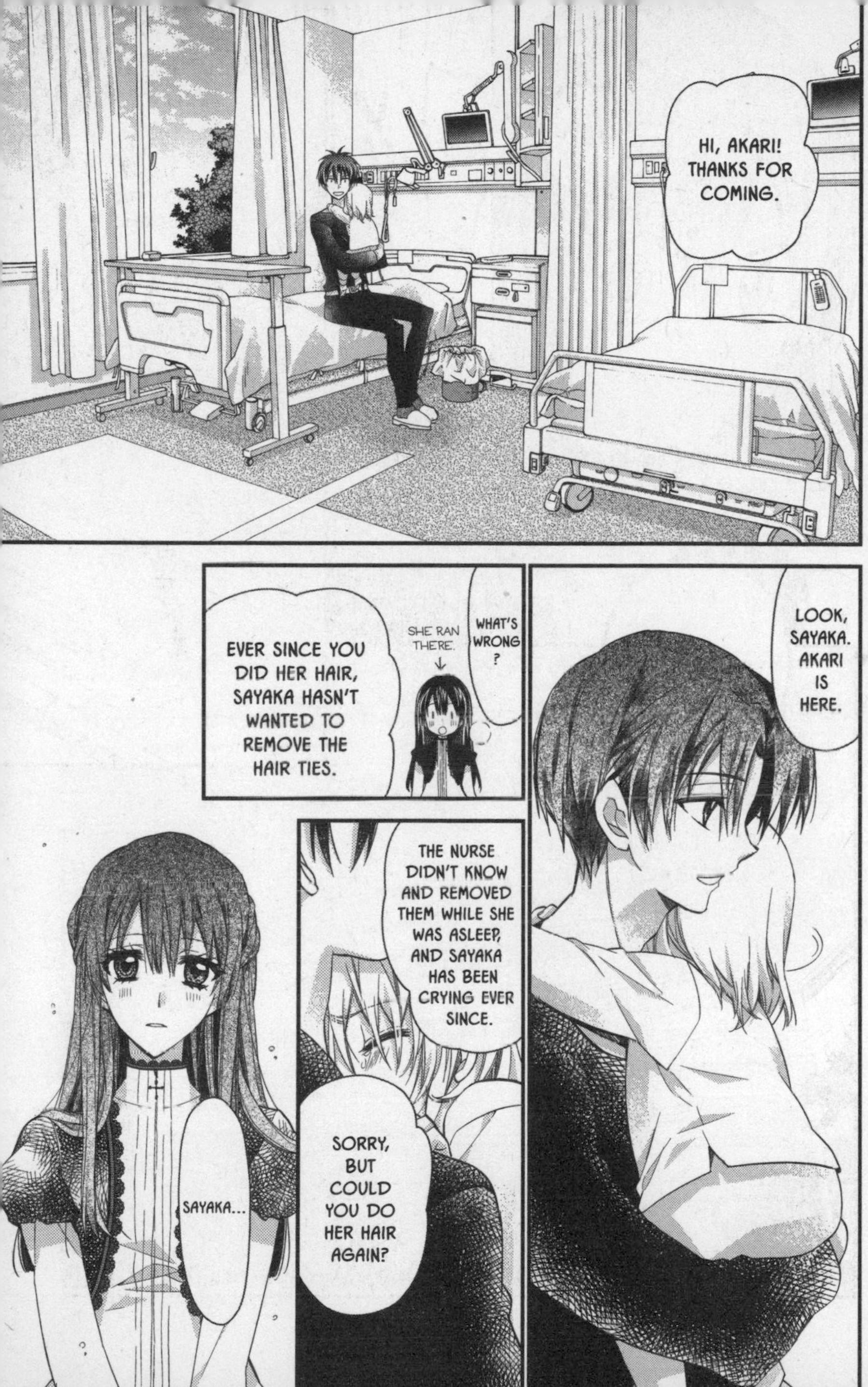
HI, AKARI! THANKS FOR COMING.
LOOK, SAYAKA. AKARI IS HERE.
WHAT'S WRONG?
SHE RAN THERE.
EVER SINCE YOU DID HER HAIR, SAYAKA HASN'T WANTED TO REMOVE THE HAIR TIES.
THE NURSE DIDN'T KNOW AND REMOVED THEM WHILE SHE WAS ASLEEP, AND SAYAKA HAS BEEN CRYING EVER SINCE.
SORRY, BUT COULD YOU DO HER HAIR AGAIN?
SAYAKA...

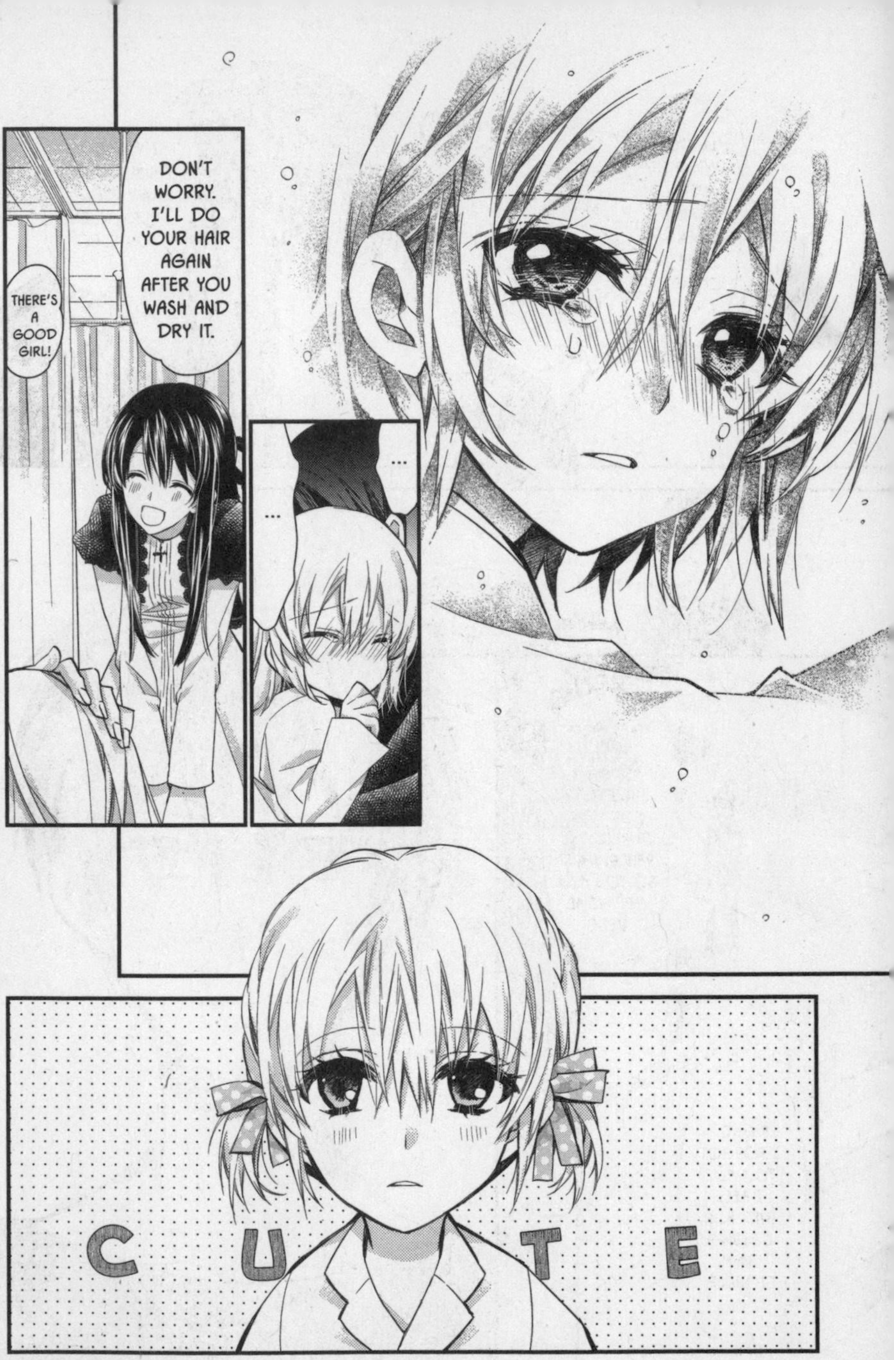
...
...
DON'T WORRY. I'LL DO YOUR HAIR AGAIN AFTER YOU WASH AND DRY IT.
THERE'S A GOOD GIRL!
CUTE

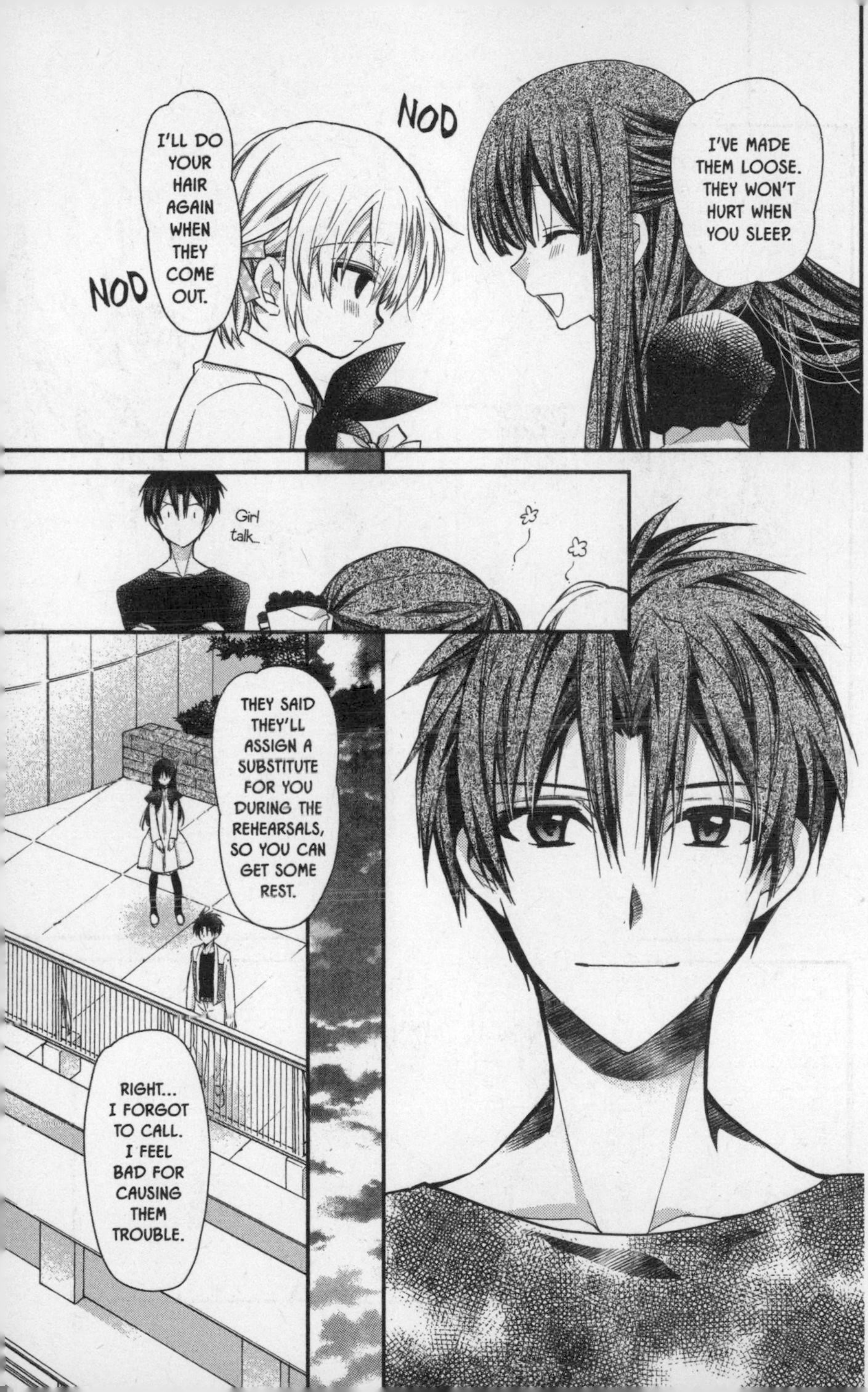
I'VE MADE THEM LOOSE. THEY WON'T HURT WHEN YOU SLEEP.
NOD
I'LL DO YOUR HAIR AGAIN WHEN THEY COME OUT.
NOD
Girl talk...
THEY SAID THEY'LL ASSIGN A SUBSTITUTE FOR YOU DURING THE REHEARSALS, SO YOU CAN GET SOME REST.
RIGHT... I FORGOT TO CALL. I FEEL BAD FOR CAUSING THEM TROUBLE.

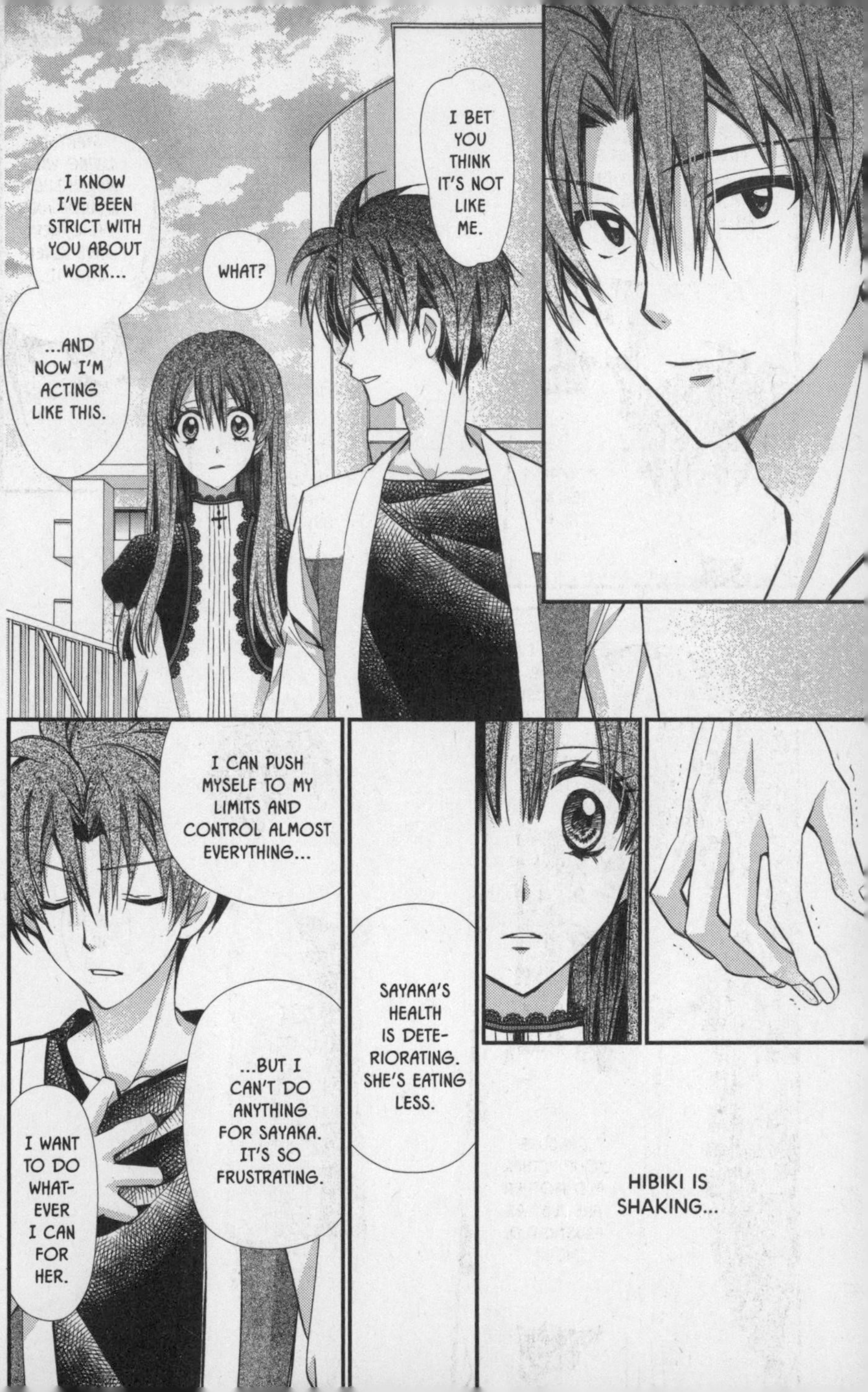
I BET YOU THINK IT'S NOT LIKE ME.
WHAT?
I KNOW I'VE BEEN STRICT WITH YOU ABOUT WORK...
...AND NOW I'M ACTING LIKE THIS.
HIBIKI IS SHAKING...
SAYAKA'S HEALTH IS DETE-RIORATING. SHE'S EATING LESS.
I CAN PUSH MYSELF TO MY LIMITS AND CONTROL ALMOST EVERYTHING...
...BUT I CAN'T DO ANYTHING FOR SAYAKA. IT'S SO FRUSTRATING.
I WANT TO DO WHAT-EVER I CAN FOR HER.

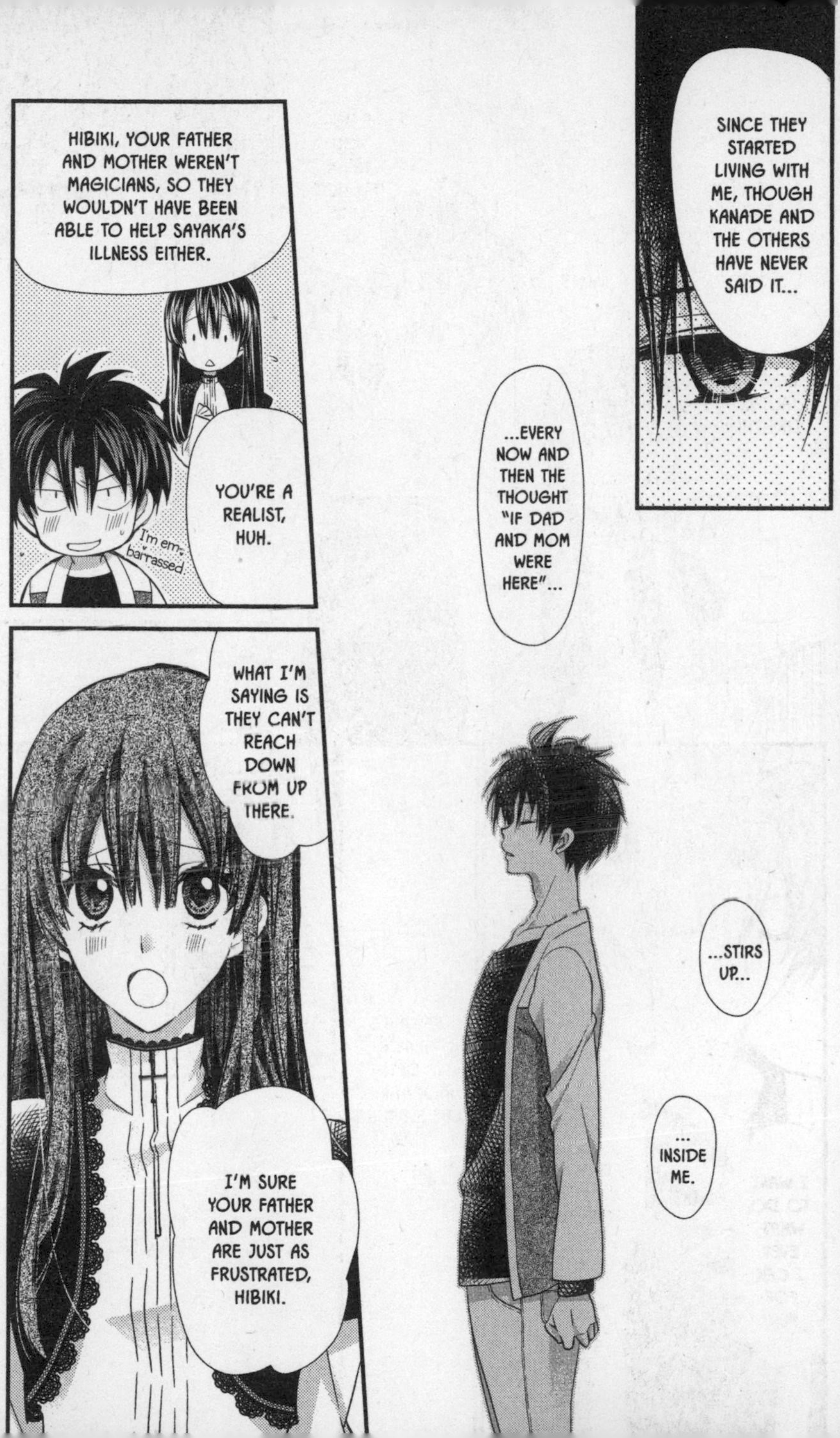
SINCE THEY STARTED LIVING WITH ME, THOUGH KANADE AND THE OTHERS HAVE NEVER SAID IT...
...EVERY NOW AND THEN THE THOUGHT "IF DAD AND MOM WERE HERE"...
...STIRS UP...
...INSIDE ME.
HIBIKI, YOUR FATHER AND MOTHER WEREN'T MAGICIANS, SO THEY WOULDN'T HAVE BEEN ABLE TO HELP SAYAKA'S ILLNESS EITHER.
YOU'RE A REALIST, HUH.
I'm embarrassed.
WHAT I'M SAYING IS THEY CAN'T REACH DOWN FROM UP THERE.
I'M SURE YOUR FATHER AND MOTHER ARE JUST AS FRUSTRATED, HIBIKI.

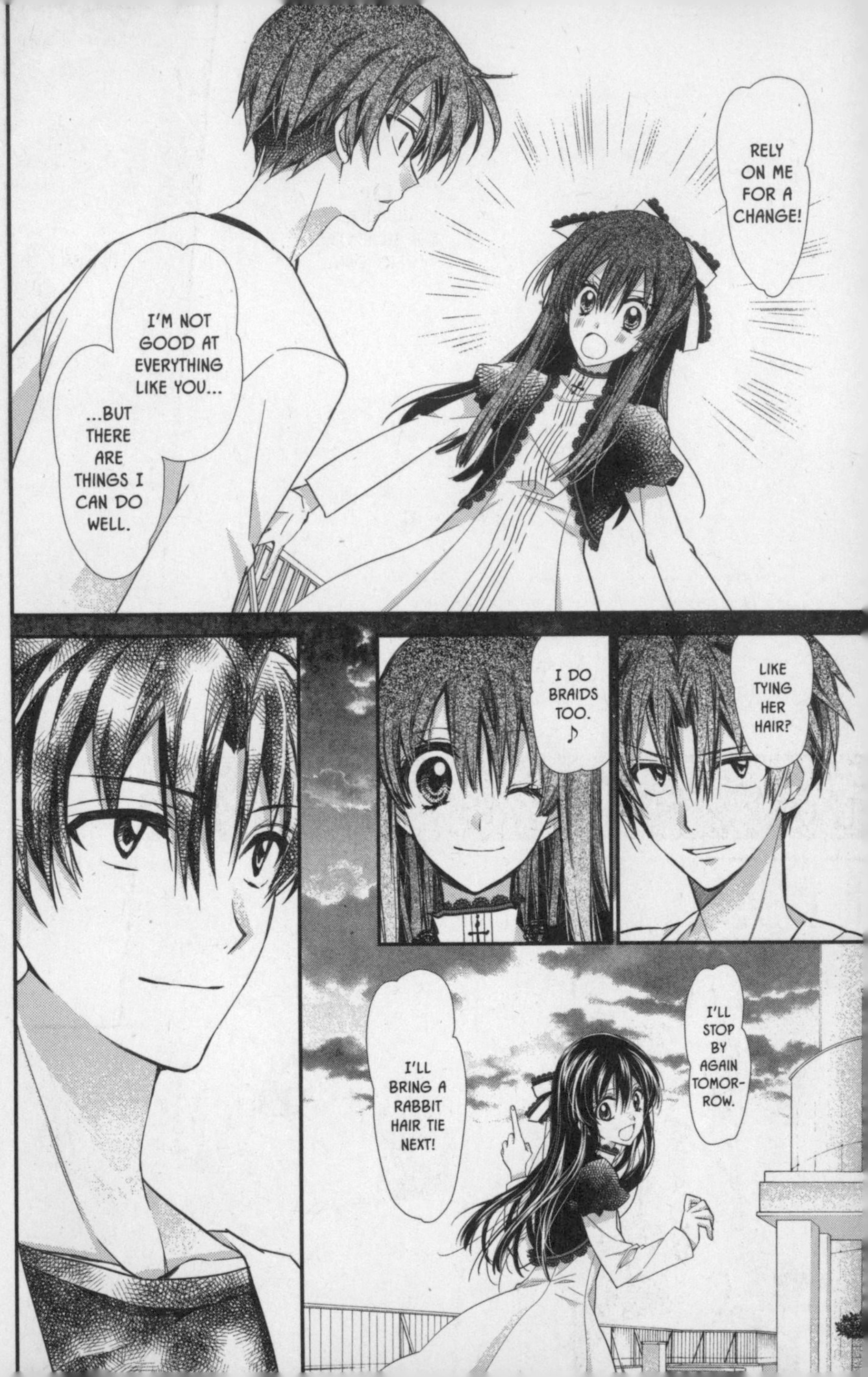
RELY ON ME FOR A CHANGE!
I'M NOT GOOD AT EVERYTHING LIKE YOU...
...BUT THERE ARE THINGS I CAN DO WELL.
LIKE TYING HER HAIR?
I DO BRAIDS TOO. ♪
I'LL STOP BY AGAIN TOMOR-ROW.
I'LL BRING A RABBIT HAIR TIE NEXT!

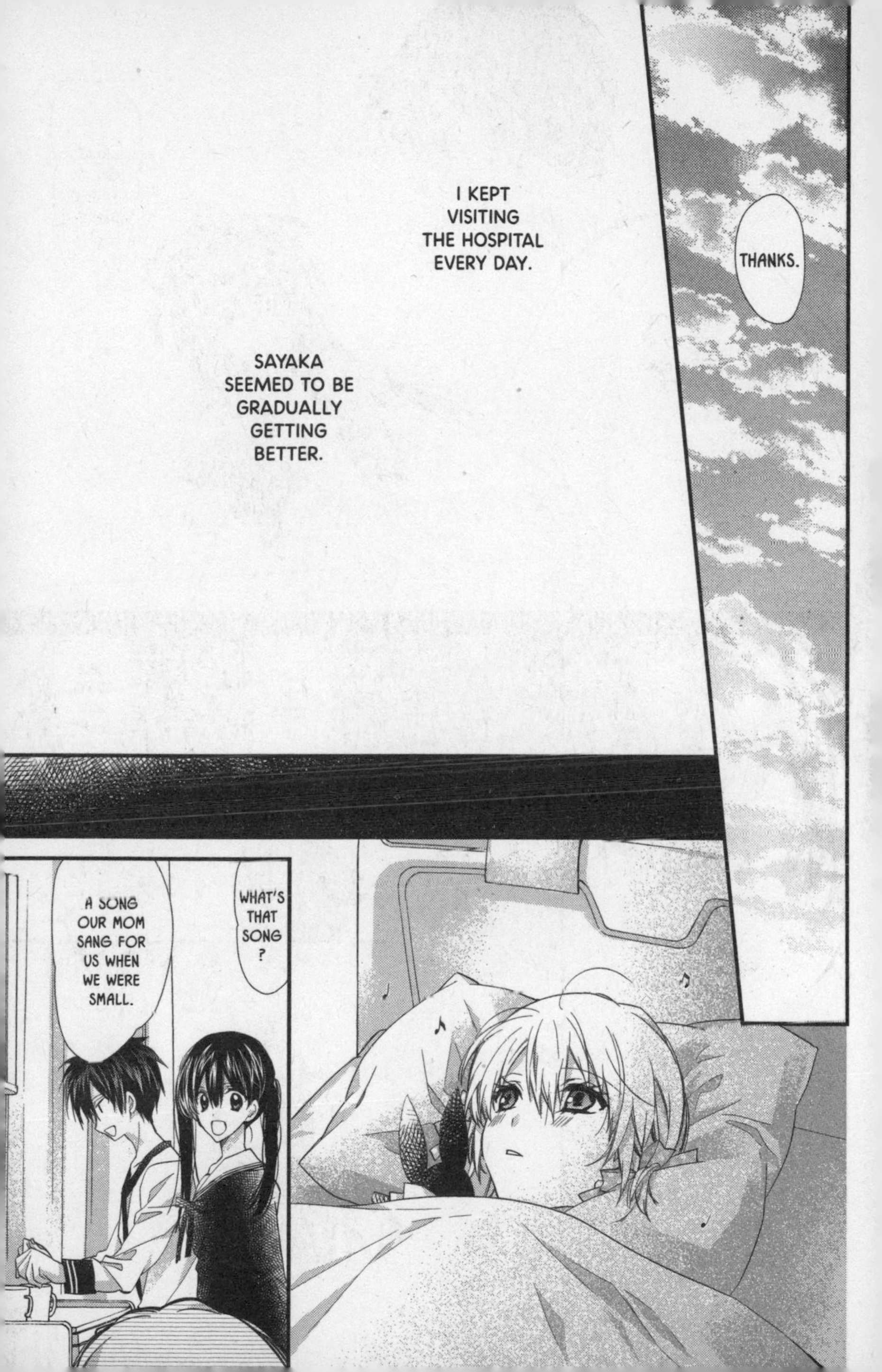
THANKS.
I KEPT VISITING THE HOSPITAL EVERY DAY.
SAYAKA SEEMED TO BE GRADUALLY GETTING BETTER.
WHAT'S THAT SONG?
A SONG OUR MOM SANG FOR US WHEN WE WERE SMALL.

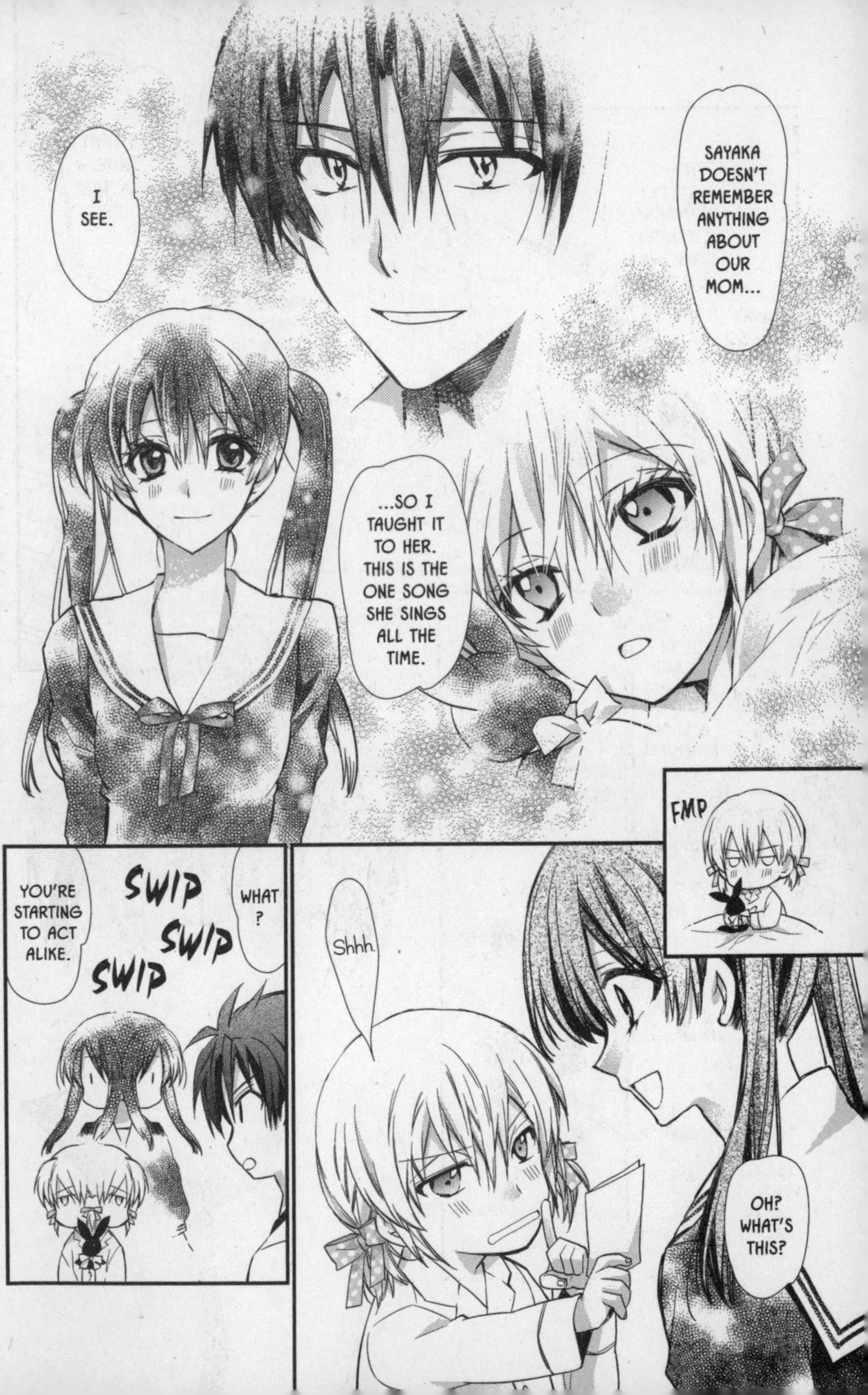
SAYAKA DOESN'T REMEMBER ANYTHING ABOUT OUR MOM...
...SO I TAUGHT IT TO HER. THIS IS THE ONE SONG SHE SINGS ALL THE TIME.
I SEE.
FMP
OH? WHAT'S THIS?
Shhh.
WHAT?
SWIP
SWIP
SWIP
YOU'RE STARTING TO ACT ALIKE.

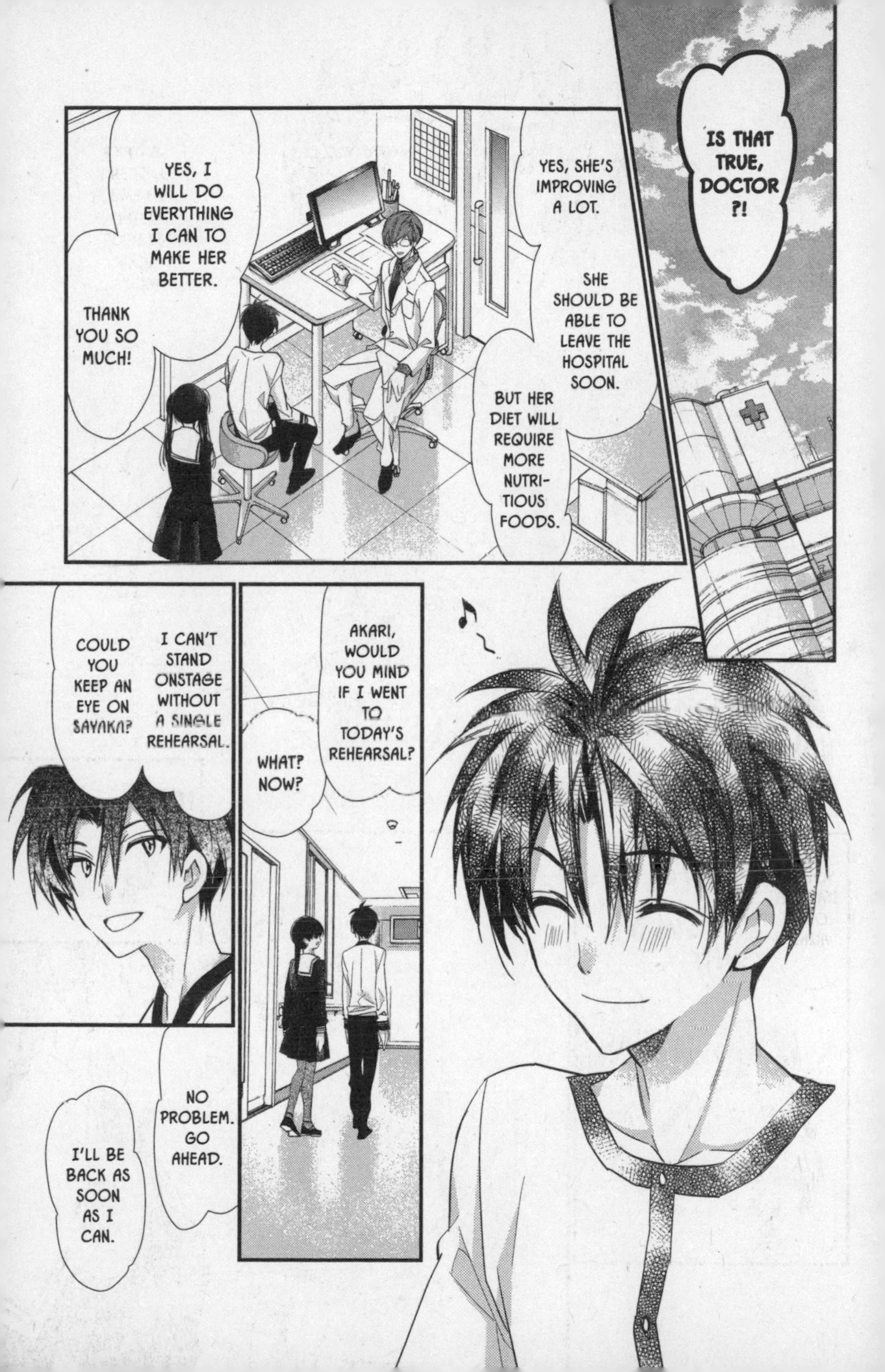
IS THAT TRUE, DOCTOR?!
YES, SHE'S IMPROVING A LOT.
SHE SHOULD BE ABLE TO LEAVE THE HOSPITAL SOON.
BUT HER DIET WILL REQUIRE MORE NUTRITIOUS FOODS.
YES, I WILL DO EVERYTHING I CAN TO MAKE HER BETTER.
THANK YOU SO MUCH!
AKARI, WOULD YOU MIND IF I WENT TO TODAY'S REHEARSAL?
WHAT? NOW?
I CAN'T STAND ONSTAGE WITHOUT A SINGLE REHEARSAL.
COULD YOU KEEP AN EYE ON SAYAKA?
NO PROBLEM. GO AHEAD.
I'LL BE BACK AS SOON AS I CAN.

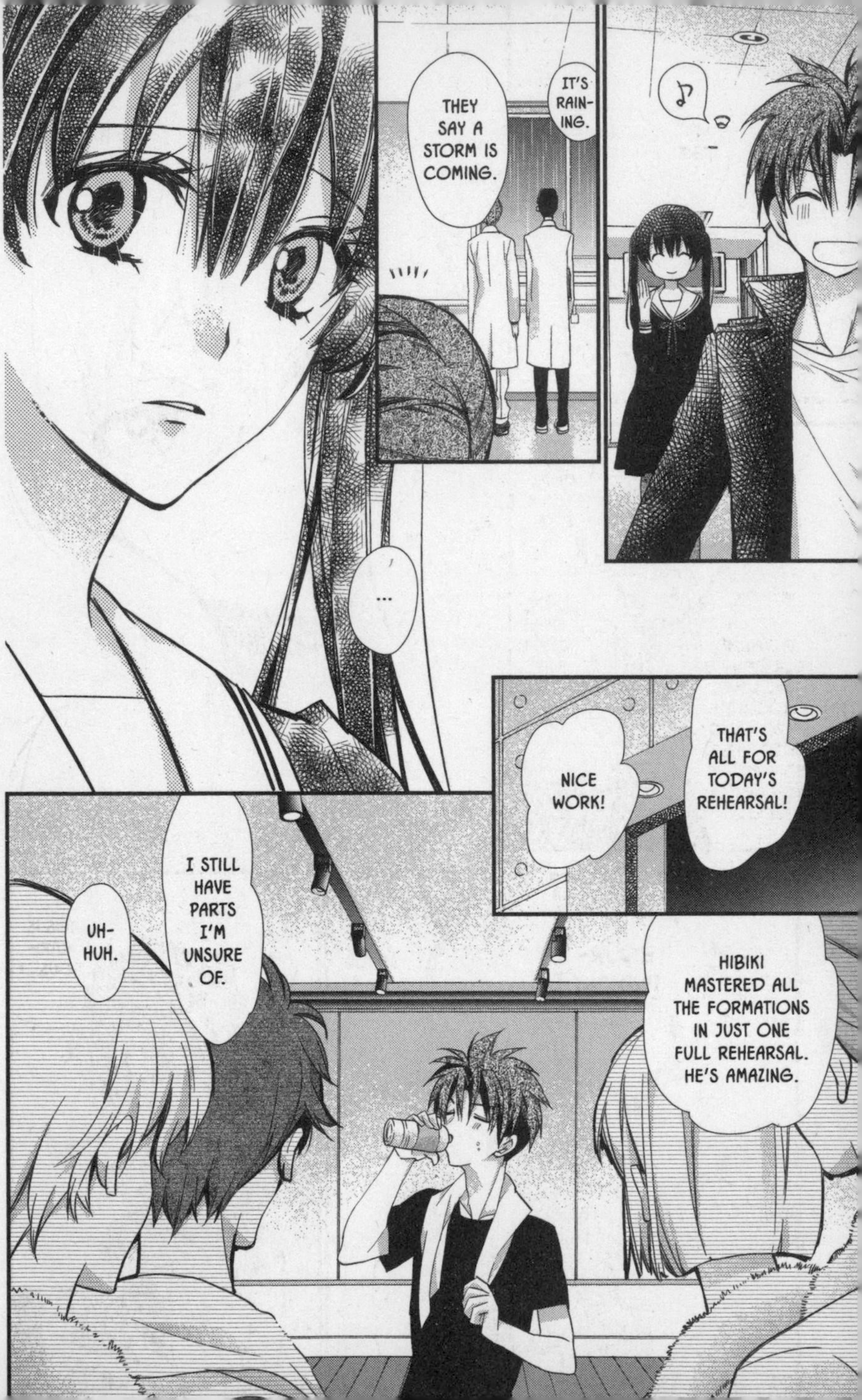
♪
IT'S RAIN-ING.
THEY SAY A STORM IS COMING.
...
THAT'S ALL FOR TODAY'S REHEARSAL!
NICE WORK!
HIBIKI MASTERED ALL THE FORMATIONS IN JUST ONE FULL REHEARSAL. HE'S AMAZING.
I STILL HAVE PARTS I'M UNSURE OF.
UH-HUH.

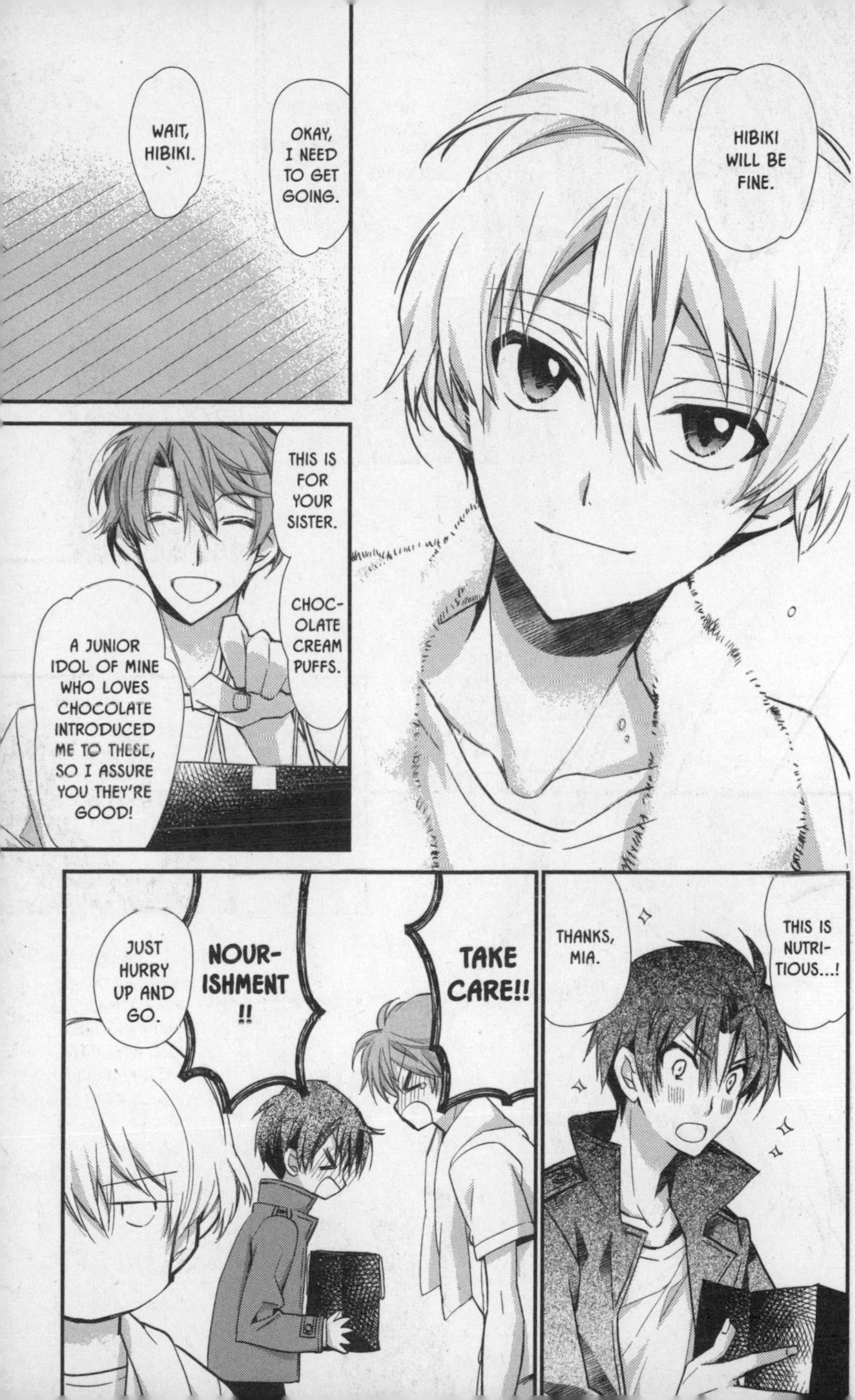

HIBIKI WILL BE FINE.
OKAY, I NEED TO GET GOING.
WAIT, HIBIKI.
THIS IS FOR YOUR SISTER.
CHOC-OLATE CREAM PUFFS.
A JUNIOR IDOL OF MINE WHO LOVES CHOCOLATE INTRODUCED ME TO THESE, SO I ASSURE YOU THEY'RE GOOD!
THIS IS NUTRI-TIOUS...!
THANKS, MIA.
TAKE CARE!!
NOUR-ISHMENT !!
JUST HURRY UP AND GO.

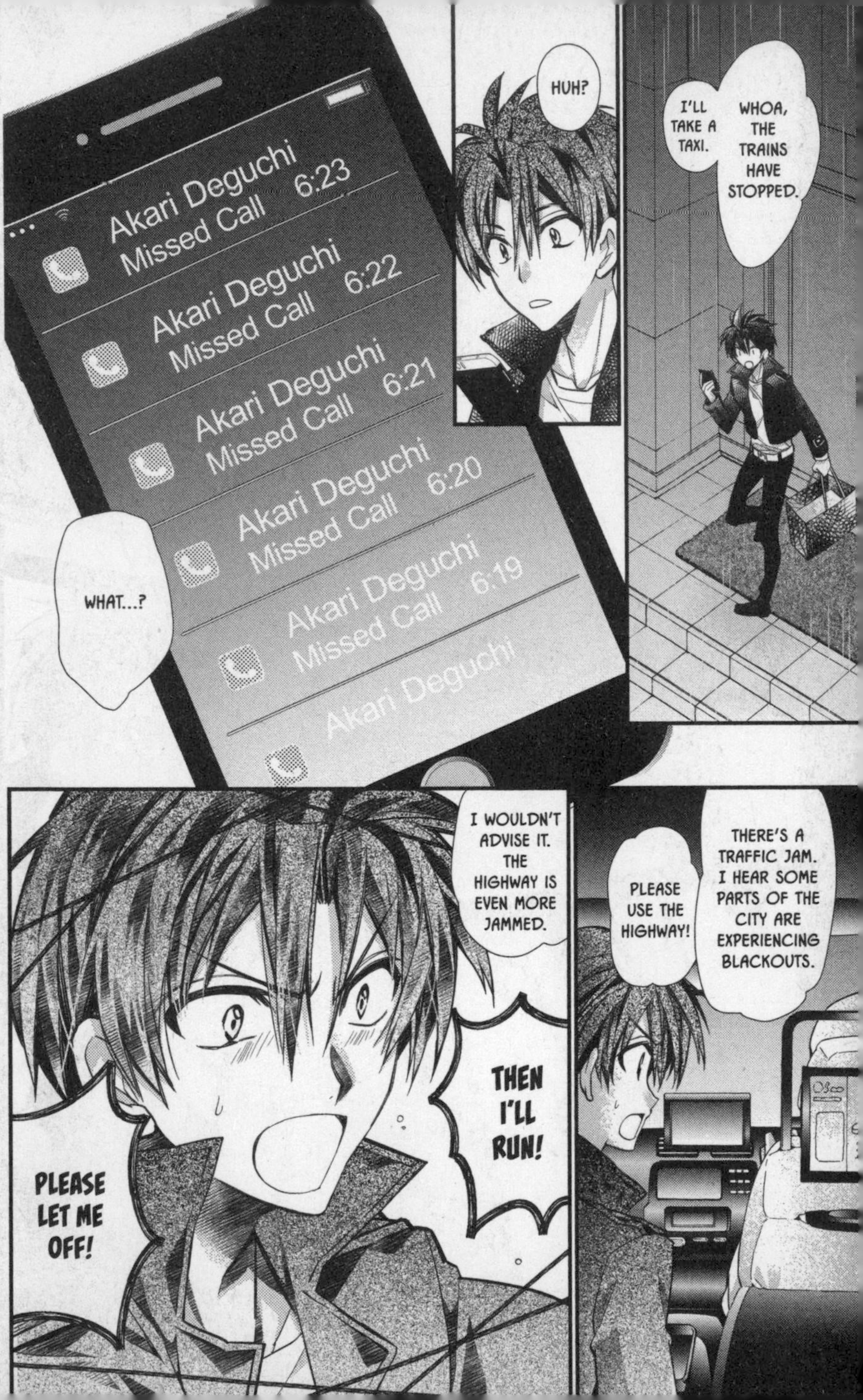
WHOA, THE TRAINS HAVE STOPPED.
I'LL TAKE A TAXI.
HUH?
Akari Deguchi
Missed Call 6:23
Akari Deguchi
Missed Call 6:22
Akari Deguchi
Missed Call 6:21
Akari Deguchi
Missed Call 6:20
Akari Deguchi
Missed Call 6:19
Akari Deguchi
WHAT...?
THERE'S A TRAFFIC JAM. I HEAR SOME PARTS OF THE CITY ARE EXPERIENCING BLACKOUTS.
PLEASE USE THE HIGHWAY!
I WOULDN'T ADVISE IT. THE HIGHWAY IS EVEN MORE JAMMED.
THEN I'LL RUN!
PLEASE LET ME OFF!

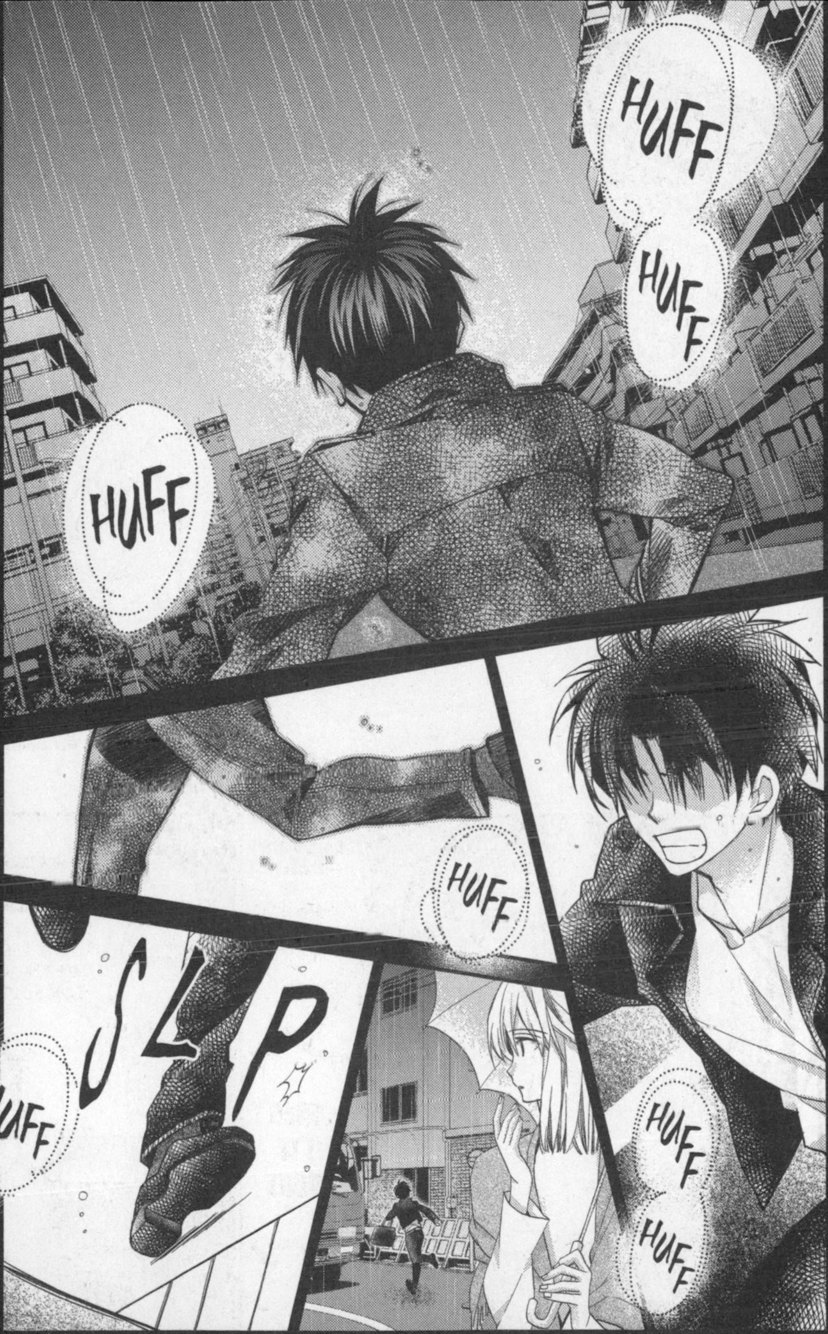
HUFF
HUFF
HUFF
HUFF
HUFF
HUFF
SLIP
HUFF

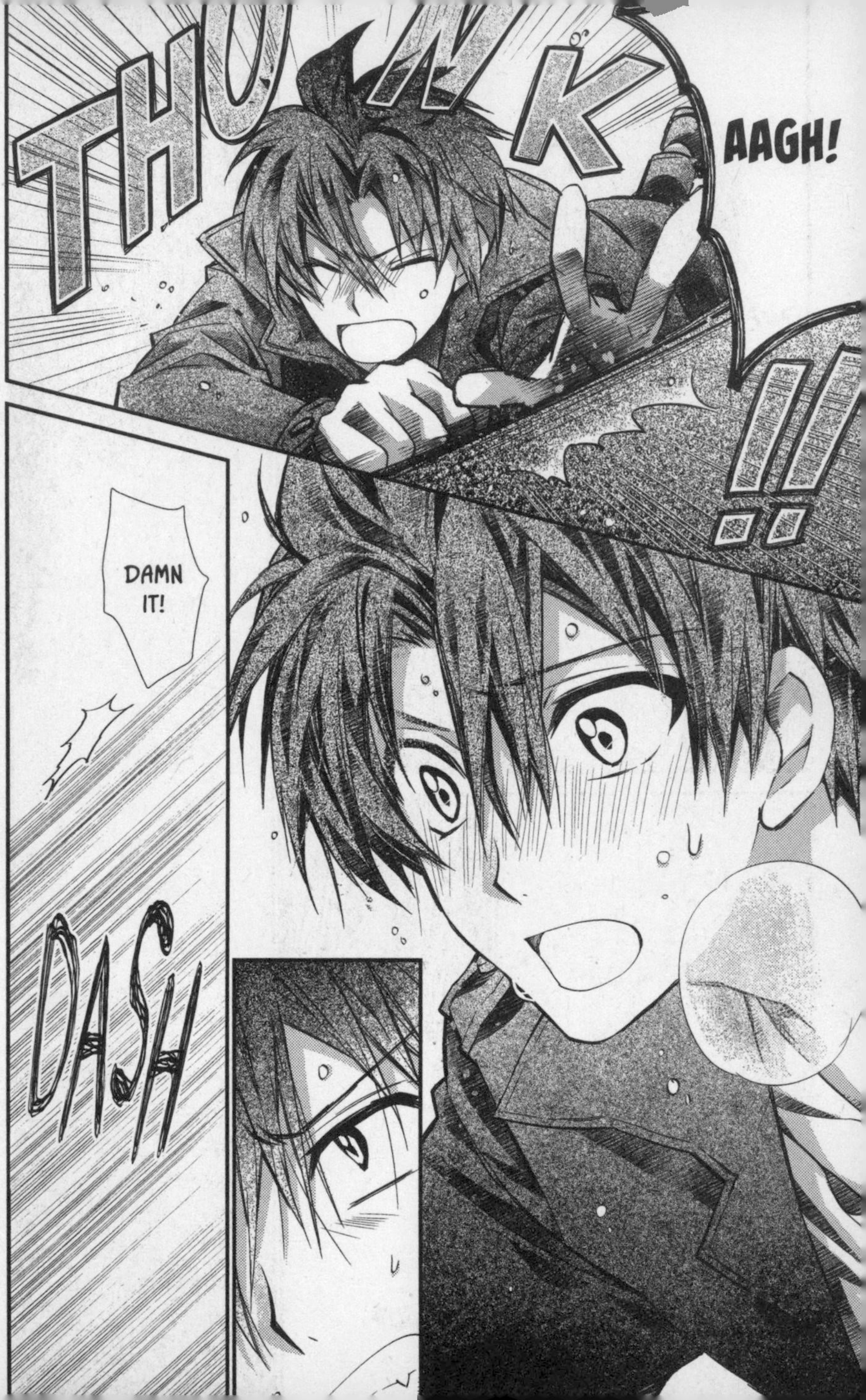
THUNK
AAGH!
!!
DAMN IT!
DASH

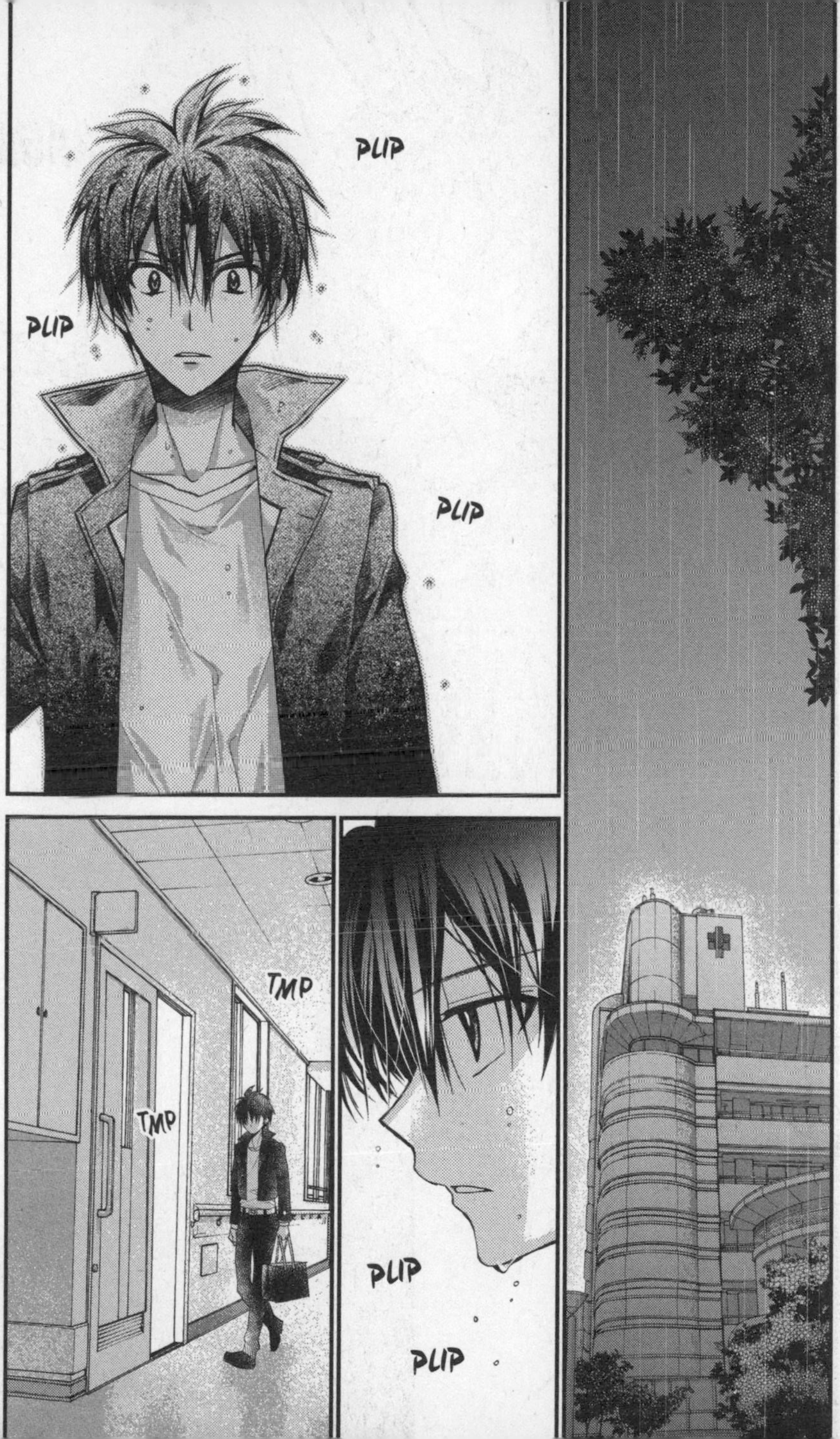
PLIP
PLIP
PLIP
PLIP
PLIP
TMP
TMP

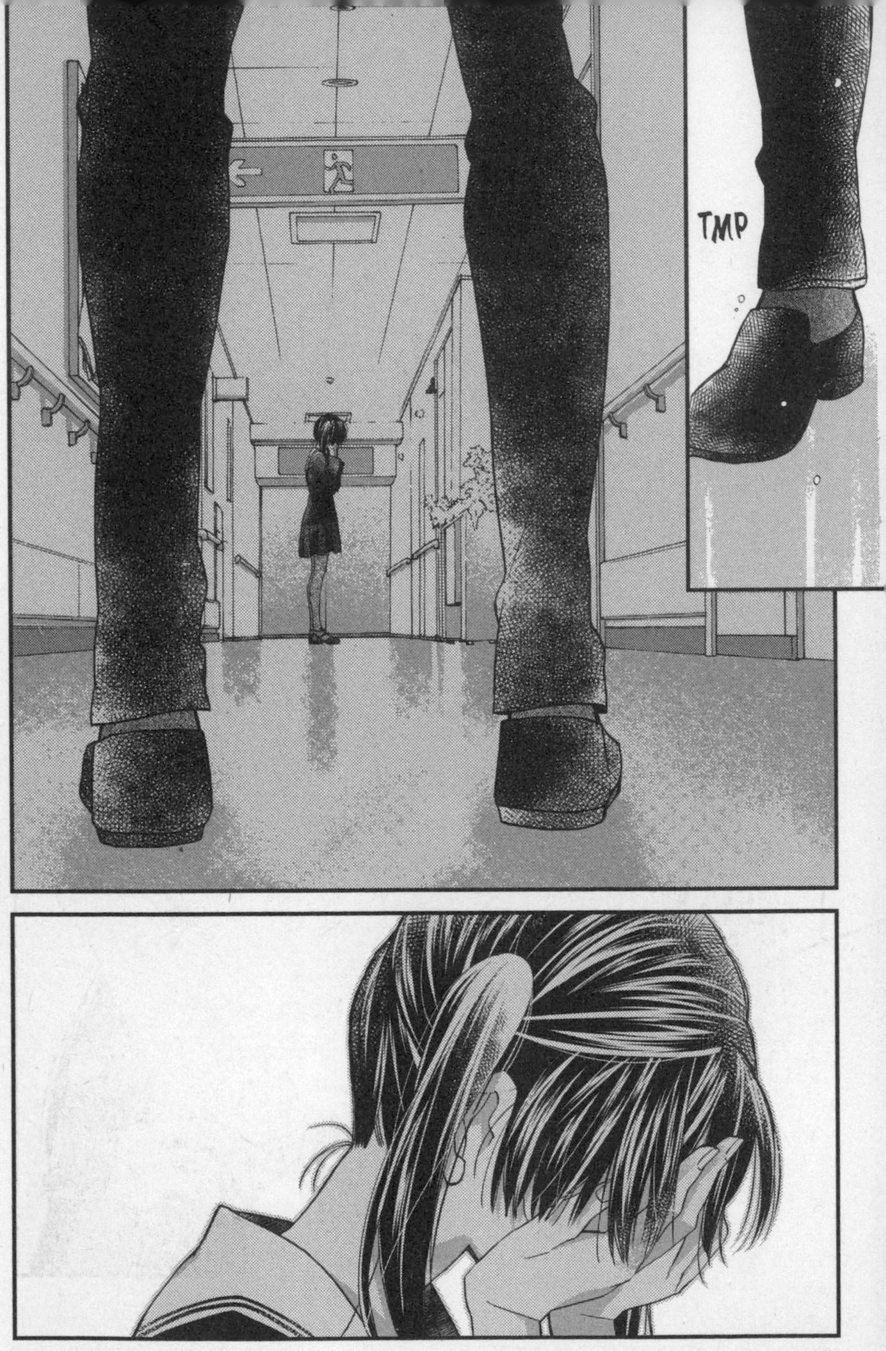
TMP

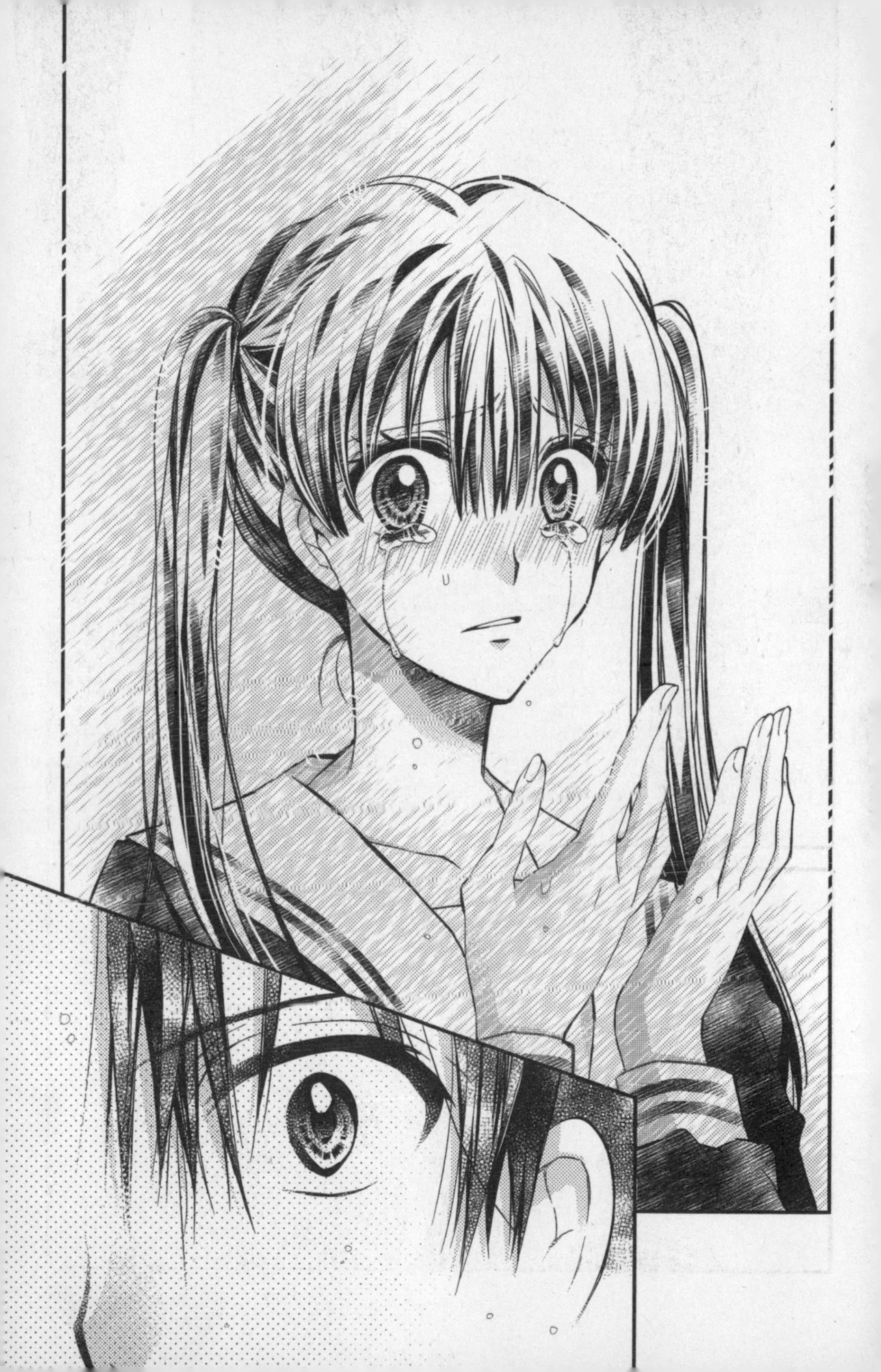

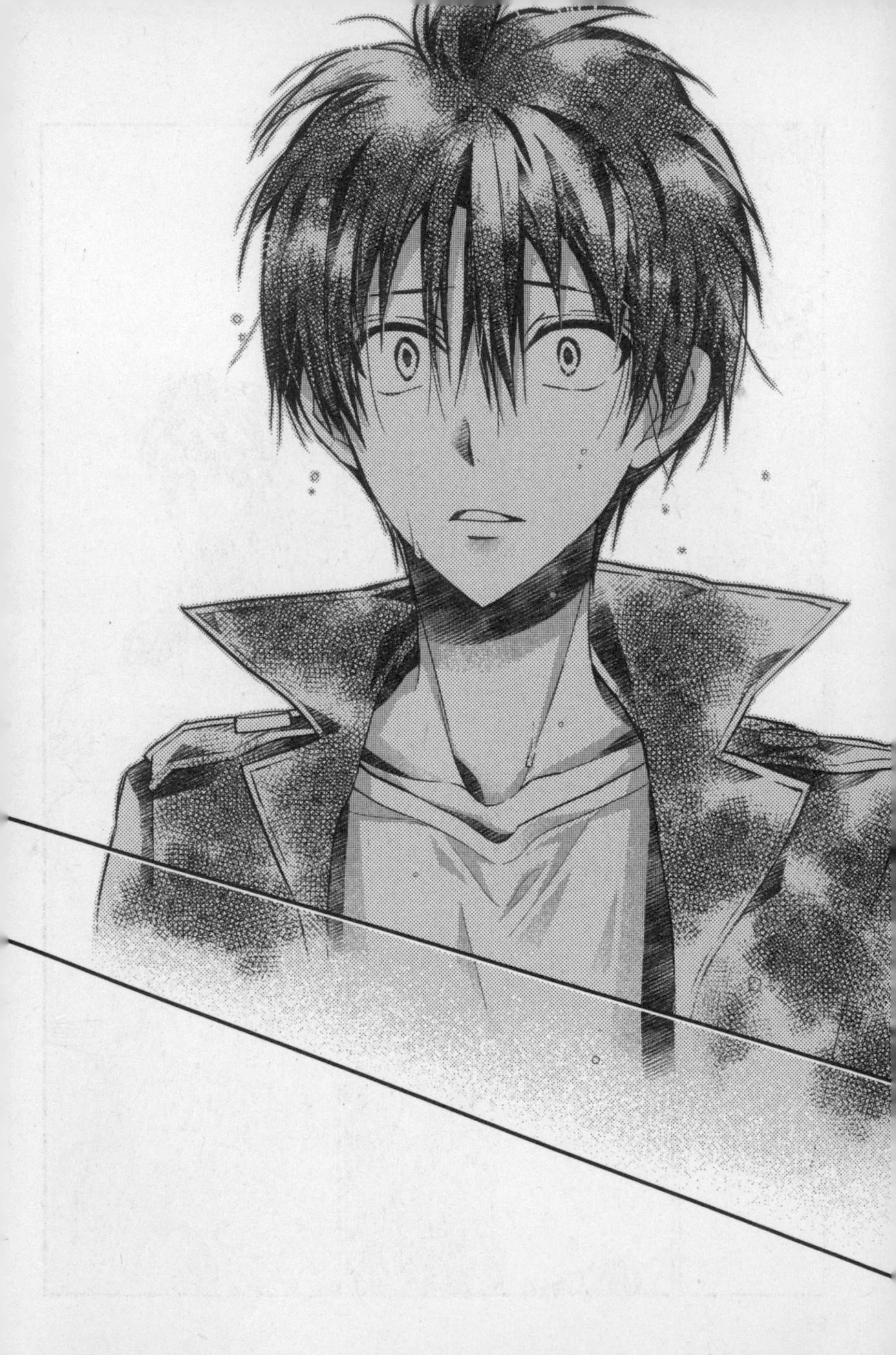

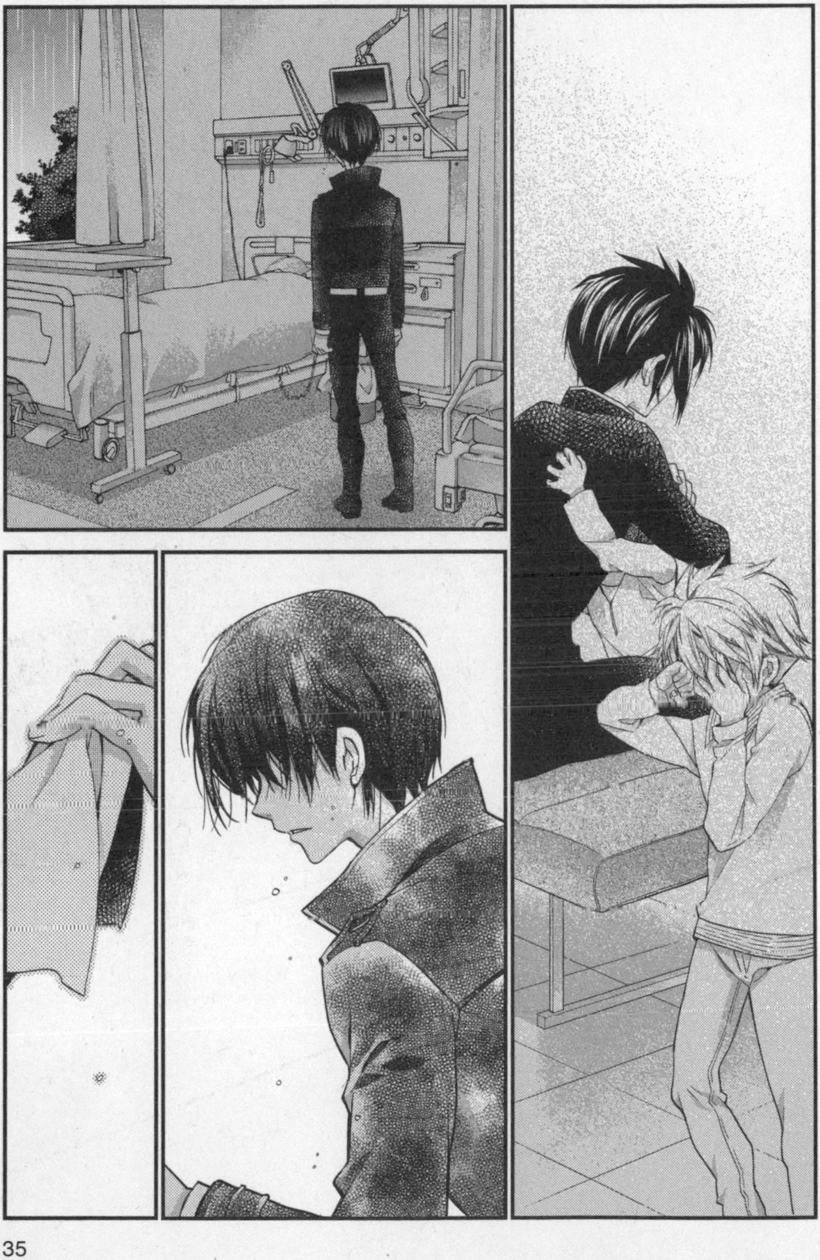

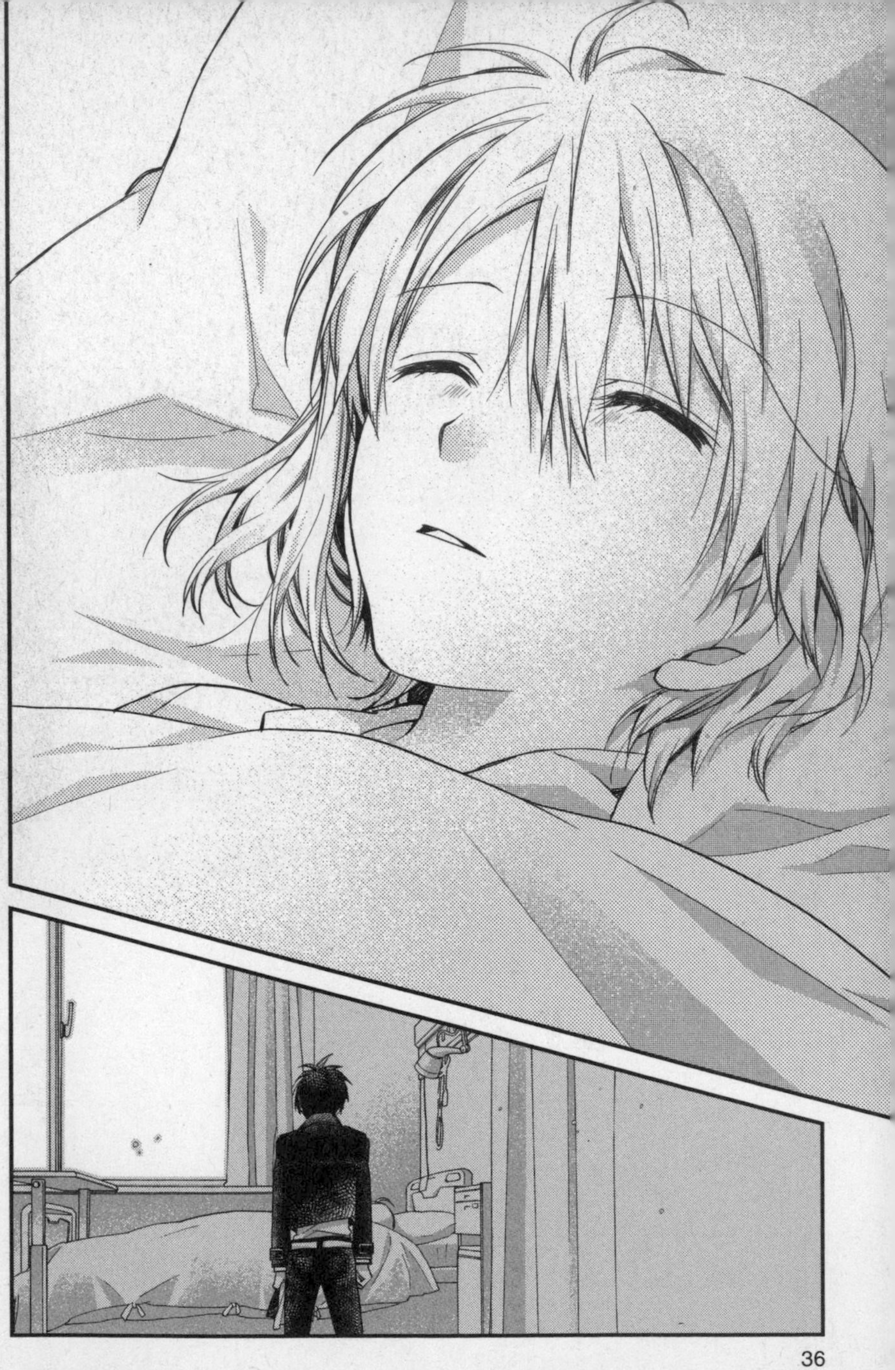

Chapter 27

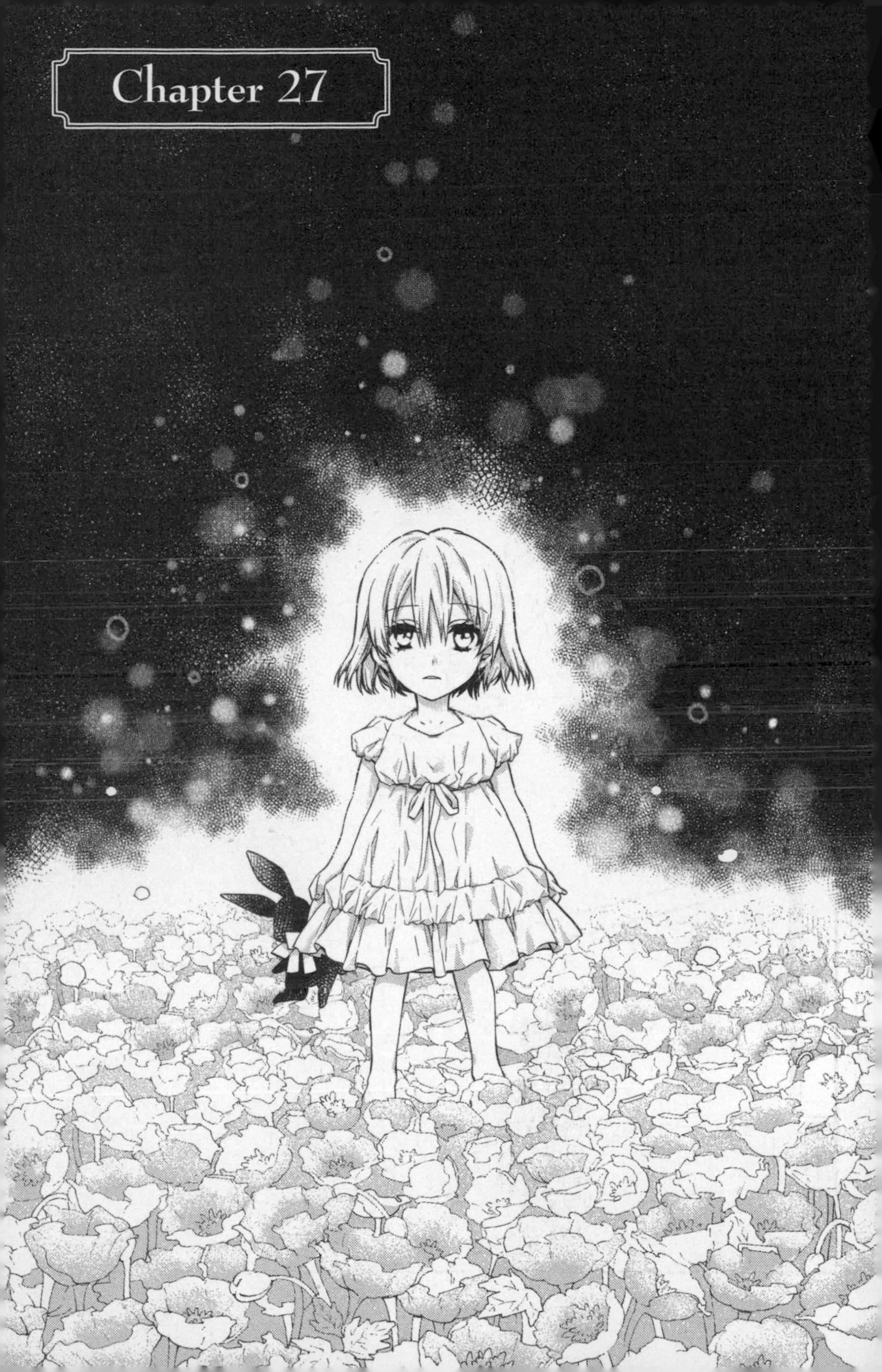

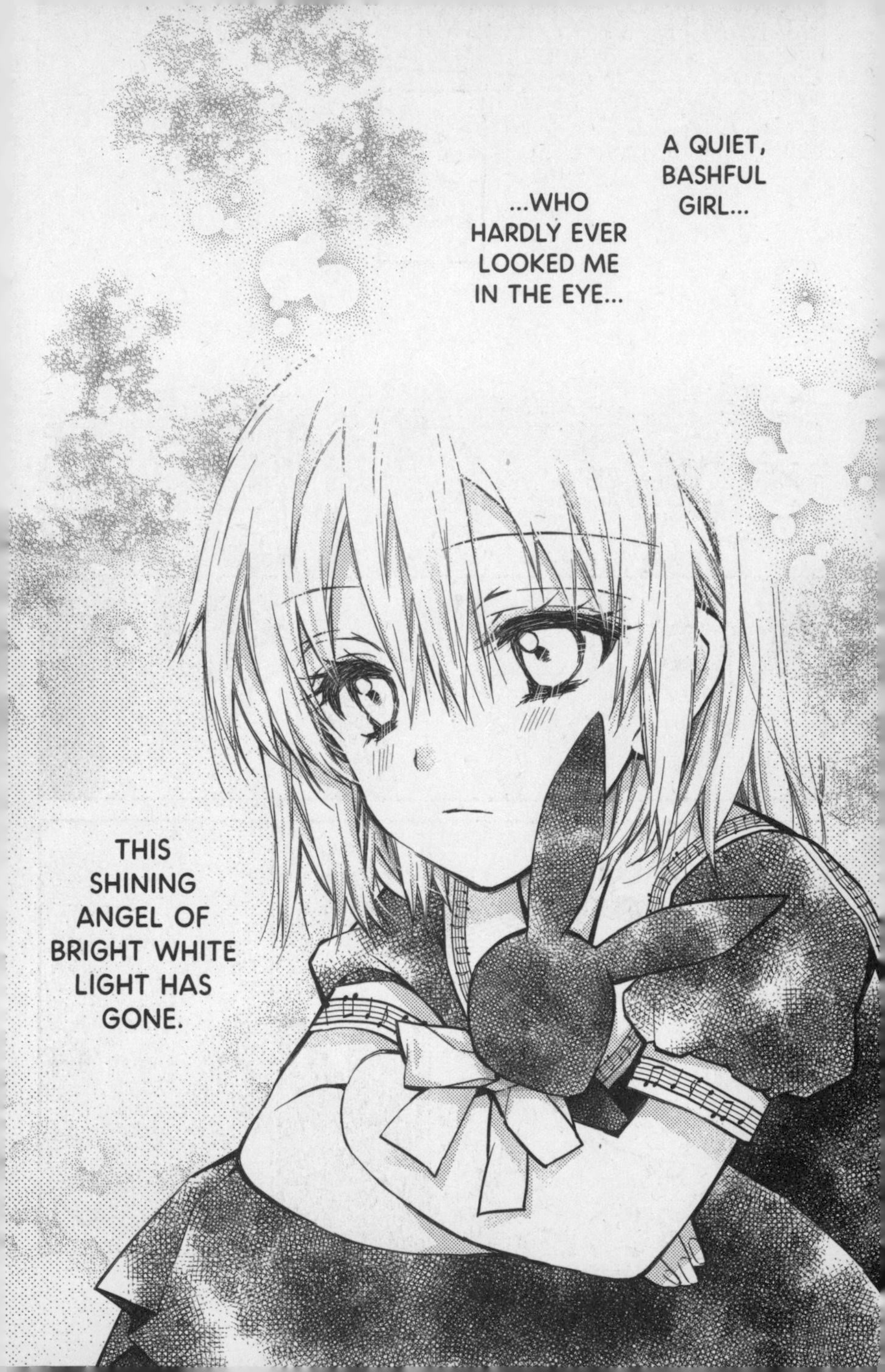
A QUIET, BASHFUL GIRL...
...WHO HARDLY EVER LOOKED ME IN THE EYE...
THIS SHINING ANGEL OF BRIGHT WHITE LIGHT HAS GONE.

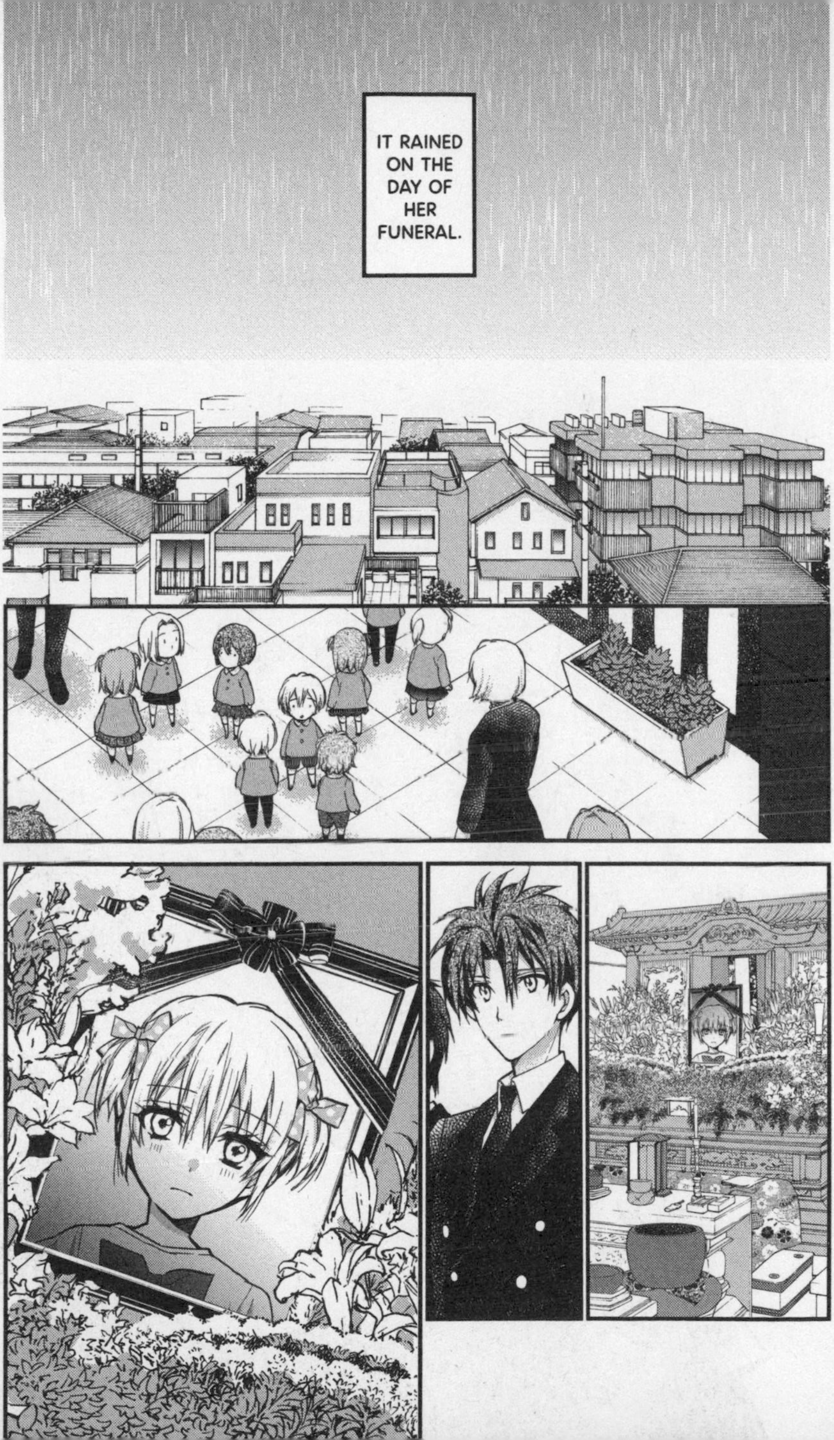
IT RAINED ON THE DAY OF HER FUNERAL.

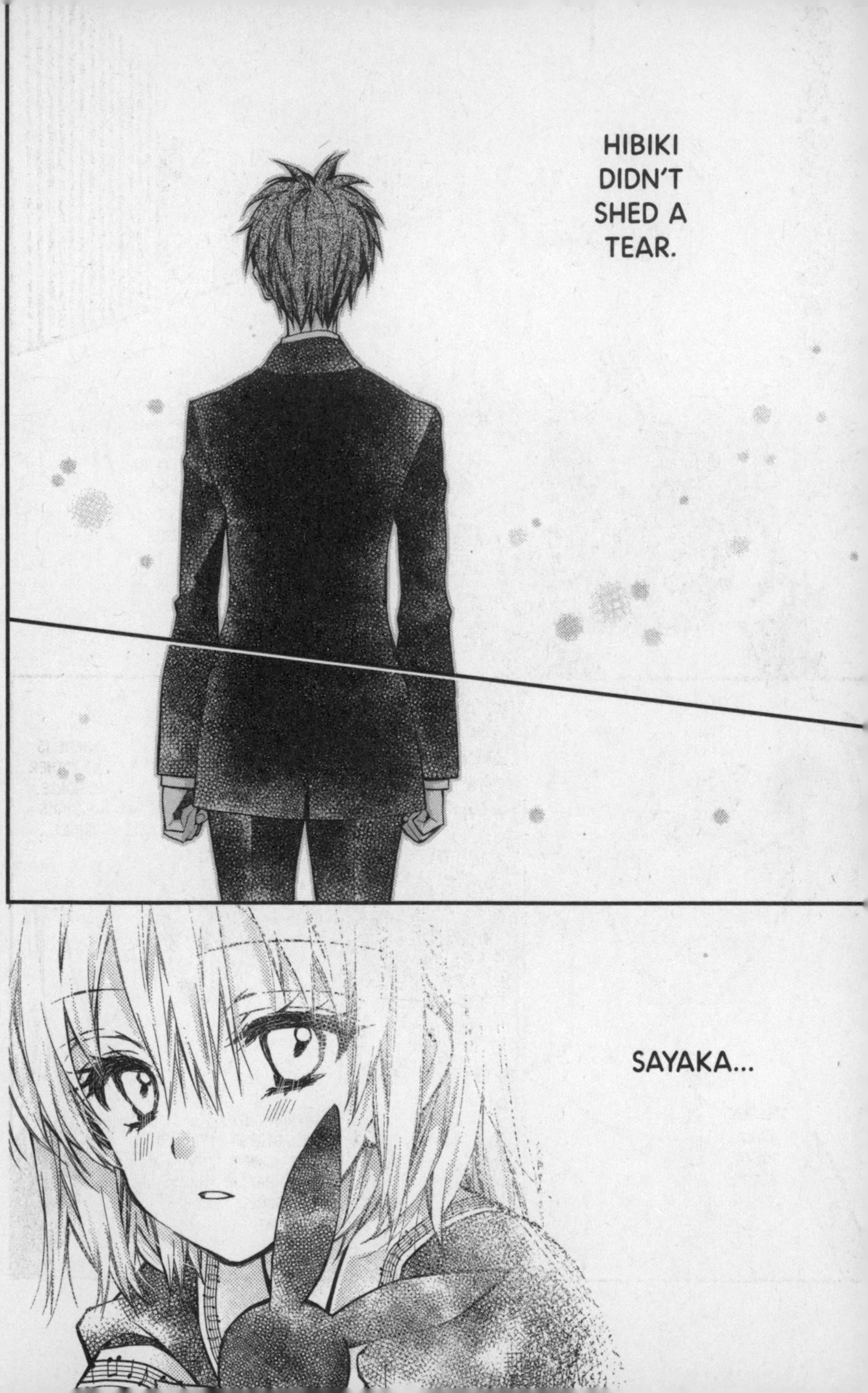
HIBIKI DIDN'T SHED A TEAR.
SAYAKA...

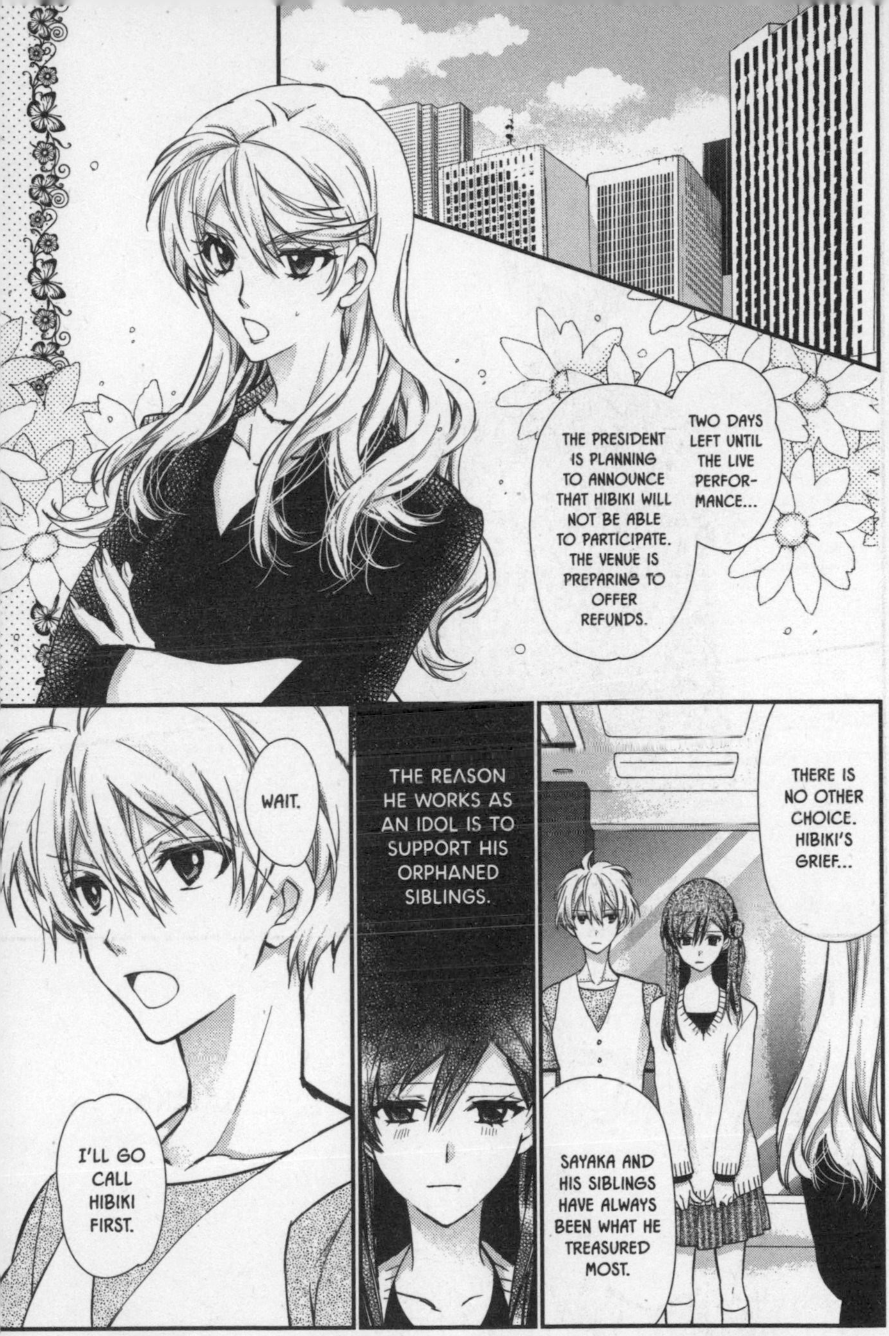
TWO DAYS LEFT UNTIL THE LIVE PERFOR- MANCE...
THE PRESIDENT IS PLANNING TO ANNOUNCE THAT HIBIKI WILL NOT BE ABLE TO PARTICIPATE. THE VENUE IS PREPARING TO OFFER REFUNDS.
THERE IS NO OTHER CHOICE. HIBIKI'S GRIEF...
SAYAKA AND HIS SIBLINGS HAVE ALWAYS BEEN WHAT HE TREASURED MOST.
THE REASON HE WORKS AS AN IDOL IS TO SUPPORT HIS ORPHANED SIBLINGS.
WAIT.
I'LL GO CALL HIBIKI FIRST.

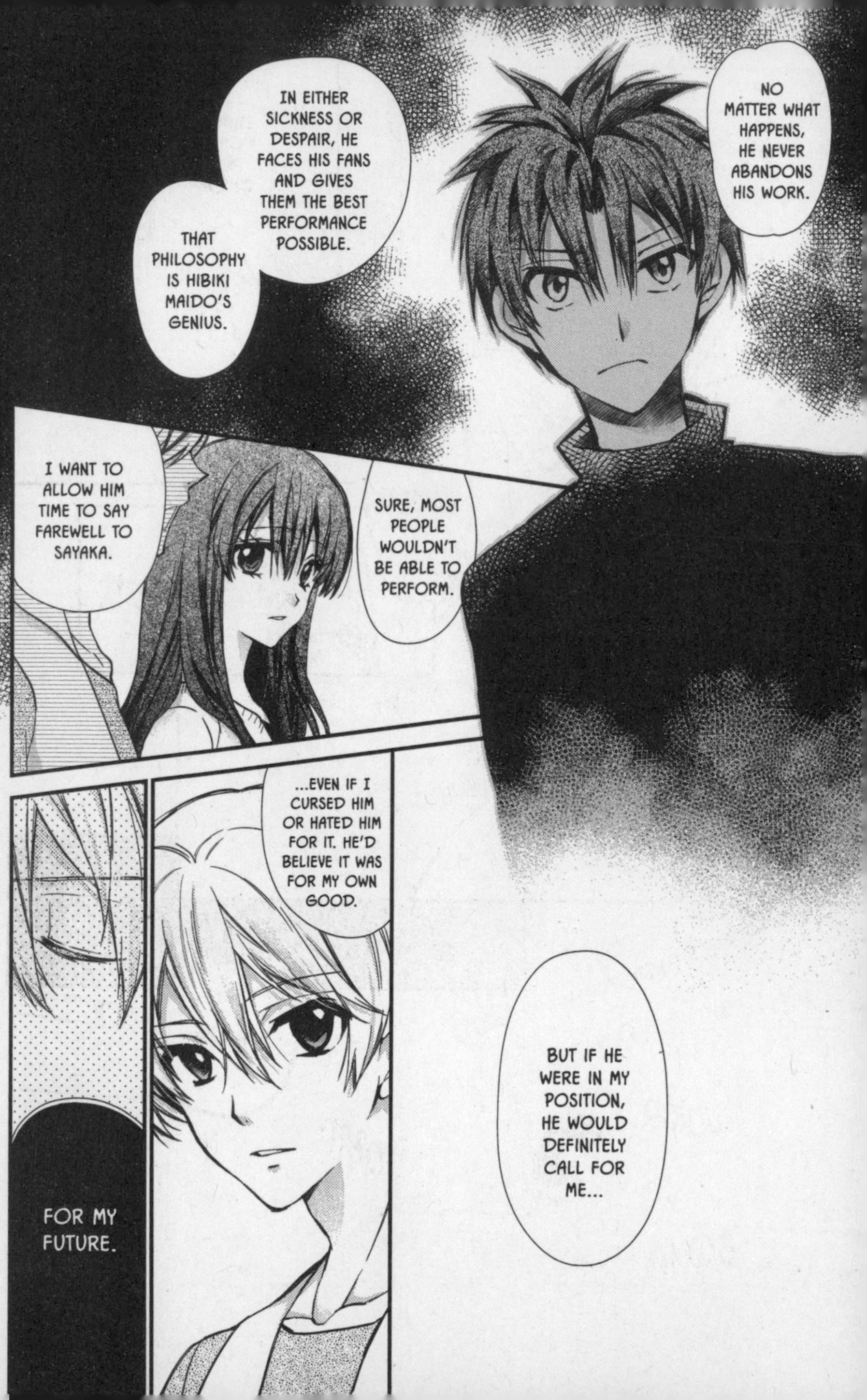
NO MATTER WHAT HAPPENS, HE NEVER ABANDONS HIS WORK.
IN EITHER SICKNESS OR DESPAIR, HE FACES HIS FANS AND GIVES THEM THE BEST PERFORMANCE POSSIBLE.
THAT PHILOSOPHY IS HIBIKI MAIDO'S GENIUS.
SURE, MOST PEOPLE WOULDN'T BE ABLE TO PERFORM.
I WANT TO ALLOW HIM TIME TO SAY FAREWELL TO SAYAKA.
BUT IF HE WERE IN MY POSITION, HE WOULD DEFINITELY CALL FOR ME...
...EVEN IF I CURSED HIM OR HATED HIM FOR IT. HE'D BELIEVE IT WAS FOR MY OWN GOOD.
FOR MY FUTURE.

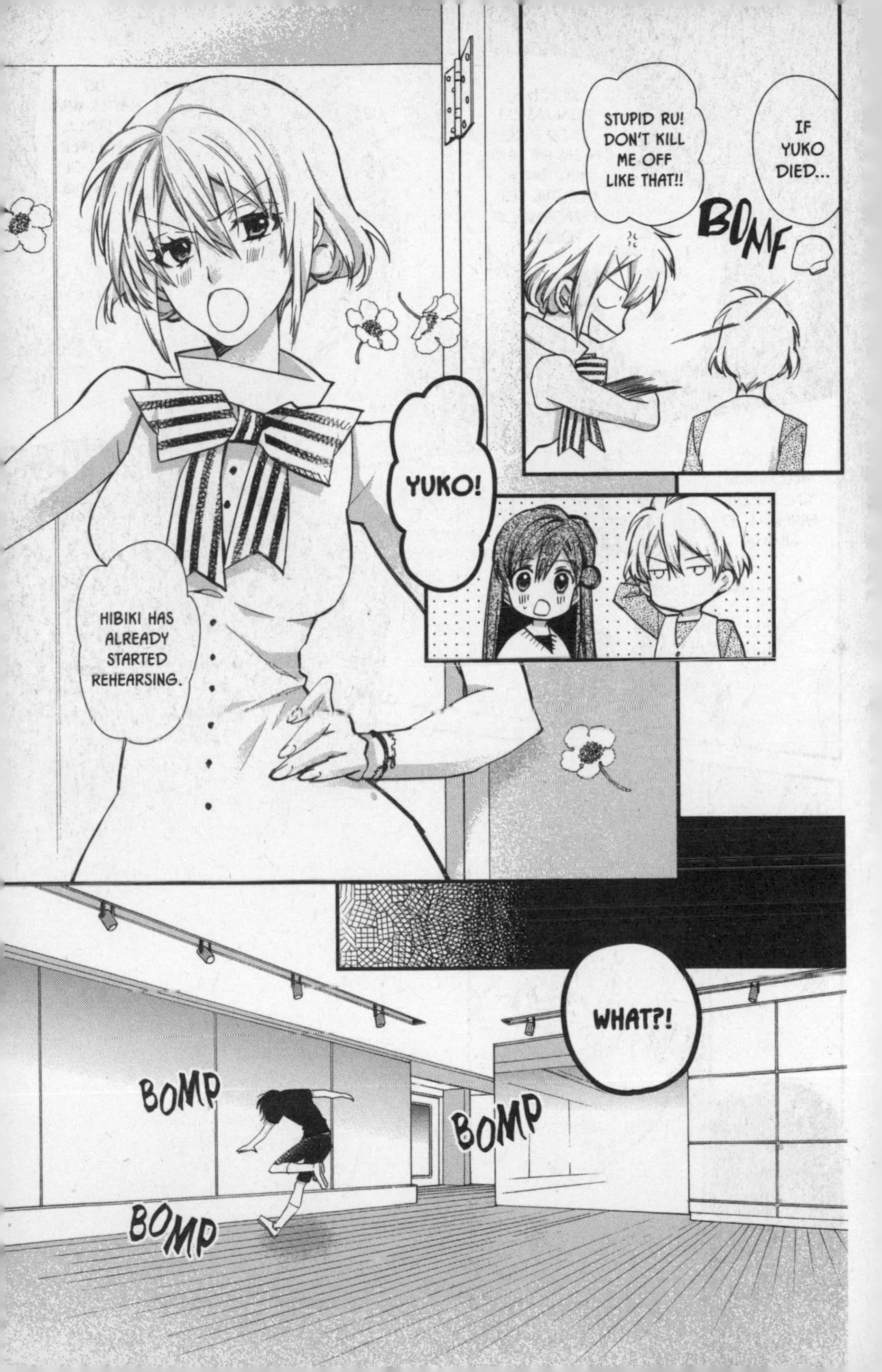
IF YUKO DIED...
STUPID RU! DON'T KILL ME OFF LIKE THAT!!
BOMF
YUKO!
HIBIKI HAS ALREADY STARTED REHEARSING.
WHAT?!
BOMP
BOMP
BOMP

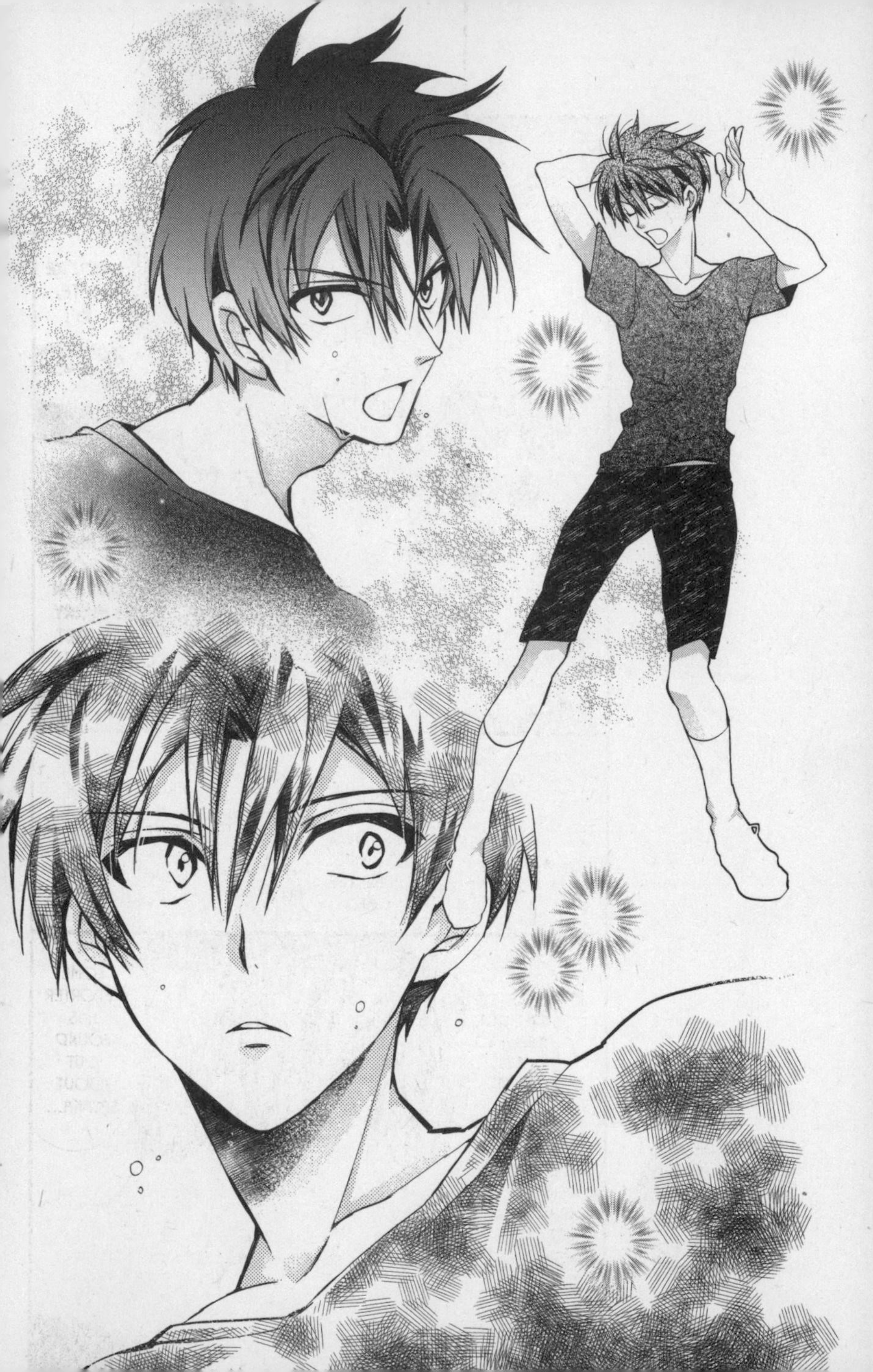

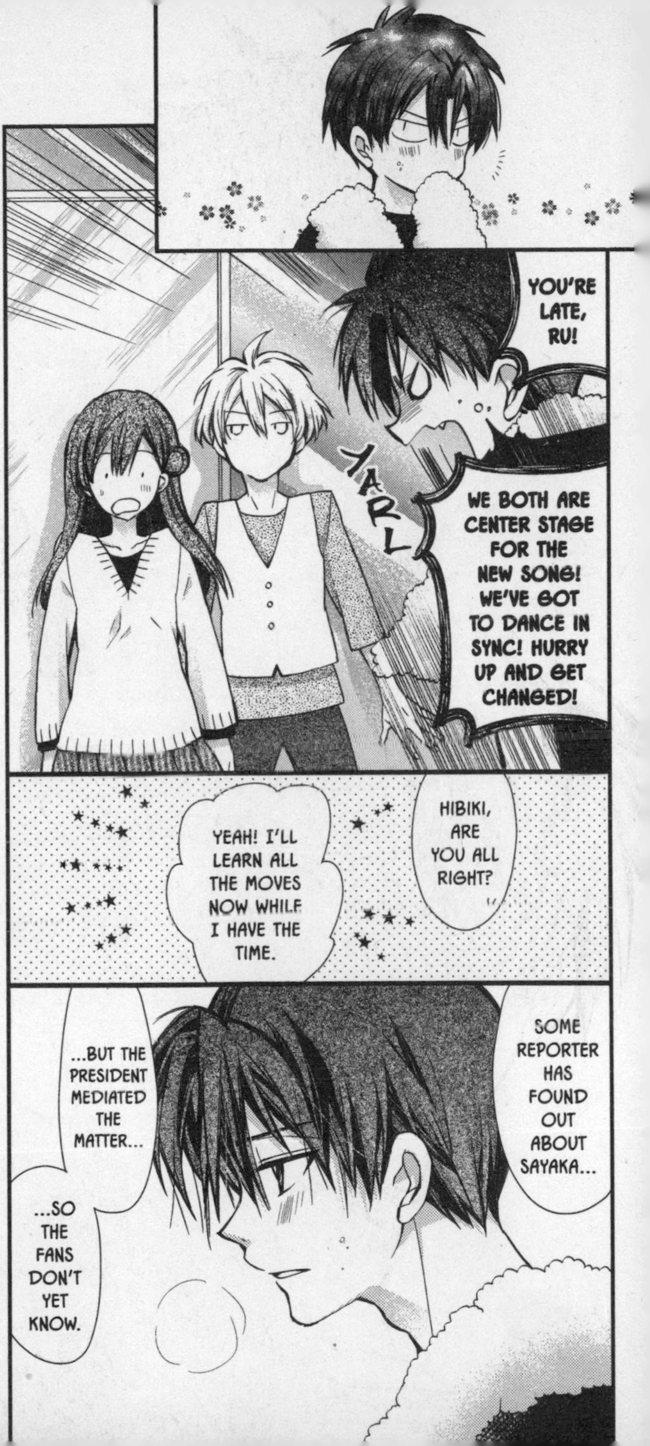
YOU'RE LATE, RU!
YARL
WE BOTH ARE CENTER STAGE FOR THE NEW SONG! WE'VE GOT TO DANCE IN SYNC! HURRY UP AND GET CHANGED!
HIBIKI, ARE YOU ALL RIGHT?
YEAH! I'LL LEARN ALL THE MOVES NOW WHILE I HAVE THE TIME.
SOME REPORTER HAS FOUND OUT ABOUT SAYAKA...
...BUT THE PRESIDENT MEDIATED THE MATTER...
...SO THE FANS DON'T YET KNOW.

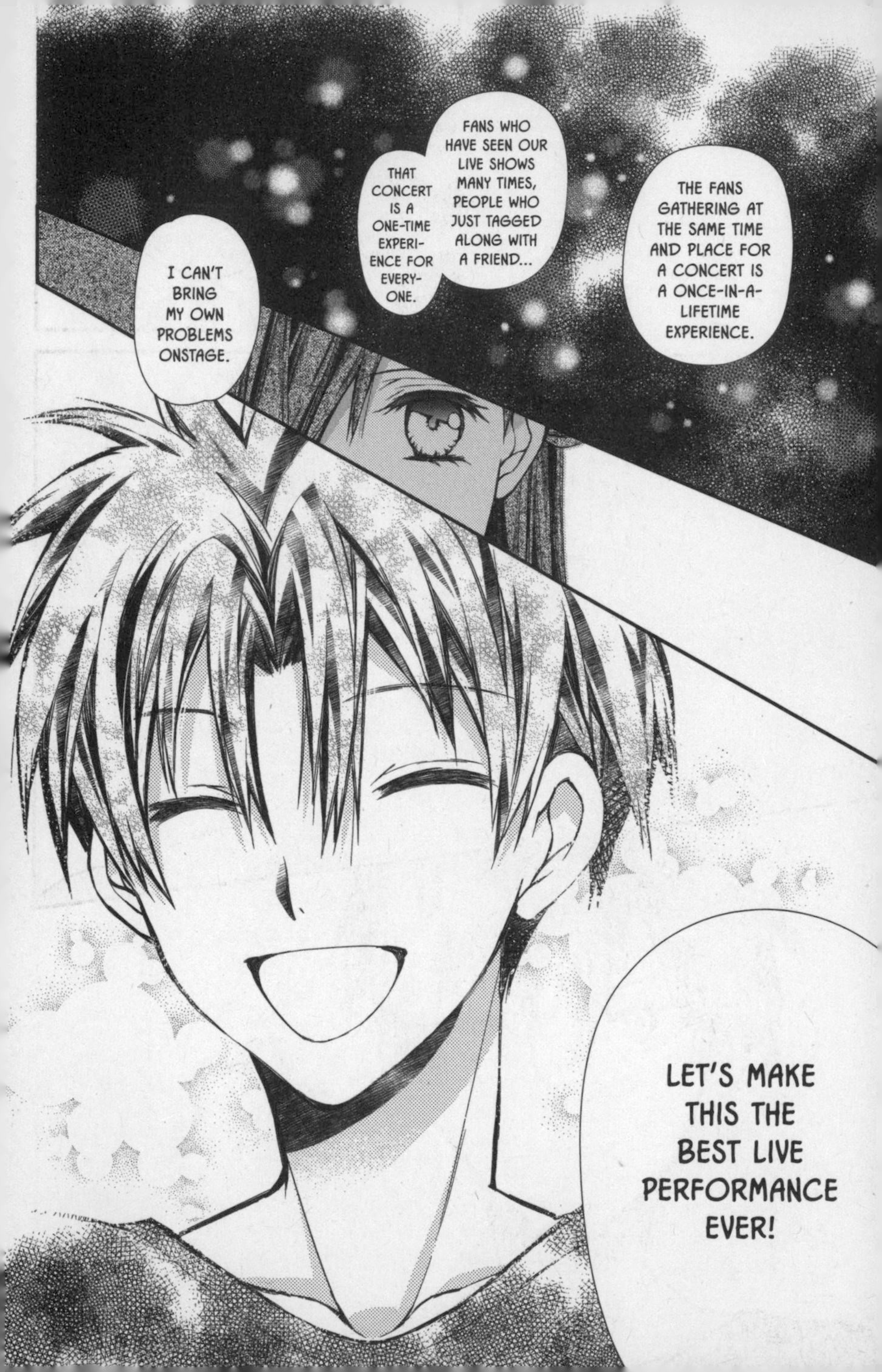
THE FANS GATHERING AT THE SAME TIME AND PLACE FOR A CONCERT IS A ONCE-IN-A-LIFETIME EXPERIENCE.
FANS WHO HAVE SEEN OUR LIVE SHOWS MANY TIMES, PEOPLE WHO JUST TAGGED ALONG WITH A FRIEND...
THAT CONCERT IS A ONE-TIME EXPERIENCE FOR EVERYONE.
I CAN'T BRING MY OWN PROBLEMS ONSTAGE.
LET'S MAKE THIS THE BEST LIVE PERFORMANCE EVER!

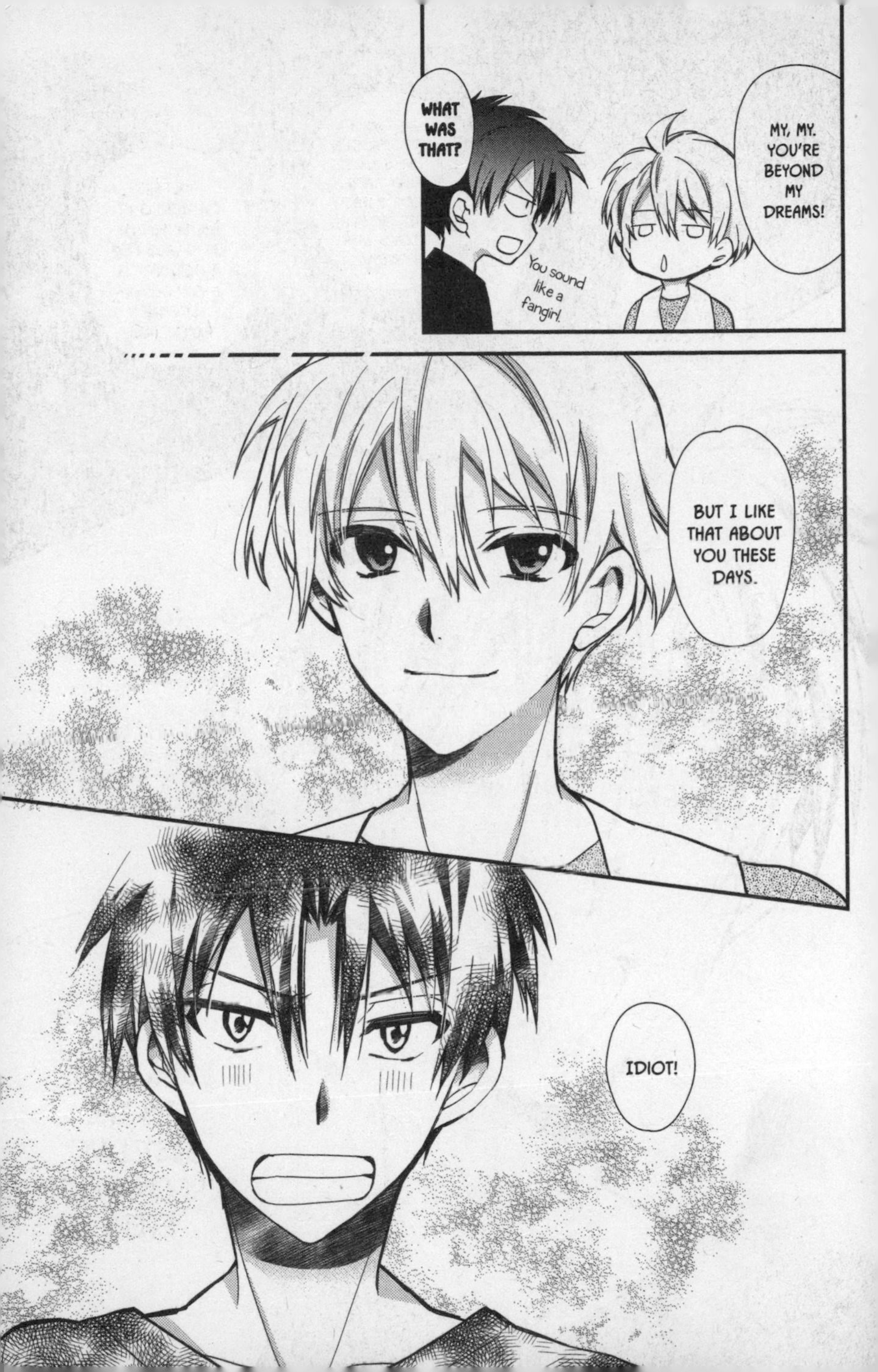

MY, MY. YOU'RE BEYOND MY DREAMS!
WHAT WAS THAT?
You sound like a fangirl.
BUT I LIKE THAT ABOUT YOU THESE DAYS.
IDIOT!

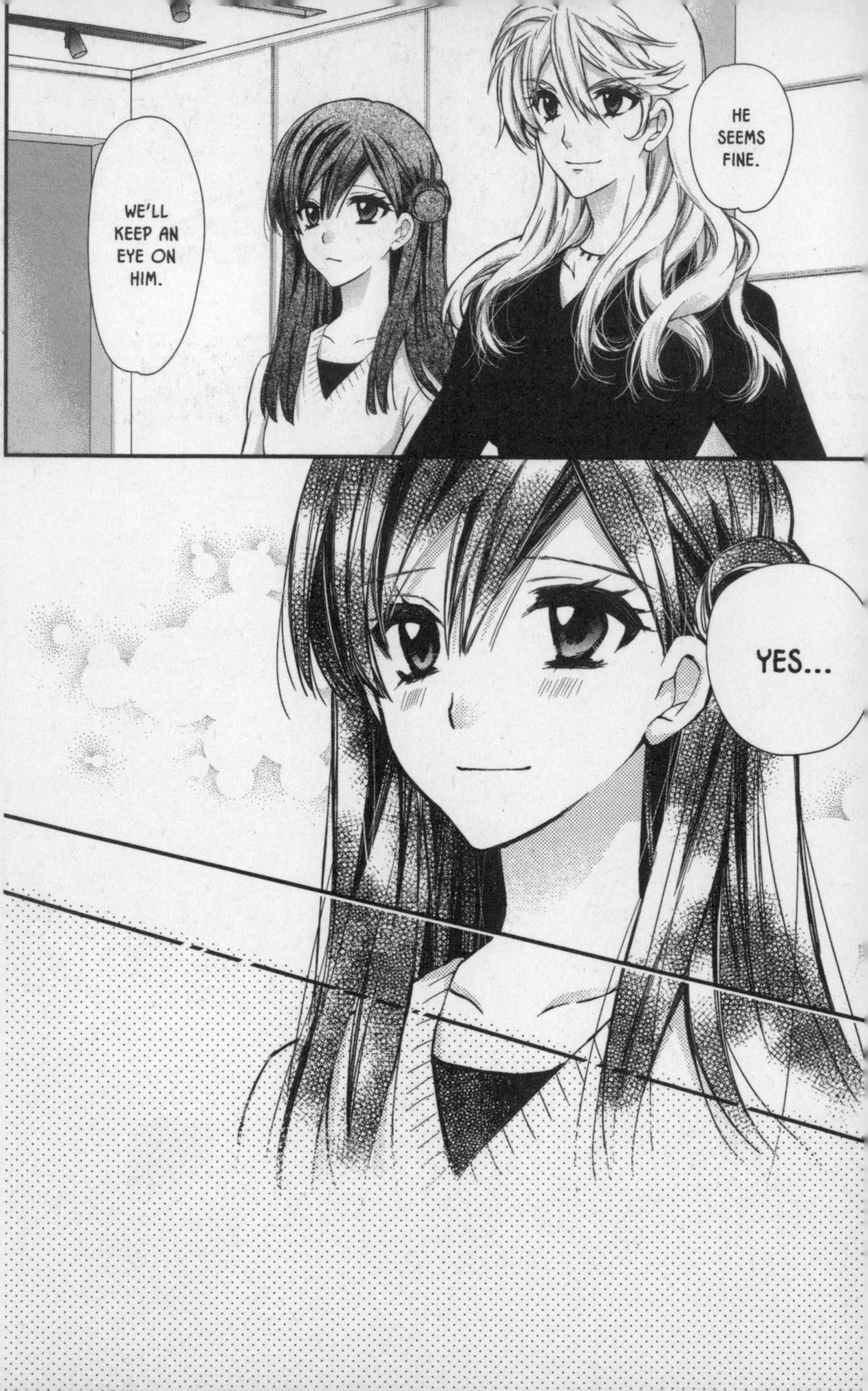
HE SEEMS FINE.
WE'LL KEEP AN EYE ON HIM.
YES...

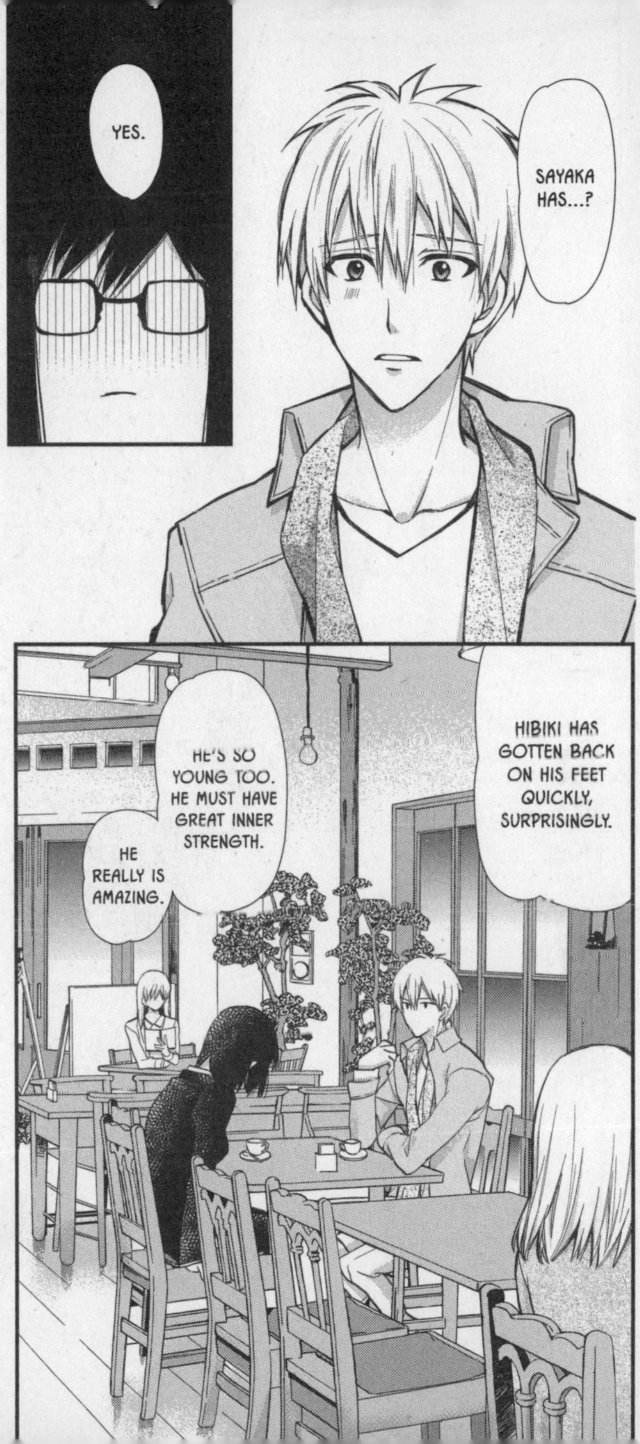
SAYAKA HAS...?
YES.
HIBIKI HAS GOTTEN BACK ON HIS FEET QUICKLY, SURPRISINGLY.
HE'S SO YOUNG TOO. HE MUST HAVE GREAT INNER STRENGTH.
HE REALLY IS AMAZING.

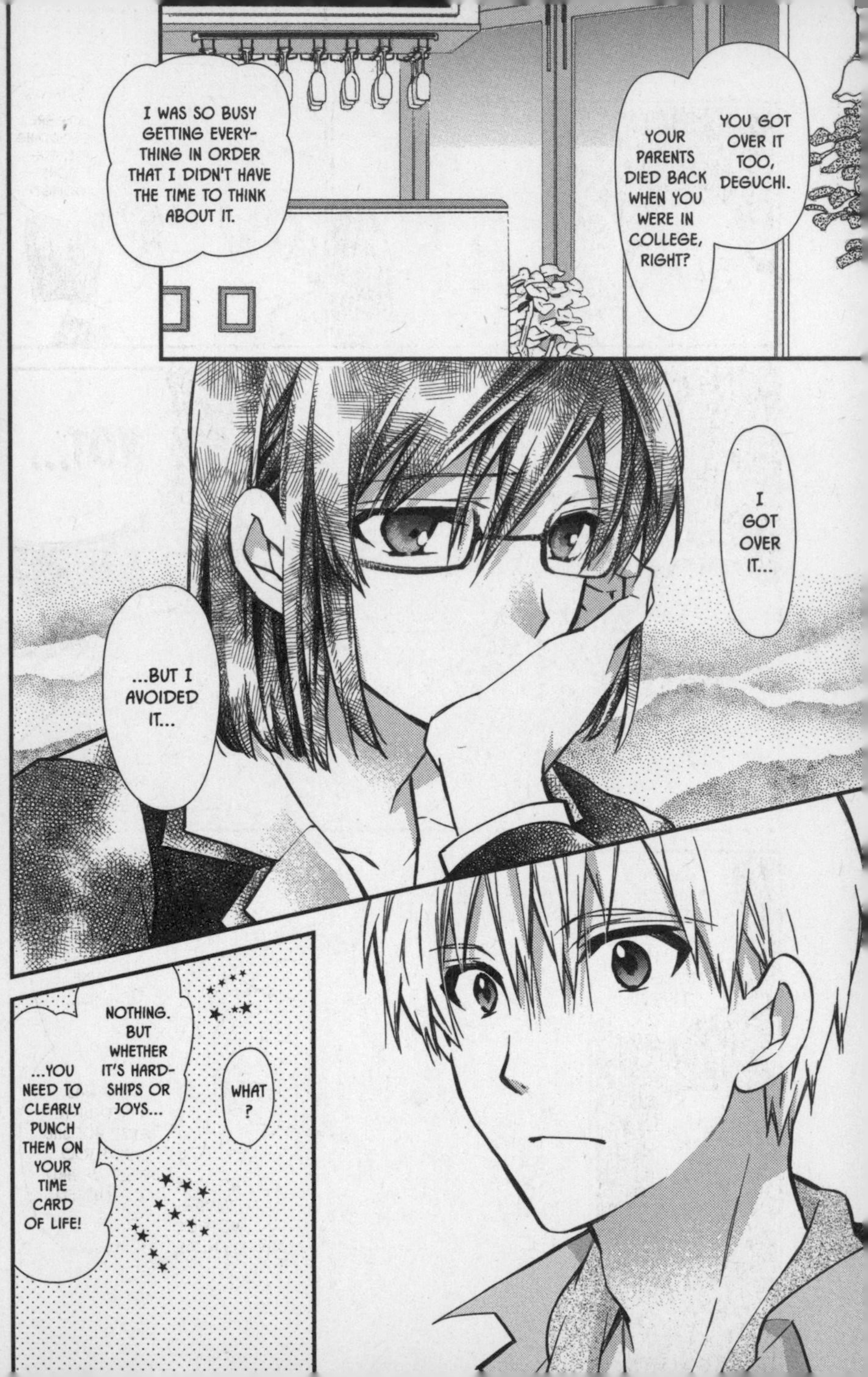
YOU GOT OVER IT TOO, DEGUCHI.
YOUR PARENTS DIED BACK WHEN YOU WERE IN COLLEGE, RIGHT?
I WAS SO BUSY GETTING EVERY-THING IN ORDER THAT I DIDN'T HAVE THE TIME TO THINK ABOUT IT.
I GOT OVER IT...
...BUT I AVOIDED IT...
WHAT?
NOTHING. BUT WHETHER IT'S HARD-SHIPS OR JOYS...
...YOU NEED TO CLEARLY PUNCH THEM ON YOUR TIME CARD OF LIFE!

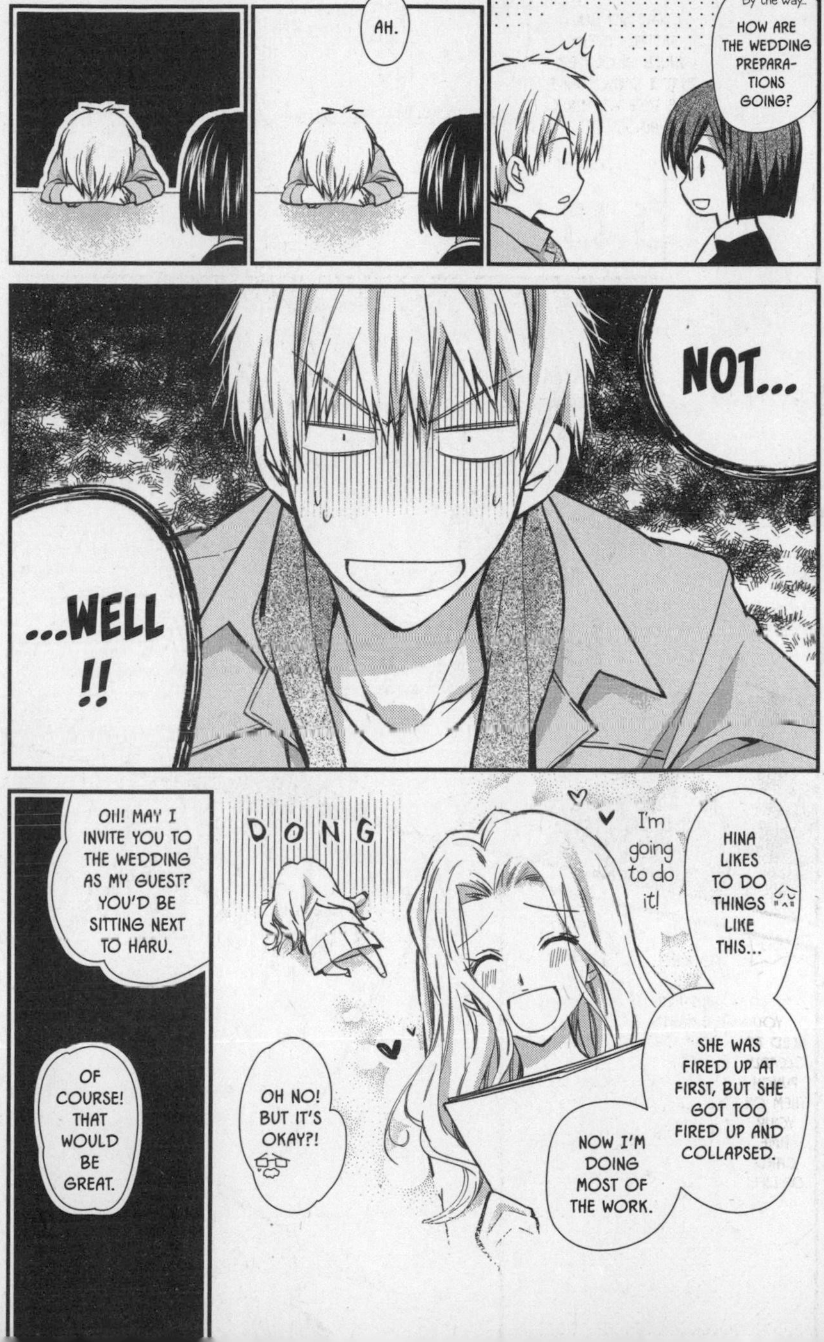
By the way...
HOW ARE THE WEDDING PREPARATIONS GOING?
AH.
NOT...
...WELL !!
HINA LIKES TO DO THINGS LIKE THIS...
I'm going to do it!
SHE WAS FIRED UP AT FIRST, BUT SHE GOT TOO FIRED UP AND COLLAPSED.
NOW I'M DOING MOST OF THE WORK.
DONG
OH NO! BUT IT'S OKAY?!
OH! MAY I INVITE YOU TO THE WEDDING AS MY GUEST? YOU'D BE SITTING NEXT TO HARU.
OF COURSE! THAT WOULD BE GREAT.

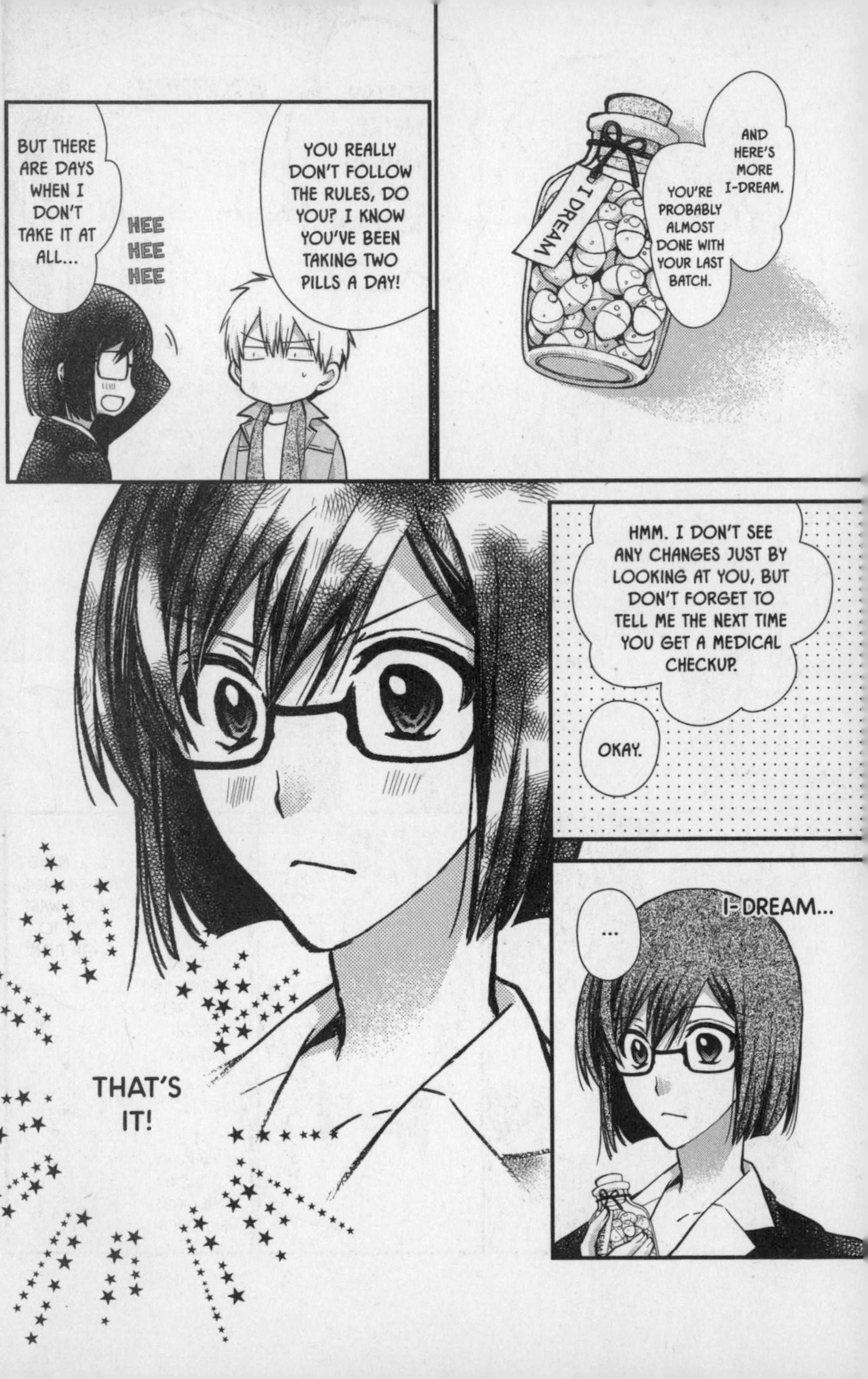
AND HERE'S MORE I-DREAM.
YOU'RE PROBABLY ALMOST DONE WITH YOUR LAST BATCH.
I DREAM
YOU REALLY DON'T FOLLOW THE RULES, DO YOU? I KNOW YOU'VE BEEN TAKING TWO PILLS A DAY!
HEE HEE HEE
BUT THERE ARE DAYS WHEN I DON'T TAKE IT AT ALL...
HMM. I DON'T SEE ANY CHANGES JUST BY LOOKING AT YOU, BUT DON'T FORGET TO TELL ME THE NEXT TIME YOU GET A MEDICAL CHECKUP.
OKAY.
I-DREAM...
...
THAT'S IT!

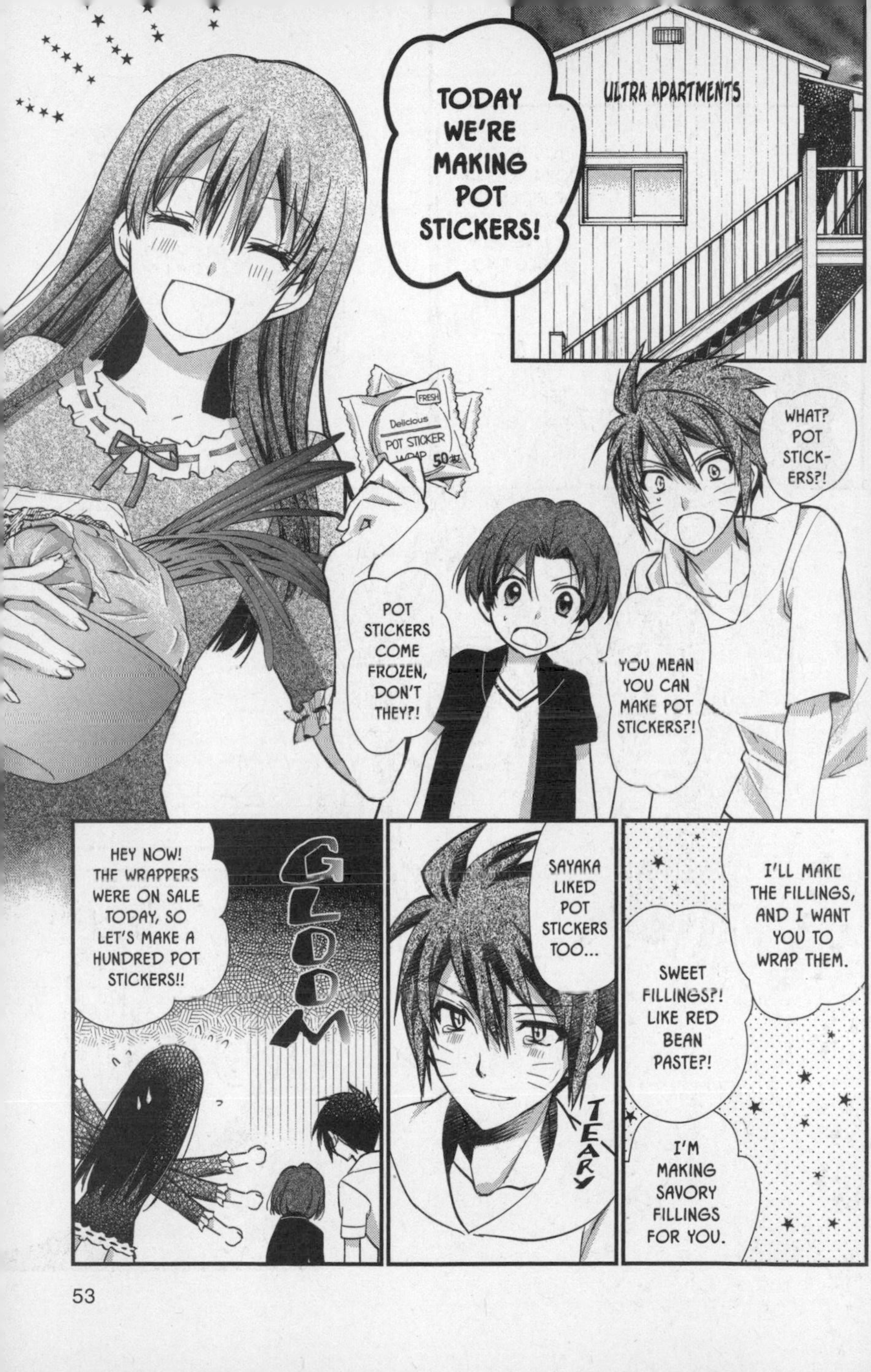
ULTRA APARTMENTS
TODAY WE'RE MAKING POT STICKERS!
FRESH
Delicious
POT STICKER WRAP
50
WHAT? POT STICK-ERS?!
YOU MEAN YOU CAN MAKE POT STICKERS?!
POT STICKERS COME FROZEN, DON'T THEY?!
I'LL MAKE THE FILLINGS, AND I WANT YOU TO WRAP THEM.
SWEET FILLINGS?! LIKE RED BEAN PASTE?!
I'M MAKING SAVORY FILLINGS FOR YOU.
SAYAKA LIKED POT STICKERS TOO...
TEARY
GLOOM
HEY NOW! THE WRAPPERS WERE ON SALE TODAY, SO LET'S MAKE A HUNDRED POT STICKERS!!

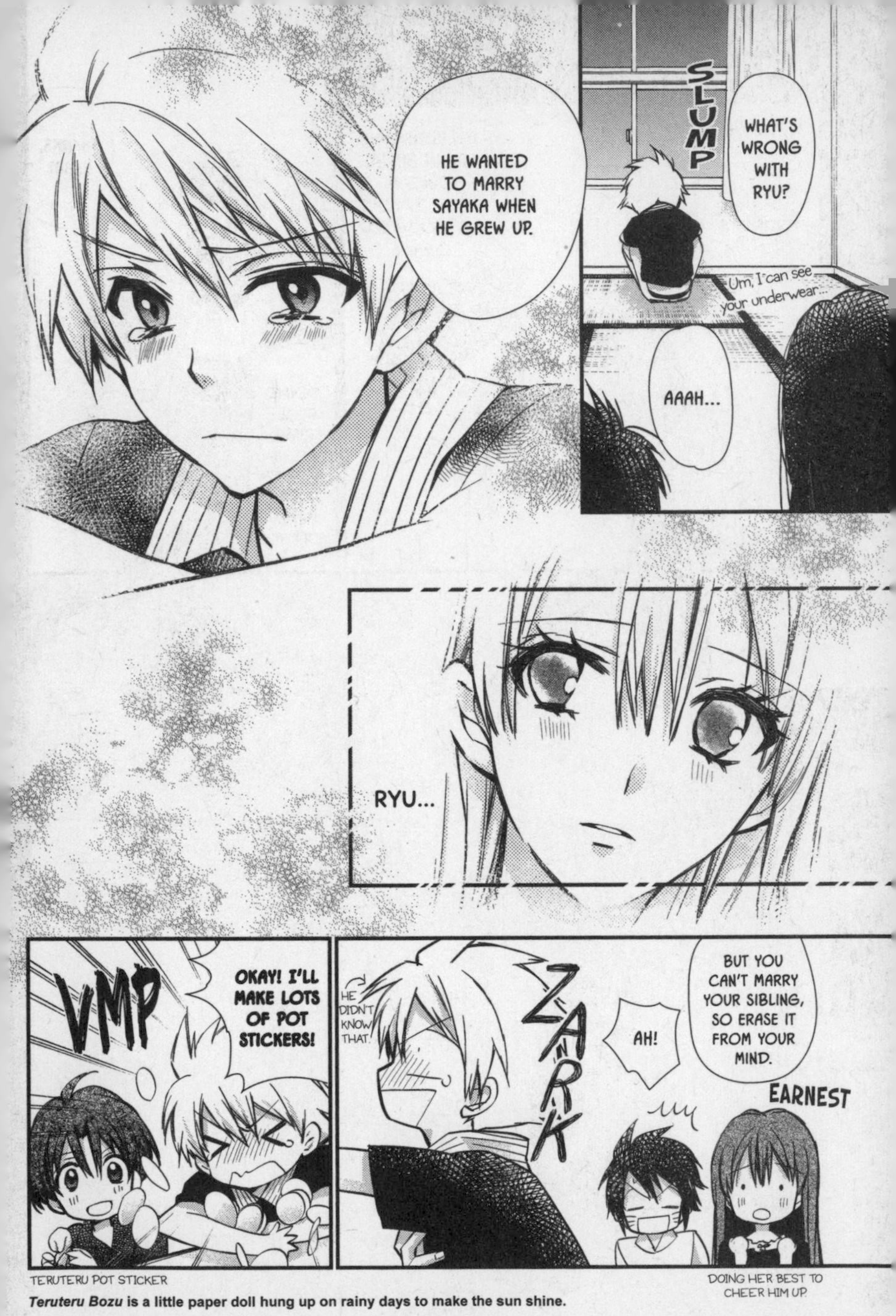
SLUMP
WHAT'S WRONG WITH RYU?
Um, I can see your underwear...
AAAH...
HE WANTED TO MARRY SAYAKA WHEN HE GREW UP.
RYU...
BUT YOU CAN'T MARRY YOUR SIBLING, SO ERASE IT FROM YOUR MIND.
EARNEST
AH!
ZARK
HE DIDN'T KNOW THAT.
OKAY! I'LL MAKE LOTS OF POT STICKERS!
VMP

DOING HER BEST TO CHEER HIM UP.

TERUTERU POT STICKER

Teruteru Bozu **is a little paper doll hung up on rainy days to make the sun shine.**

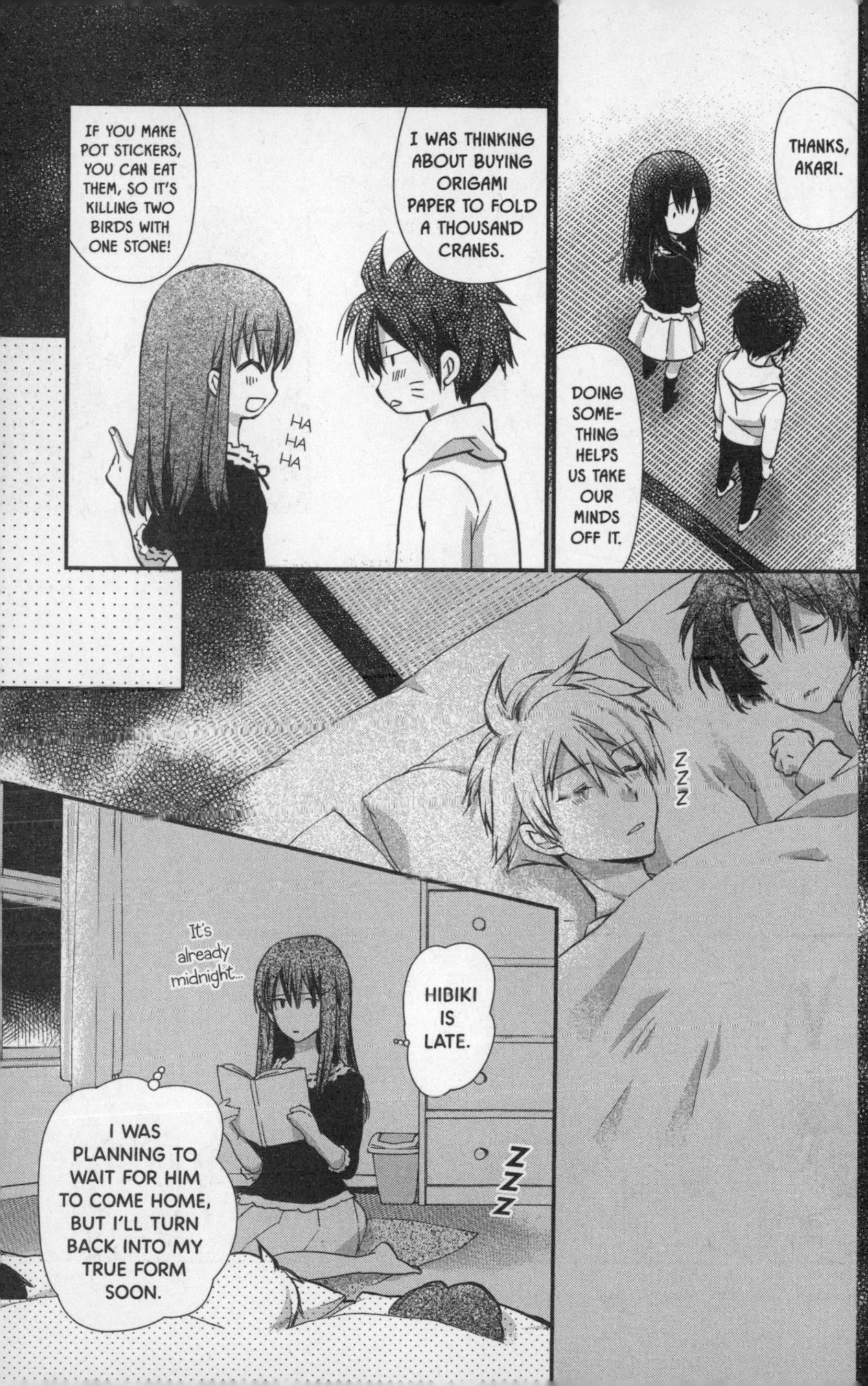
THANKS, AKARI.
DOING SOME-THING HELPS US TAKE OUR MINDS OFF IT.
I WAS THINKING ABOUT BUYING ORIGAMI PAPER TO FOLD A THOUSAND CRANES.
IF YOU MAKE POT STICKERS, YOU CAN EAT THEM, SO IT'S KILLING TWO BIRDS WITH ONE STONE!
HA HA HA
ZZZ
It's already midnight...
HIBIKI IS LATE.
I WAS PLANNING TO WAIT FOR HIM TO COME HOME, BUT I'LL TURN BACK INTO MY TRUE FORM SOON.
ZZZ

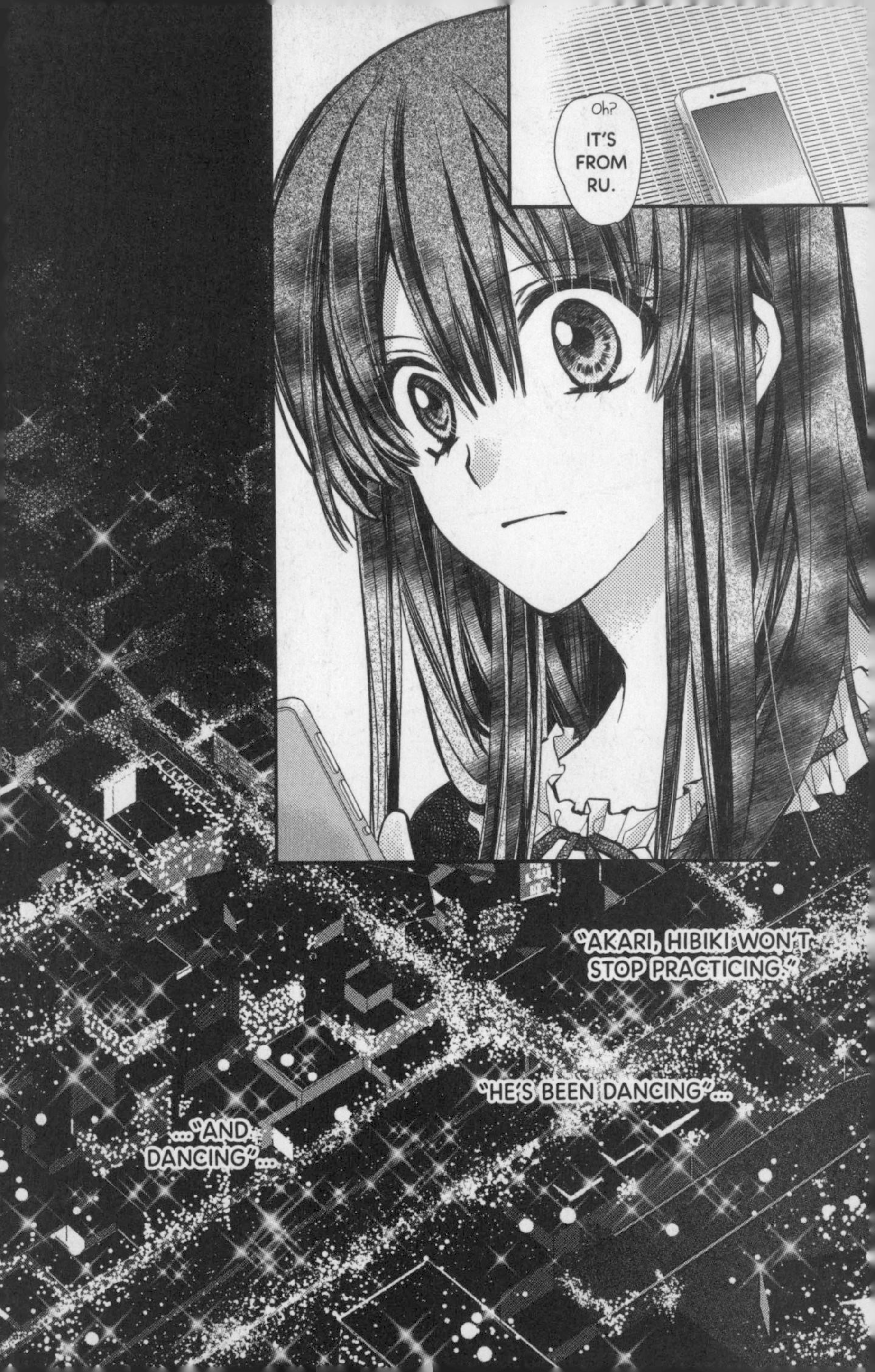
Oh?
IT'S FROM RU.
"AKARI, HIBIKI WON'T STOP PRACTICING."
"HE'S BEEN DANCING"...
..."AND DANCING"...

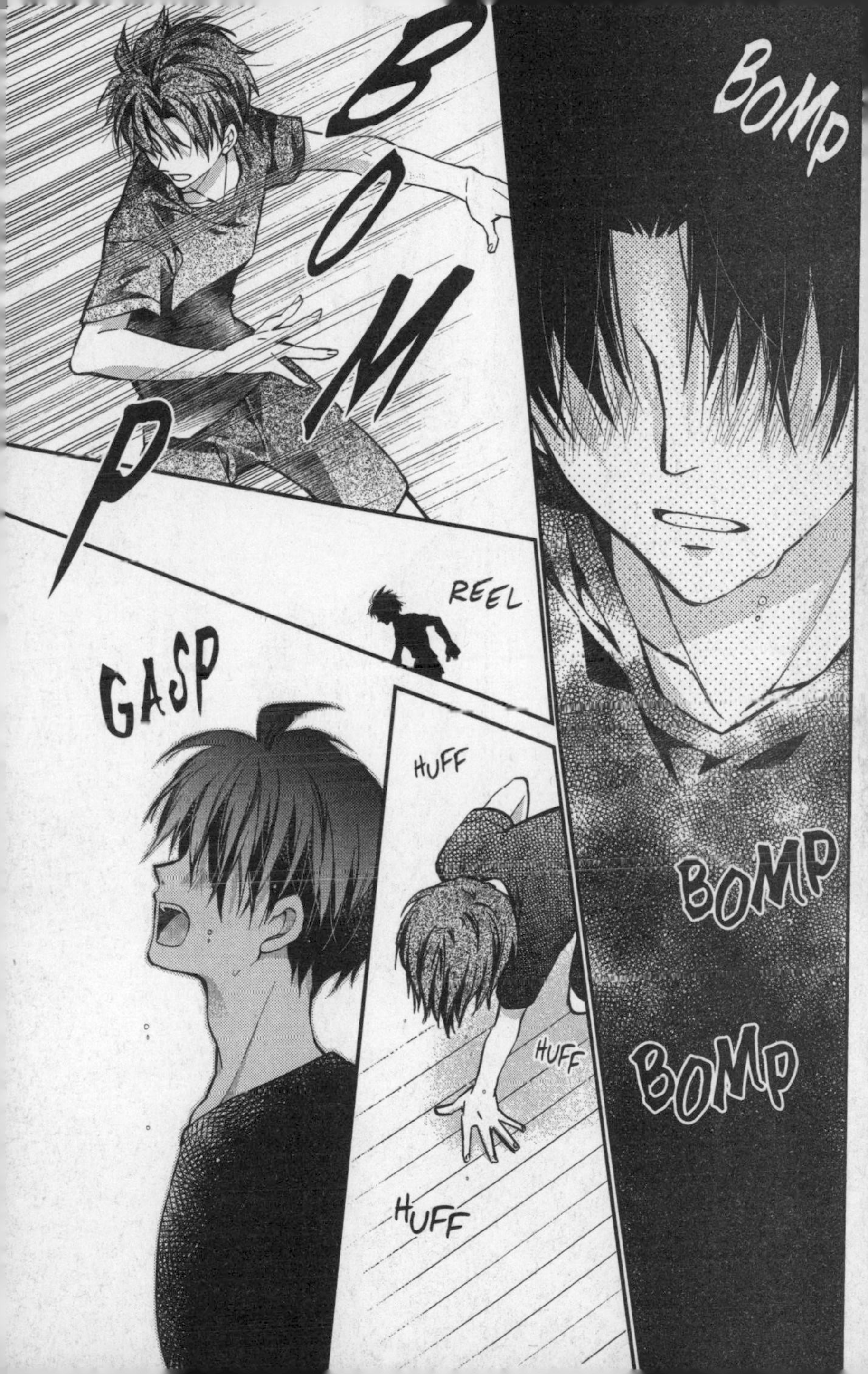

BOMP
BOMP
BOMP
BOMP
REEL
HUFF
HUFF
HUFF
GASP

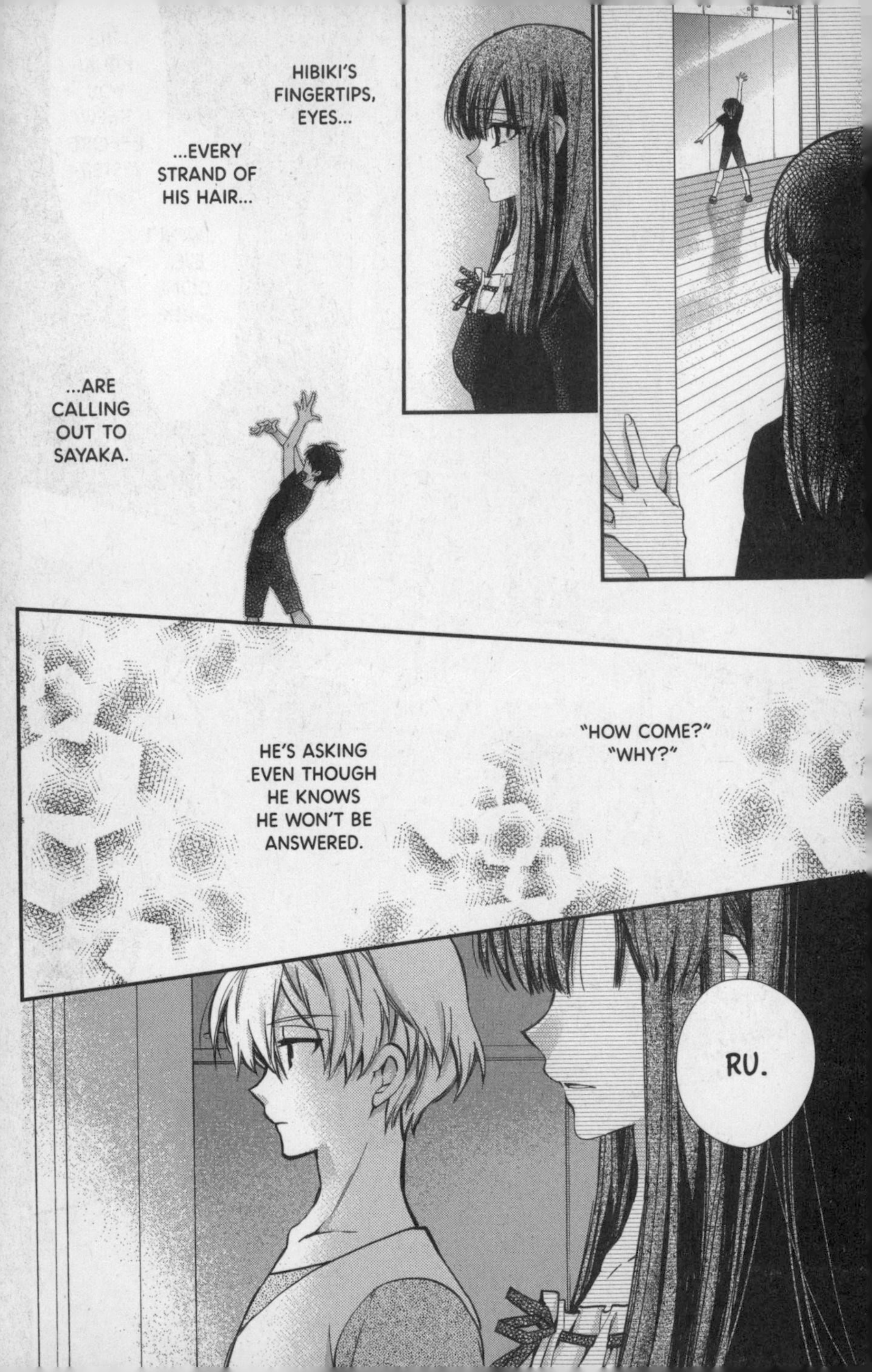
HIBIKI'S FINGERTIPS, EYES...
...EVERY STRAND OF HIS HAIR...
...ARE CALLING OUT TO SAYAKA.
"HOW COME?" "WHY?"
HE'S ASKING EVEN THOUGH HE KNOWS HE WON'T BE ANSWERED.
RU.

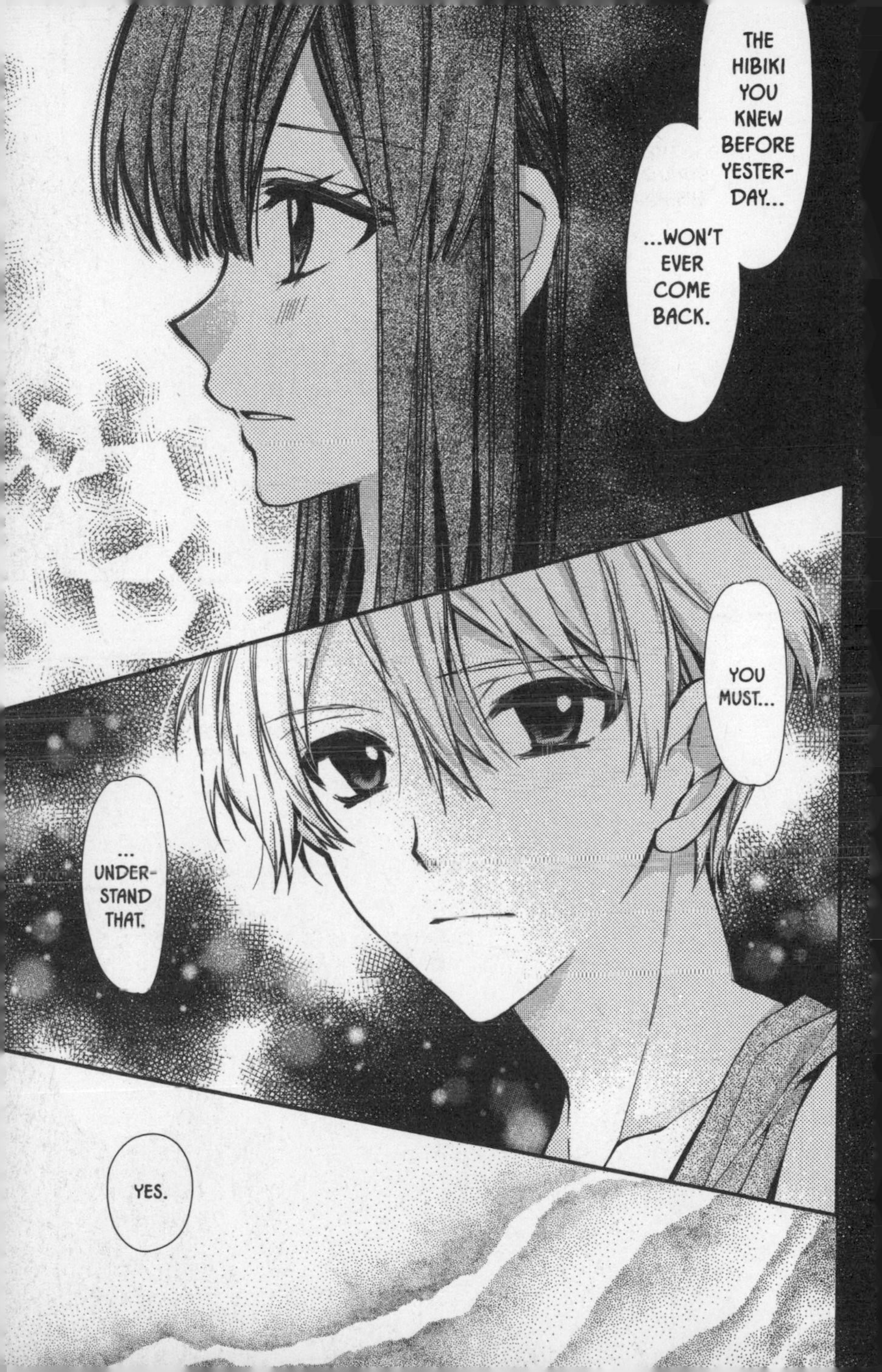
THE HIBIKI YOU KNEW BEFORE YESTER-DAY...
...WON'T EVER COME BACK.
YOU MUST...
...UNDER-STAND THAT.
YES.

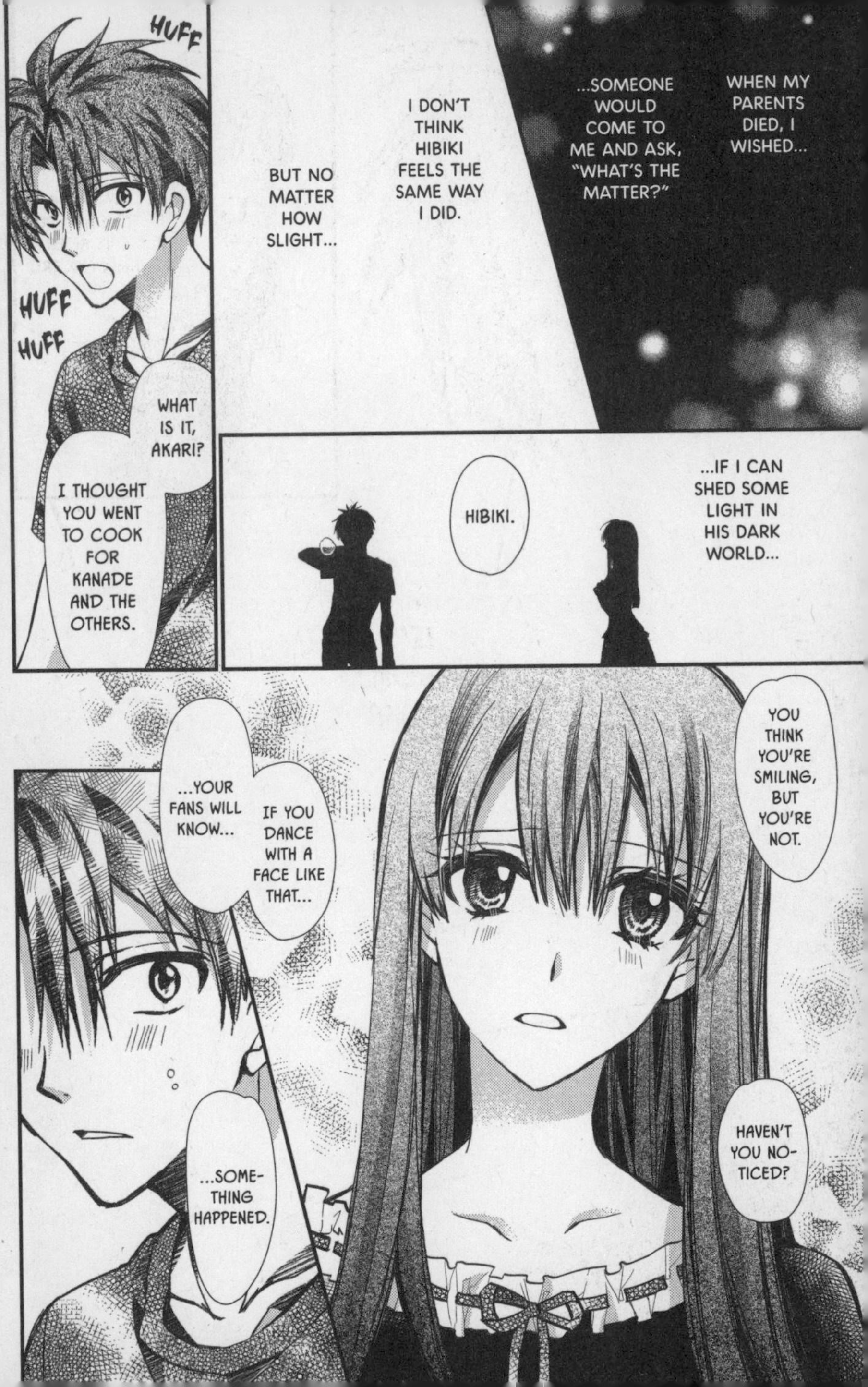
WHEN MY PARENTS DIED, I WISHED...
...SOMEONE WOULD COME TO ME AND ASK, "WHAT'S THE MATTER?"
I DON'T THINK HIBIKI FEELS THE SAME WAY I DID.
BUT NO MATTER HOW SLIGHT...
...IF I CAN SHED SOME LIGHT IN HIS DARK WORLD...
HIBIKI.
HUFF
HUFF
HUFF
WHAT IS IT, AKARI?
I THOUGHT YOU WENT TO COOK FOR KANADE AND THE OTHERS.
YOU THINK YOU'RE SMILING, BUT YOU'RE NOT.
HAVEN'T YOU NO-TICED?
IF YOU DANCE WITH A FACE LIKE THAT...
...YOUR FANS WILL KNOW...
...SOME-THING HAPPENED.

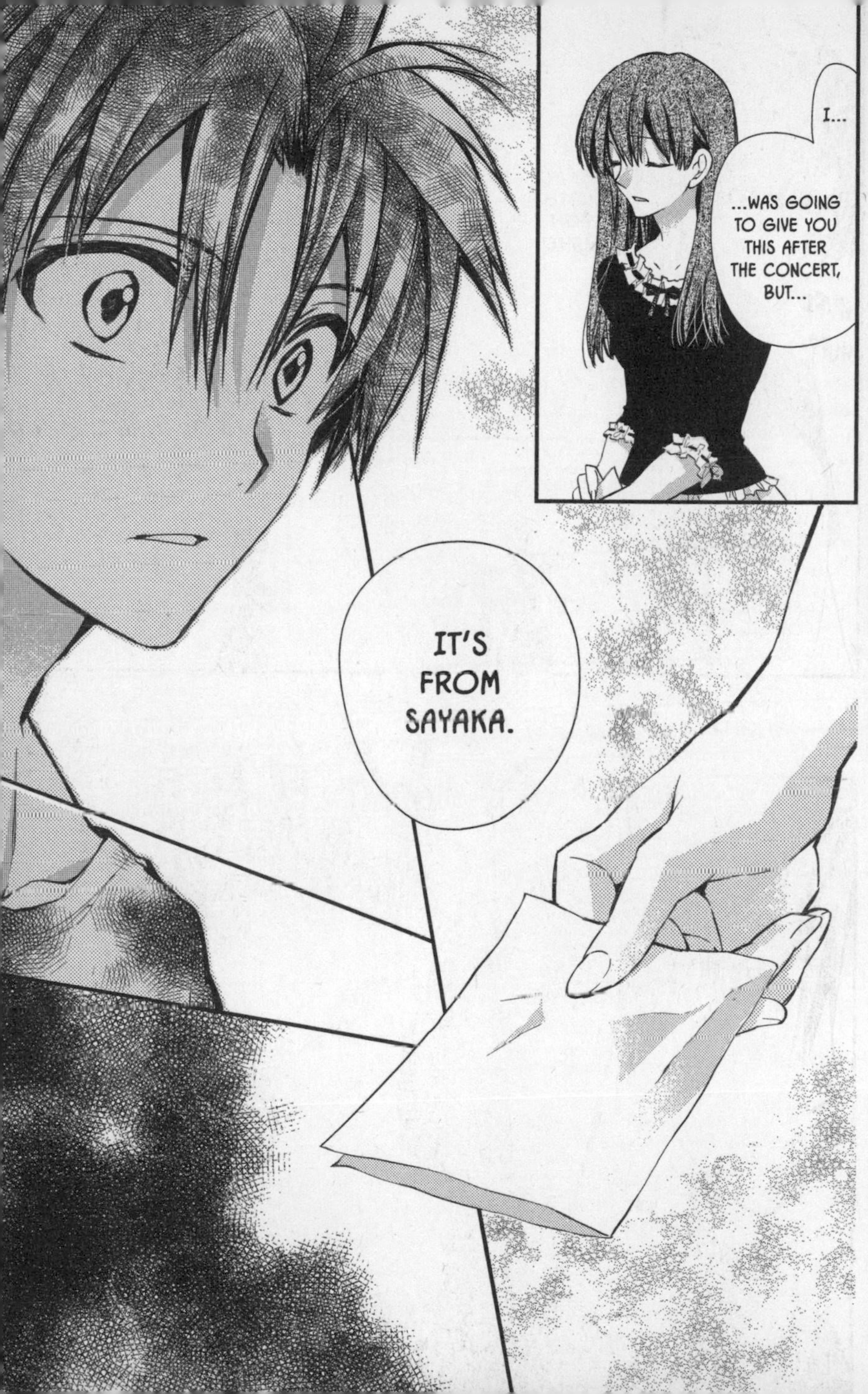
I...
...WAS GOING TO GIVE YOU THIS AFTER THE CONCERT, BUT...
IT'S FROM SAYAKA.

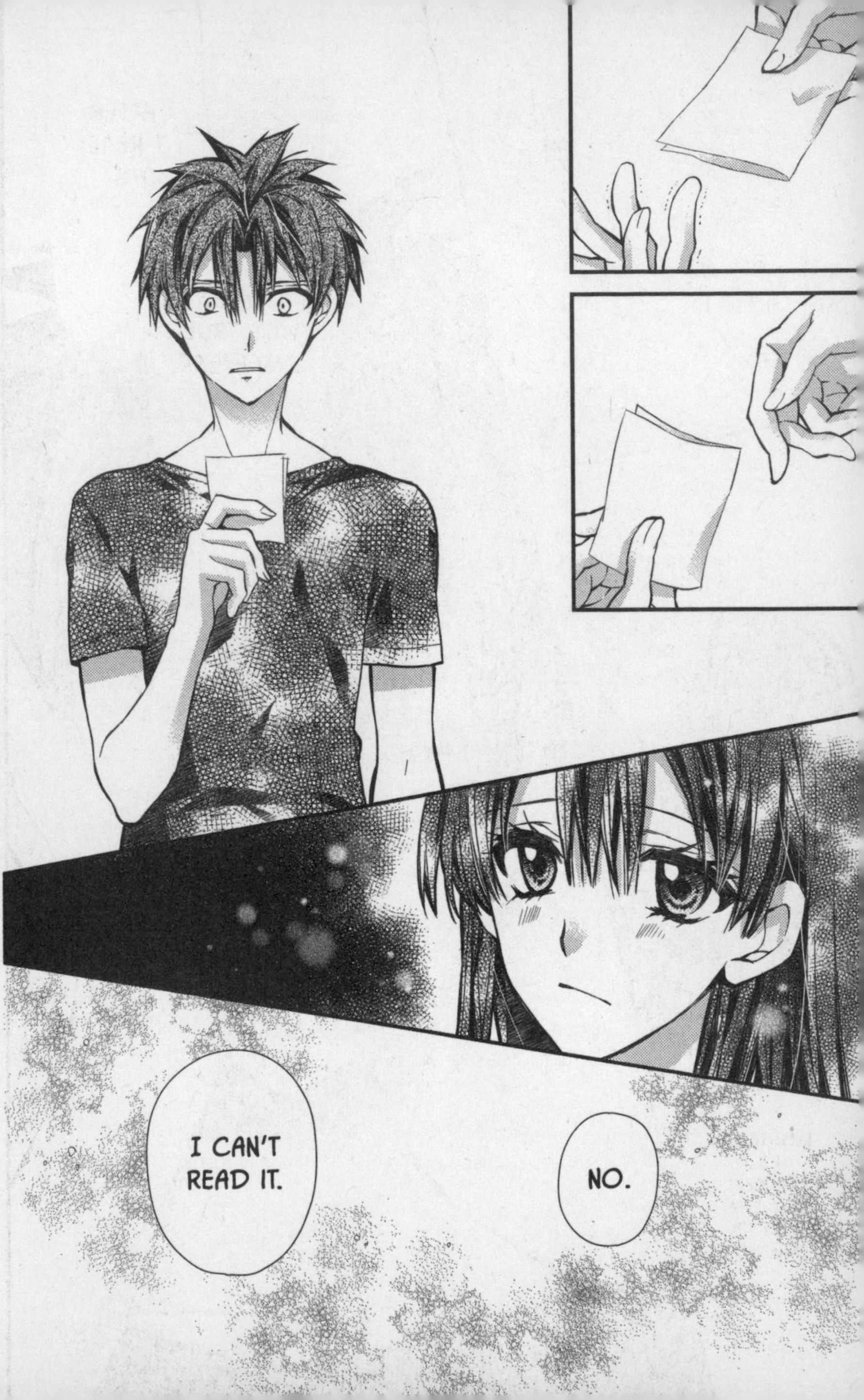
NO.
I CAN'T READ IT.

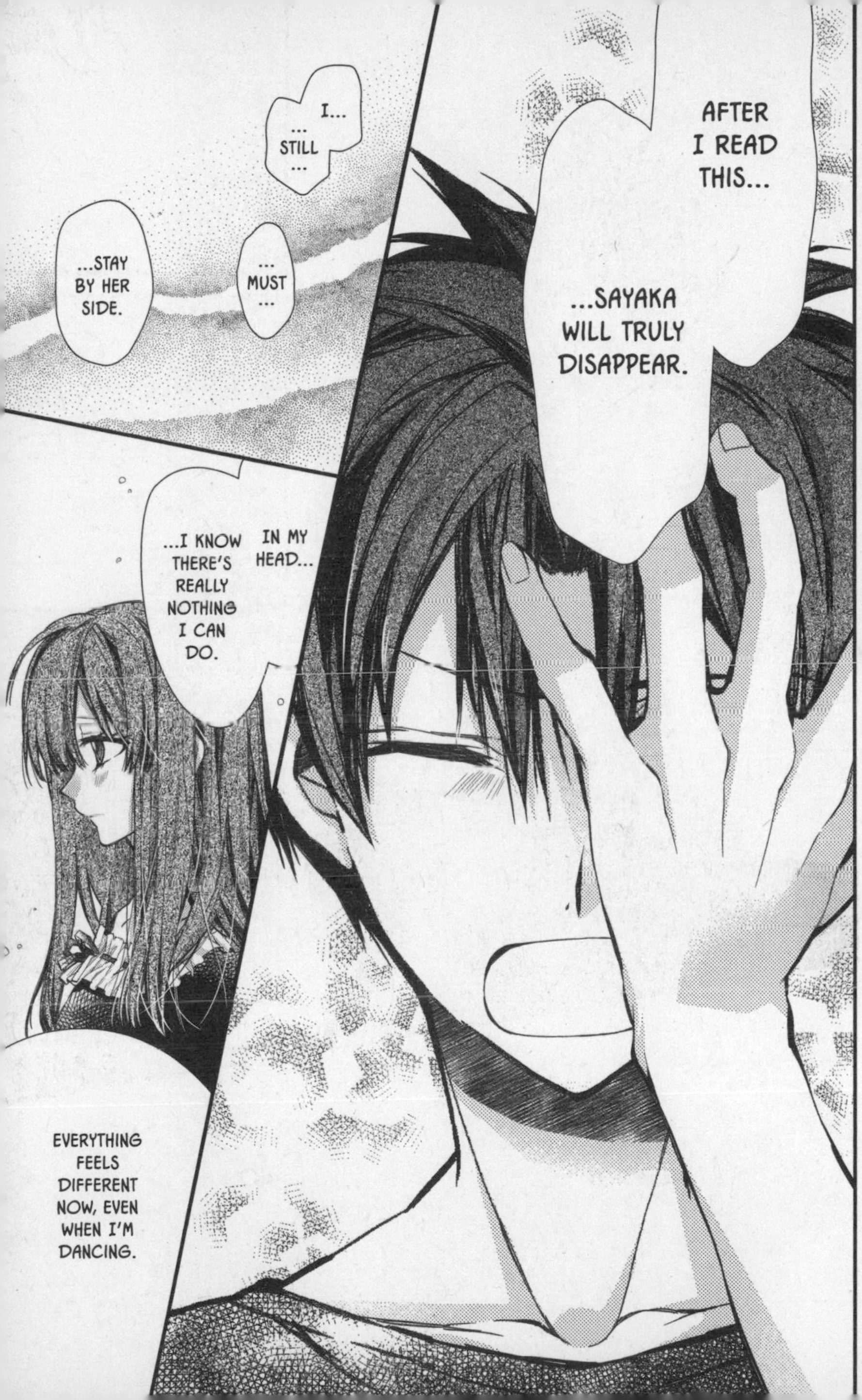
AFTER I READ THIS...
...SAYAKA WILL TRULY DISAPPEAR.
I... ...STILL...
...MUST...
...STAY BY HER SIDE.
IN MY HEAD...
...I KNOW THERE'S REALLY NOTHING I CAN DO.
EVERYTHING FEELS DIFFERENT NOW, EVEN WHEN I'M DANCING.

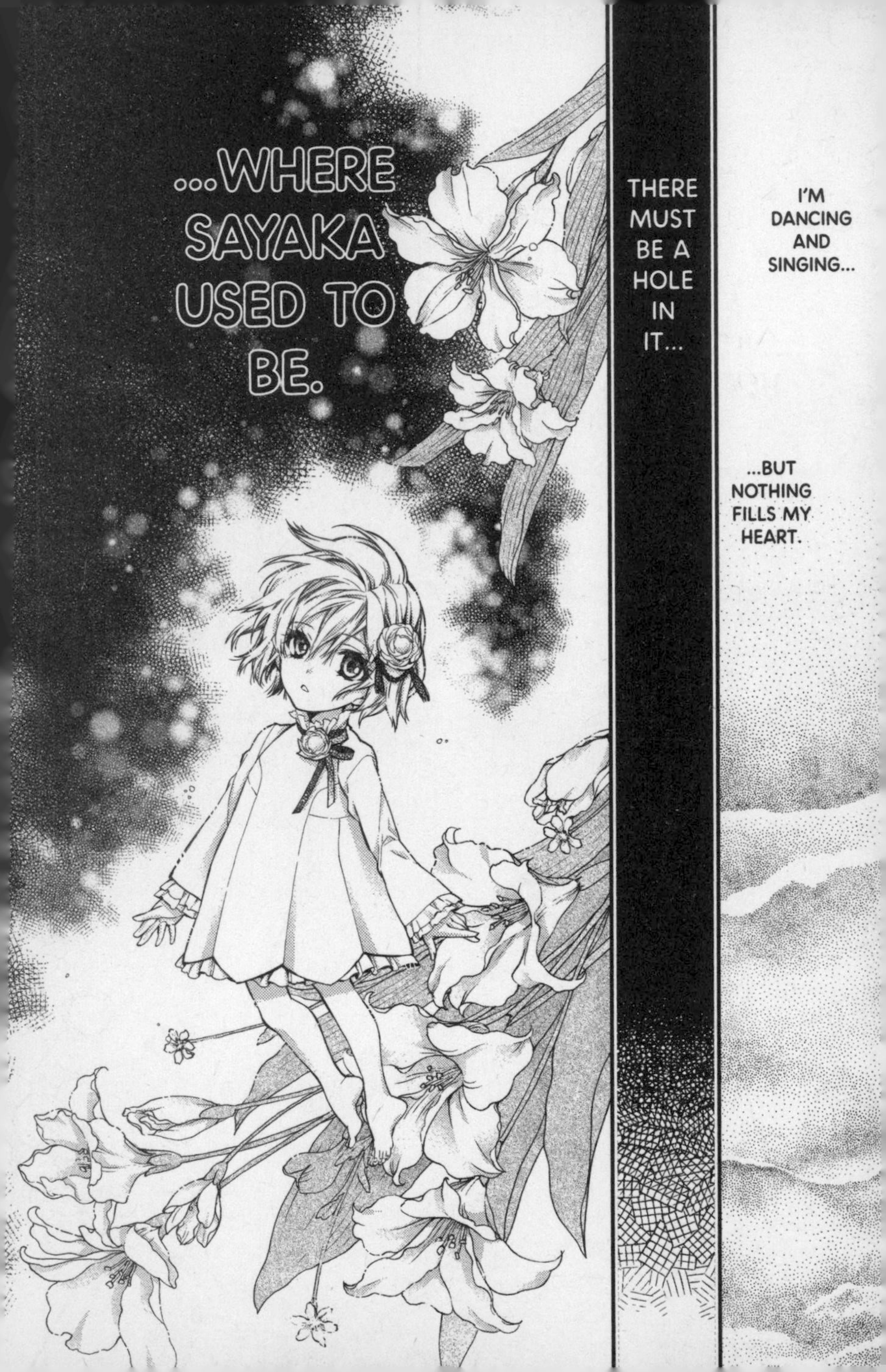
I'M DANCING AND SINGING...
...BUT NOTHING FILLS MY HEART.
THERE MUST BE A HOLE IN IT...
...WHERE SAYAKA USED TO BE.

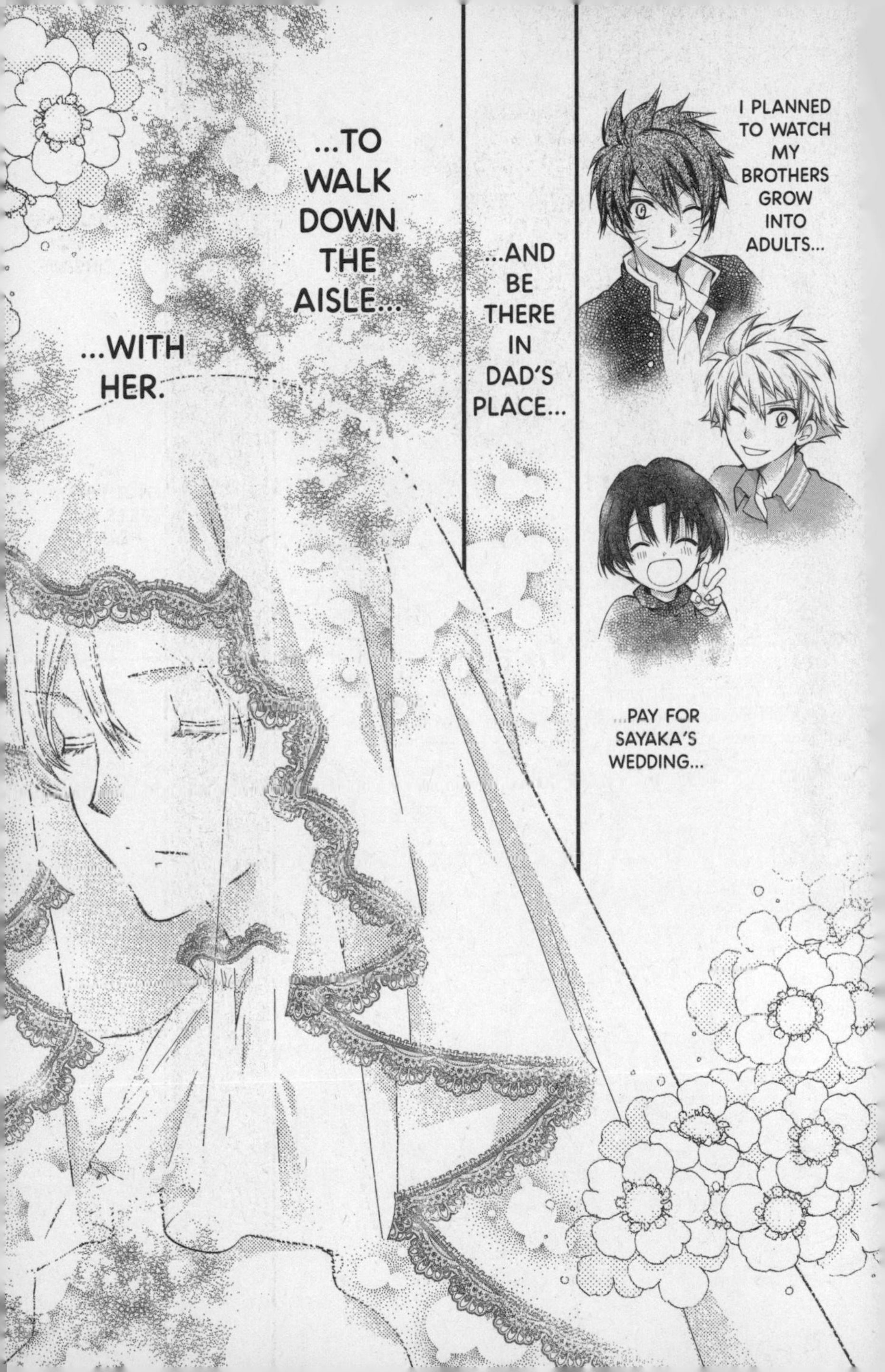
I PLANNED TO WATCH MY BROTHERS GROW INTO ADULTS...
...PAY FOR SAYAKA'S WEDDING...
...AND BE THERE IN DAD'S PLACE...
...TO WALK DOWN THE AISLE...
...WITH HER.

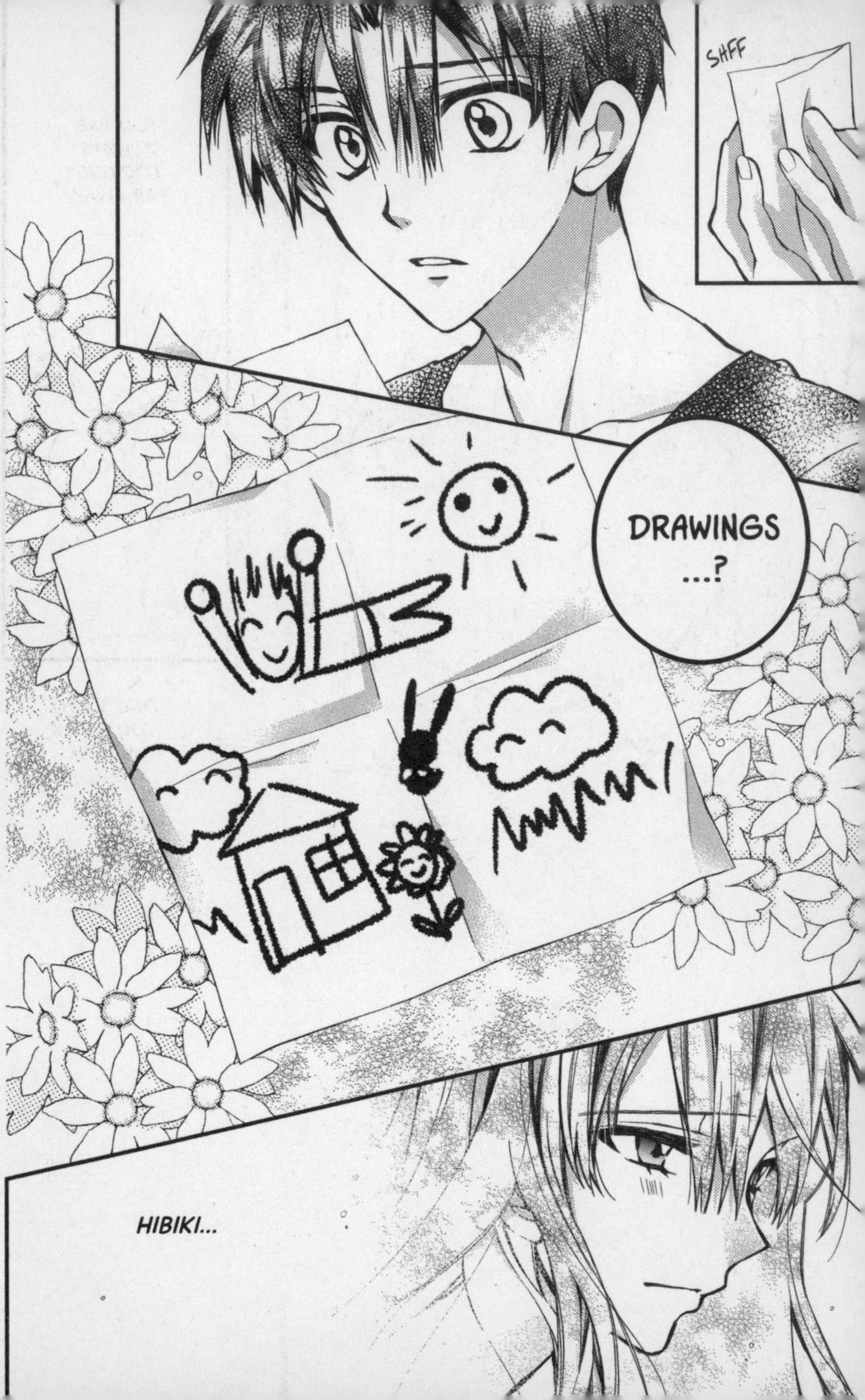
SHFF
DRAWINGS ...?
HIBIKI...

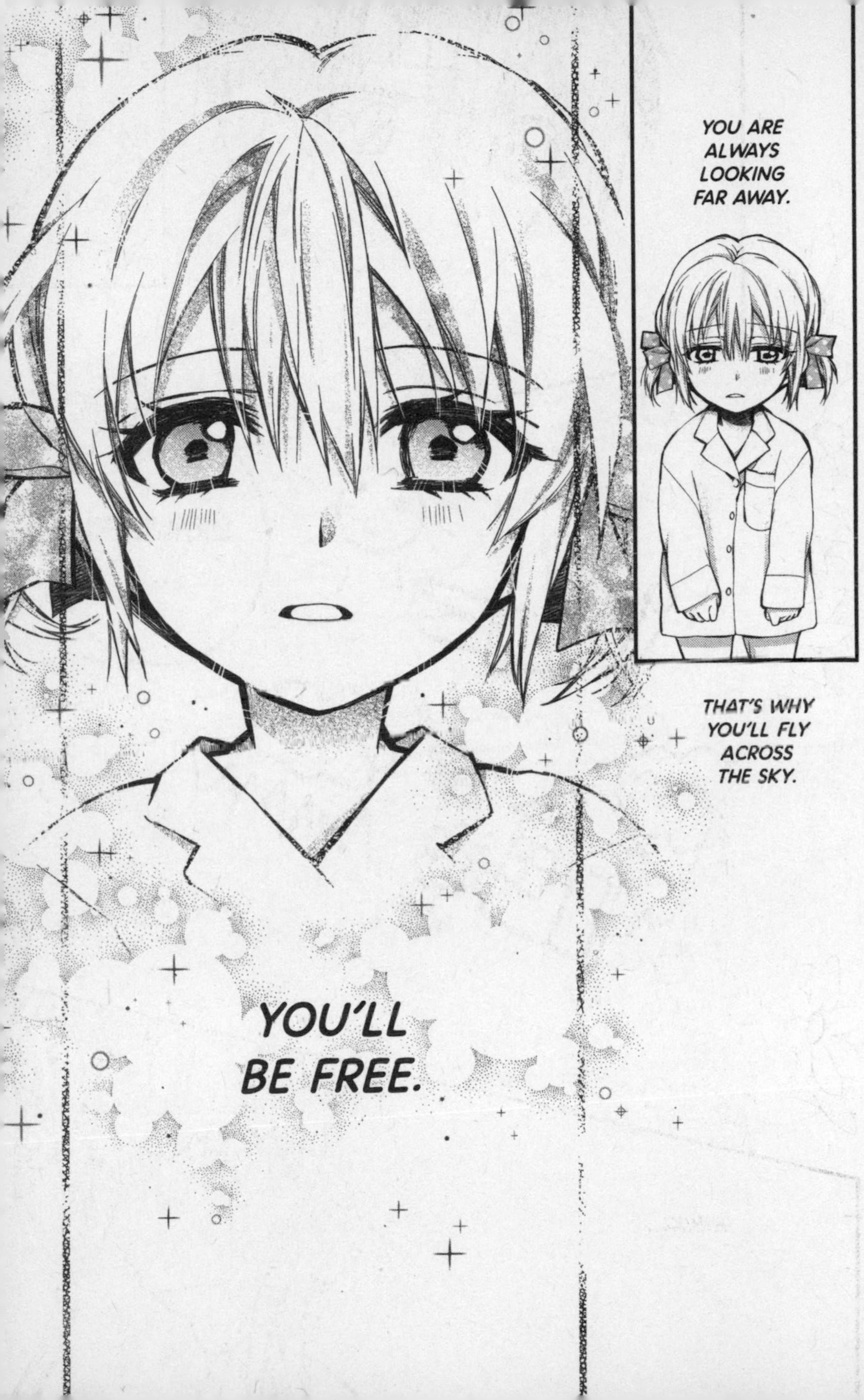
YOU ARE ALWAYS LOOKING FAR AWAY.
THAT'S WHY YOU'LL FLY ACROSS THE SKY.
YOU'LL BE FREE.

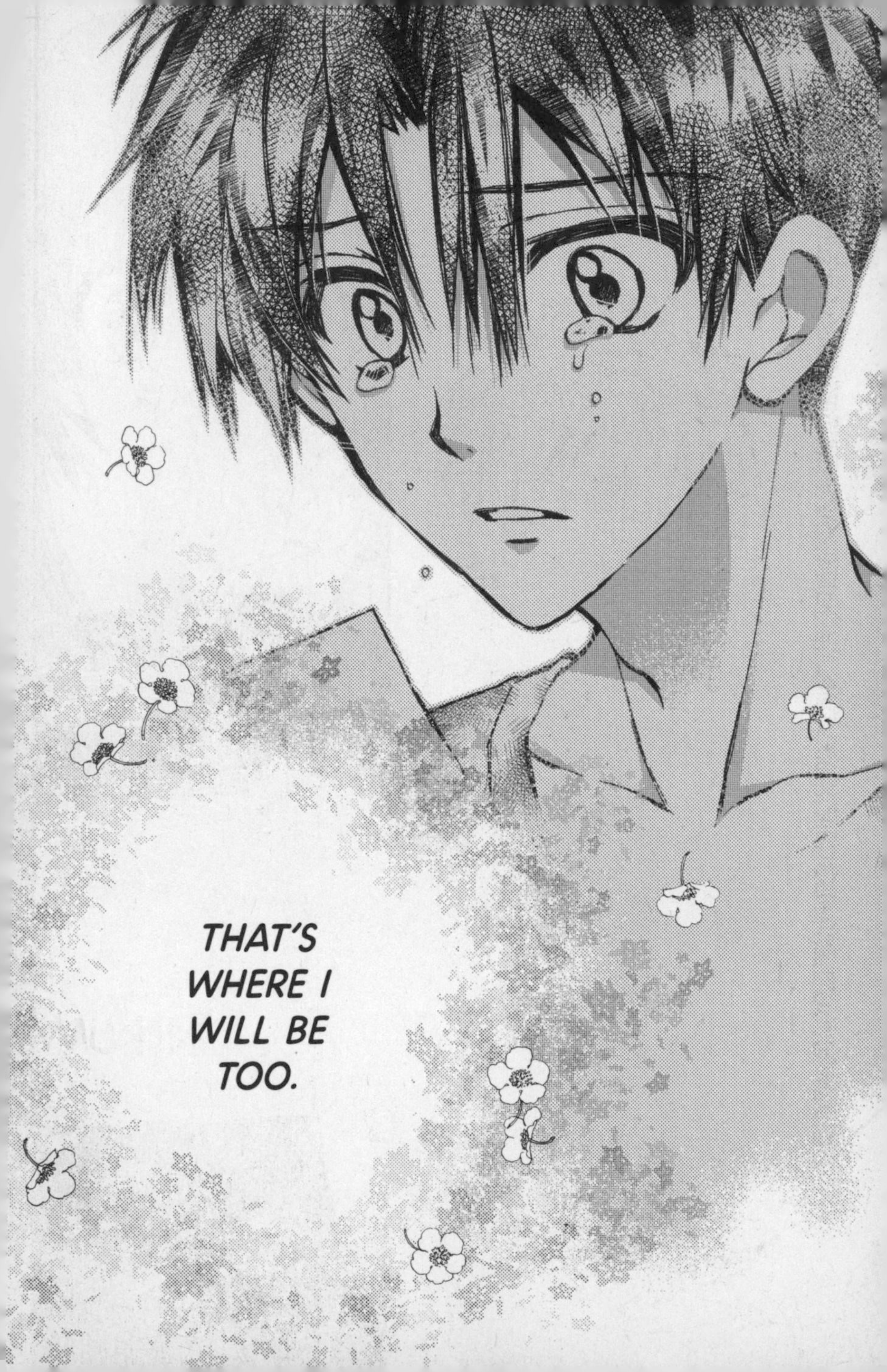
THAT'S WHERE I WILL BE TOO.

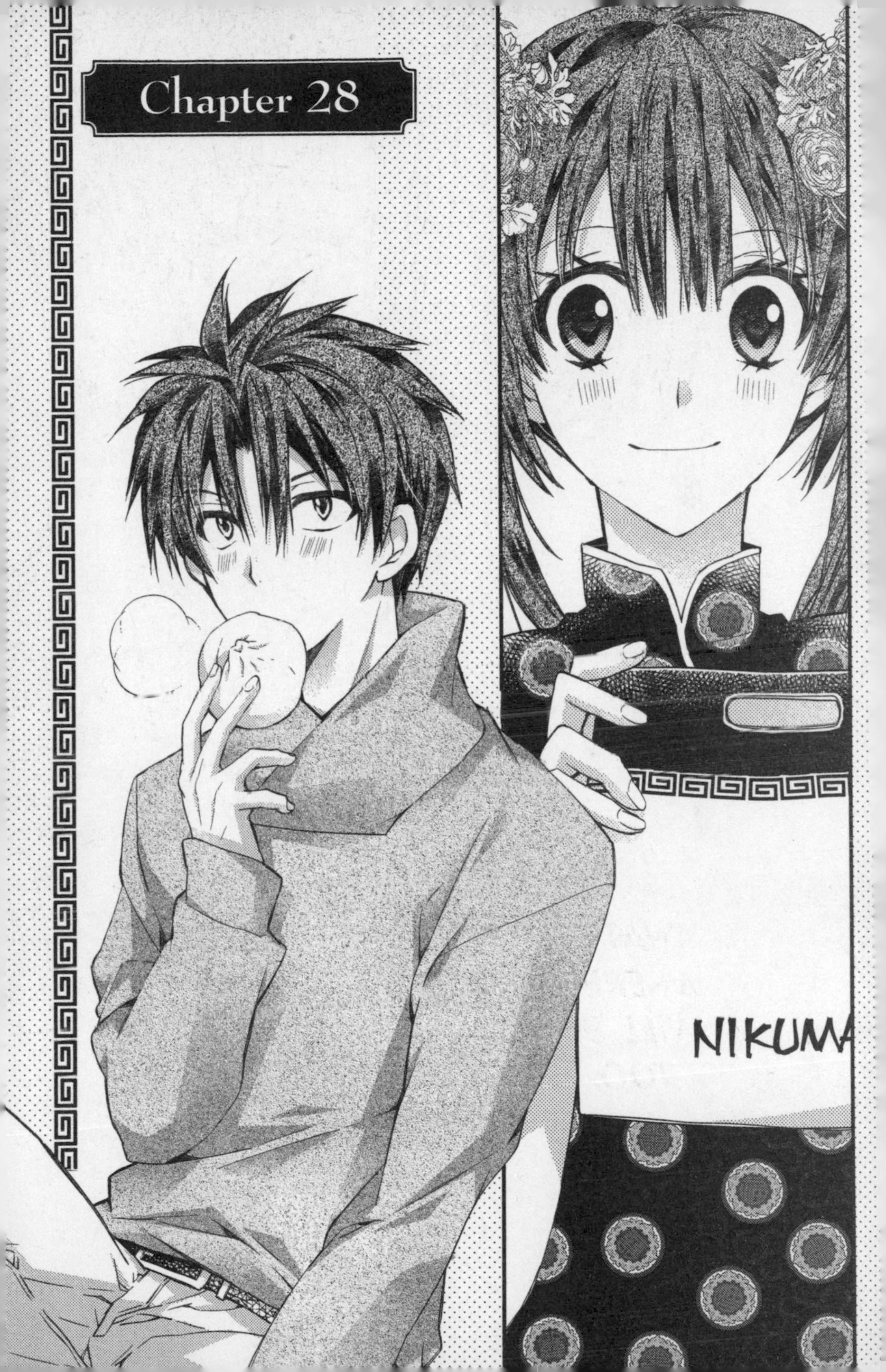
Chapter 28
NIKUMA

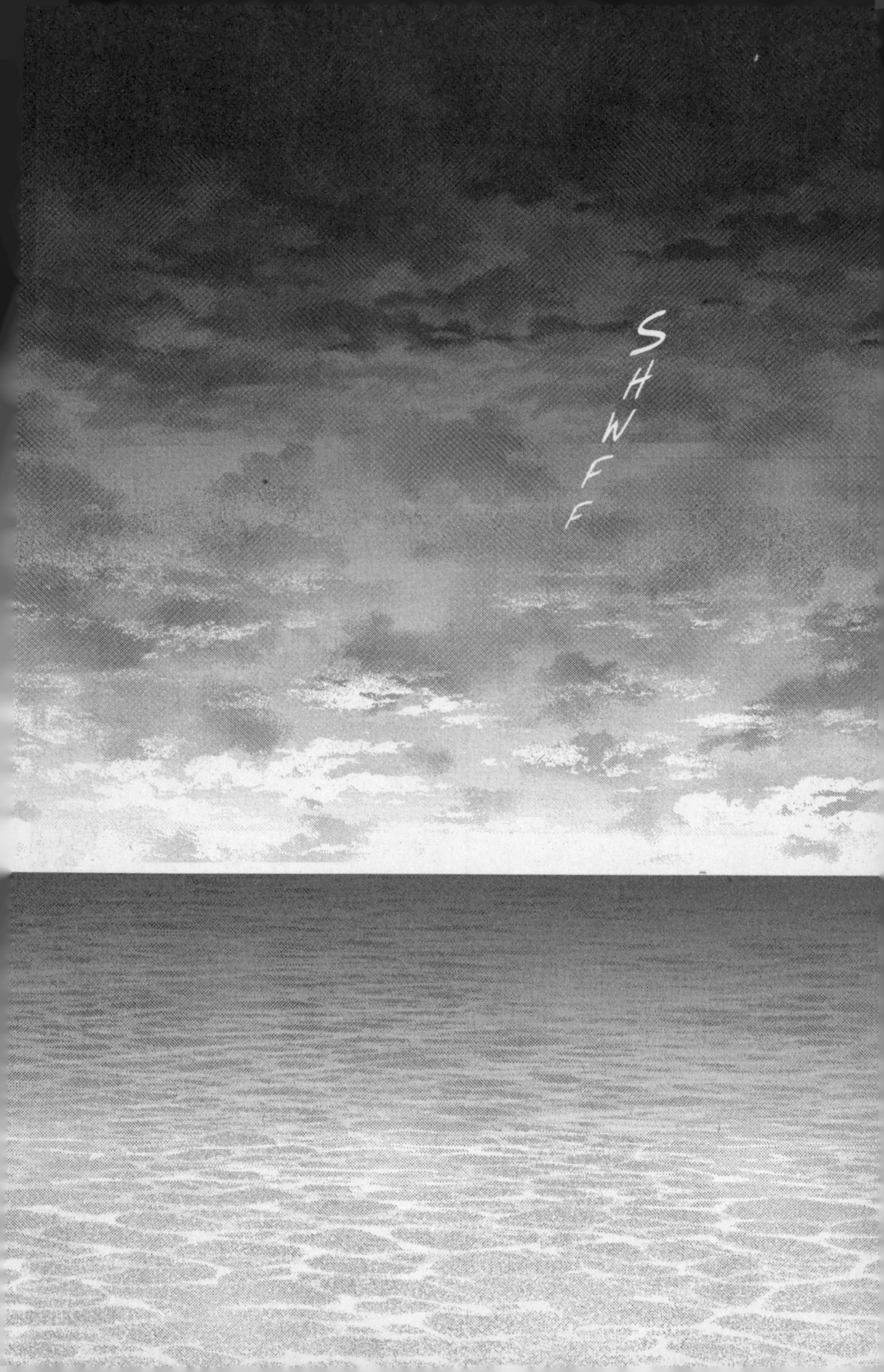
SHWFF

SHWFF

I WONDER WHY LOOKING AT THE SEA MAKES ME NOSTALGIC.

THE CREATURES ON EARTH WERE BORN FROM THE SEA.

DEEP DOWN WE PROBABLY HAVE A YEARNING TO RETURN.

AND WE LONG FOR THE SKY BECAUSE WE CANNOT FLY.

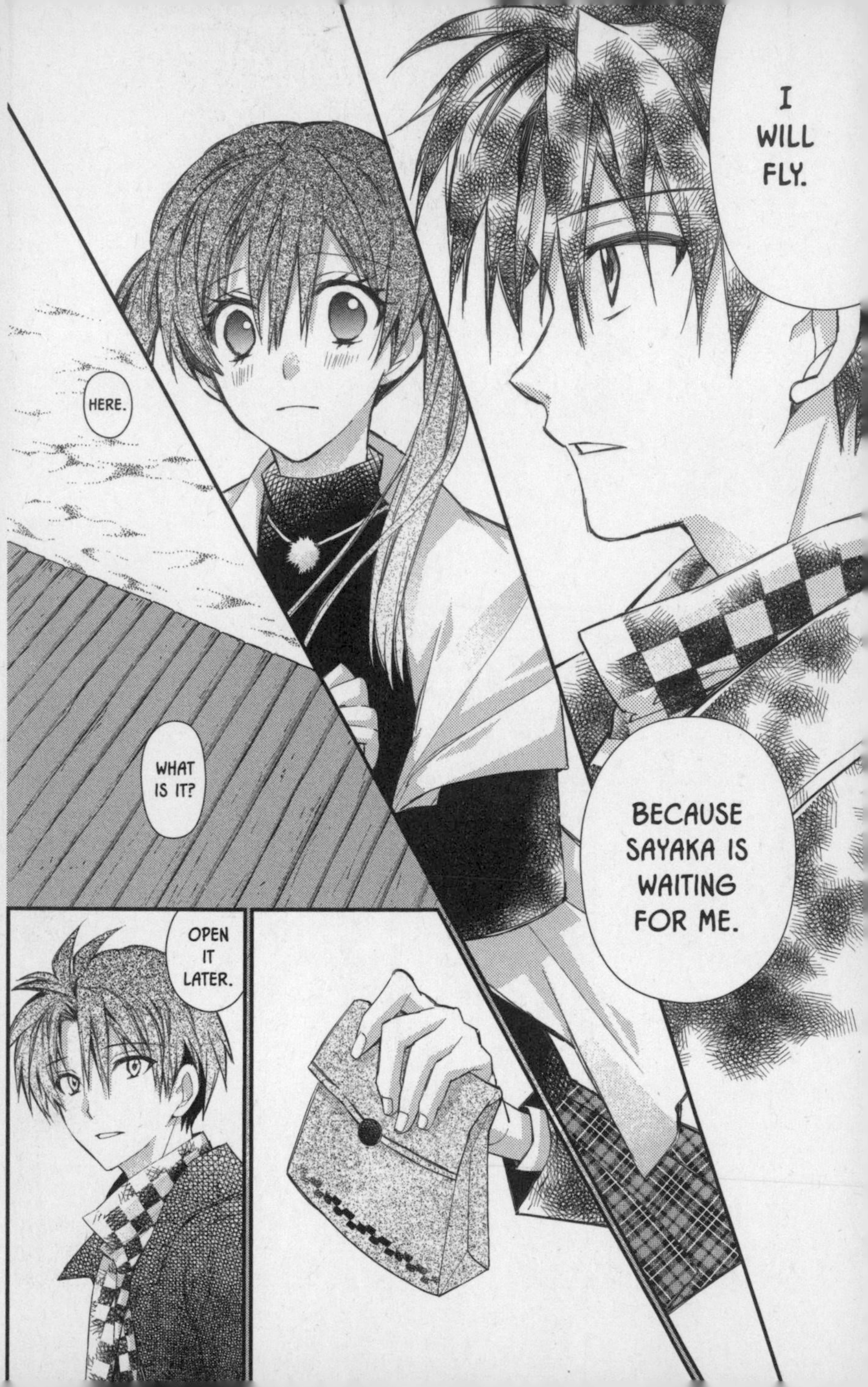
I WILL FLY.
BECAUSE SAYAKA IS WAITING FOR ME.
HERE.
WHAT IS IT?
OPEN IT LATER.

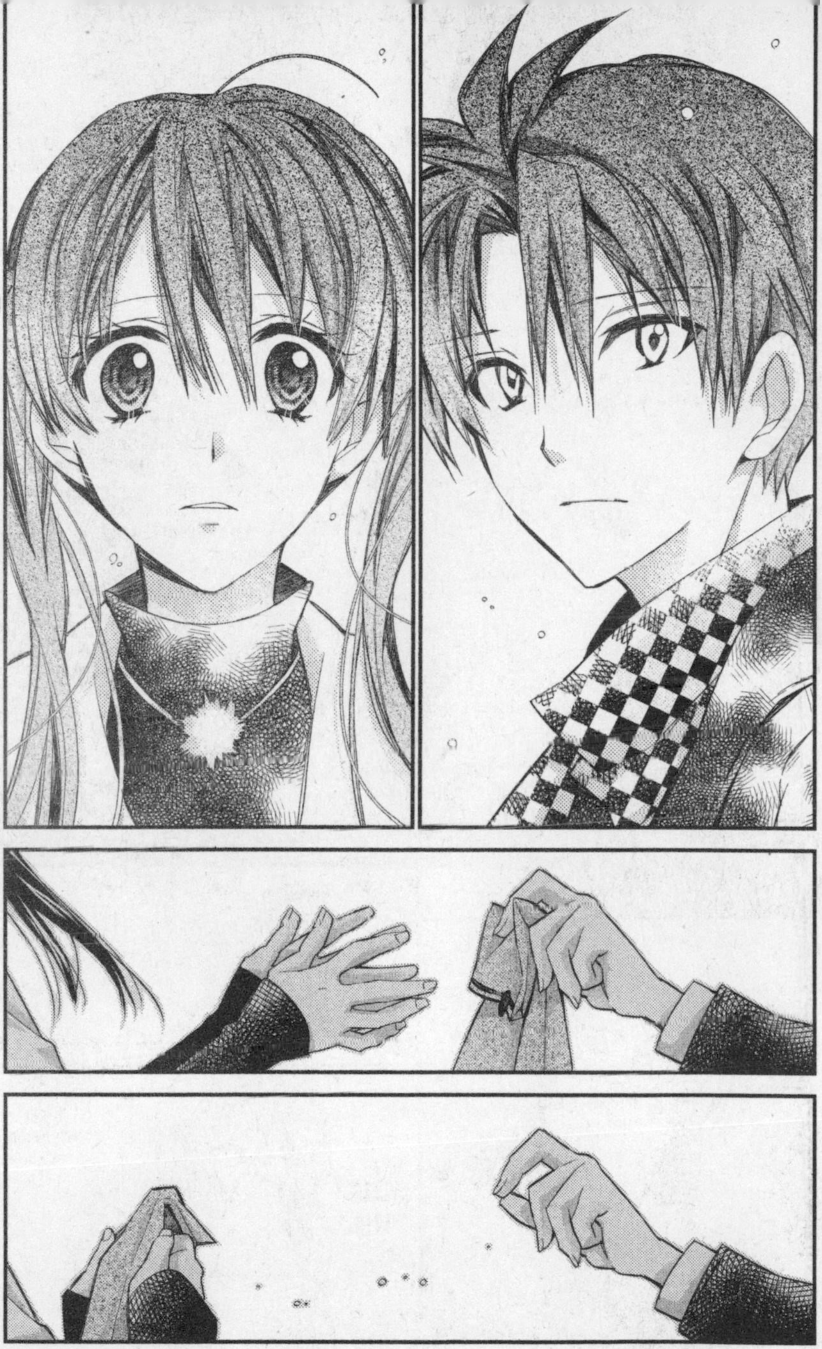

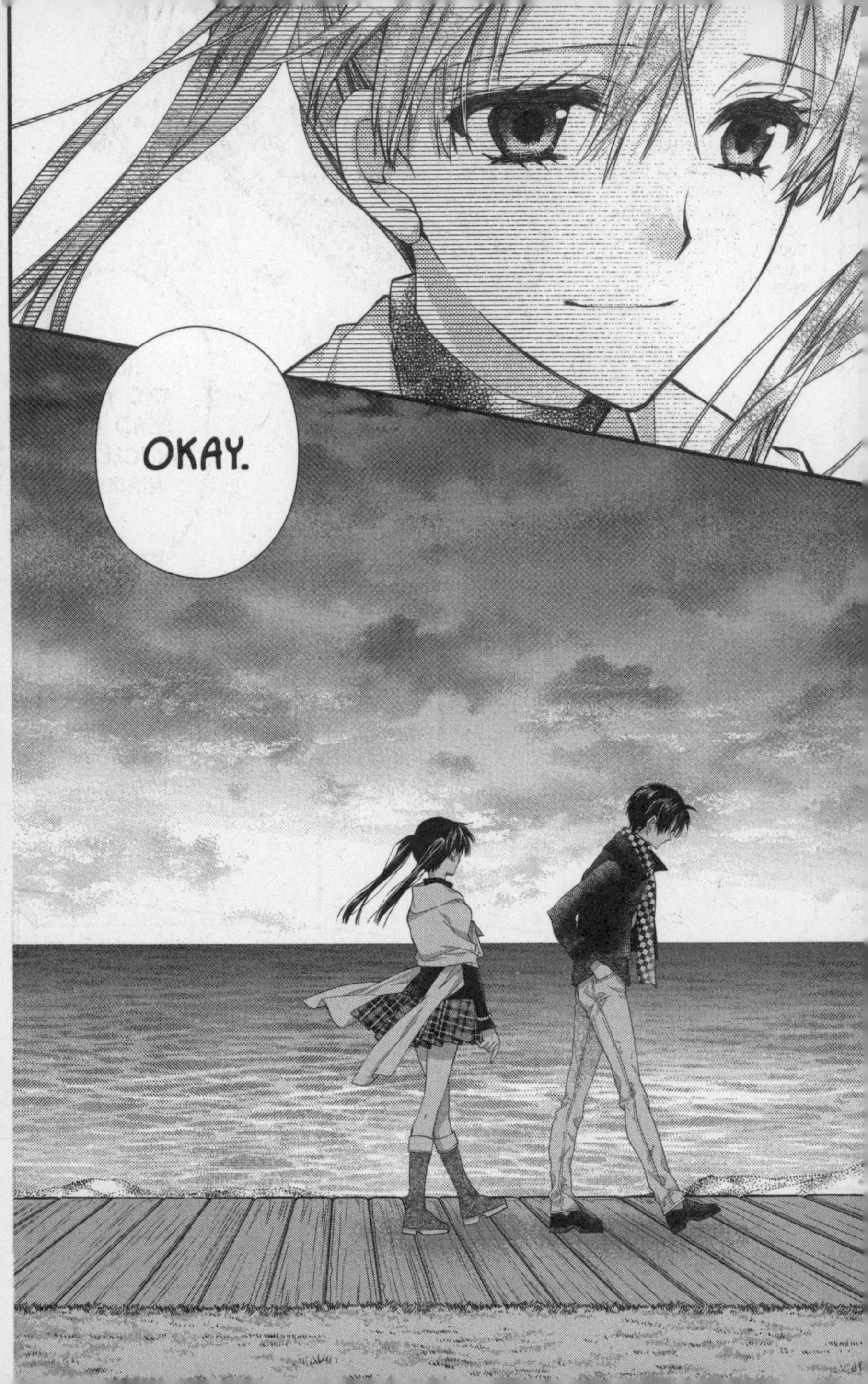
OKAY.

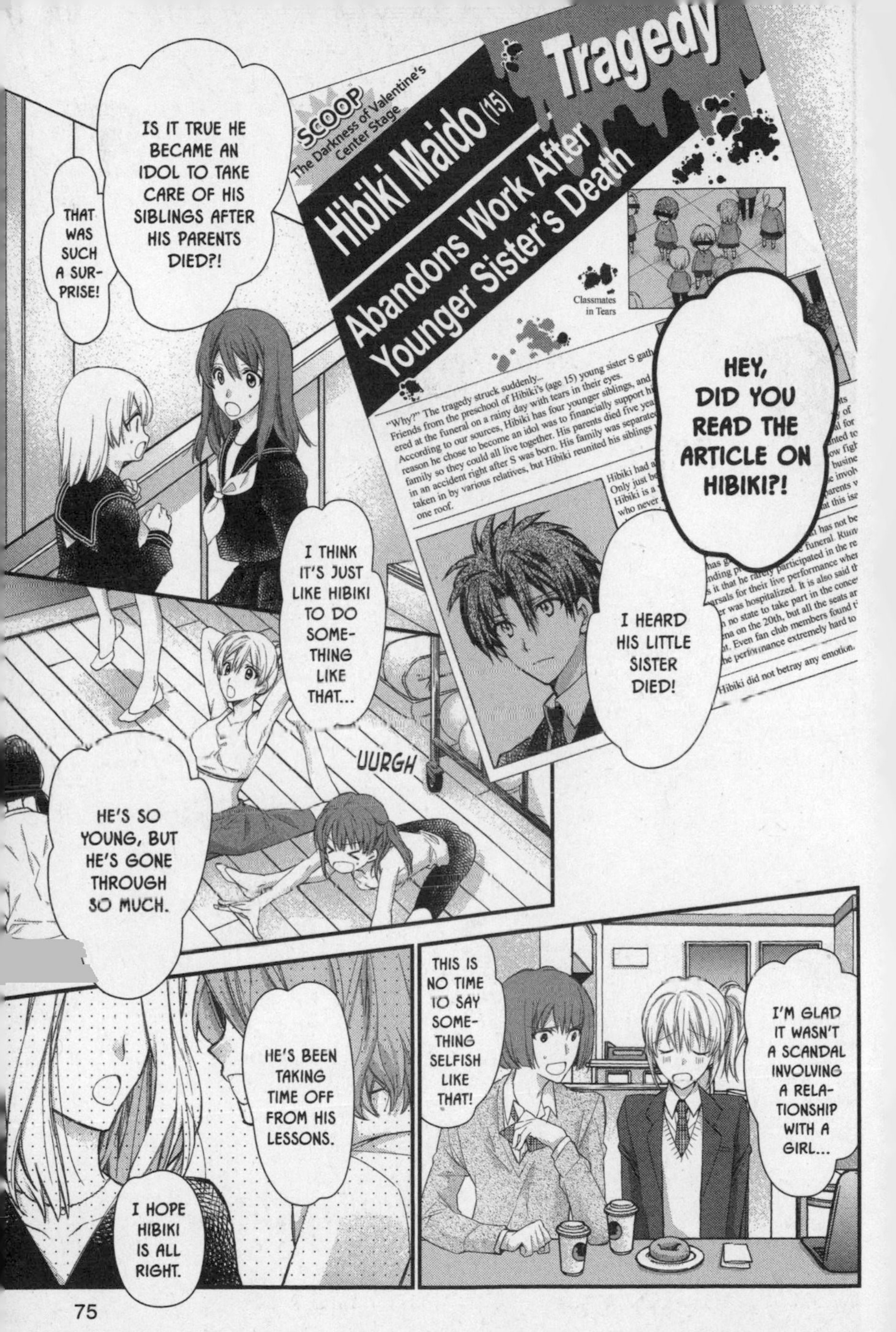
HEY, DID YOU READ THE ARTICLE ON HIBIKI?!
Tragedy
SCOOP
The Darkness of Valentine's Center Stage
Hibiki Maido (15)
Abandons Work After Younger Sister's Death
Classmates in Tears
IS IT TRUE HE BECAME AN IDOL TO TAKE CARE OF HIS SIBLINGS AFTER HIS PARENTS DIED?!
THAT WAS SUCH A SUR-PRISE!
I HEARD HIS LITTLE SISTER DIED!
I THINK IT'S JUST LIKE HIBIKI TO DO SOME-THING LIKE THAT...
UURGH
HE'S SO YOUNG, BUT HE'S GONE THROUGH SO MUCH.
I'M GLAD IT WASN'T A SCANDAL INVOLVING A RELA-TIONSHIP WITH A GIRL...
THIS IS NO TIME TO SAY SOME-THING SELFISH LIKE THAT!
HE'S BEEN TAKING TIME OFF FROM HIS LESSONS.
I HOPE HIBIKI IS ALL RIGHT.

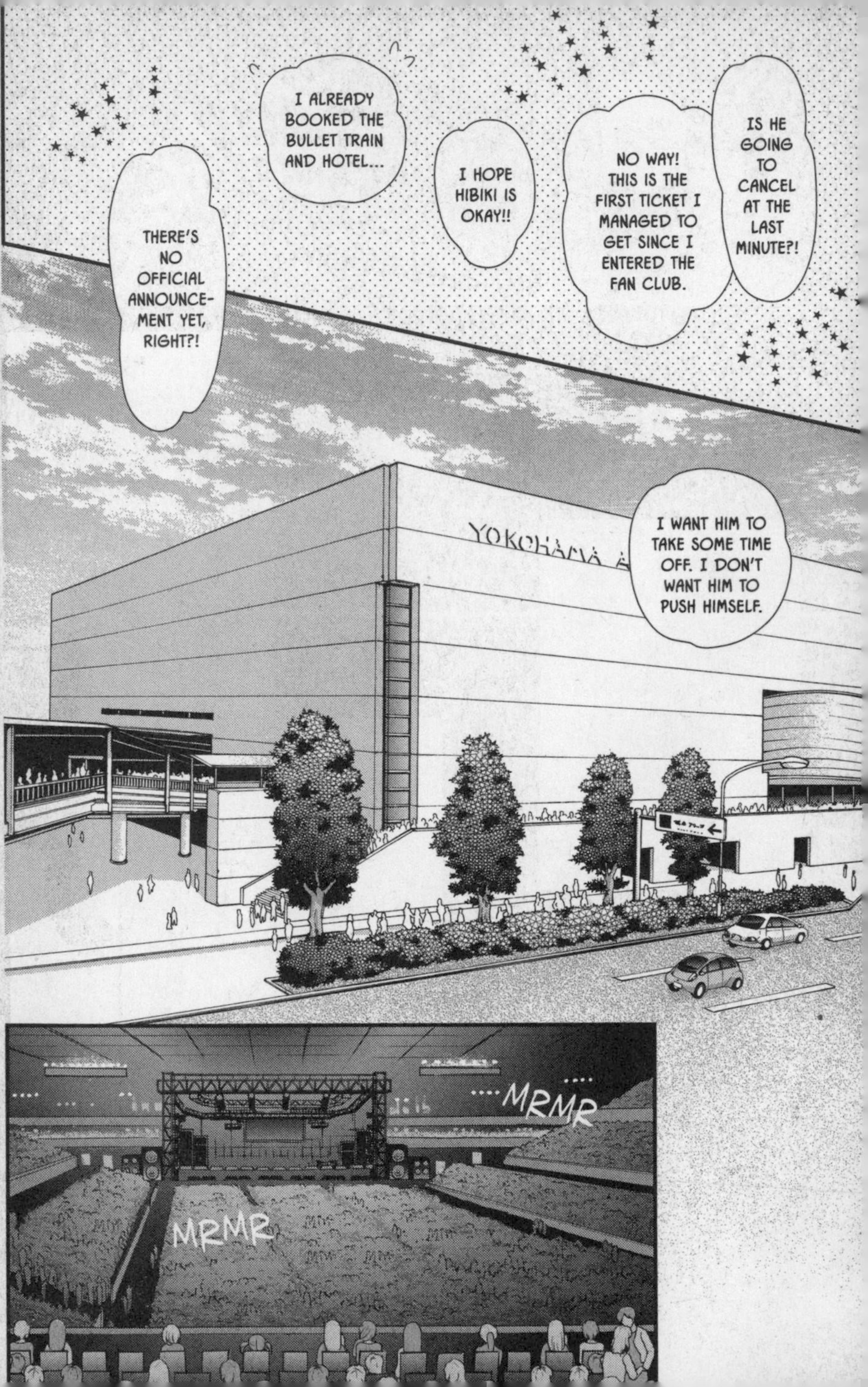
IS HE GOING TO CANCEL AT THE LAST MINUTE?!
NO WAY! THIS IS THE FIRST TICKET I MANAGED TO GET SINCE I ENTERED THE FAN CLUB.
I HOPE HIBIKI IS OKAY!!
I ALREADY BOOKED THE BULLET TRAIN AND HOTEL...
THERE'S NO OFFICIAL ANNOUNCEMENT YET, RIGHT?!
I WANT HIM TO TAKE SOME TIME OFF. I DON'T WANT HIM TO PUSH HIMSELF.
...MRMR
MRMR

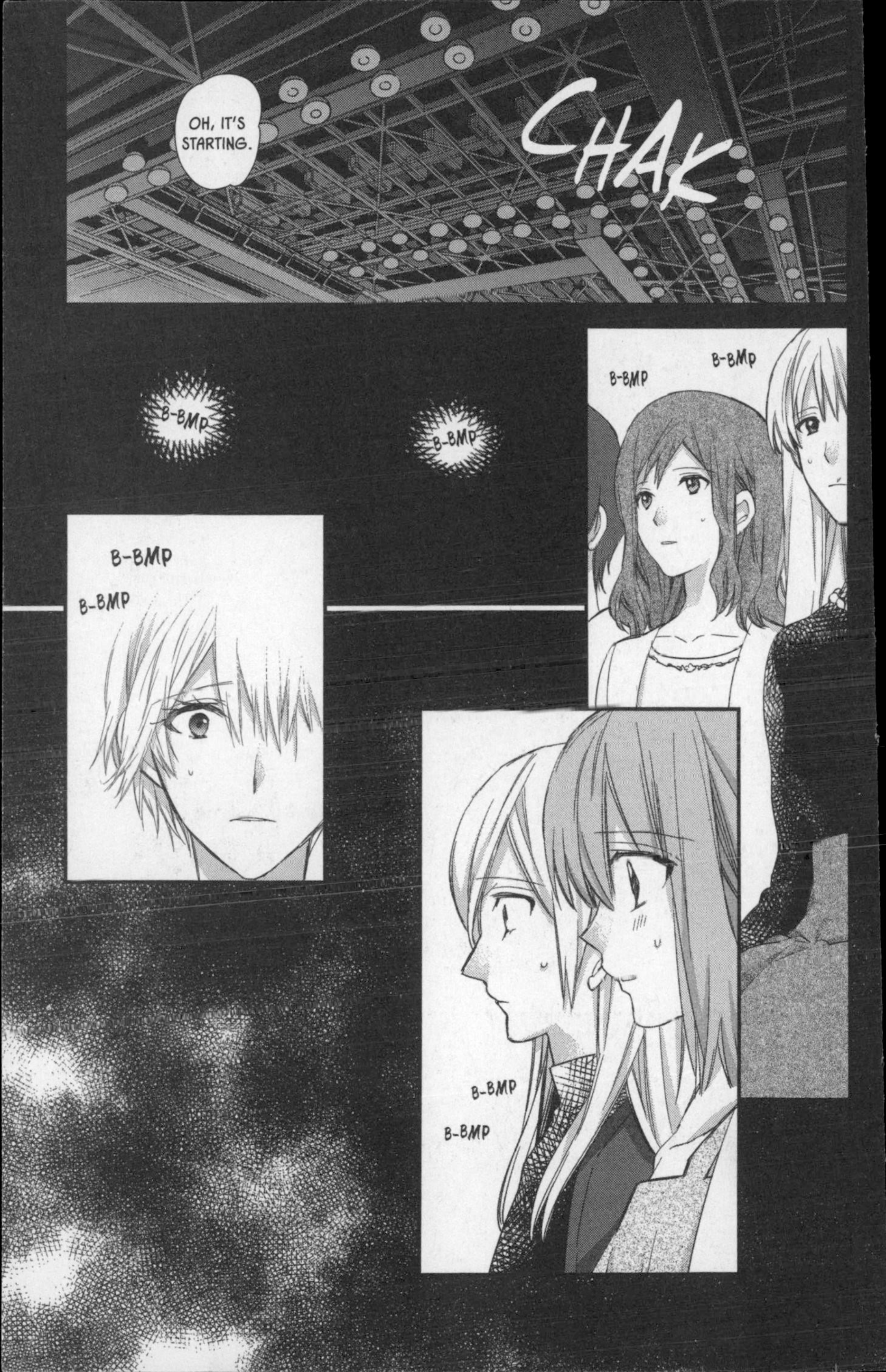
CHAK
OH, IT'S STARTING.
B-BMP
B-BMP
B-BMP
B-BMP
B-BMP
B-BMP
B-BMP
B-BMP

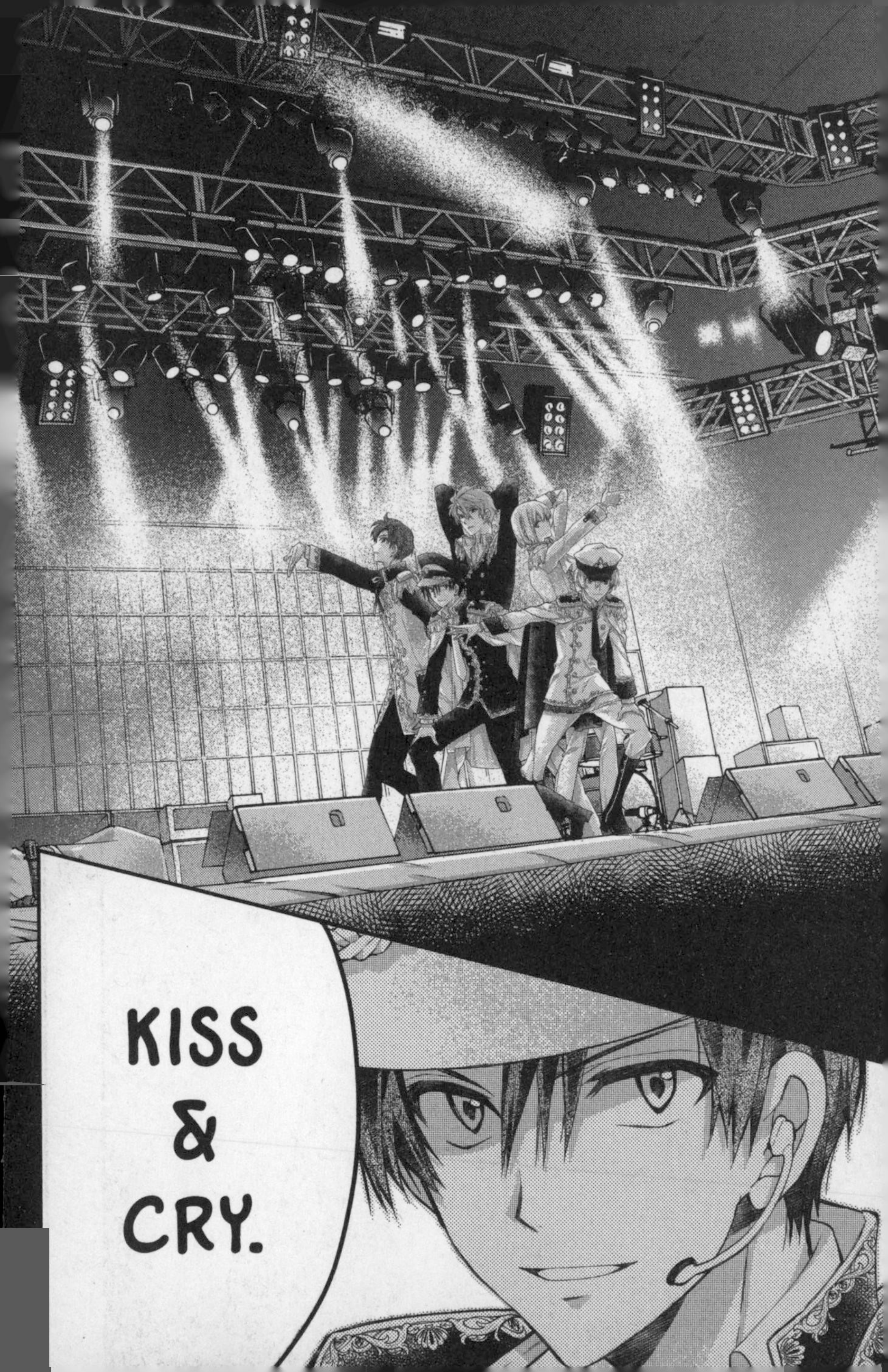
KISS & CRY.

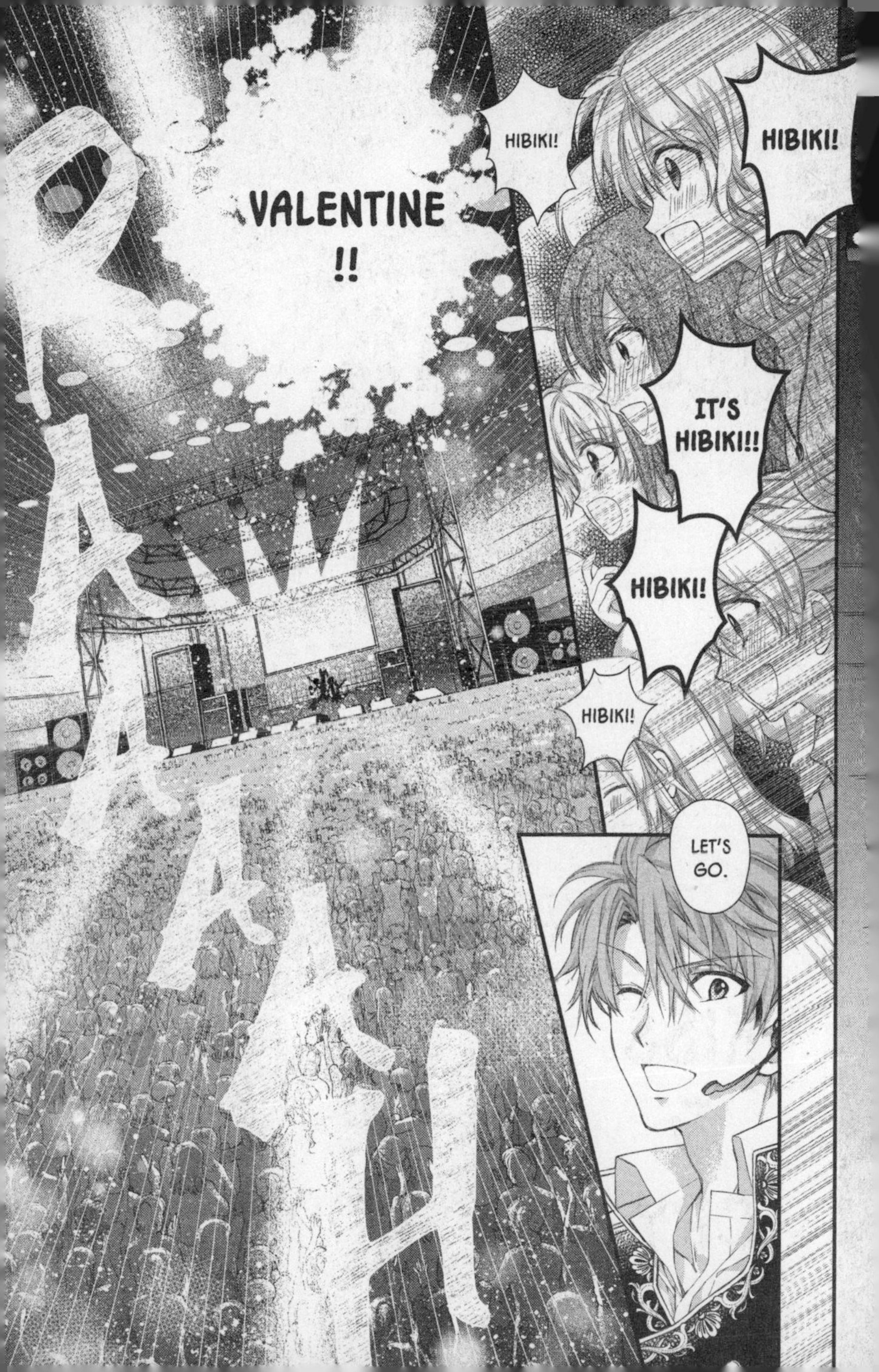
HIBIKI!
HIBIKI!
IT'S HIBIKI!!!
HIBIKI!
HIBIKI!
LET'S GO.
VALENTINE !!

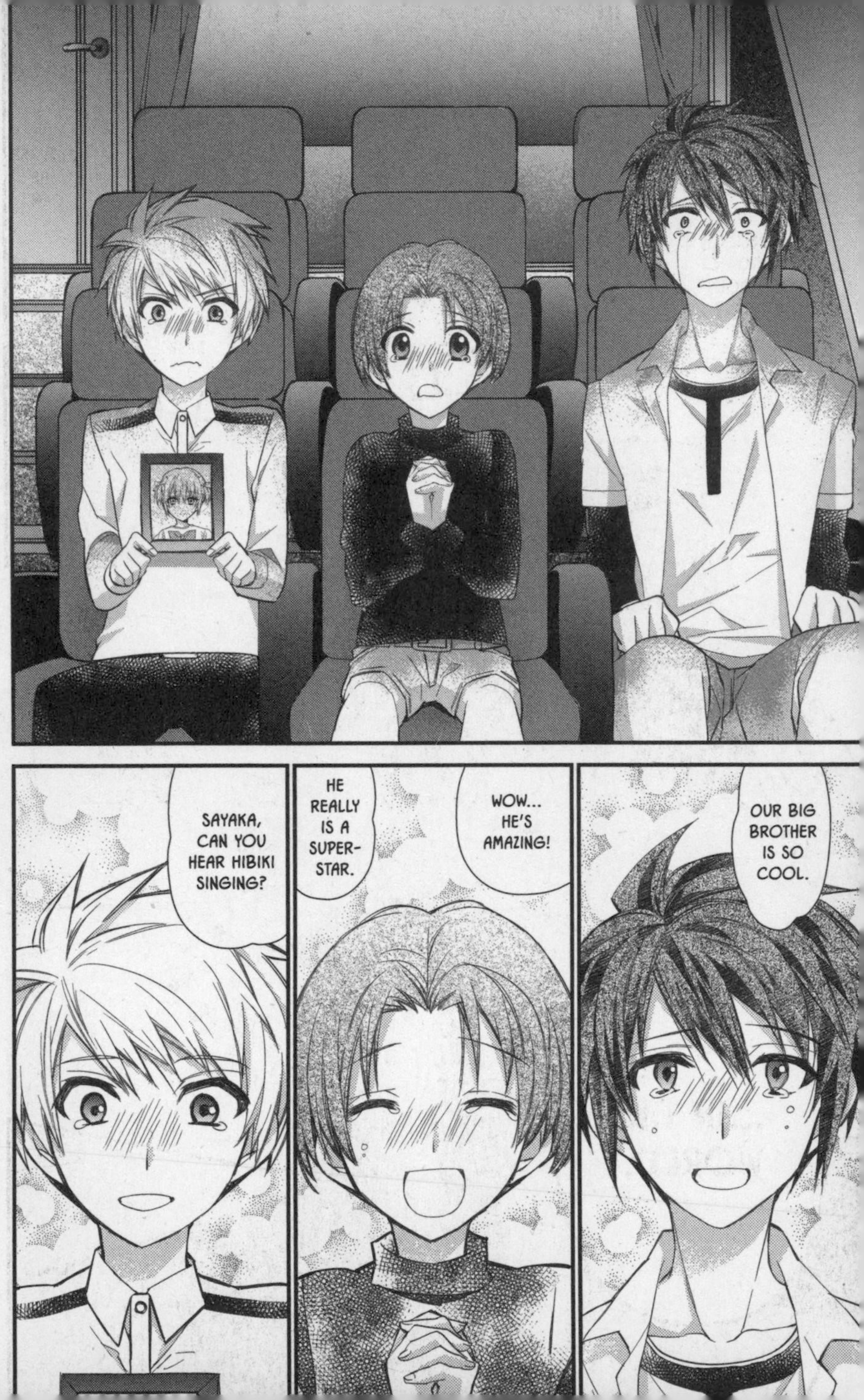
OUR BIG BROTHER IS SO COOL.
WOW... HE'S AMAZING!
HE REALLY IS A SUPER-STAR.
SAYAKA, CAN YOU HEAR HIBIKI SINGING?

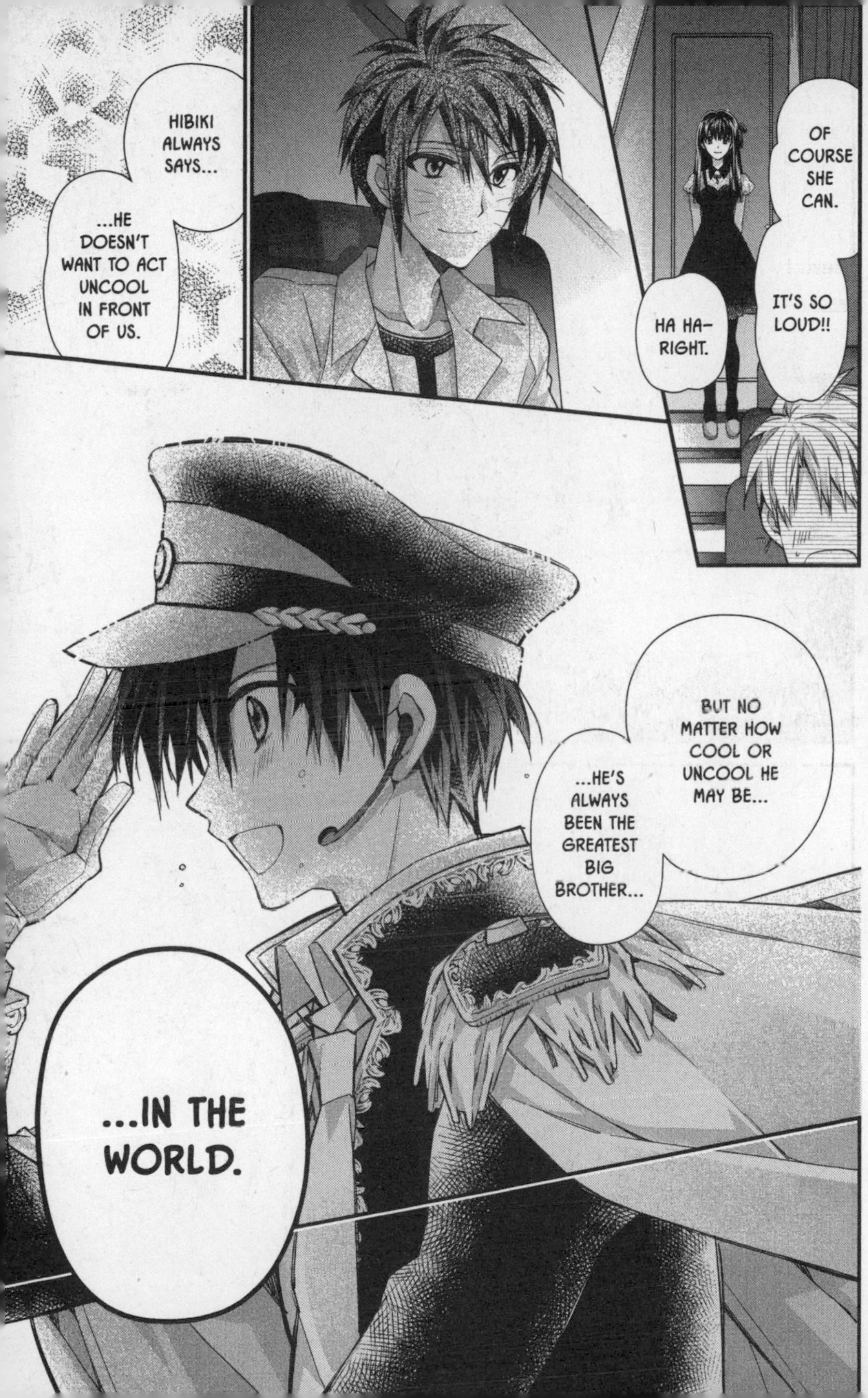
OF COURSE SHE CAN.
IT'S SO LOUD!!
HA HA-RIGHT.
HIBIKI ALWAYS SAYS...
...HE DOESN'T WANT TO ACT UNCOOL IN FRONT OF US.
BUT NO MATTER HOW COOL OR UNCOOL HE MAY BE...
...HE'S ALWAYS BEEN THE GREATEST BIG BROTHER...
...IN THE WORLD.

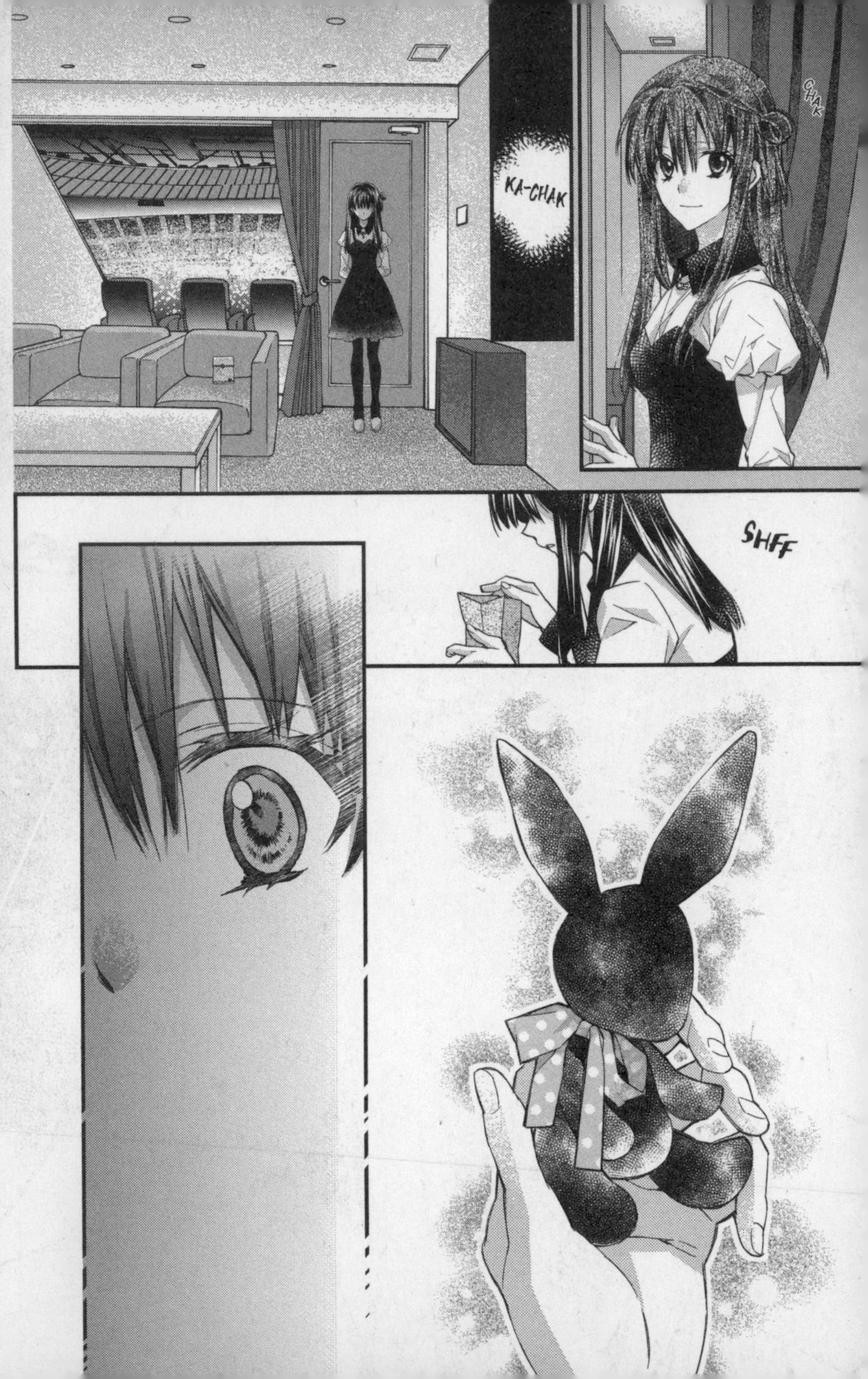
CHAK
KA-CHAK
SHFF

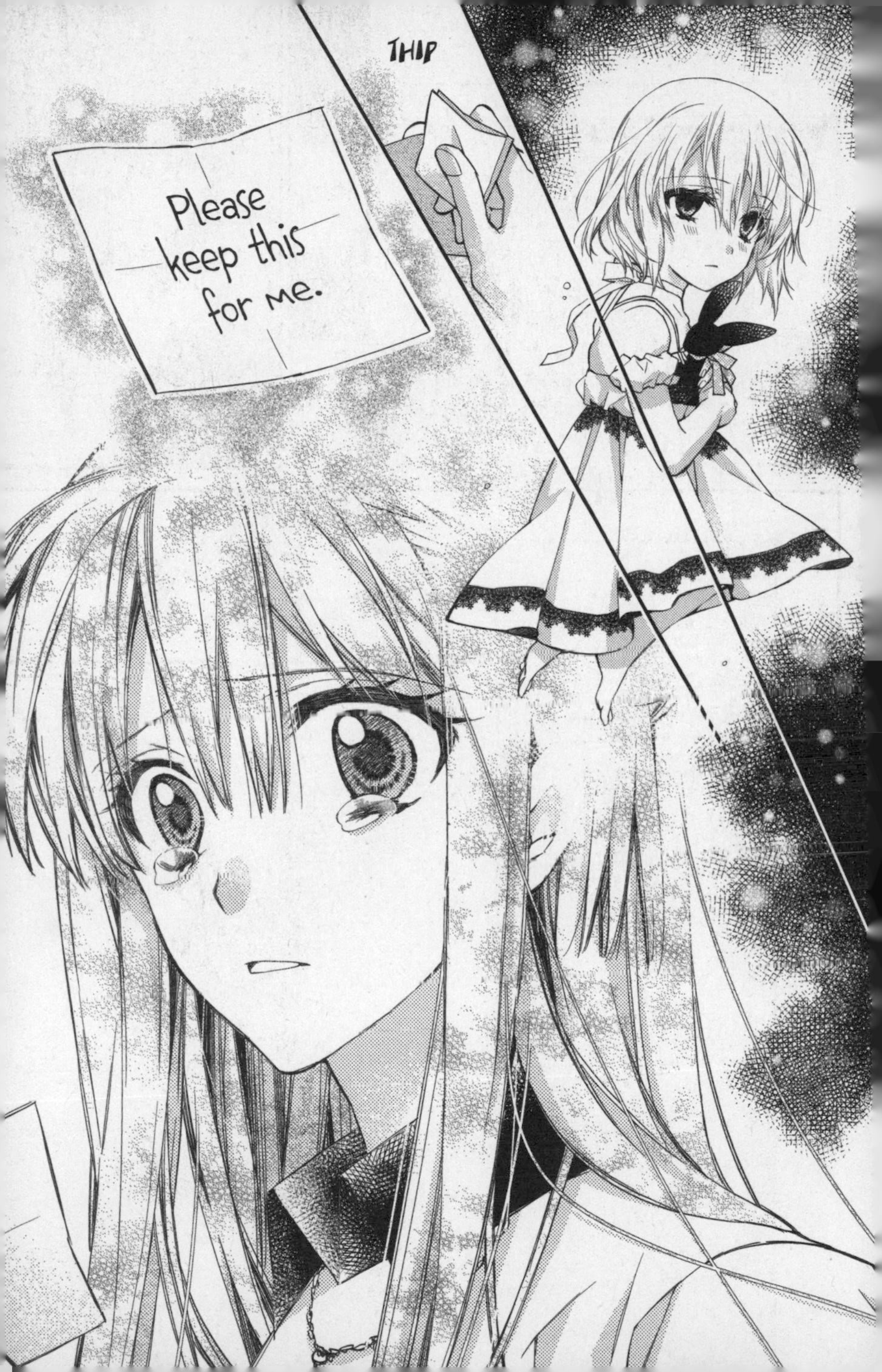
THIP
Please keep this for me.

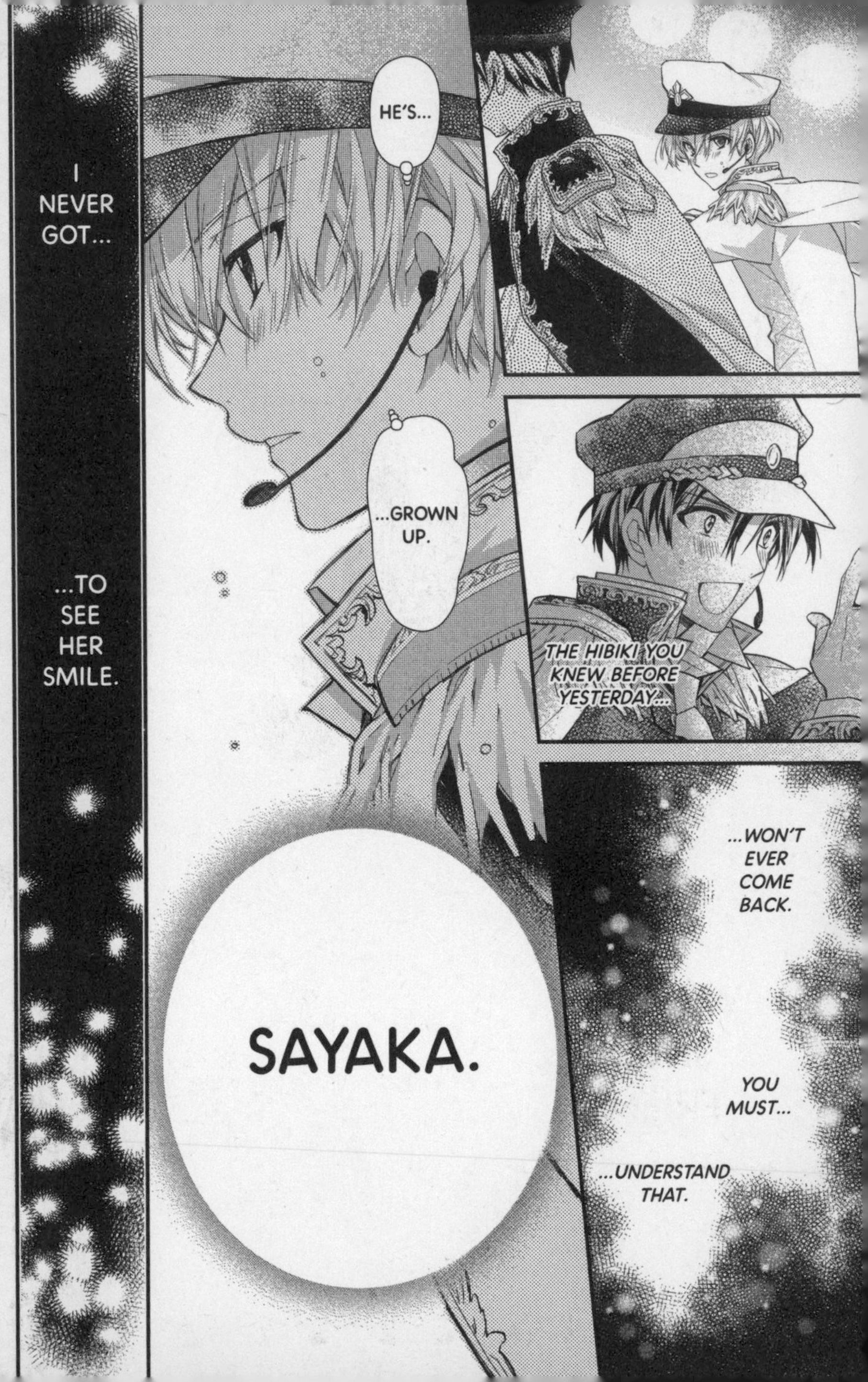
THE HIBIKI YOU KNEW BEFORE YESTERDAY...
...WON'T EVER COME BACK.
YOU MUST...
...UNDERSTAND THAT.
HE'S...
...GROWN UP.
SAYAKA.
I NEVER GOT...
...TO SEE HER SMILE.

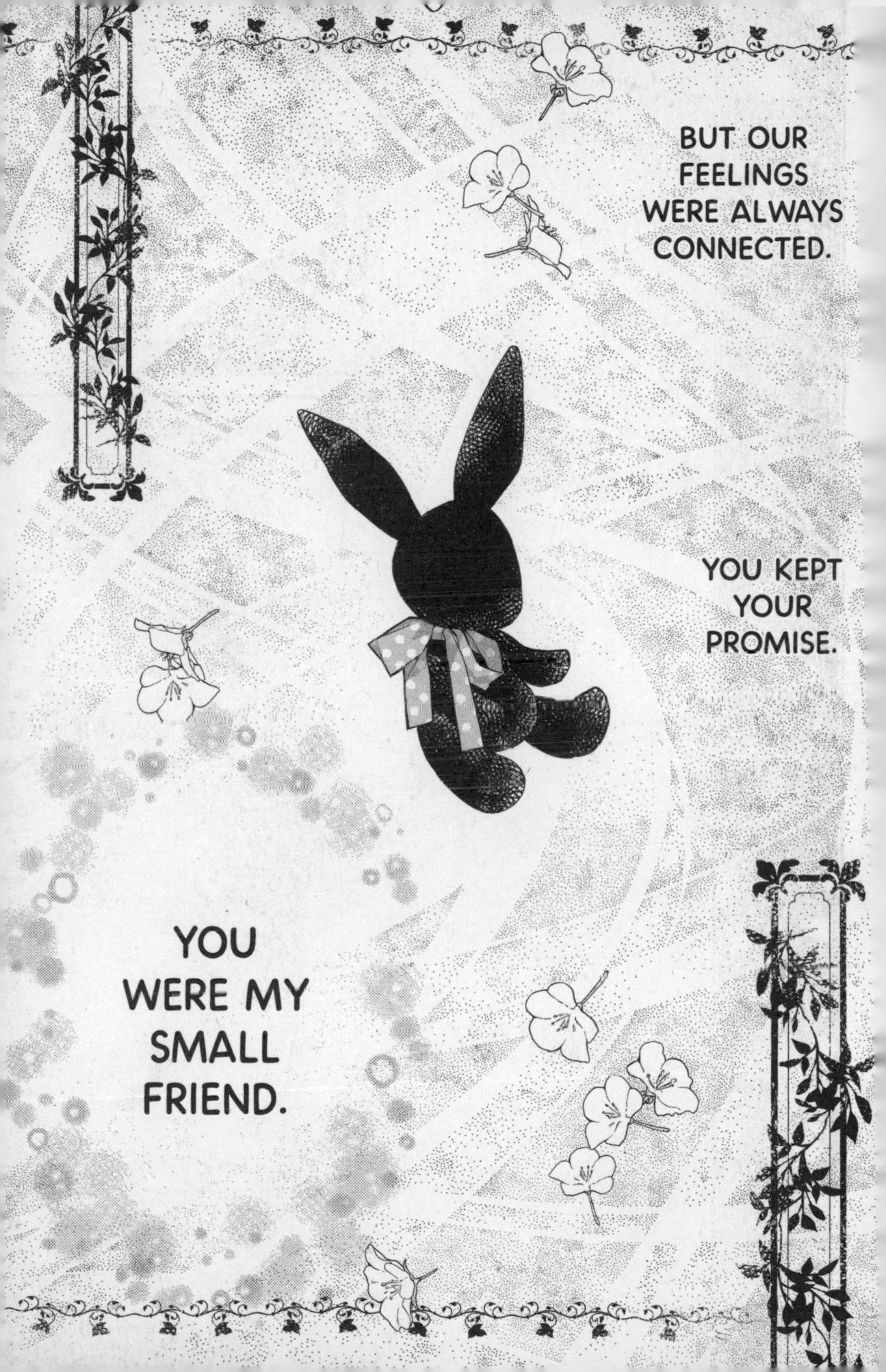
BUT OUR FEELINGS WERE ALWAYS CONNECTED.
YOU KEPT YOUR PROMISE.
YOU WERE MY SMALL FRIEND.

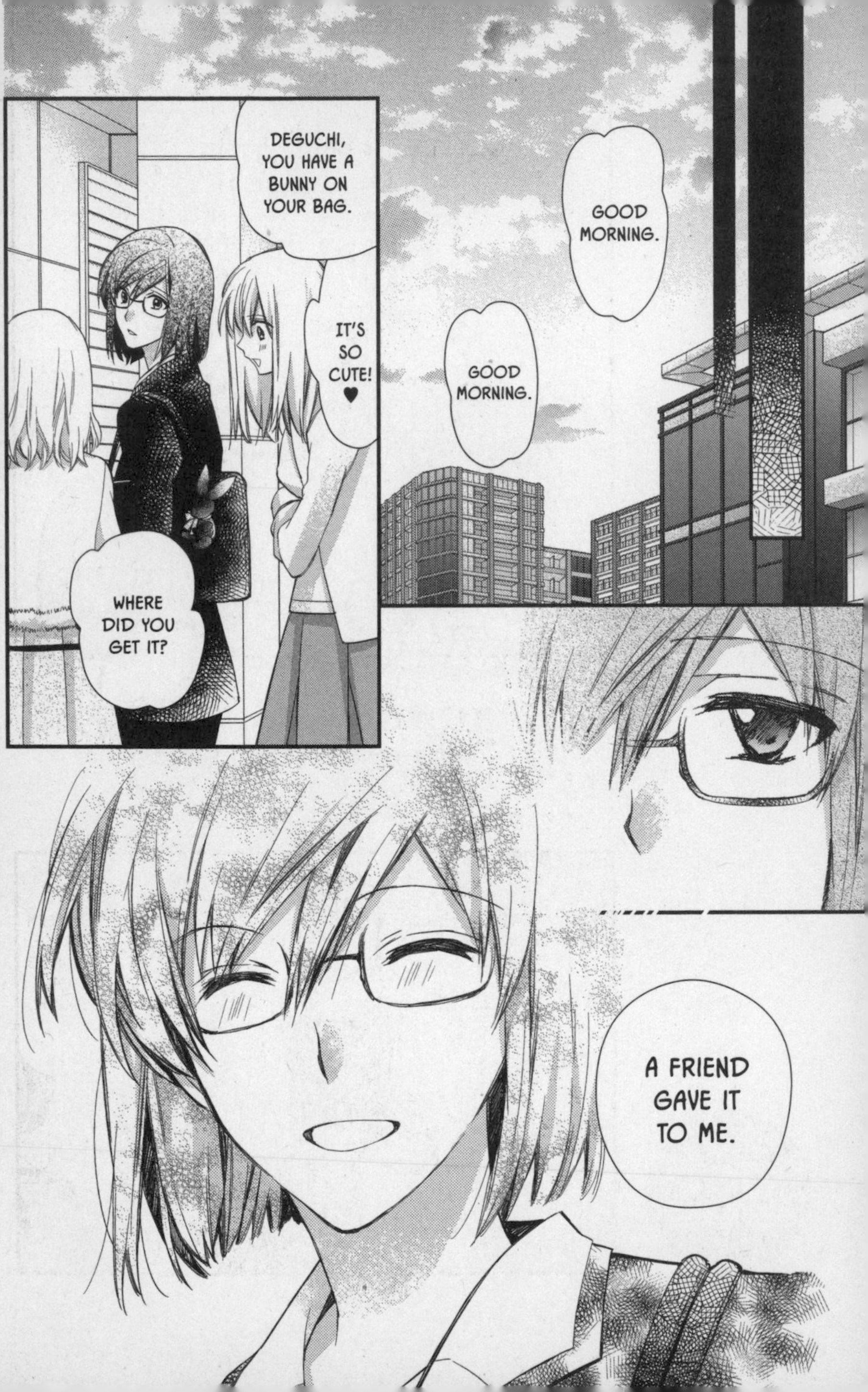
GOOD MORNING.
GOOD MORNING.
DEGUCHI, YOU HAVE A BUNNY ON YOUR BAG.
IT'S SO CUTE! ♥
WHERE DID YOU GET IT?
A FRIEND GAVE IT TO ME.

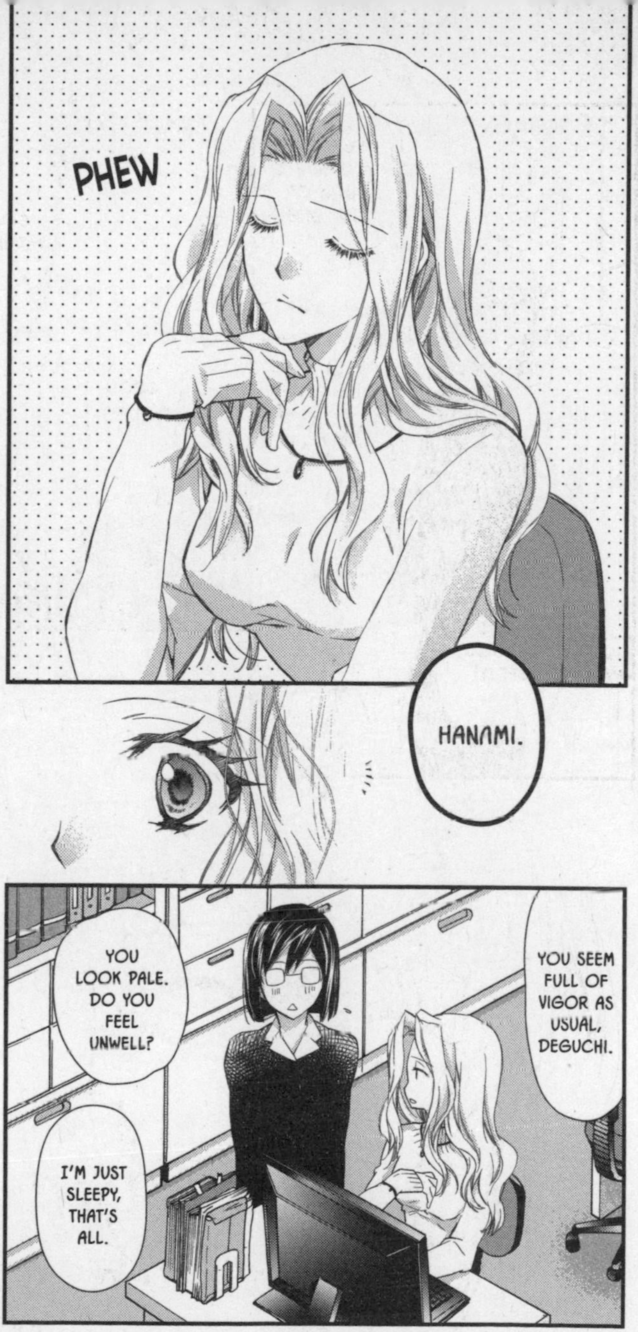
PHEW
HANAMI.
YOU SEEM FULL OF VIGOR AS USUAL, DEGUCHI.
YOU LOOK PALE. DO YOU FEEL UNWELL?
I'M JUST SLEEPY, THAT'S ALL.

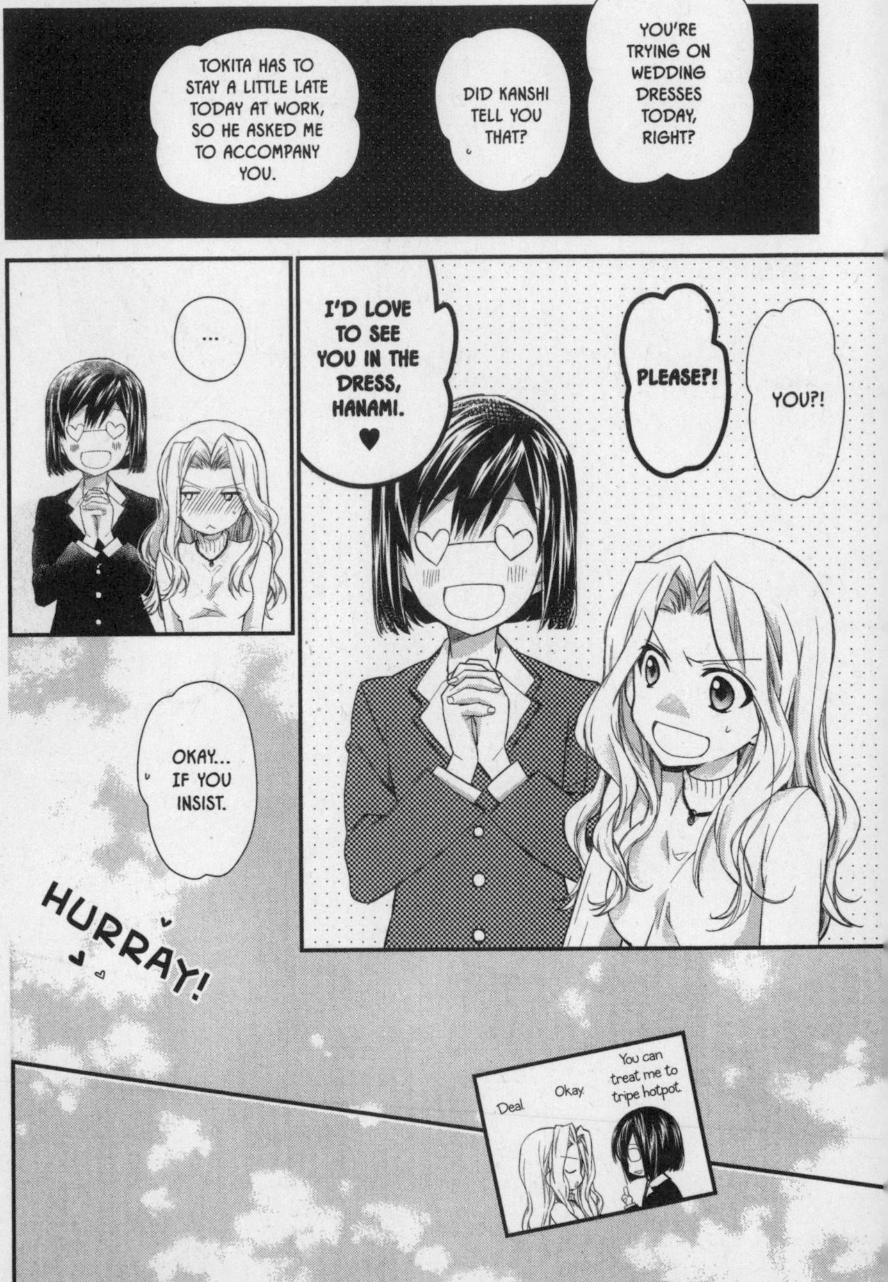
YOU'RE TRYING ON WEDDING DRESSES TODAY, RIGHT?
DID KANSHI TELL YOU THAT?
TOKITA HAS TO STAY A LITTLE LATE TODAY AT WORK, SO HE ASKED ME TO ACCOMPANY YOU.
YOU?!
PLEASE?!
I'D LOVE TO SEE YOU IN THE DRESS, HANAMI. ♥
...
OKAY... IF YOU INSIST.
HURRAY!
You can treat me to tripe hotpot.
Okay.
Deal.

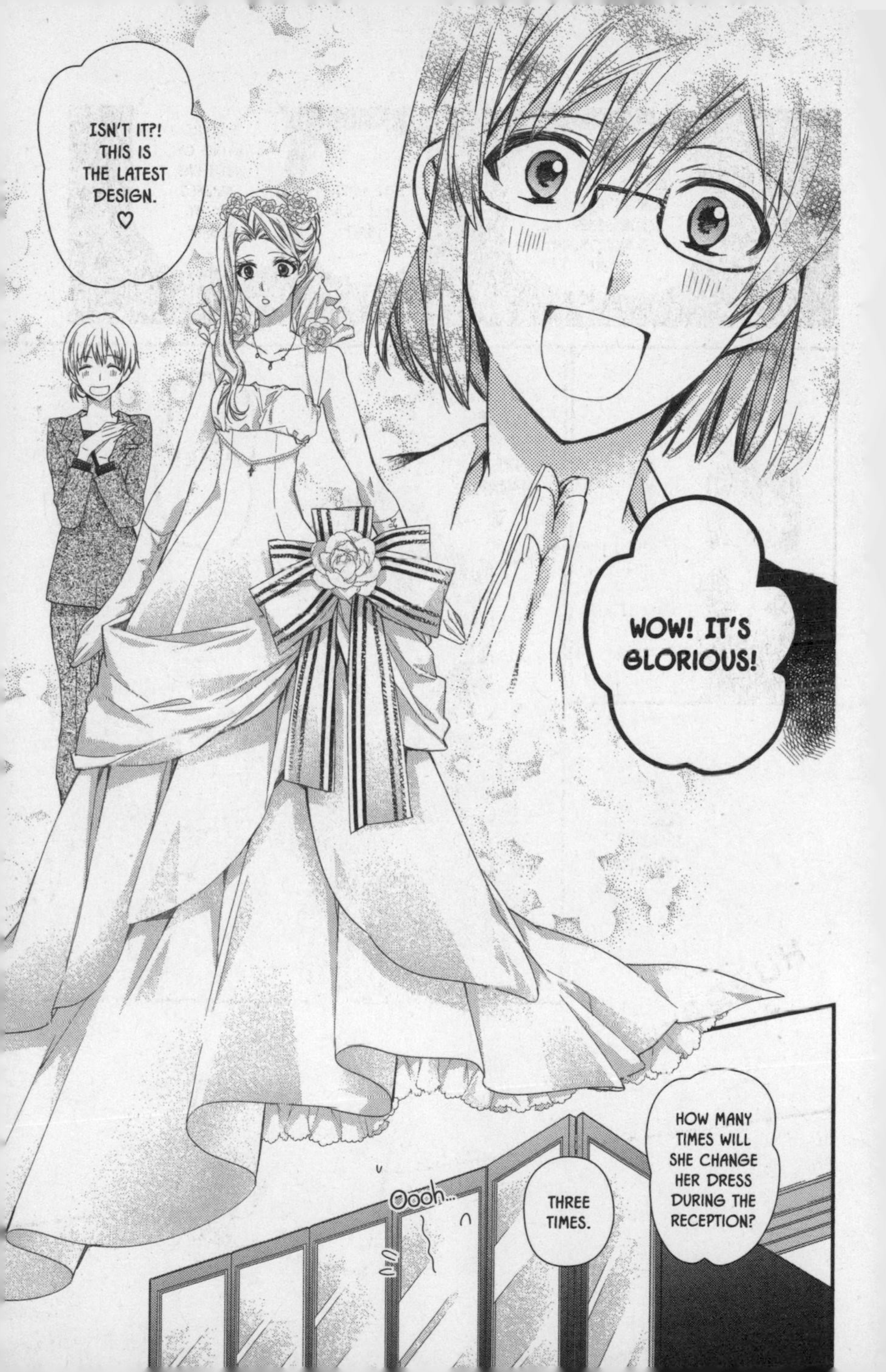
WOW! IT'S GLORIOUS!
ISN'T IT?! THIS IS THE LATEST DESIGN. ♡
HOW MANY TIMES WILL SHE CHANGE HER DRESS DURING THE RECEPTION?
THREE TIMES.
Oooh...

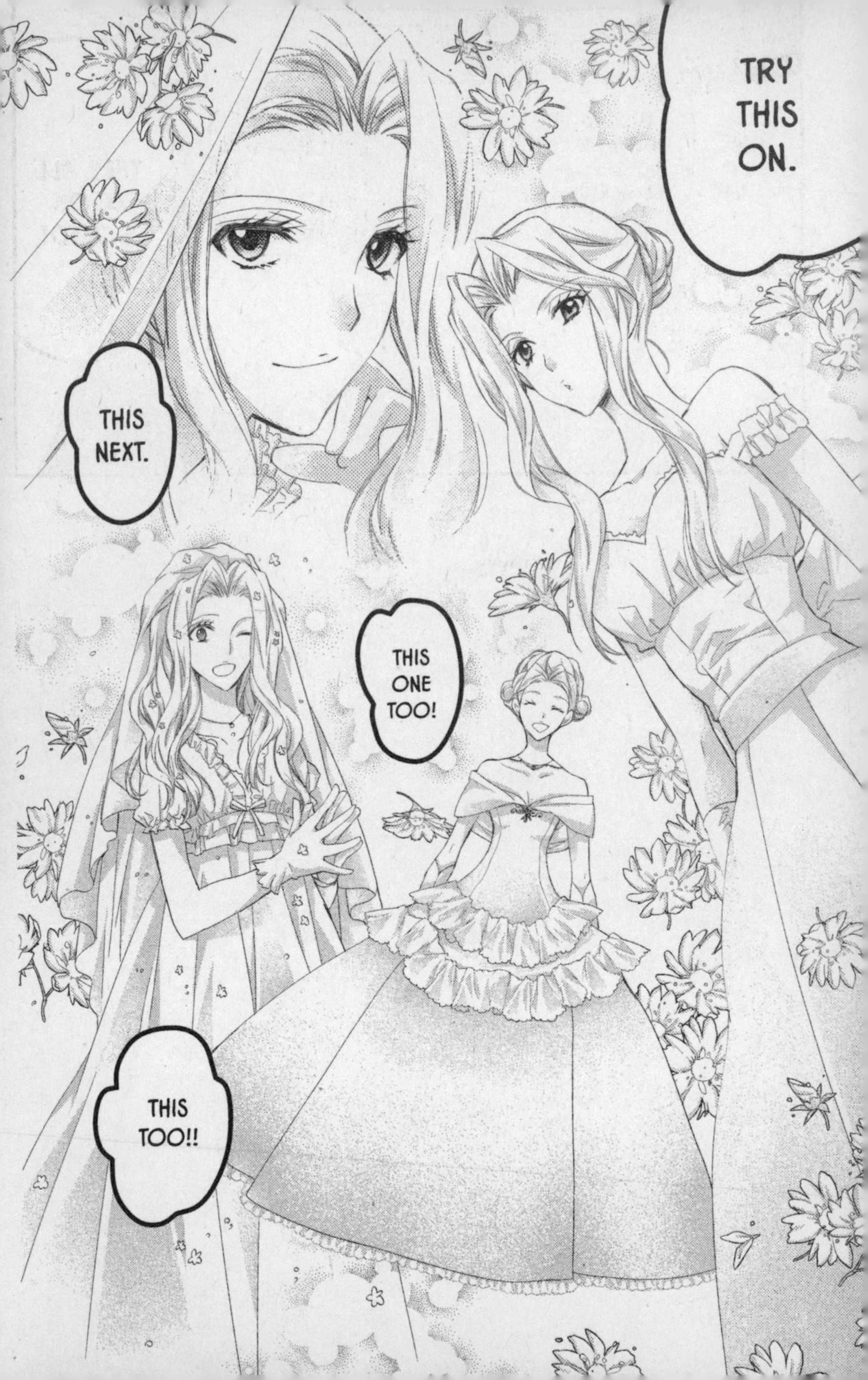
TRY THIS ON.
THIS NEXT.
THIS ONE TOO!
THIS TOO!!

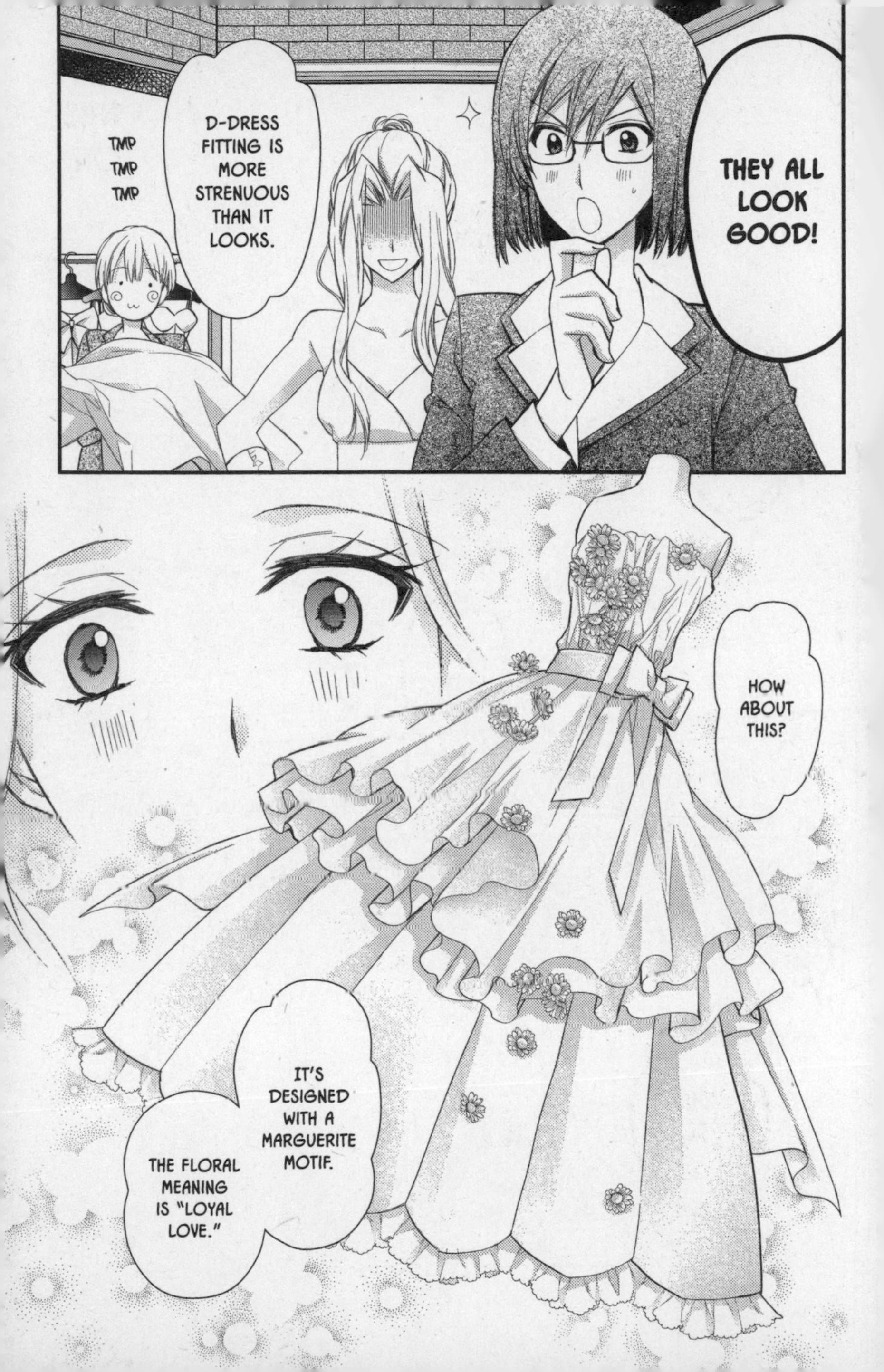
THEY ALL LOOK GOOD!
D-DRESS FITTING IS MORE STRENUOUS THAN IT LOOKS.
TMP TMP TMP
HOW ABOUT THIS?
IT'S DESIGNED WITH A MARGUERITE MOTIF.
THE FLORAL MEANING IS "LOYAL LOVE."

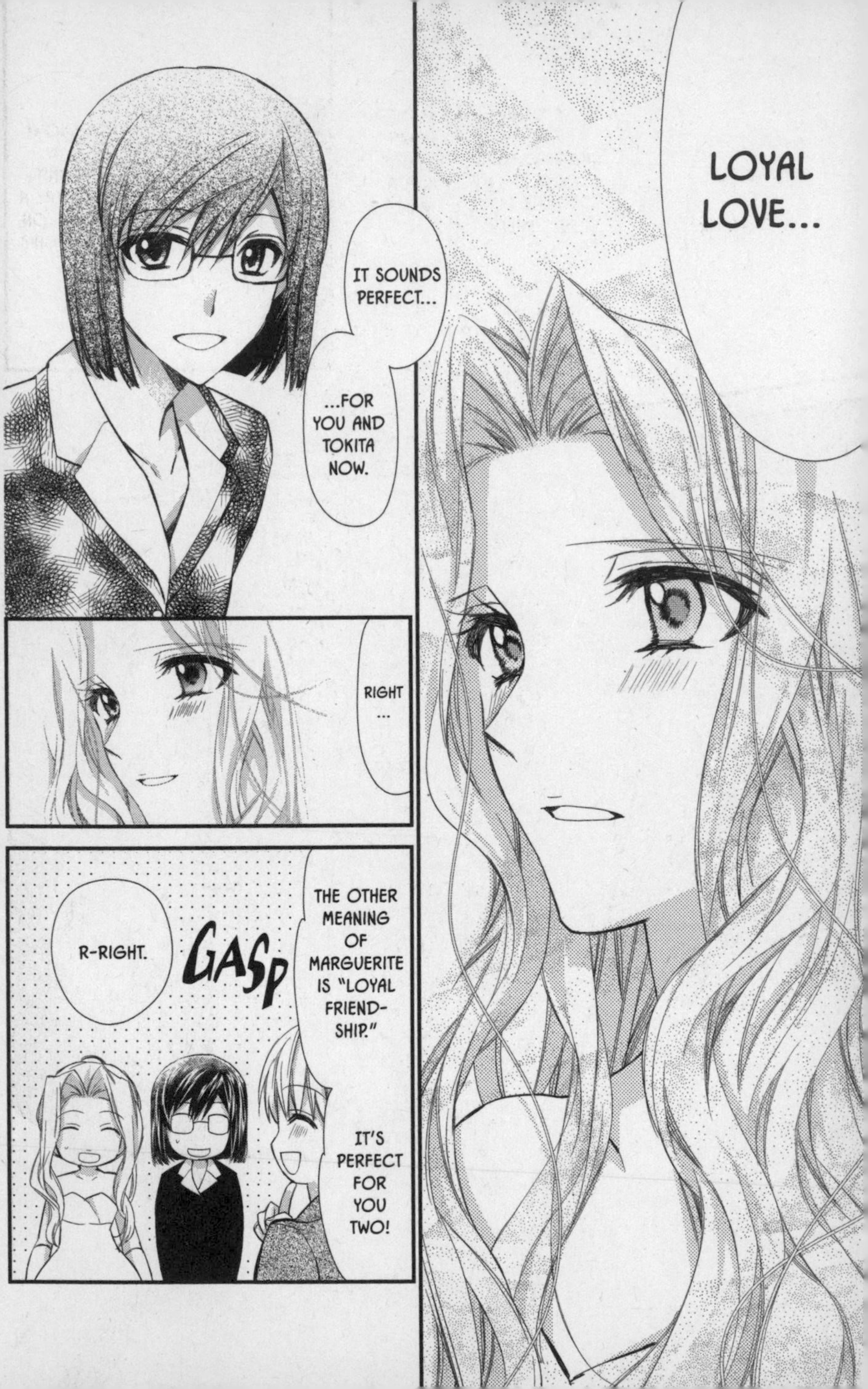
LOYAL LOVE...
IT SOUNDS PERFECT...
...FOR YOU AND TOKITA NOW.
RIGHT ...
THE OTHER MEANING OF MARGUERITE IS "LOYAL FRIEND-SHIP."
GASP
R-RIGHT.
IT'S PERFECT FOR YOU TWO!

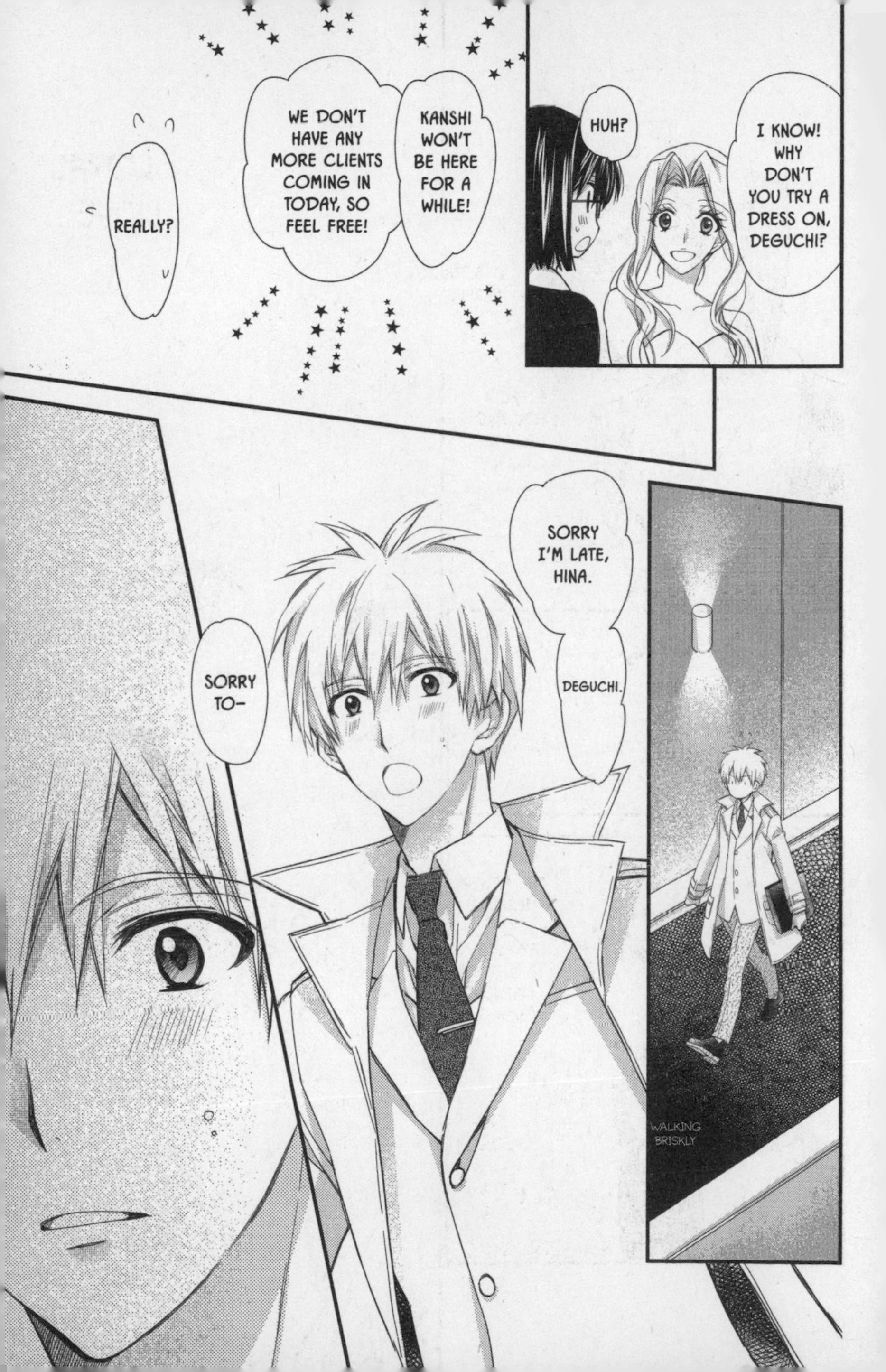
I KNOW! WHY DON'T YOU TRY A DRESS ON, DEGUCHI?
HUH?
KANSHI WON'T BE HERE FOR A WHILE!
WE DON'T HAVE ANY MORE CLIENTS COMING IN TODAY, SO FEEL FREE!
REALLY?
WALKING BRISKLY
SORRY I'M LATE, HINA.
DEGUCHI.
SORRY TO-

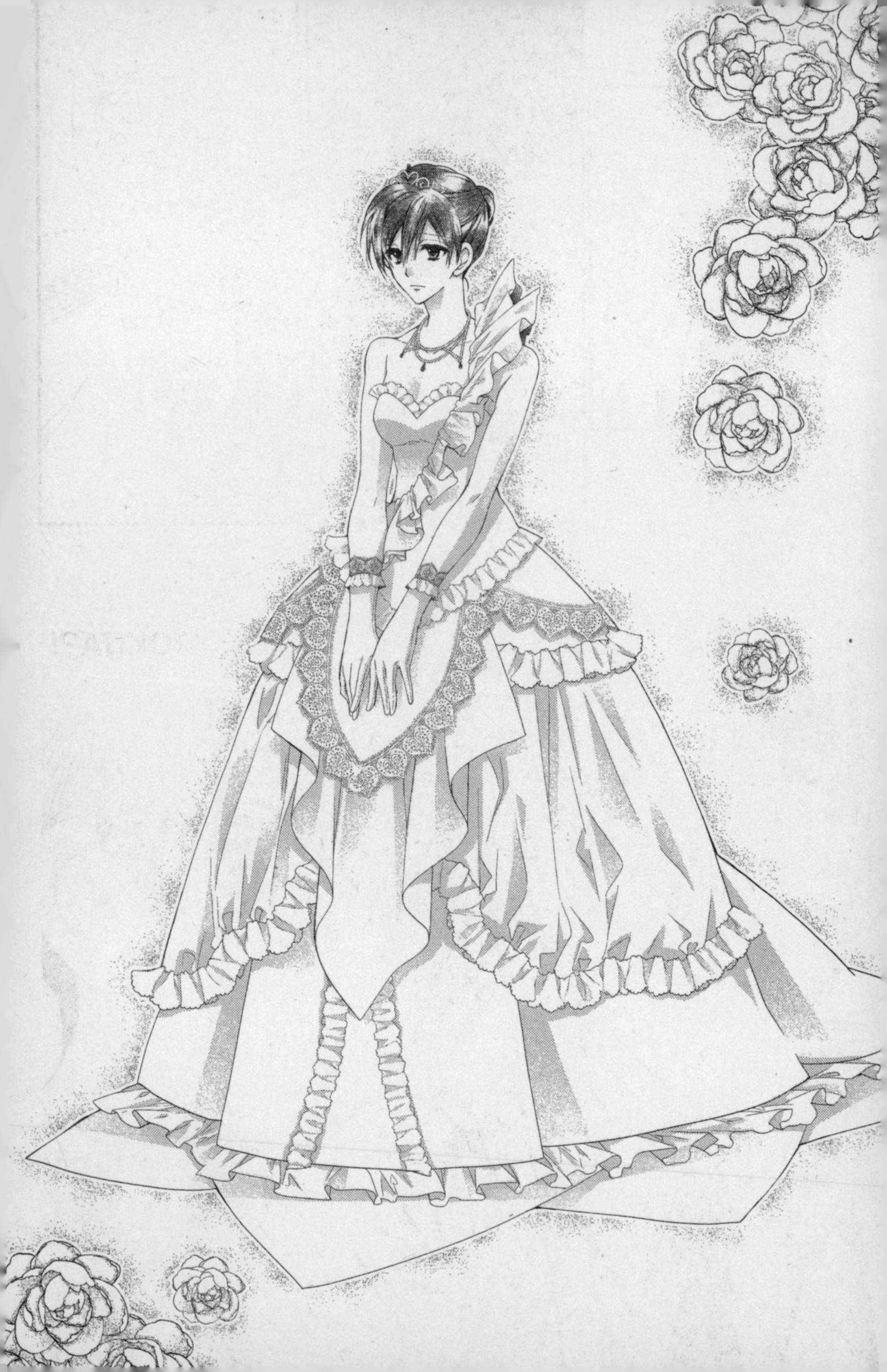

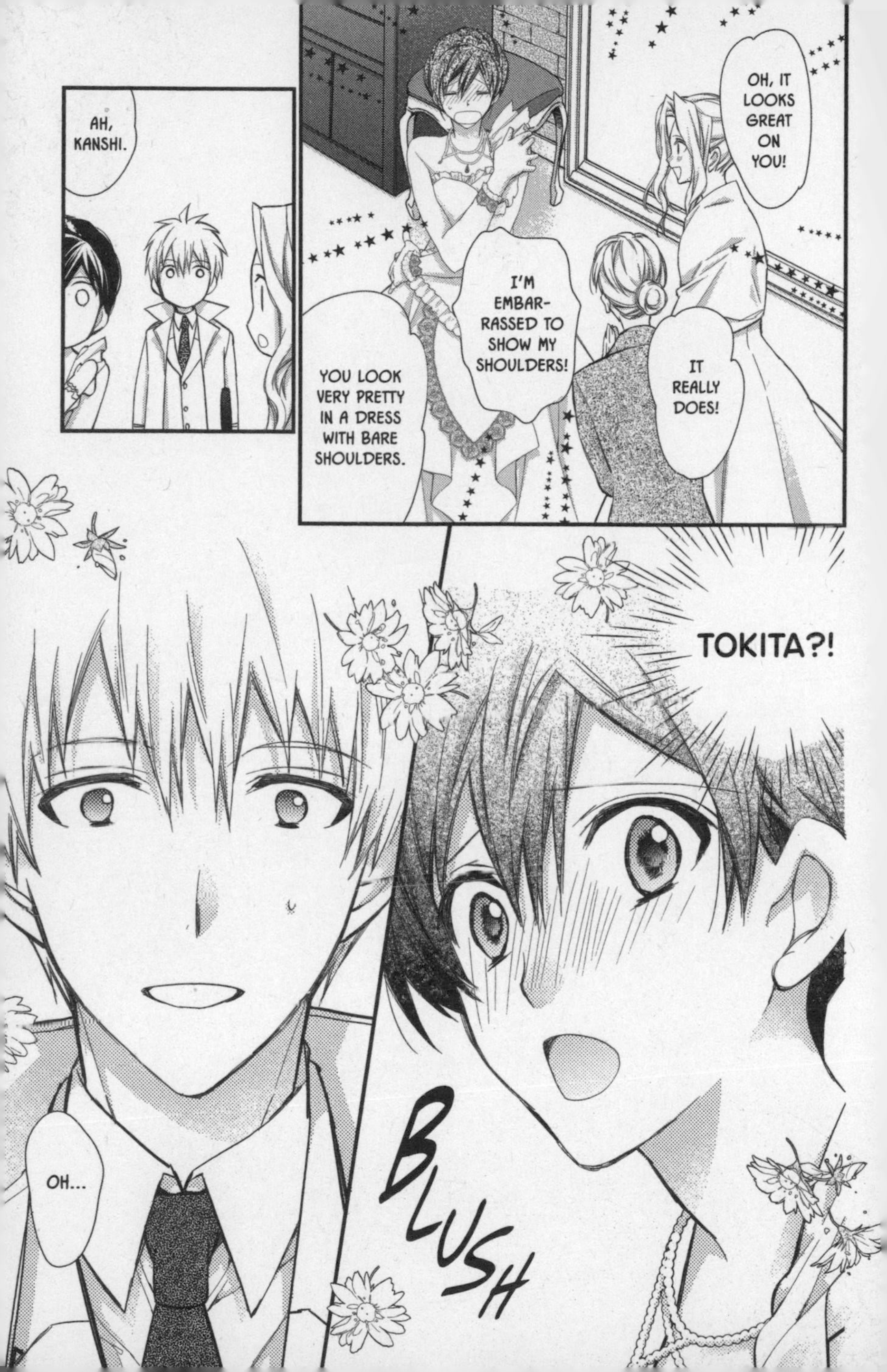
OH, IT LOOKS GREAT ON YOU!
IT REALLY DOES!
I'M EMBAR-RASSED TO SHOW MY SHOULDERS!
YOU LOOK VERY PRETTY IN A DRESS WITH BARE SHOULDERS.
AH, KANSHI.
TOKITA?!
BLUSH
OH...

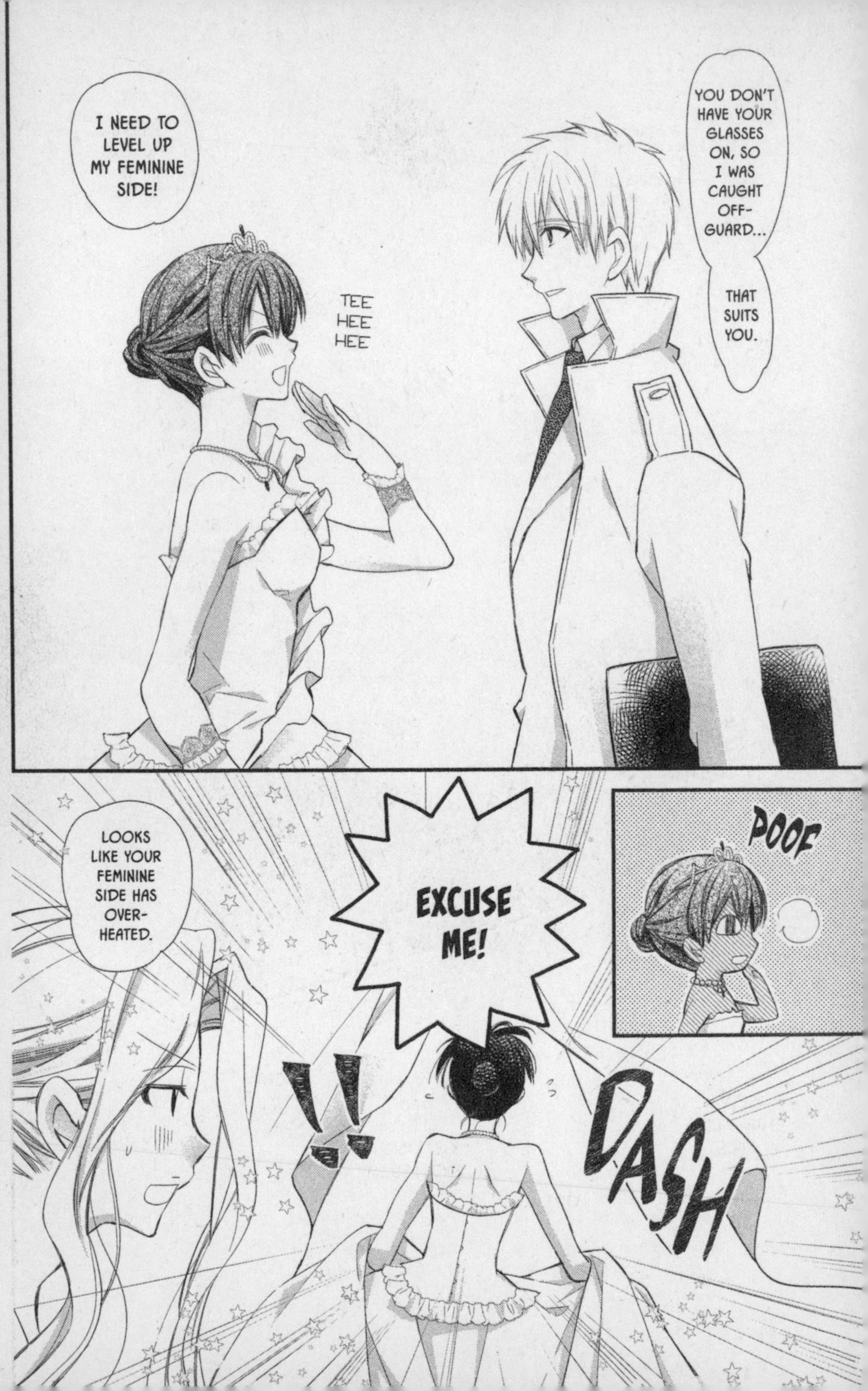
YOU DON'T HAVE YOUR GLASSES ON, SO I WAS CAUGHT OFF-GUARD...
THAT SUITS YOU.
TEE HEE HEE
I NEED TO LEVEL UP MY FEMININE SIDE!
POOF
DASH
EXCUSE ME!
!!
LOOKS LIKE YOUR FEMININE SIDE HAS OVER-HEATED.

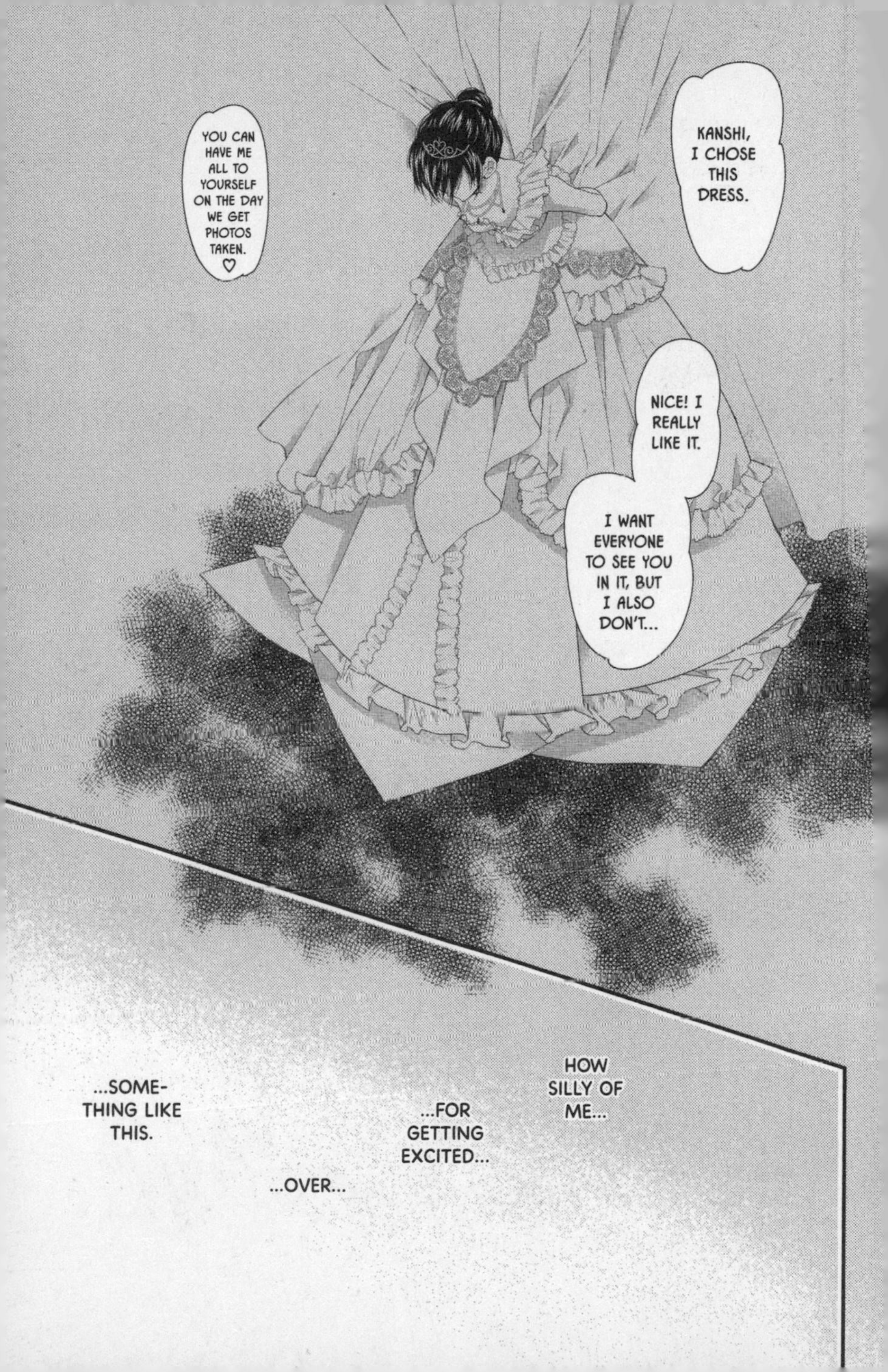
KANSHI, I CHOSE THIS DRESS.
NICE! I REALLY LIKE IT.
I WANT EVERYONE TO SEE YOU IN IT, BUT I ALSO DON'T...
YOU CAN HAVE ME ALL TO YOURSELF ON THE DAY WE GET PHOTOS TAKEN. ♡
HOW SILLY OF ME...
...FOR GETTING EXCITED...
...OVER...
...SOME-THING LIKE THIS.

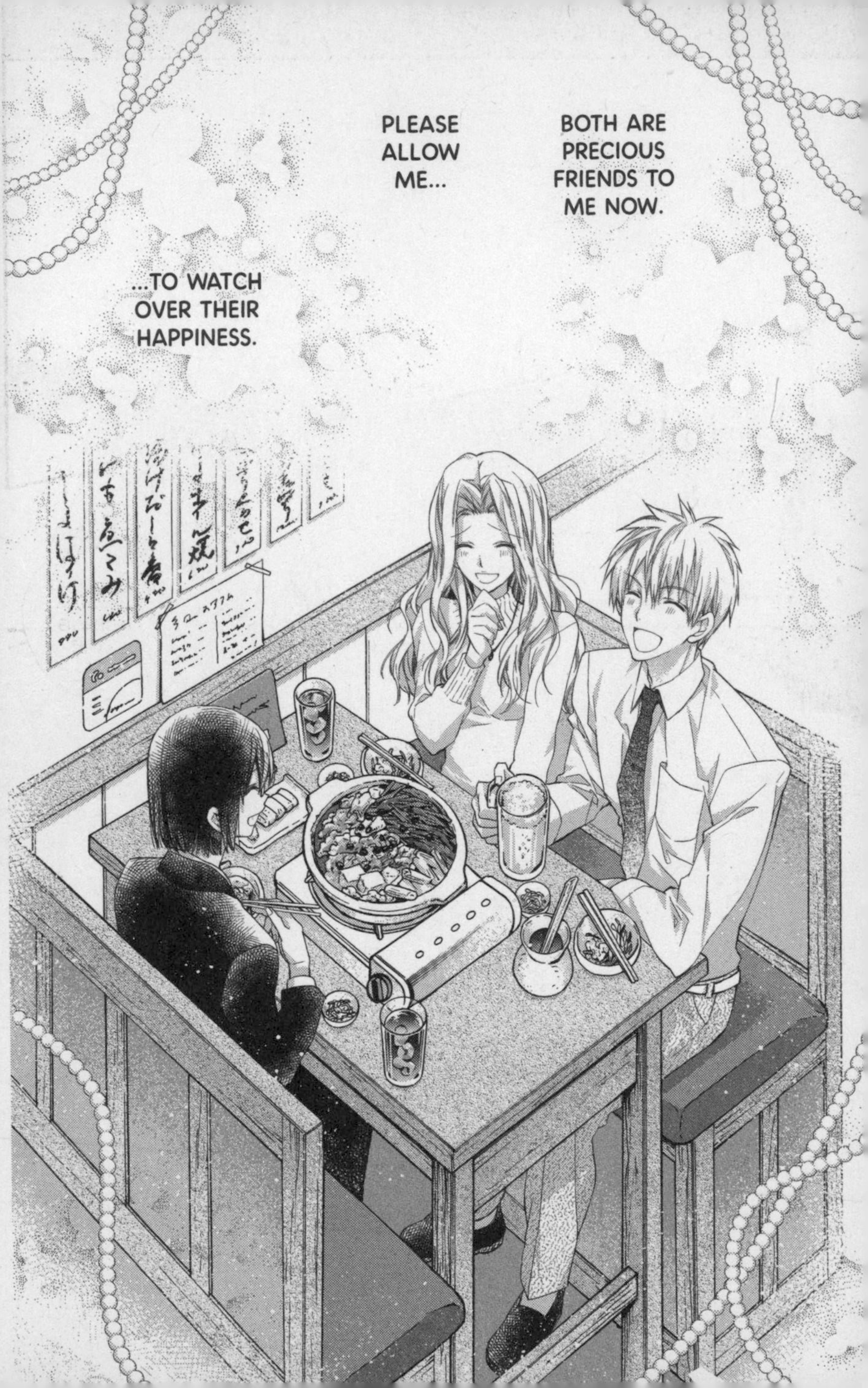
BOTH ARE PRECIOUS FRIENDS TO ME NOW.
PLEASE ALLOW ME...
...TO WATCH OVER THEIR HAPPINESS.

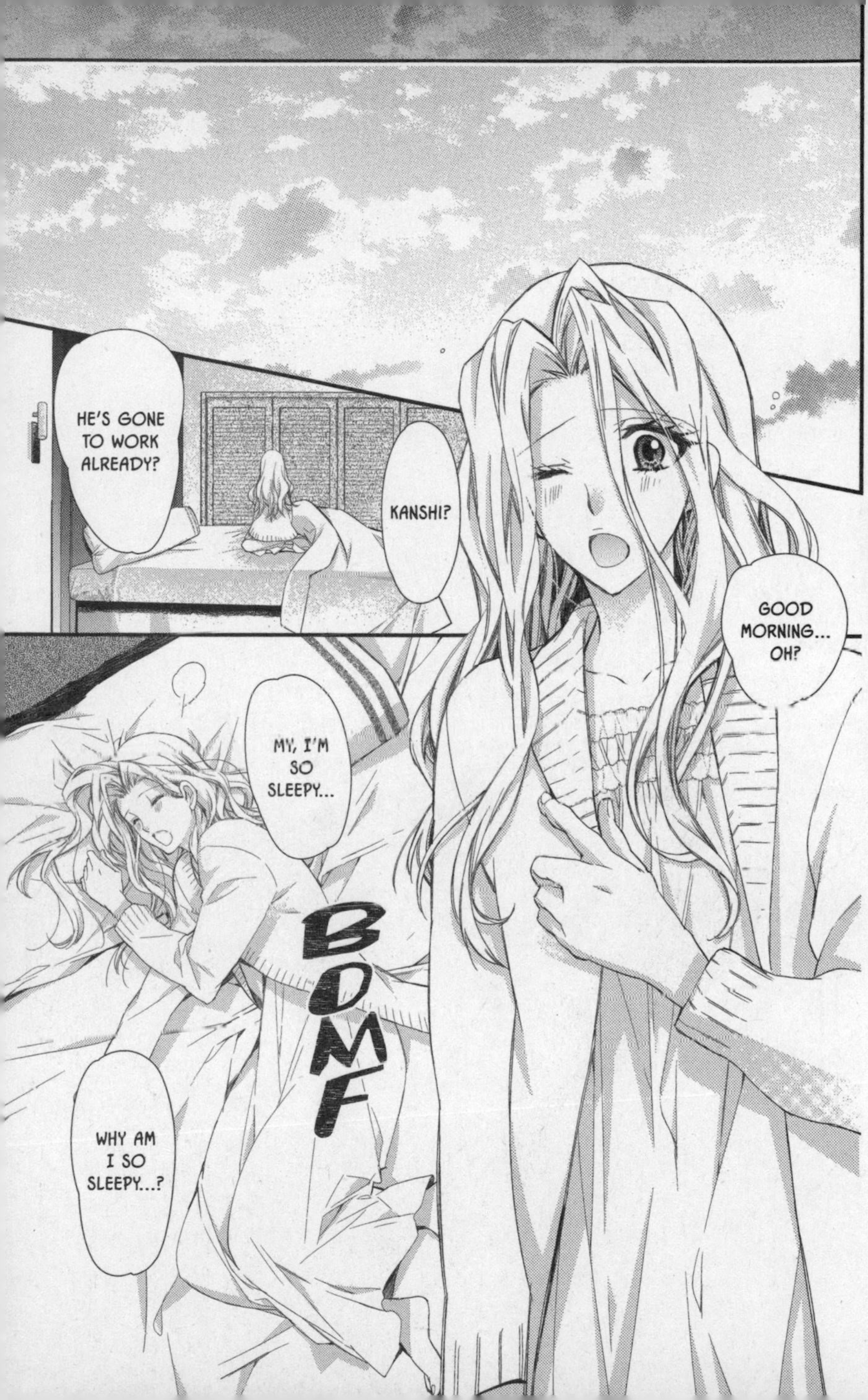
GOOD MORNING... OH?
KANSHI?
HE'S GONE TO WORK ALREADY?
MY, I'M SO SLEEPY...
BDMF
WHY AM I SO SLEEPY...?

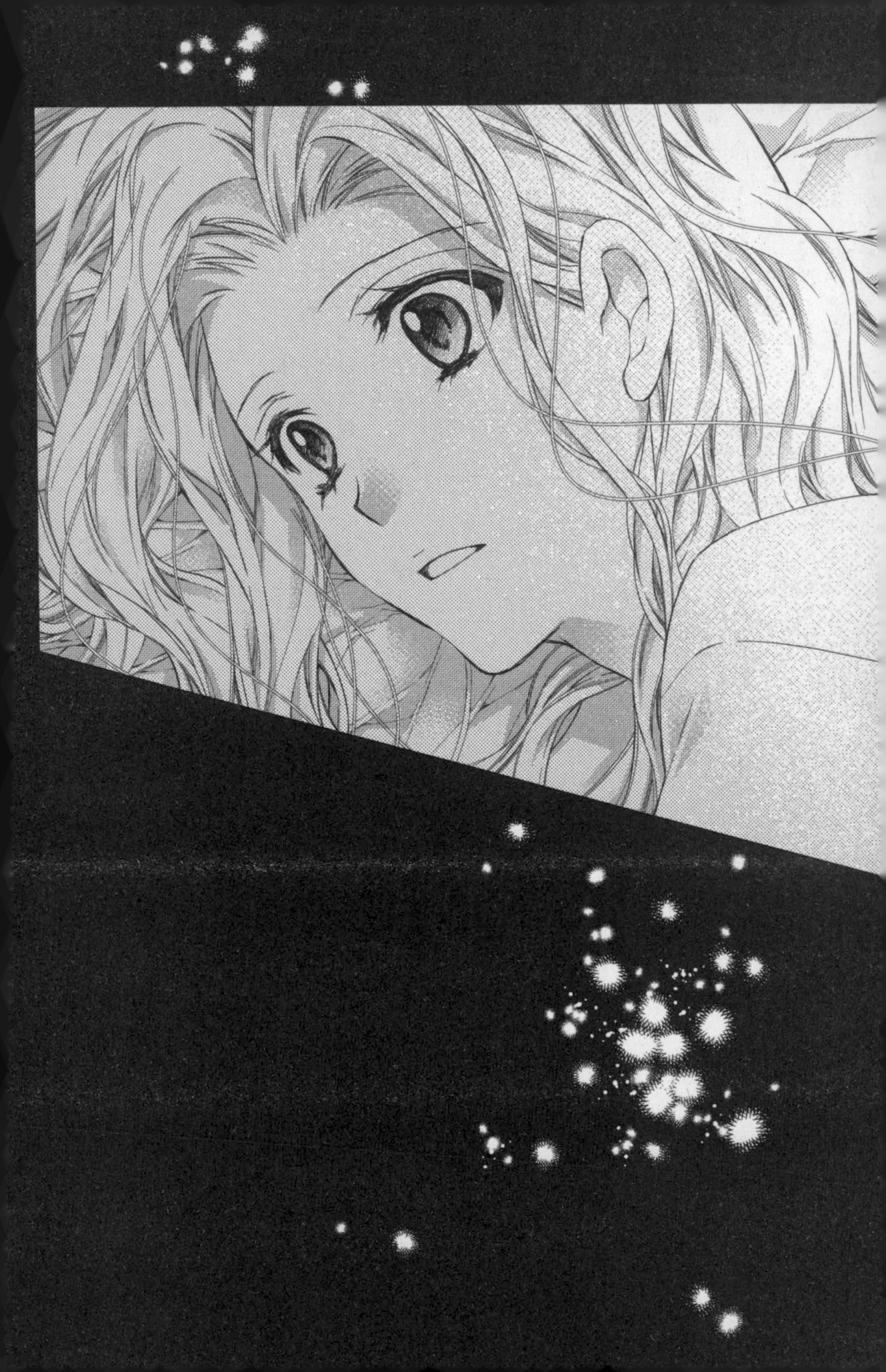

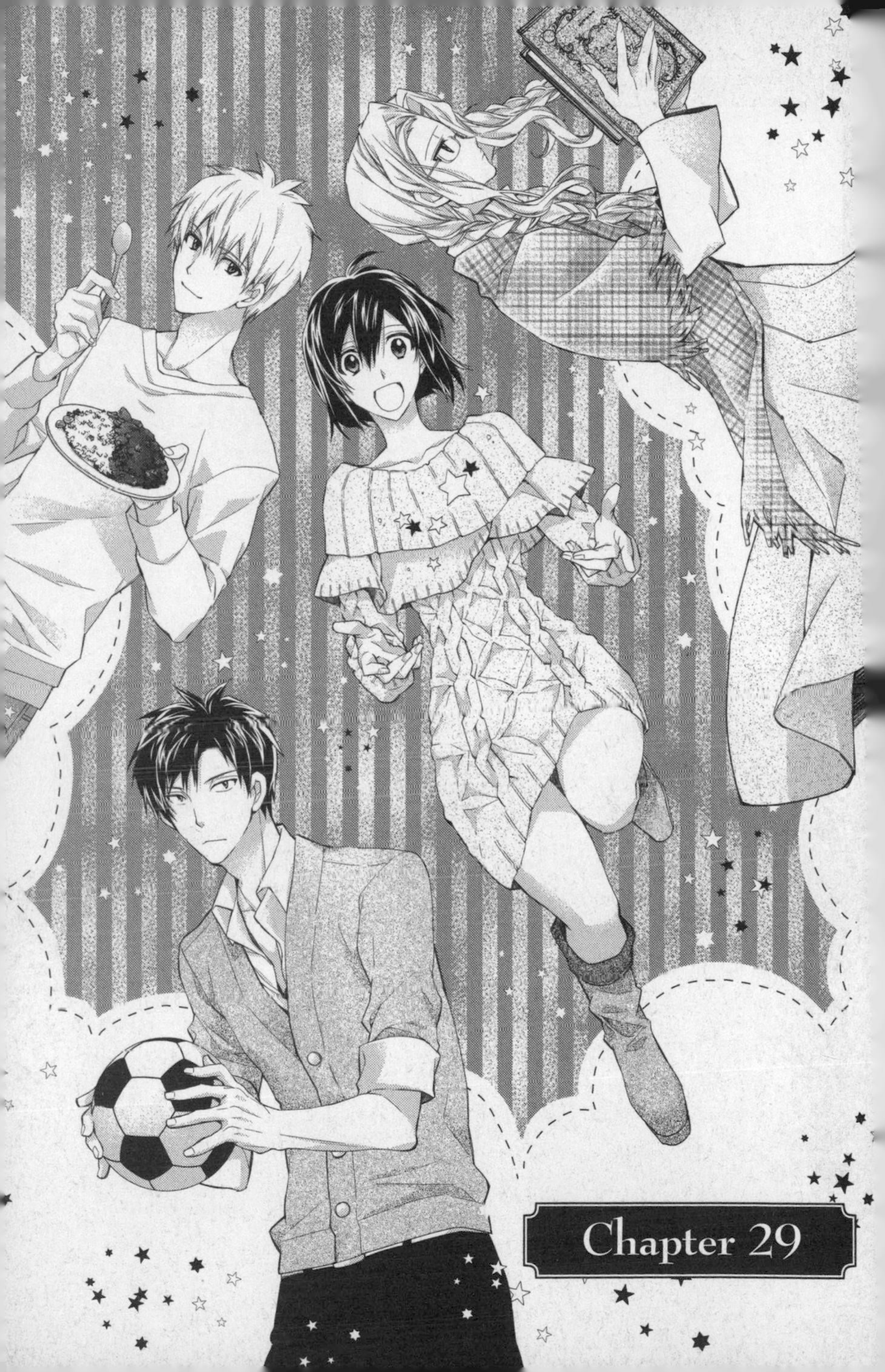
Chapter 29

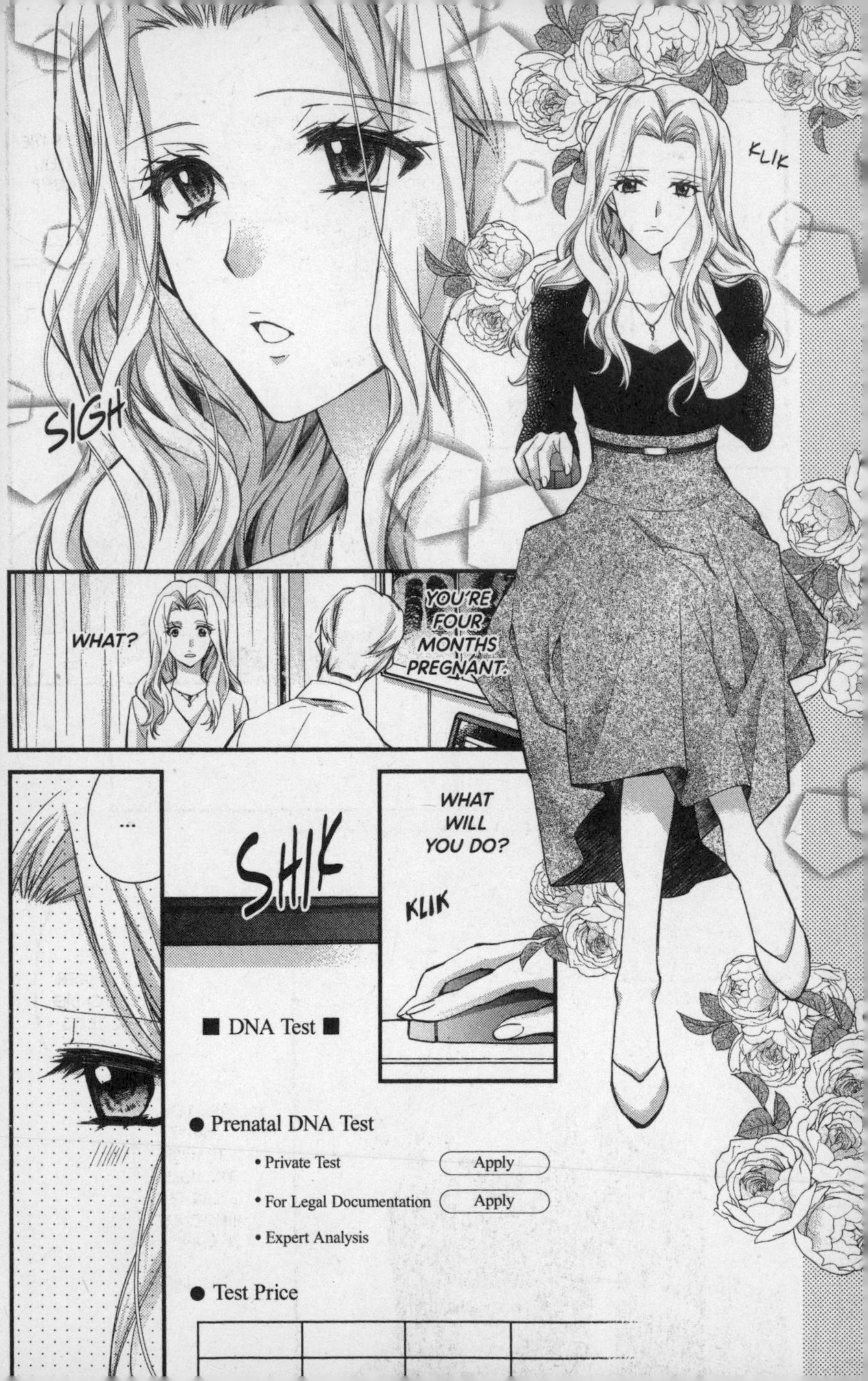
KLIK
SIGH
YOU'RE FOUR MONTHS PREGNANT.
WHAT?
WHAT WILL YOU DO?
KLIK
SHIK
■ DNA Test ■
● Prenatal DNA Test
• Private Test
Apply
• For Legal Documentation
Apply
• Expert Analysis
● Test Price
...

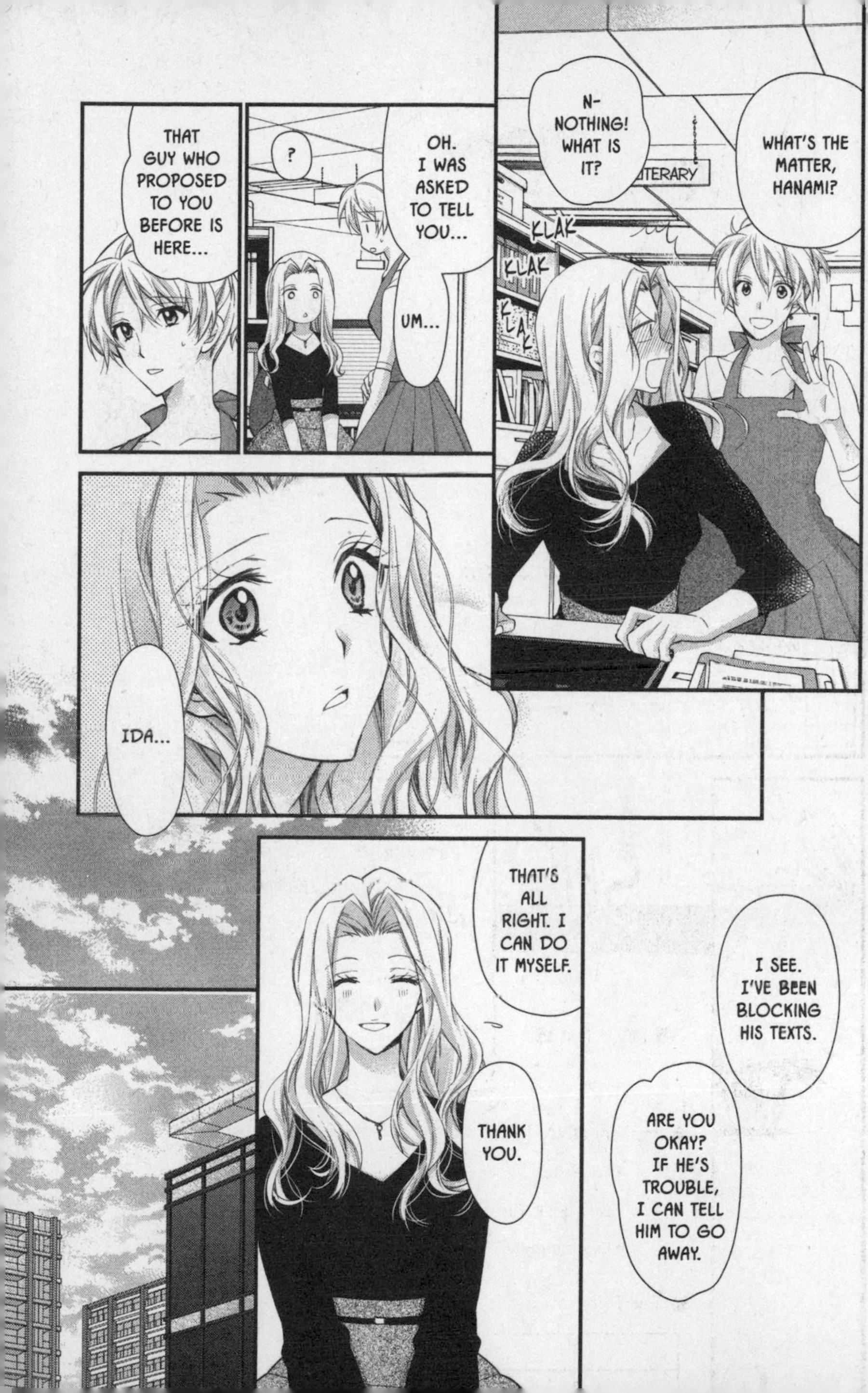
WHAT'S THE MATTER, HANAMI?
N- NOTHING! WHAT IS IT?
ITERARY
KLAK
KLAK
KLAK
OH. I WAS ASKED TO TELL YOU...
?
UM...
THAT GUY WHO PROPOSED TO YOU BEFORE IS HERE...
IDA...
I SEE. I'VE BEEN BLOCKING HIS TEXTS.
ARE YOU OKAY? IF HE'S TROUBLE, I CAN TELL HIM TO GO AWAY.
THAT'S ALL RIGHT. I CAN DO IT MYSELF.
THANK YOU.

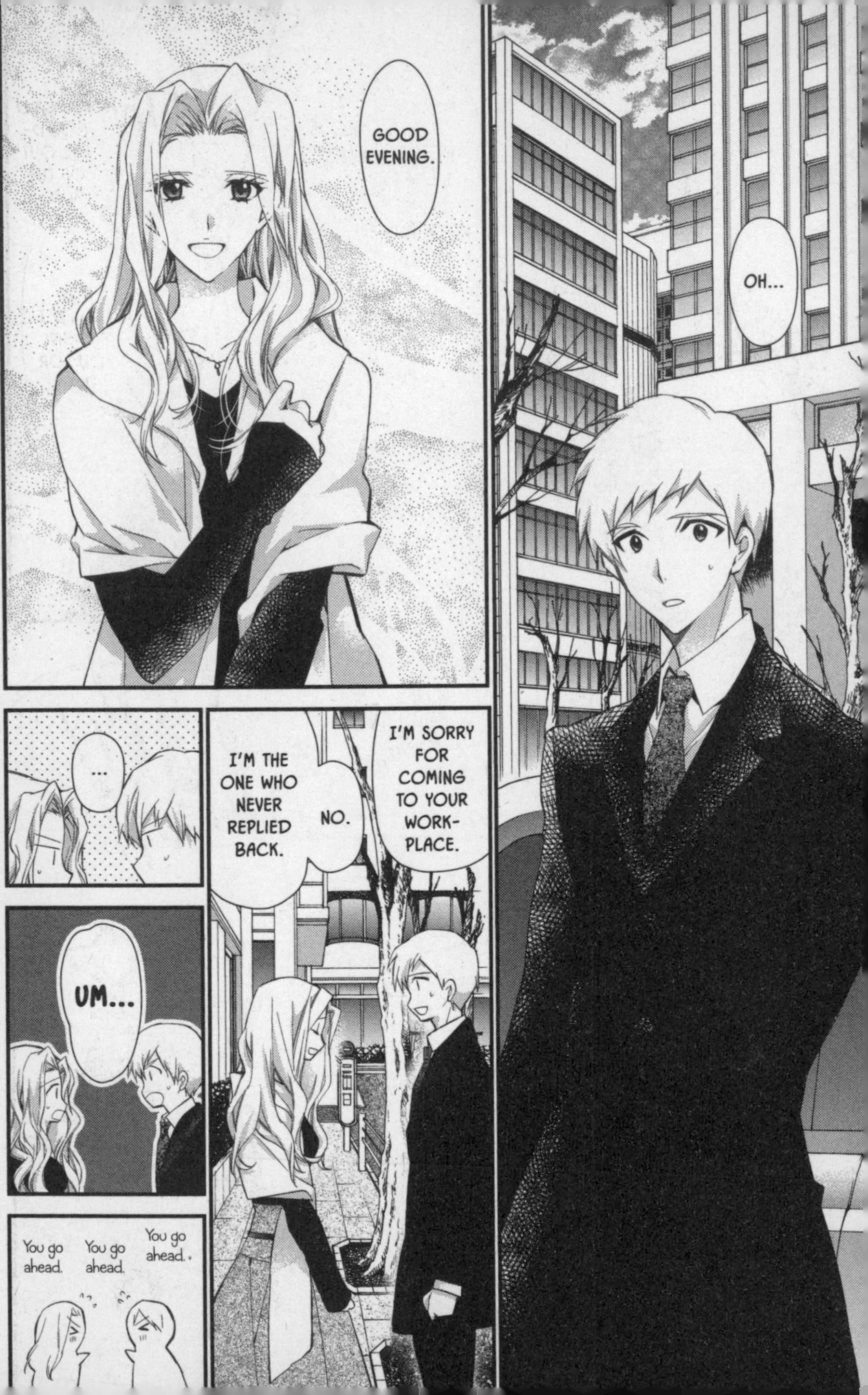

OH...
GOOD EVENING.
I'M SORRY FOR COMING TO YOUR WORK-PLACE.
NO.
I'M THE ONE WHO NEVER REPLIED BACK.
...
UM...
You go ahead.
You go ahead.
You go ahead.

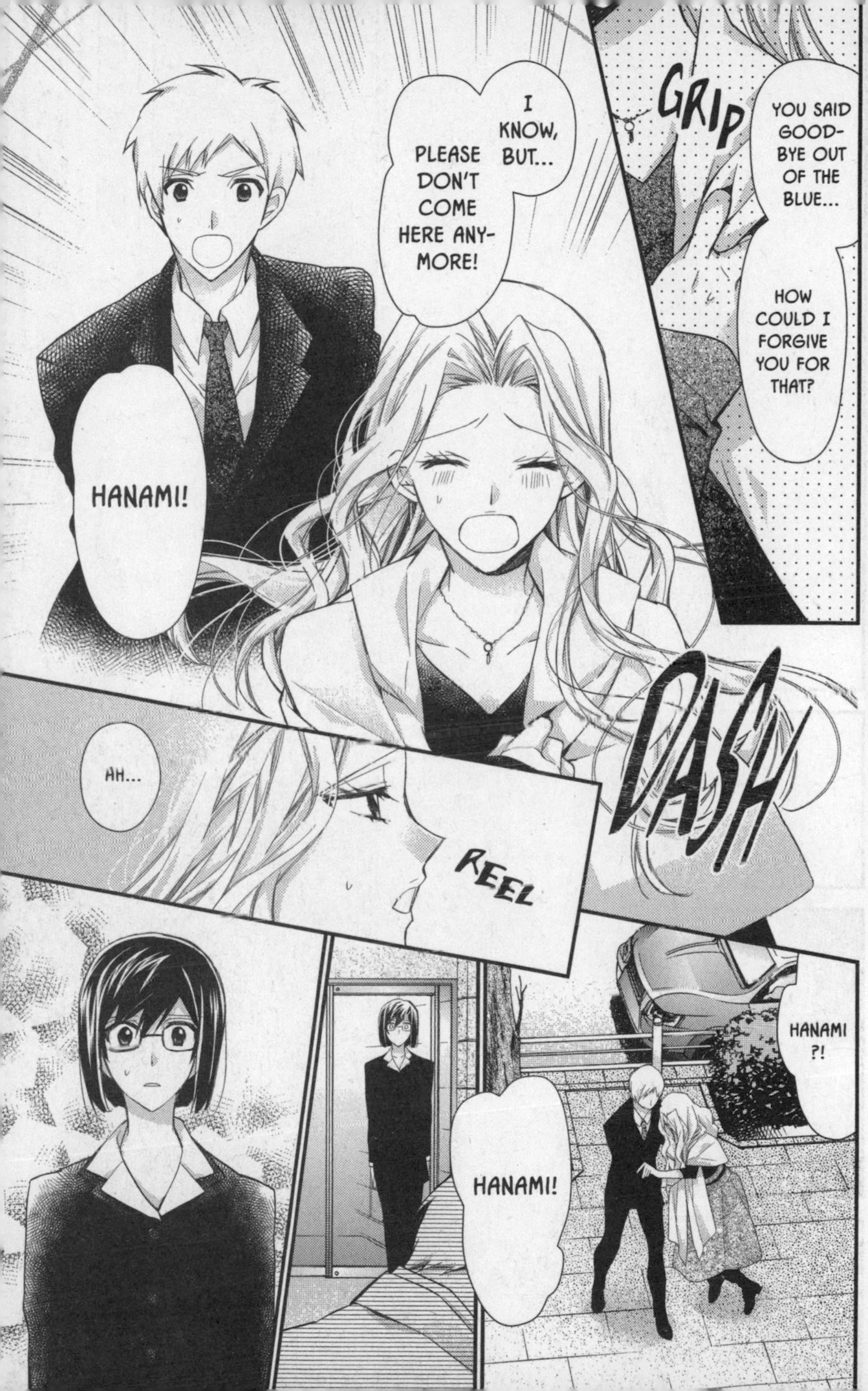
GRIP
YOU SAID GOOD-BYE OUT OF THE BLUE...
HOW COULD I FORGIVE YOU FOR THAT?!
I KNOW, BUT...
PLEASE DON'T COME HERE ANY-MORE!
DASH
HANAMI!
AH...
REEL
HANAMI ?!
HANAMI!

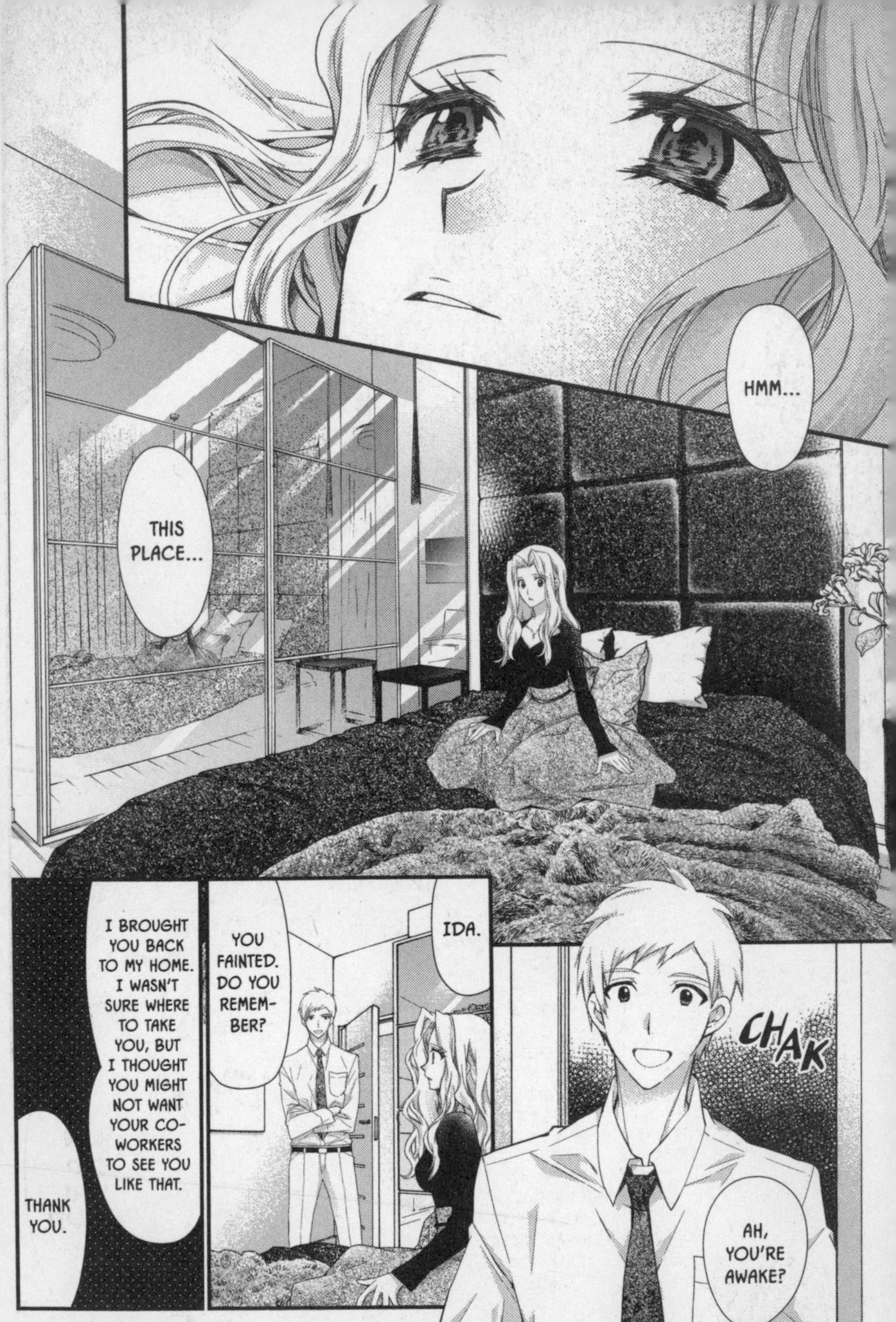
HMM...
THIS PLACE...
CHAK
AH, YOU'RE AWAKE?
IDA.
YOU FAINTED. DO YOU REMEMBER?
I BROUGHT YOU BACK TO MY HOME. I WASN'T SURE WHERE TO TAKE YOU, BUT I THOUGHT YOU MIGHT NOT WANT YOUR CO-WORKERS TO SEE YOU LIKE THAT.
THANK YOU.

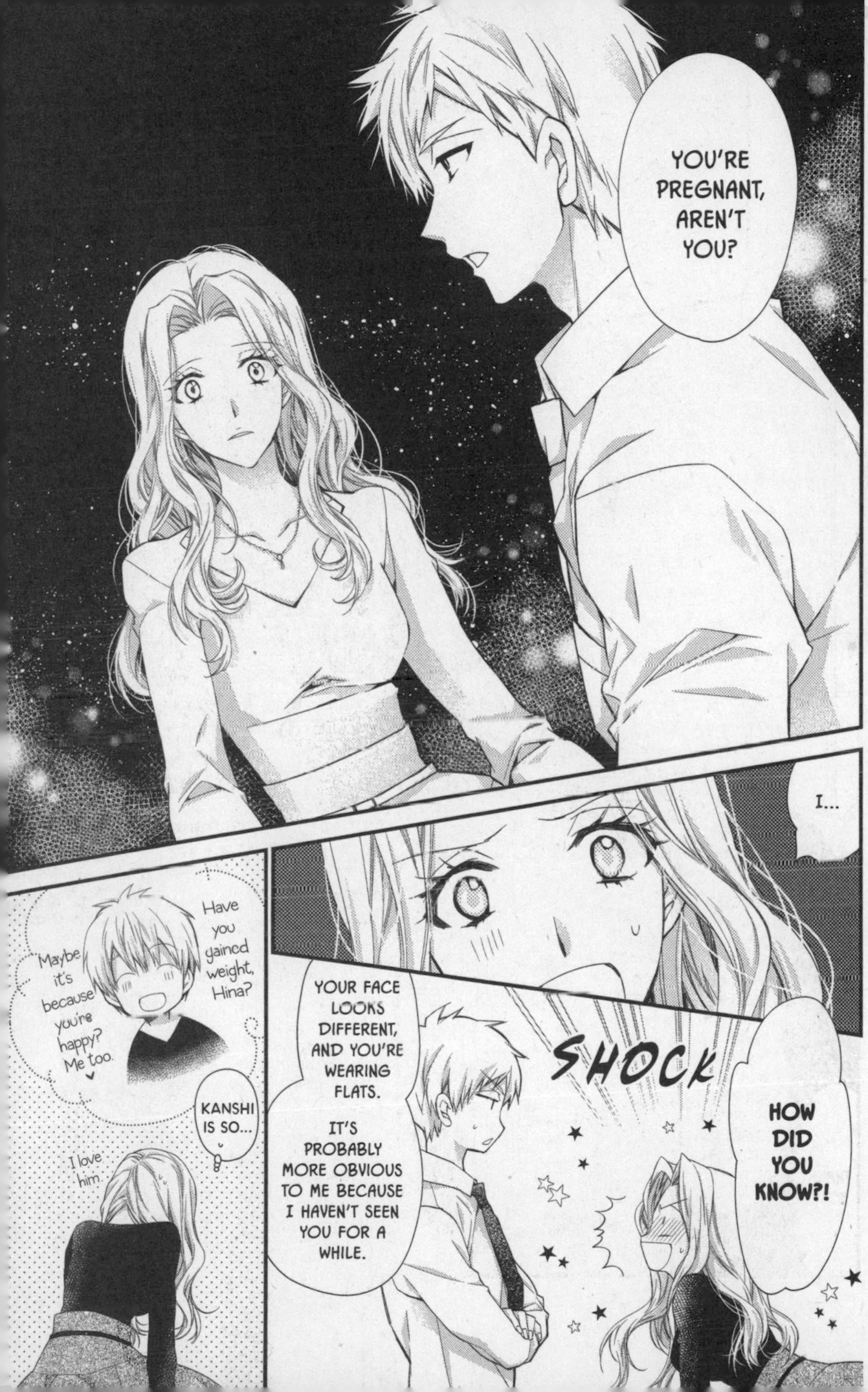
YOU'RE PREGNANT, AREN'T YOU?
I...
HOW DID YOU KNOW?!
SHOCK
YOUR FACE LOOKS DIFFERENT, AND YOU'RE WEARING FLATS.
IT'S PROBABLY MORE OBVIOUS TO ME BECAUSE I HAVEN'T SEEN YOU FOR A WHILE.
Have you gained weight, Hina?
Maybe it's because you're happy? Me too.
KANSHI IS SO...
I love him.

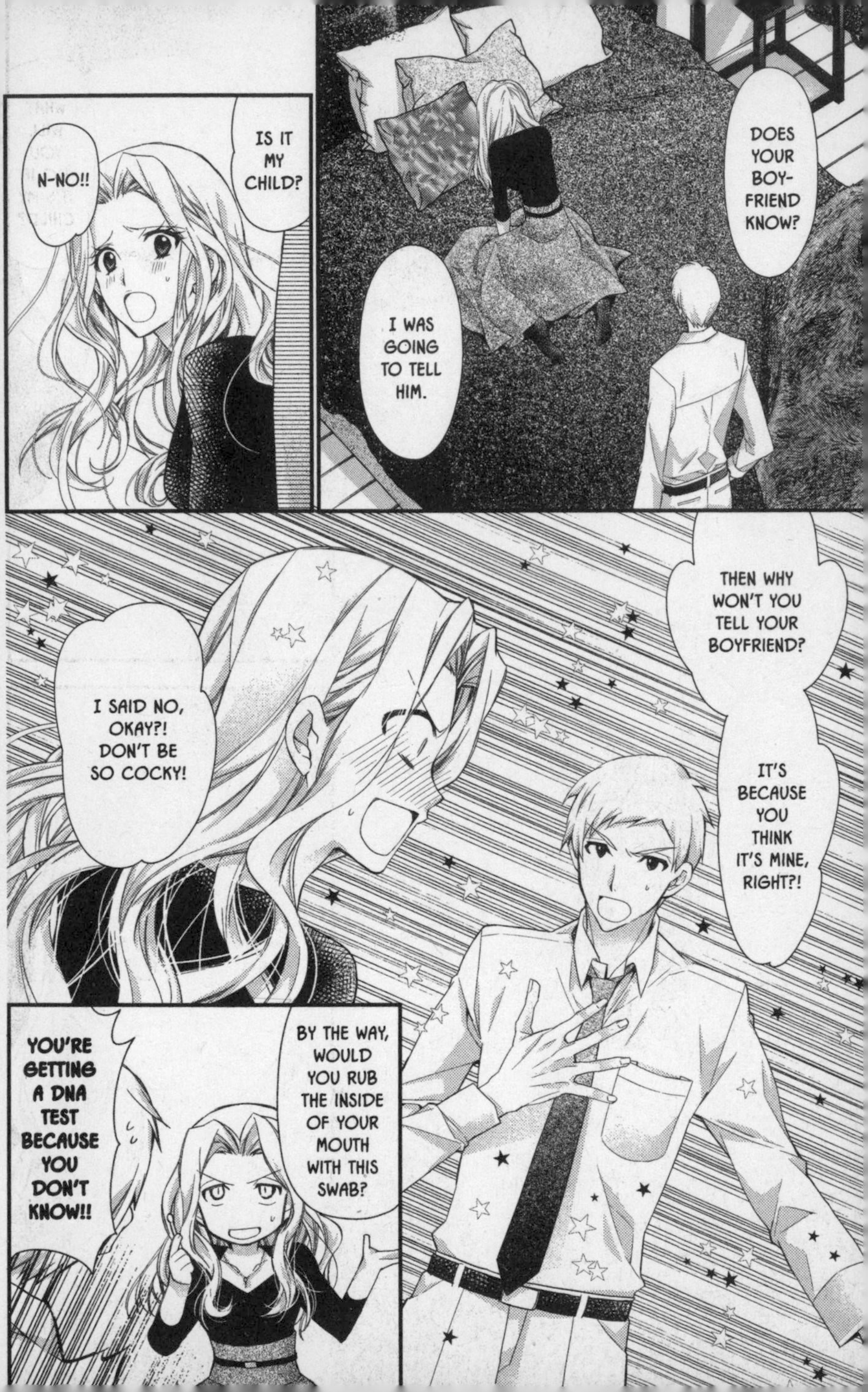
DOES YOUR BOY-FRIEND KNOW?
I WAS GOING TO TELL HIM.
IS IT MY CHILD?
N-NO!!
THEN WHY WON'T YOU TELL YOUR BOYFRIEND?
IT'S BECAUSE YOU THINK IT'S MINE, RIGHT?!
I SAID NO, OKAY?! DON'T BE SO COCKY!
BY THE WAY, WOULD YOU RUB THE INSIDE OF YOUR MOUTH WITH THIS SWAB?
YOU'RE GETTING A DNA TEST BECAUSE YOU DON'T KNOW!!

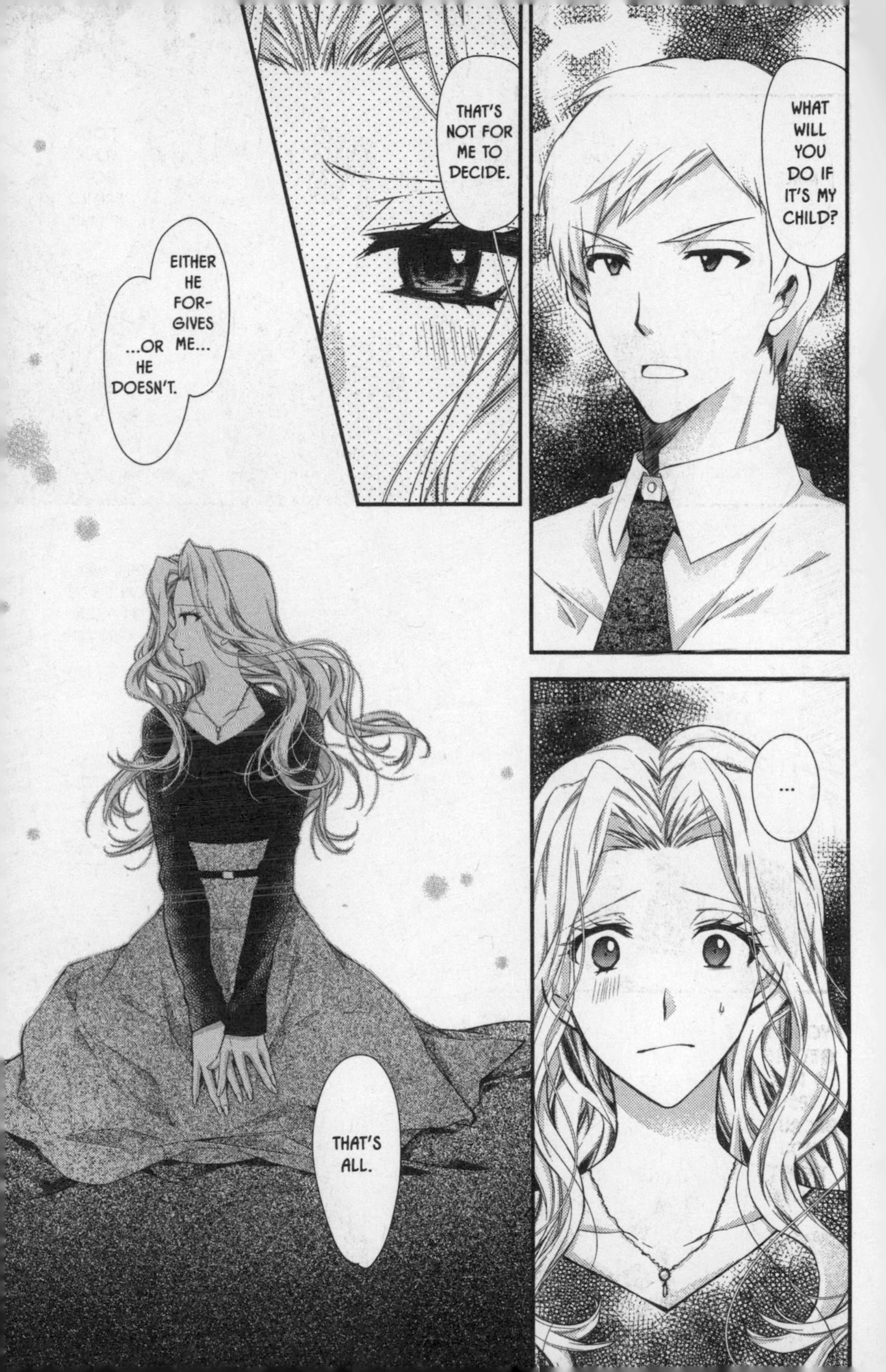
WHAT WILL YOU DO IF IT'S MY CHILD?
THAT'S NOT FOR ME TO DECIDE.
EITHER HE FOR-GIVES ME... ...OR HE DOESN'T.
THAT'S ALL.
...

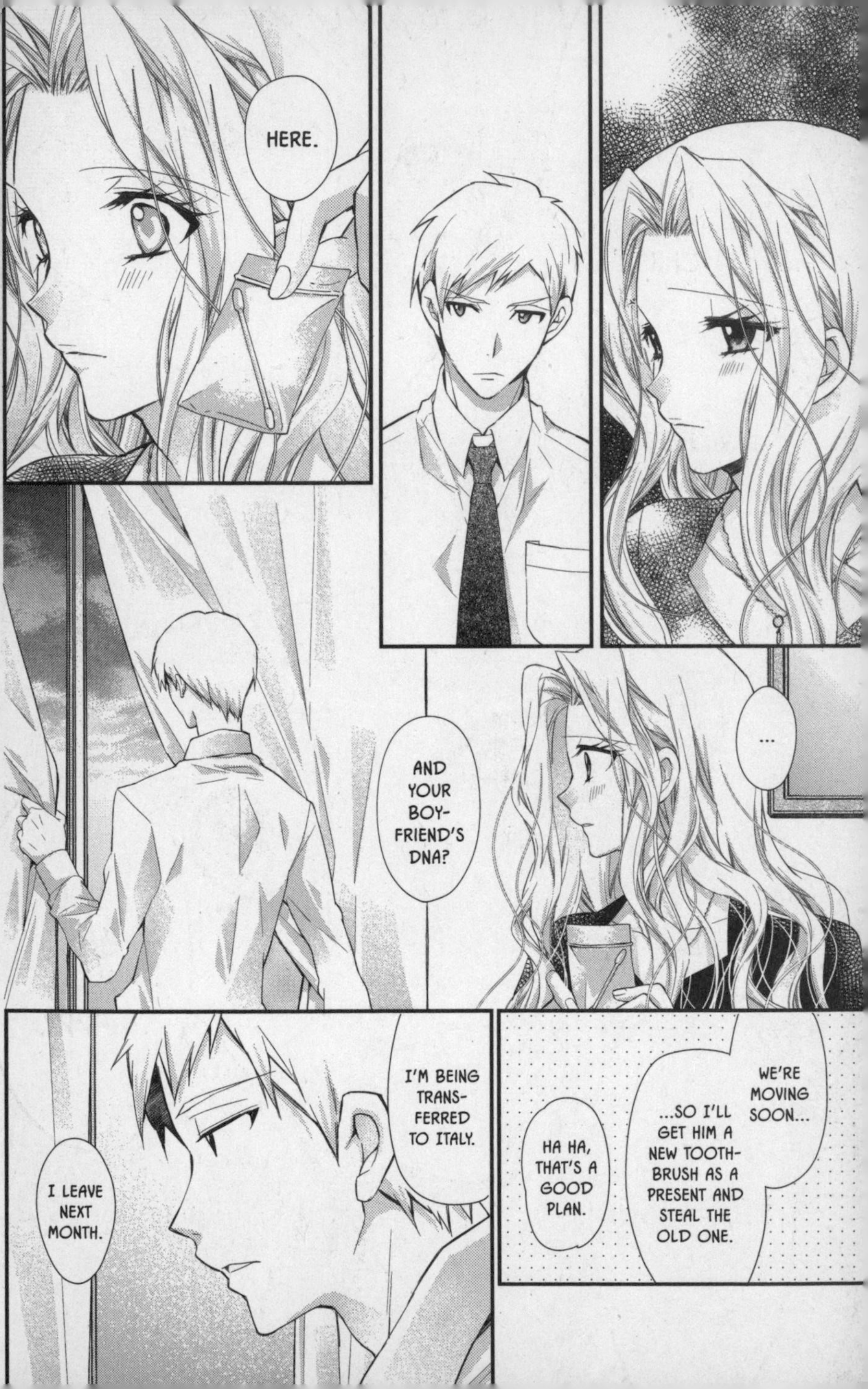
HERE.
...
AND YOUR BOY-FRIEND'S DNA?
WE'RE MOVING SOON...
...SO I'LL GET HIM A NEW TOOTH-BRUSH AS A PRESENT AND STEAL THE OLD ONE.
HA HA, THAT'S A GOOD PLAN.
I'M BEING TRANS-FERRED TO ITALY.
I LEAVE NEXT MONTH.

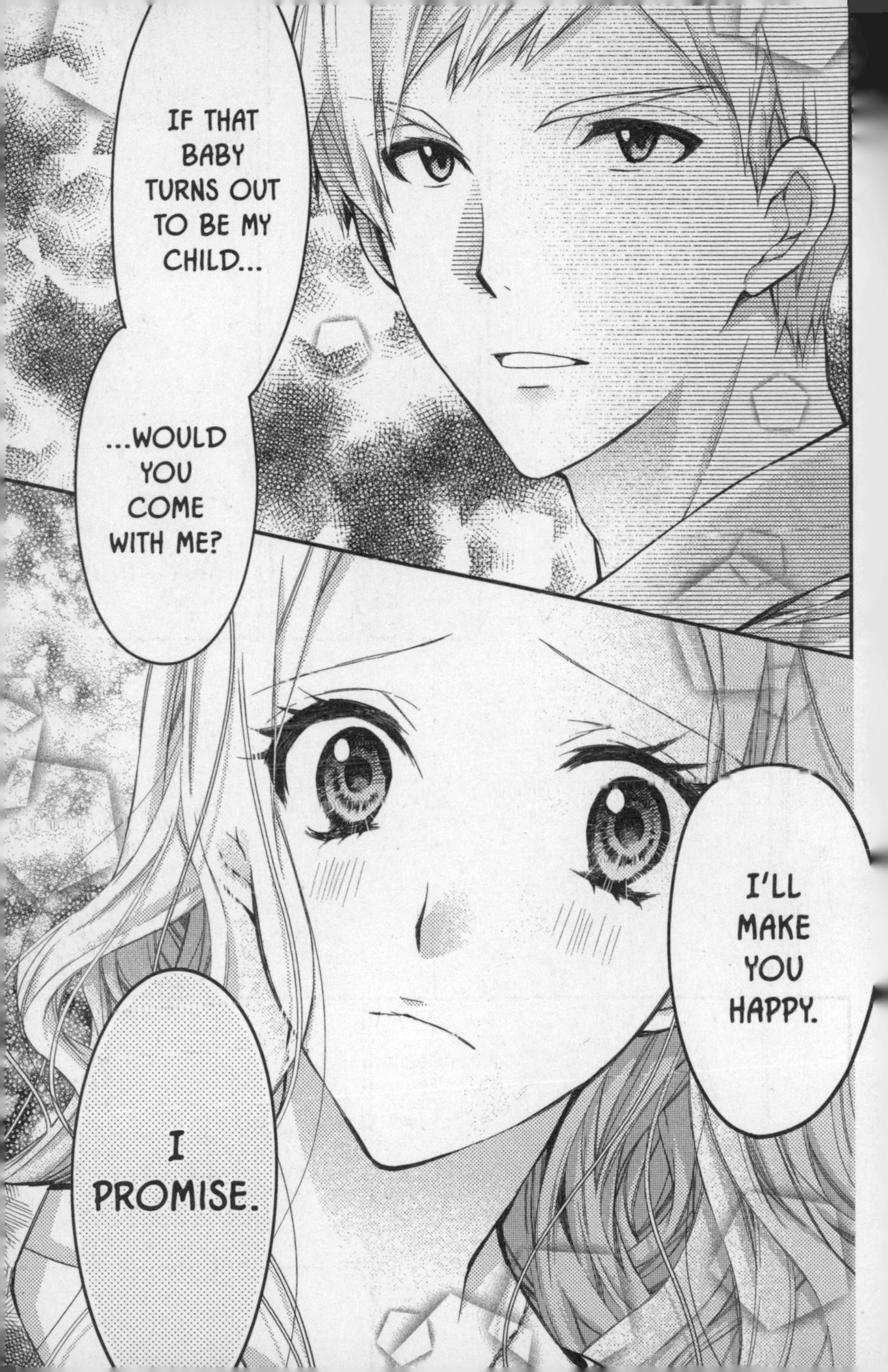
IF THAT BABY TURNS OUT TO BE MY CHILD...
...WOULD YOU COME WITH ME?
I'LL MAKE YOU HAPPY.
I PROMISE.

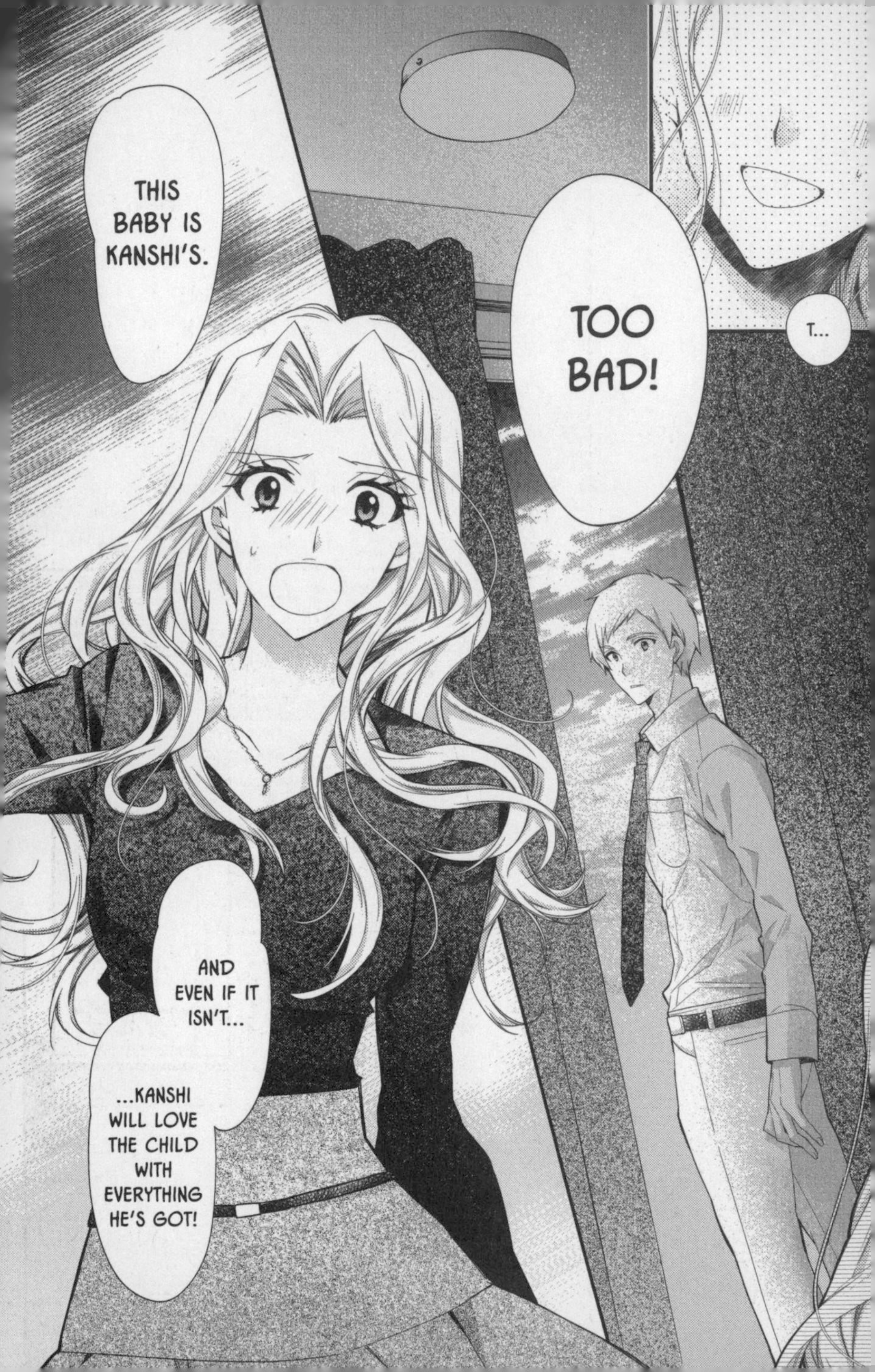
T...
TOO BAD!
THIS BABY IS KANSHI'S.
AND EVEN IF IT ISN'T...
...KANSHI WILL LOVE THE CHILD WITH EVERYTHING HE'S GOT!

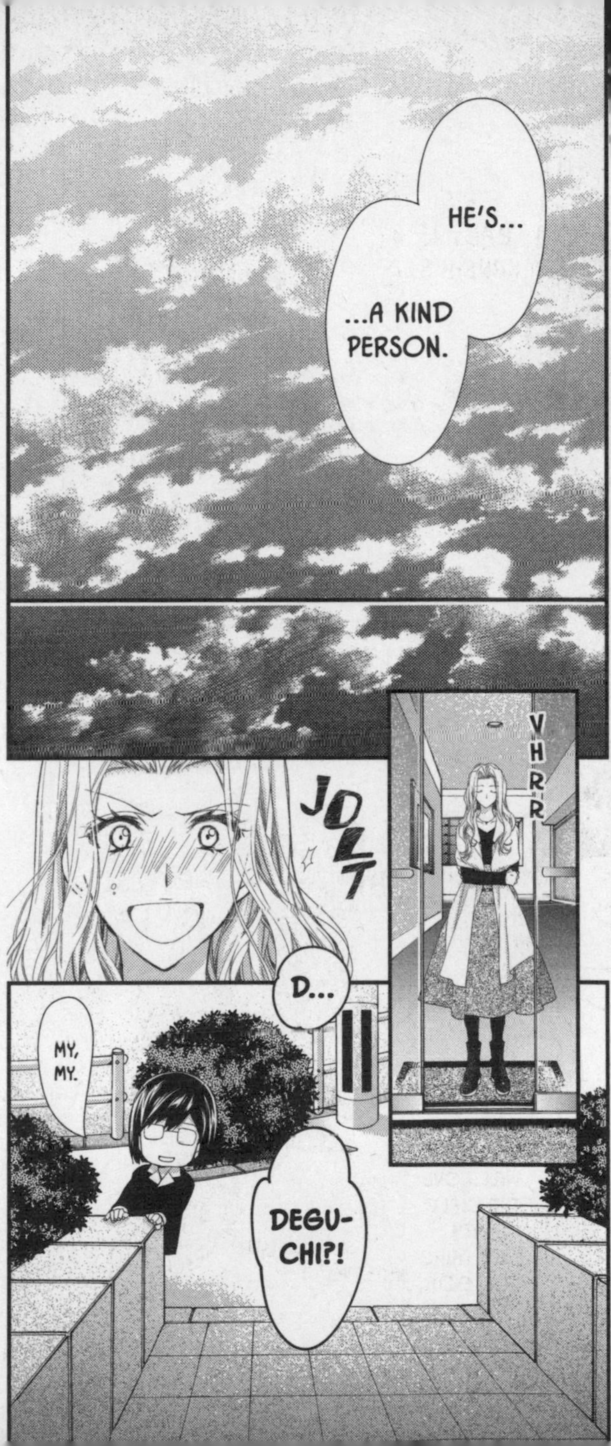
HE'S...
...A KIND PERSON.
VHRR
JOLT
D...
DEGU-CHI?!
MY, MY.

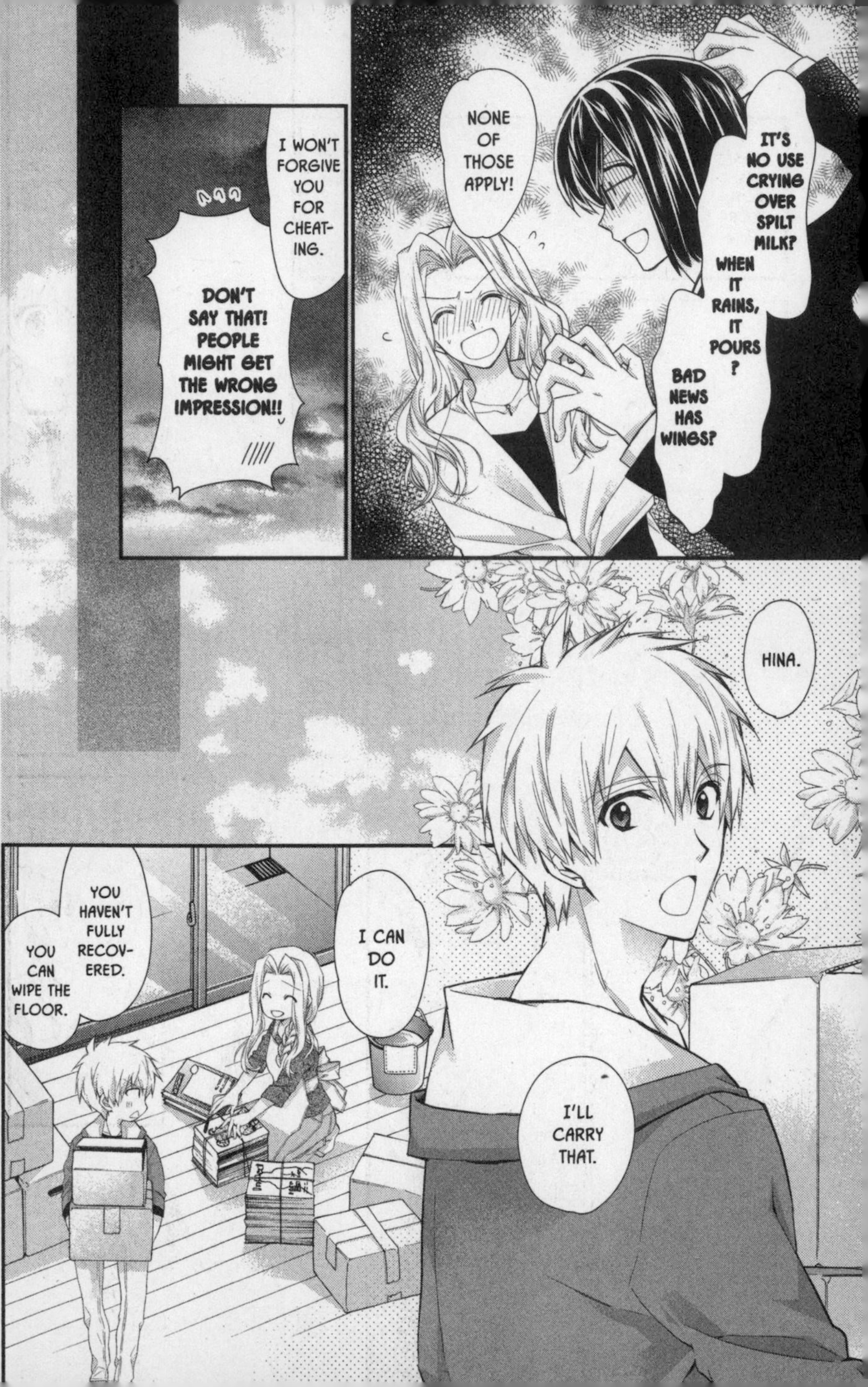

IT'S NO USE CRYING OVER SPILT MILK?
WHEN IT RAINS, IT POURS?
BAD NEWS HAS WINGS?
NONE OF THOSE APPLY!
I WON'T FORGIVE YOU FOR CHEATING.
DON'T SAY THAT! PEOPLE MIGHT GET THE WRONG IMPRESSION!!
HINA.
I'LL CARRY THAT.
I CAN DO IT.
YOU HAVEN'T FULLY RECOVERED.
YOU CAN WIPE THE FLOOR.

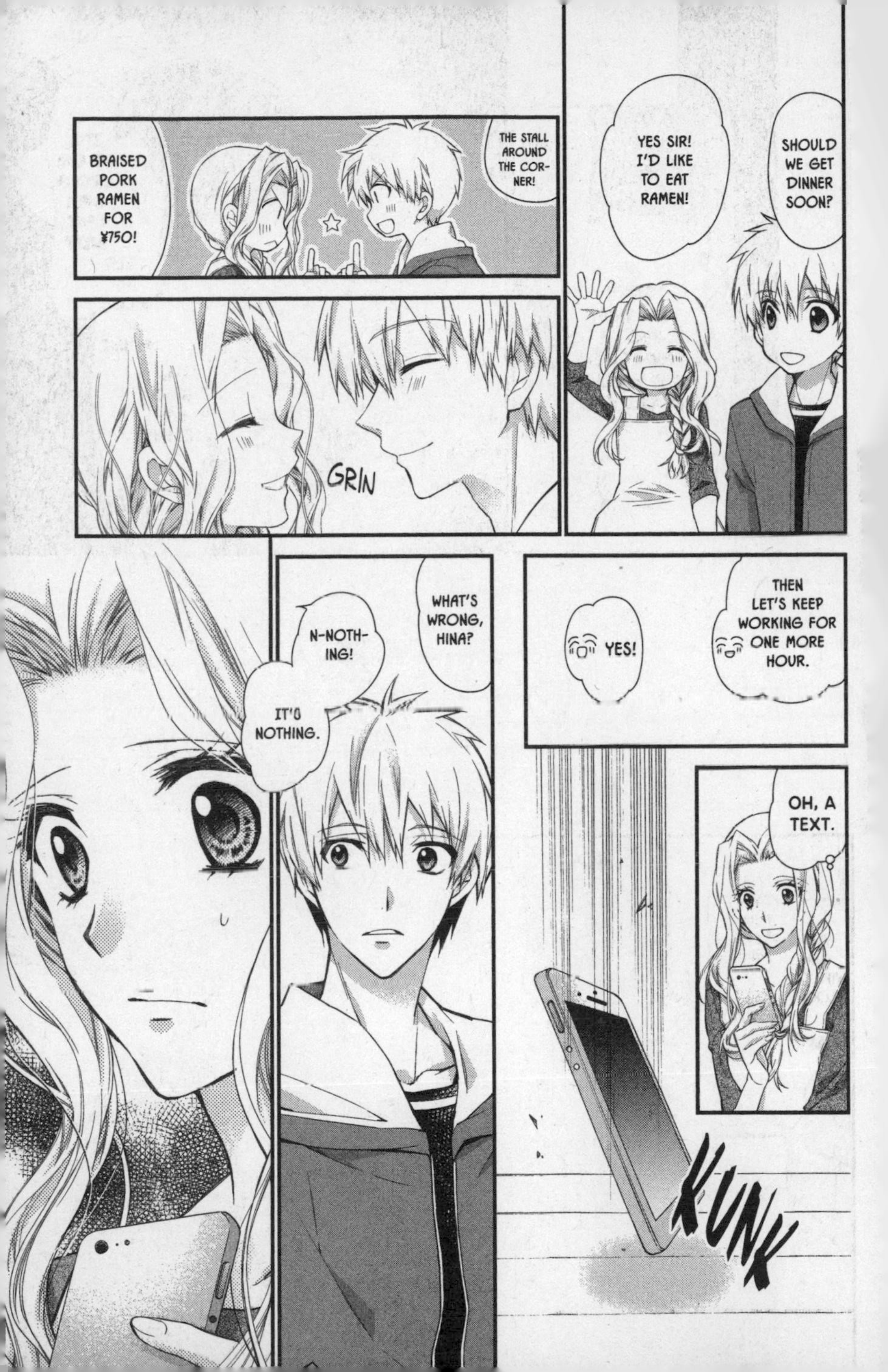
SHOULD WE GET DINNER SOON?
YES SIR! I'D LIKE TO EAT RAMEN!
THE STALL AROUND THE COR-NER!
BRAISED PORK RAMEN FOR ¥750!
GRIN
THEN LET'S KEEP WORKING FOR ONE MORE HOUR.
YES!
OH, A TEXT.
KUNK
WHAT'S WRONG, HINA?
N-NOTHING!
IT'S NOTHING.

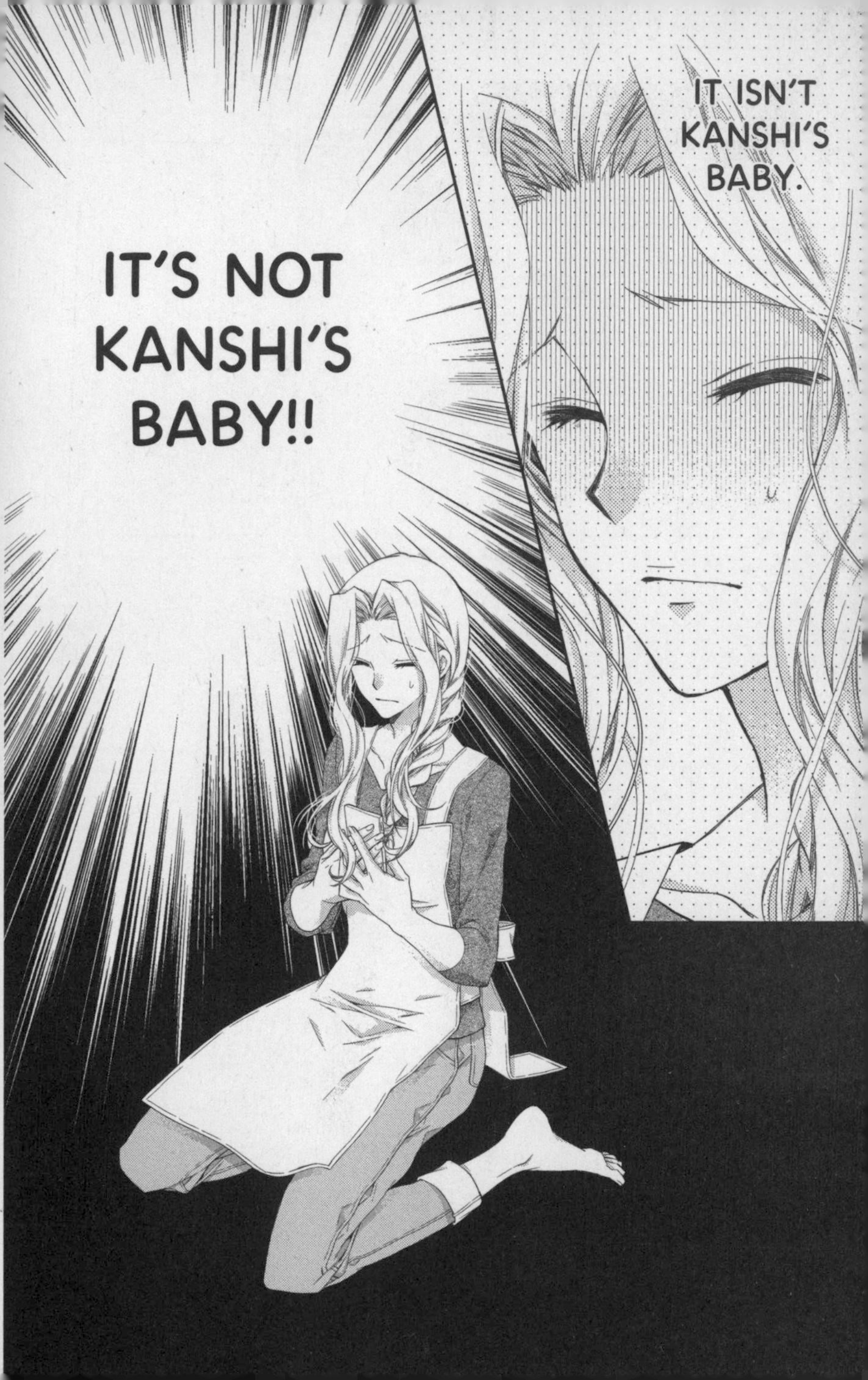
IT ISN'T KANSHI'S BABY.
IT'S NOT KANSHI'S BABY!!

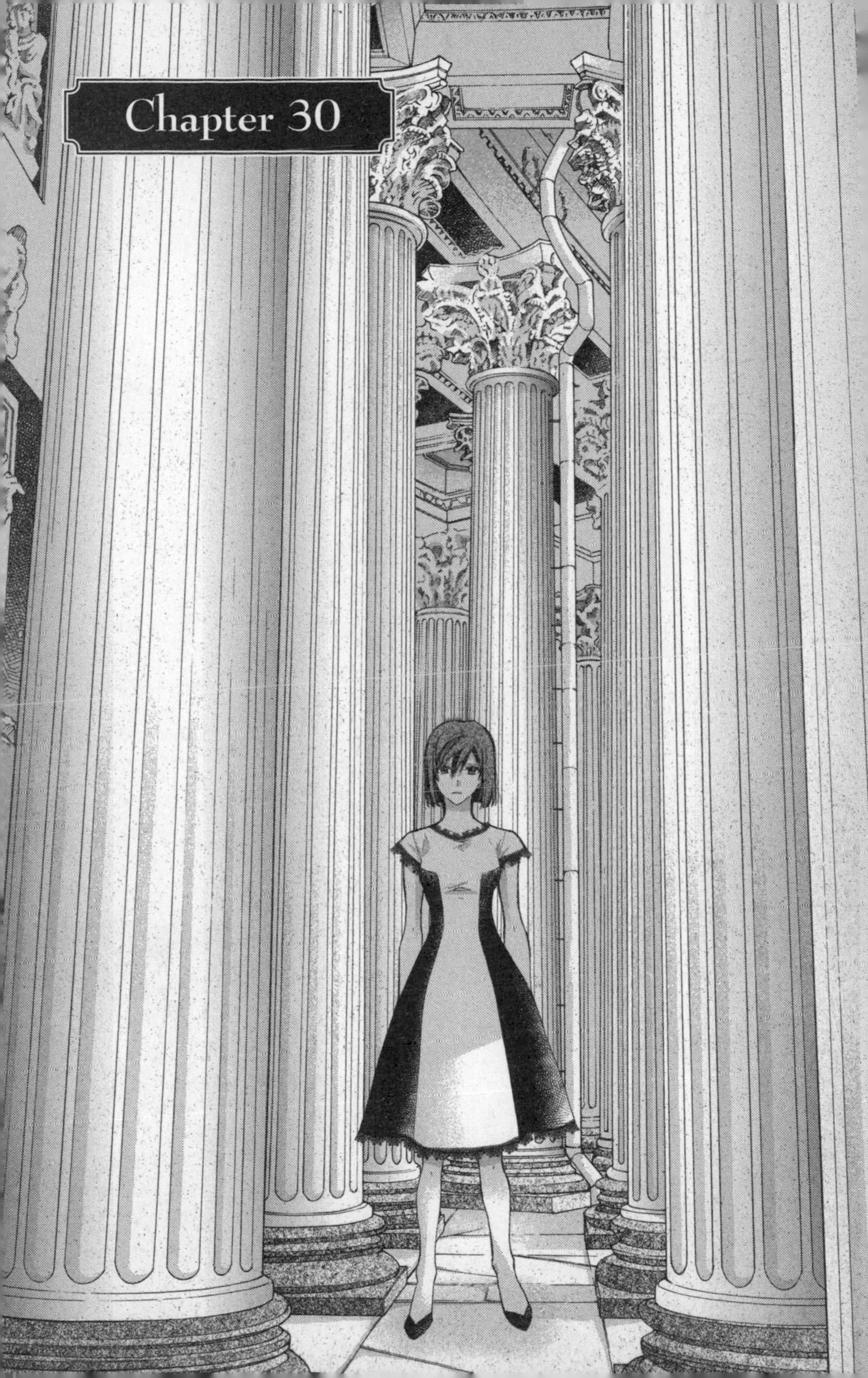
Chapter 30

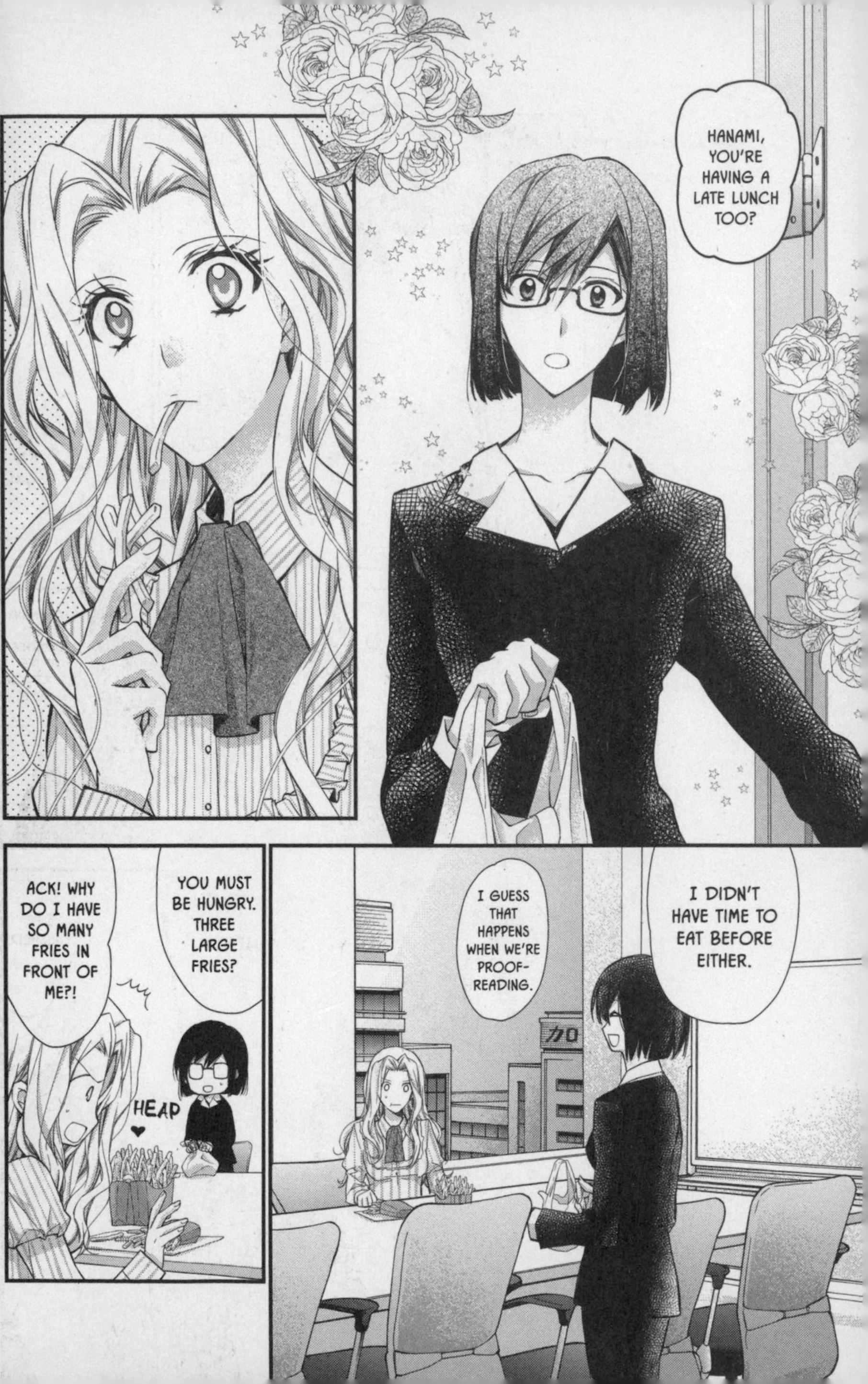

HANAMI, YOU'RE HAVING A LATE LUNCH TOO?
I DIDN'T HAVE TIME TO EAT BEFORE EITHER.
I GUESS THAT HAPPENS WHEN WE'RE PROOF-READING.
カロ
YOU MUST BE HUNGRY. THREE LARGE FRIES?
ACK! WHY DO I HAVE SO MANY FRIES IN FRONT OF ME?!
HEAP

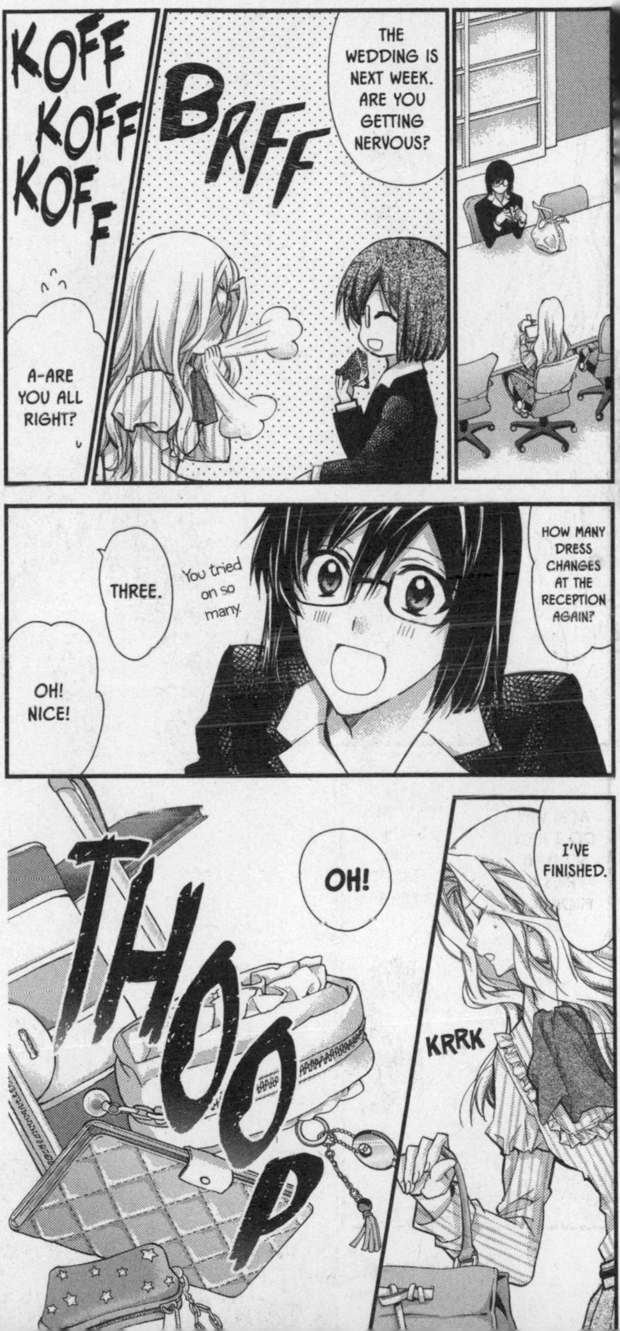
THE WEDDING IS NEXT WEEK. ARE YOU GETTING NERVOUS?
BRFF
KOFF KOFF KOFF
A-ARE YOU ALL RIGHT?
HOW MANY DRESS CHANGES AT THE RECEPTION AGAIN?
You tried on so many.
THREE.
OH! NICE!
I'VE FINISHED.
KRRK
OH!
THOOP

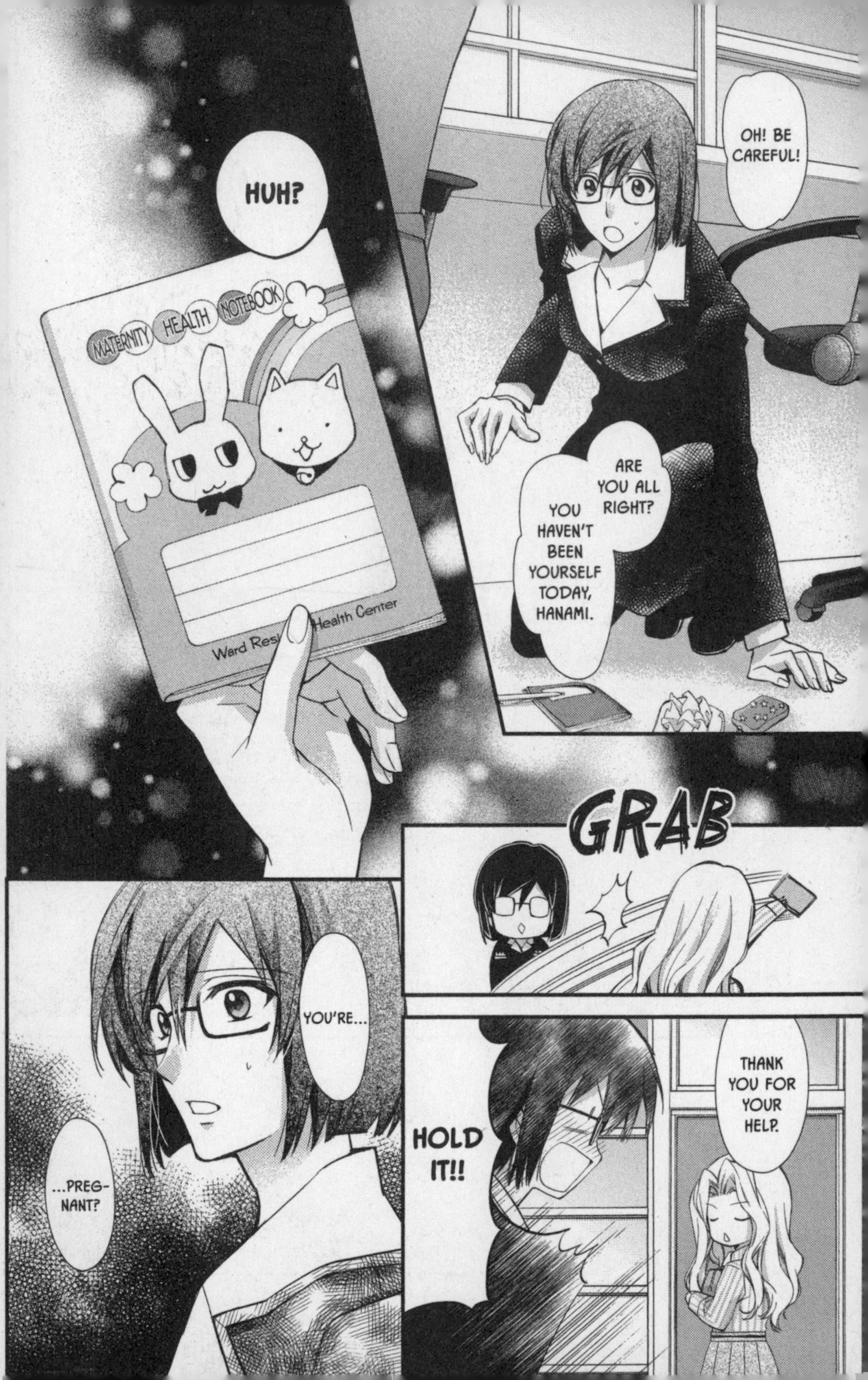
OH! BE CAREFUL!
ARE YOU ALL RIGHT?
YOU HAVEN'T BEEN YOURSELF TODAY, HANAMI.
HUH?
MATERNITY HEALTH NOTEBOOK
Ward Res
Health Center
GRAB
THANK YOU FOR YOUR HELP.
HOLD IT!!
YOU'RE...
...PREG-NANT?

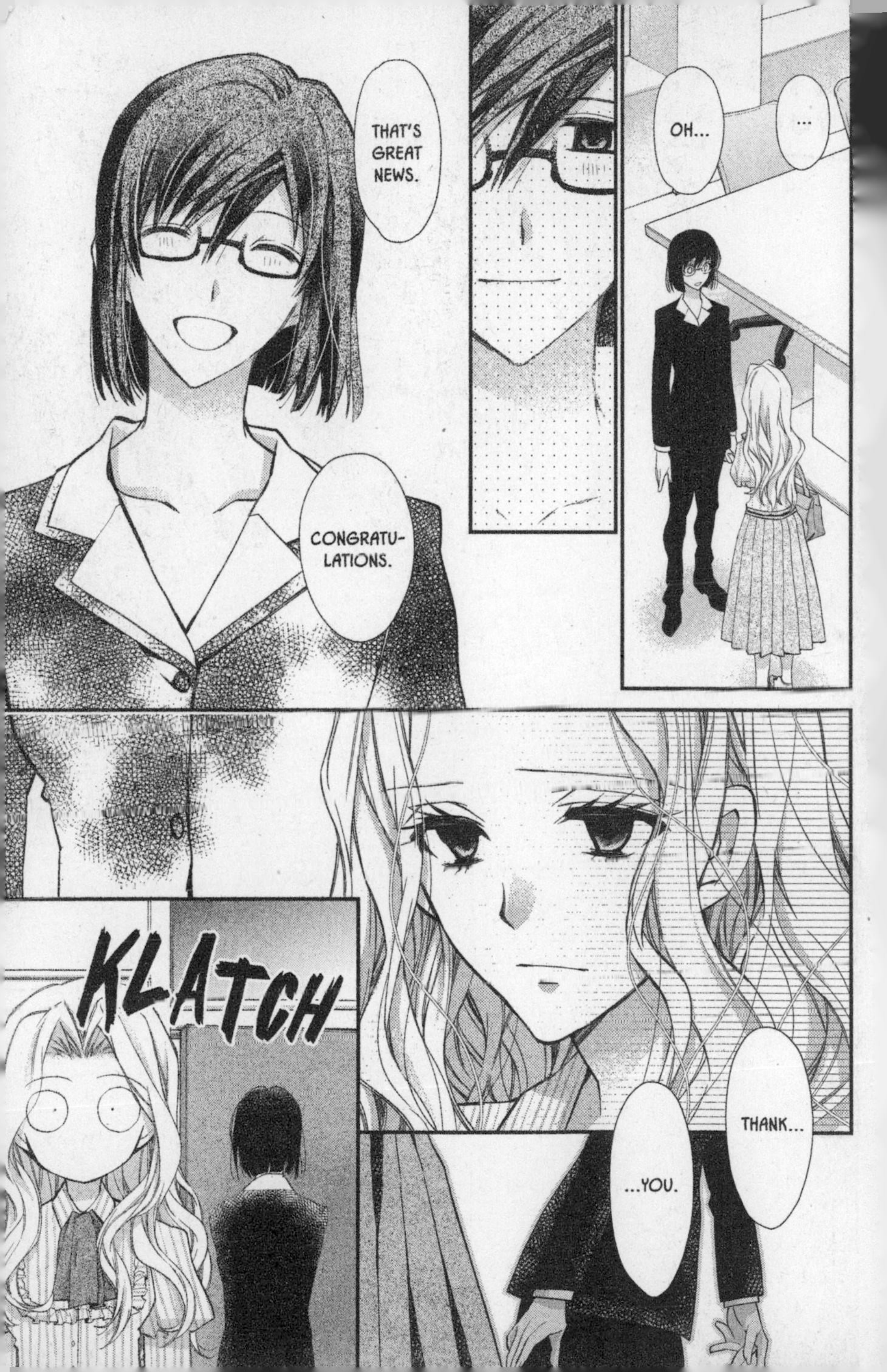
...
OH...
THAT'S GREAT NEWS.
CONGRATULATIONS.
THANK...
...YOU.
KLATCH

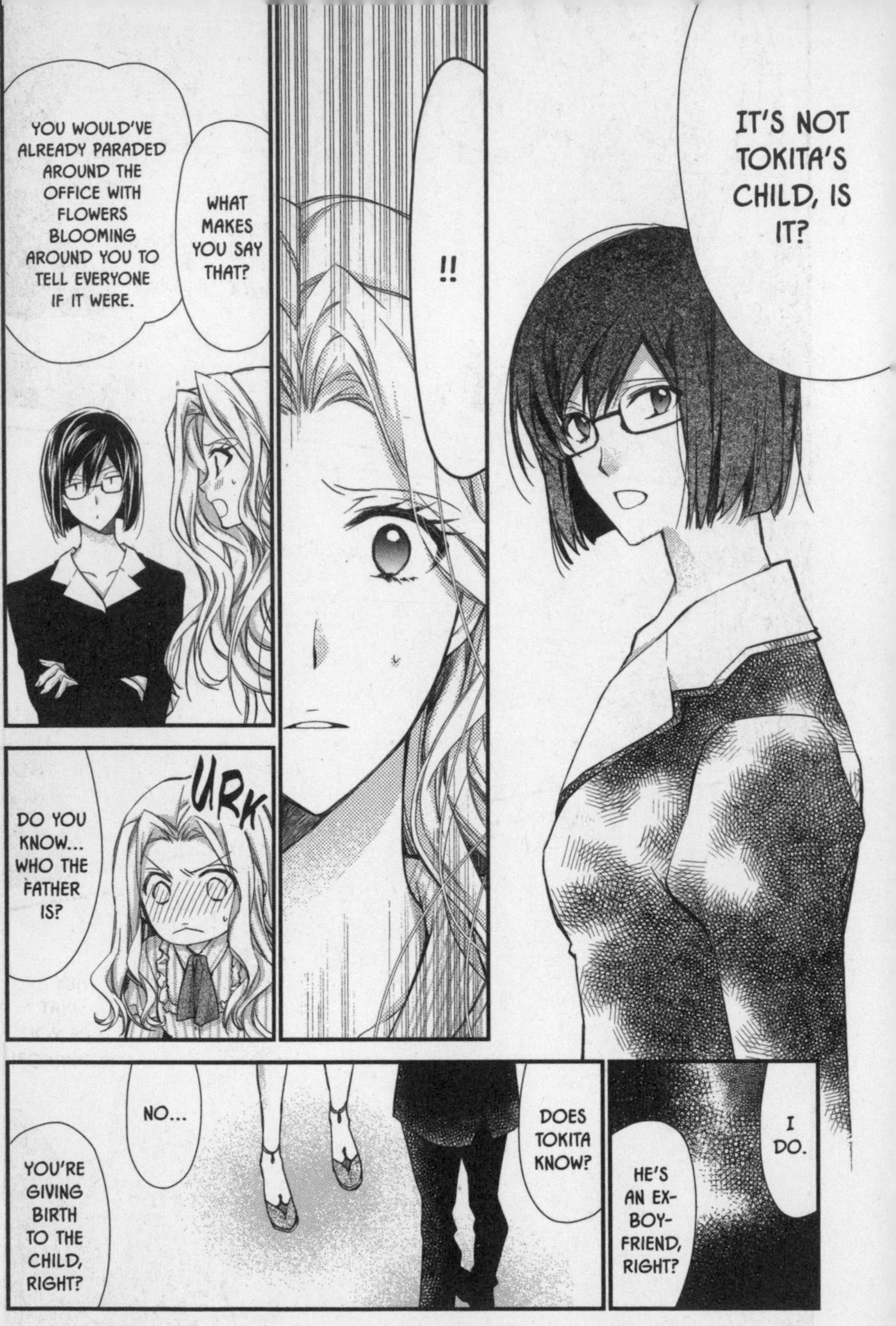
IT'S NOT TOKITA'S CHILD, IS IT?
!!
WHAT MAKES YOU SAY THAT?
YOU WOULD'VE ALREADY PARADED AROUND THE OFFICE WITH FLOWERS BLOOMING AROUND YOU TO TELL EVERYONE IF IT WERE.
URK
DO YOU KNOW... WHO THE FATHER IS?
I DO.
HE'S AN EX-BOYFRIEND, RIGHT?
DOES TOKITA KNOW?
NO...
YOU'RE GIVING BIRTH TO THE CHILD, RIGHT?

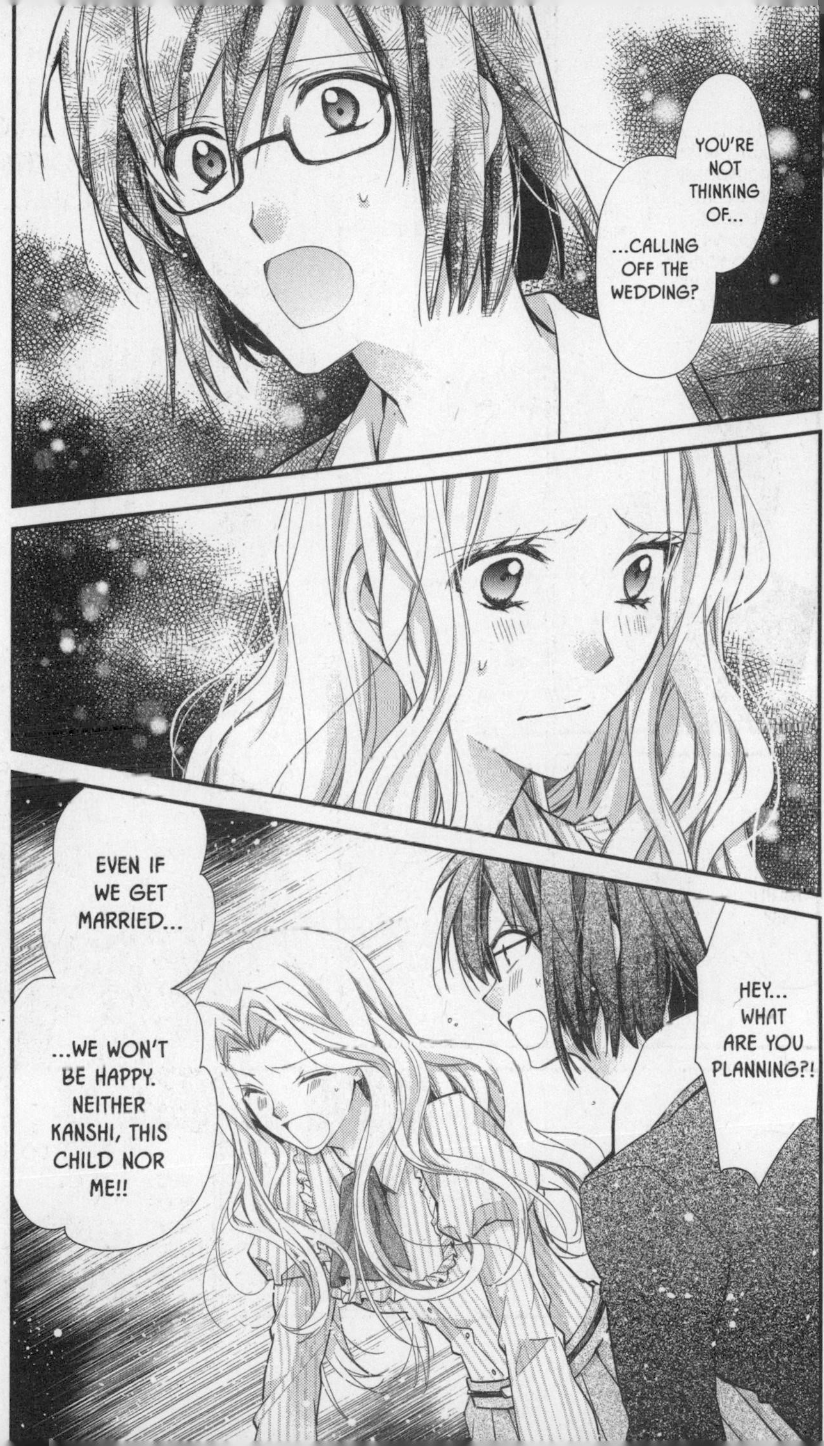
YOU'RE NOT THINKING OF...
...CALLING OFF THE WEDDING?
HEY... WHAT ARE YOU PLANNING?!
EVEN IF WE GET MARRIED...
...WE WON'T BE HAPPY. NEITHER KANSHI, THIS CHILD NOR ME!!

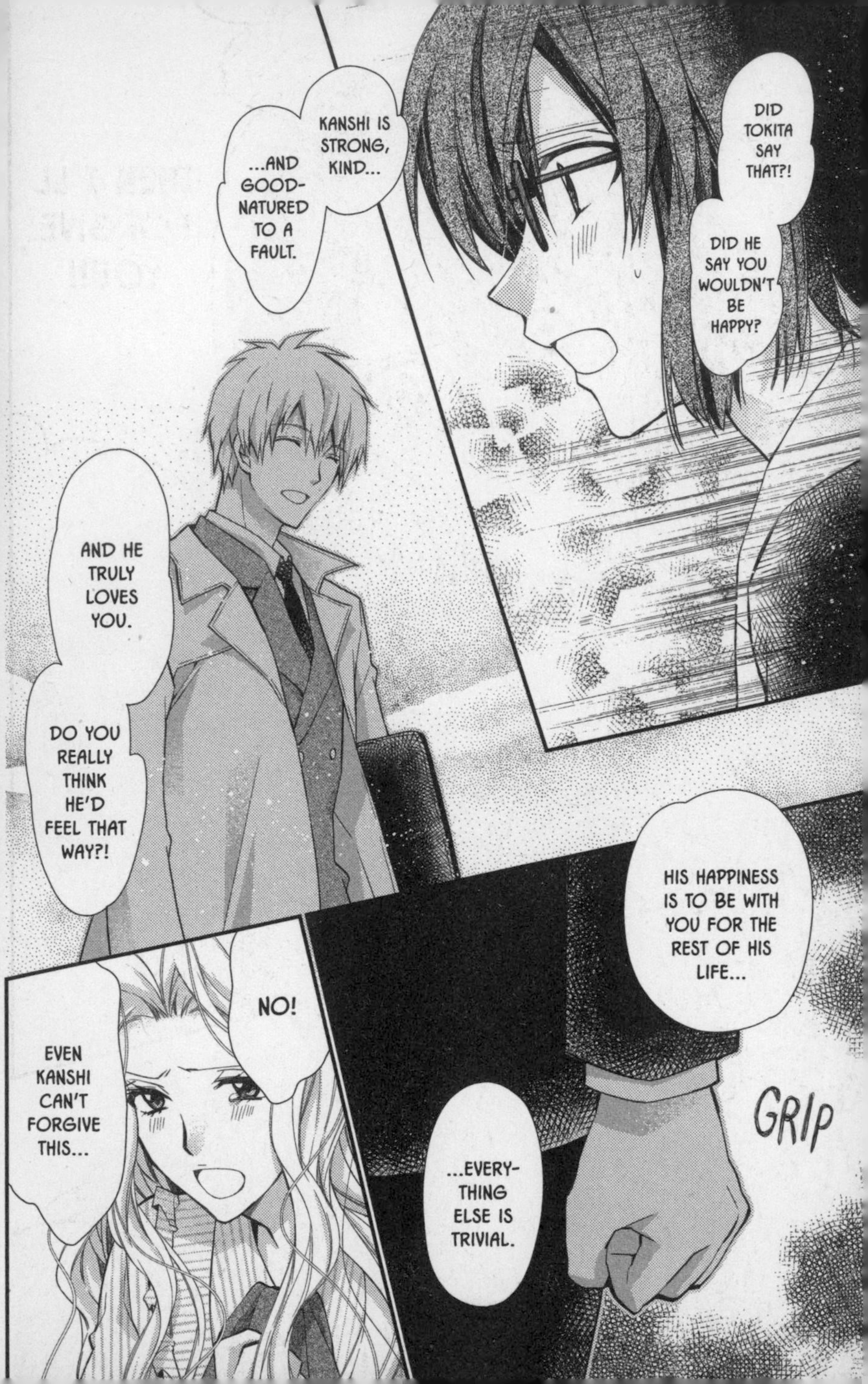
DID TOKITA SAY THAT?!
DID HE SAY YOU WOULDN'T BE HAPPY?
KANSHI IS STRONG, KIND...
...AND GOOD-NATURED TO A FAULT.
AND HE TRULY LOVES YOU.
DO YOU REALLY THINK HE'D FEEL THAT WAY?!
HIS HAPPINESS IS TO BE WITH YOU FOR THE REST OF HIS LIFE...
...EVERY-THING ELSE IS TRIVIAL.
GRIP
NO!
EVEN KANSHI CAN'T FORGIVE THIS...

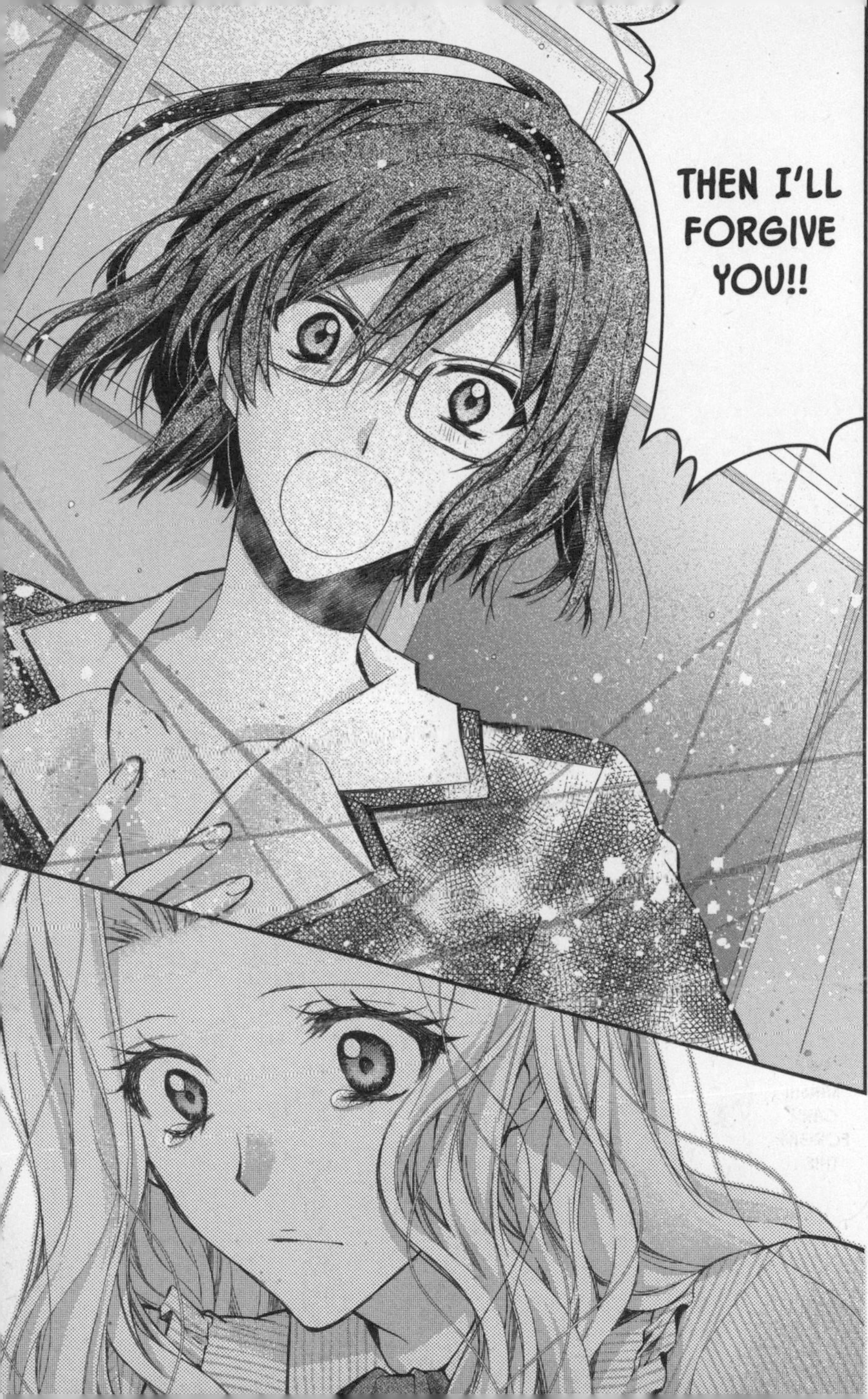
THEN I'LL FORGIVE YOU!!

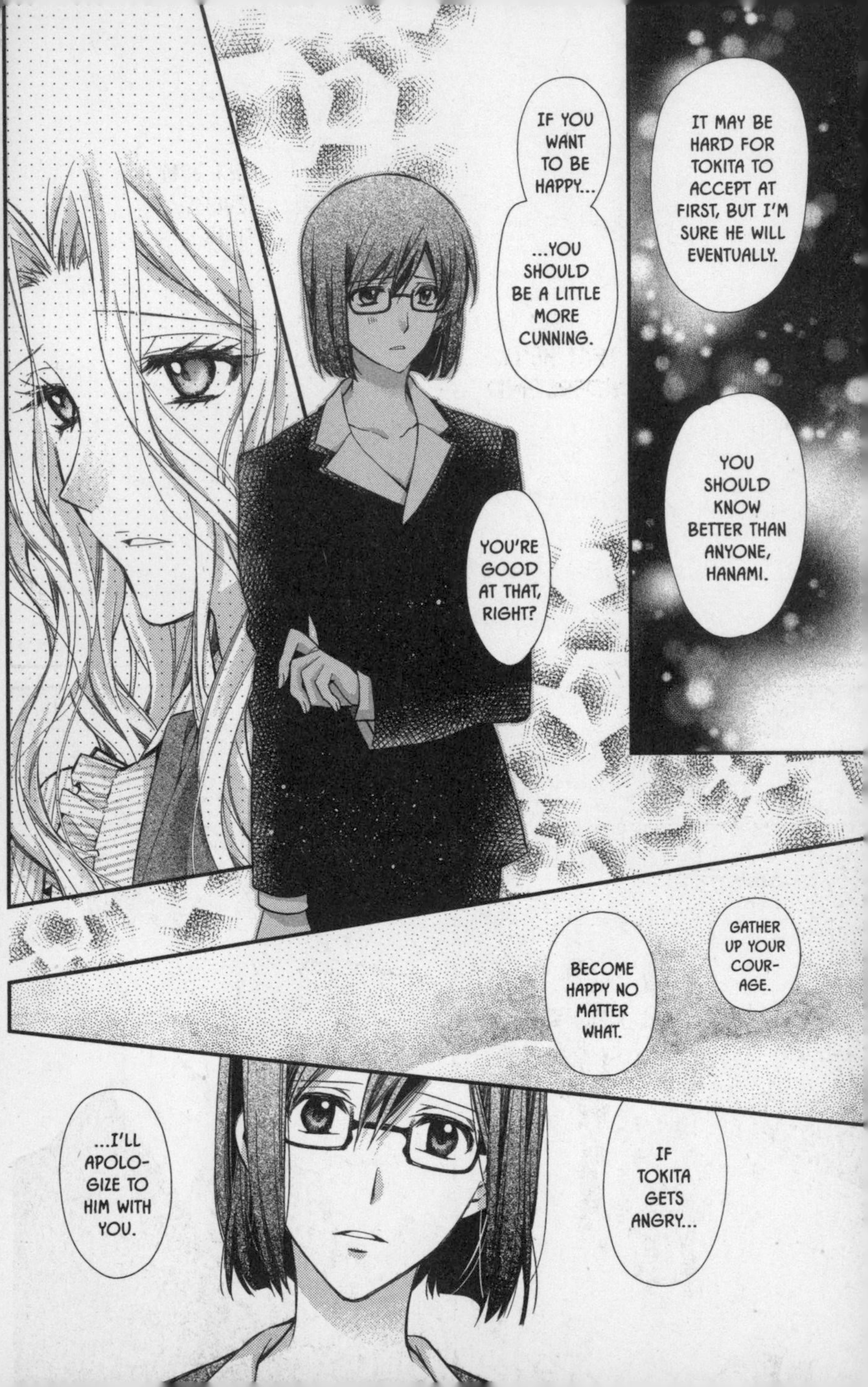
IT MAY BE HARD FOR TOKITA TO ACCEPT AT FIRST, BUT I'M SURE HE WILL EVENTUALLY.
YOU SHOULD KNOW BETTER THAN ANYONE, HANAMI.
IF YOU WANT TO BE HAPPY...
...YOU SHOULD BE A LITTLE MORE CUNNING.
YOU'RE GOOD AT THAT, RIGHT?
GATHER UP YOUR COUR-AGE.
BECOME HAPPY NO MATTER WHAT.
IF TOKITA GETS ANGRY...
...I'LL APOLO-GIZE TO HIM WITH YOU.

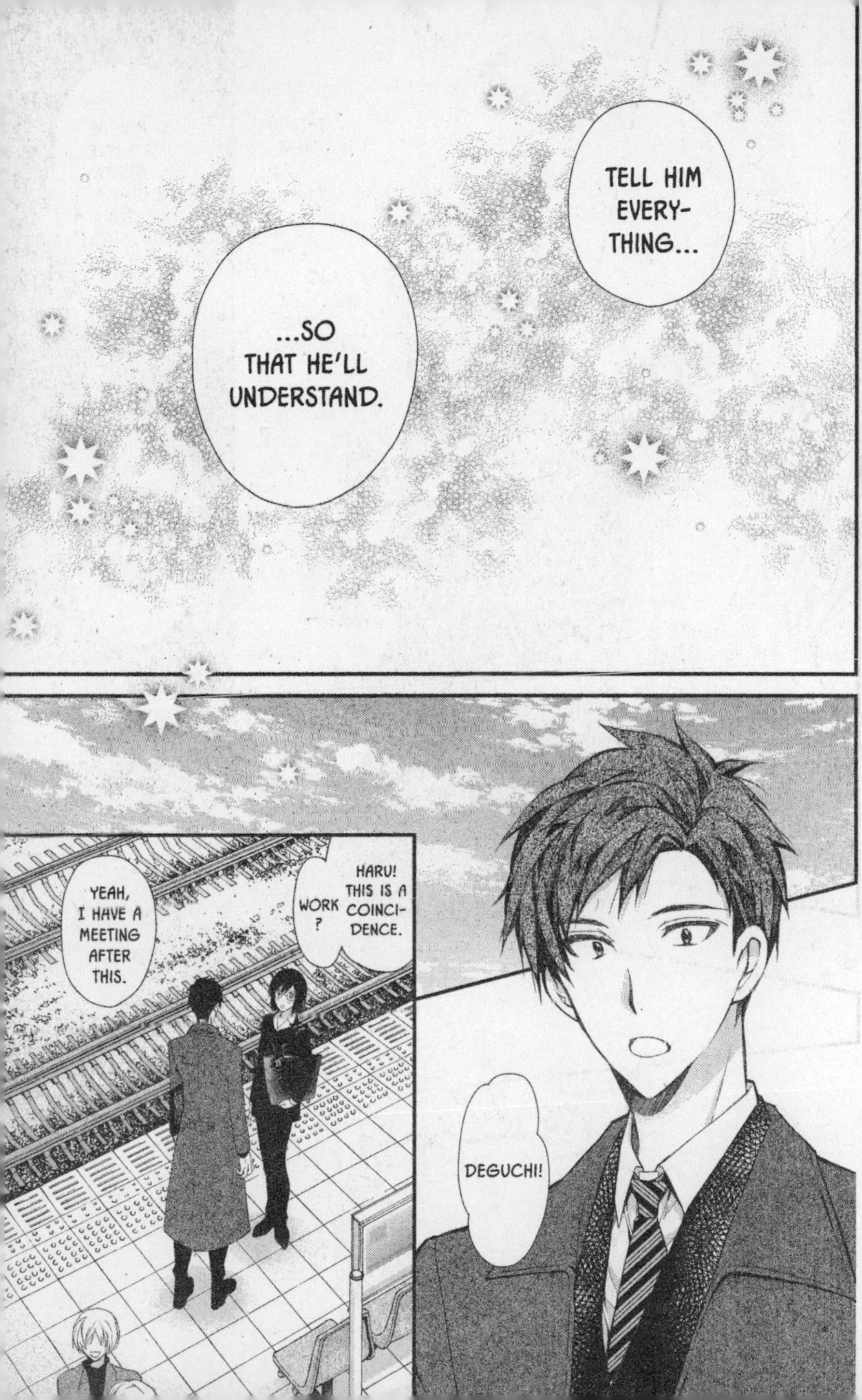
TELL HIM EVERY-THING...
...SO THAT HE'LL UNDERSTAND.
DEGUCHI!
HARU! THIS IS A COINCI-DENCE.
WORK?
YEAH, I HAVE A MEETING AFTER THIS.

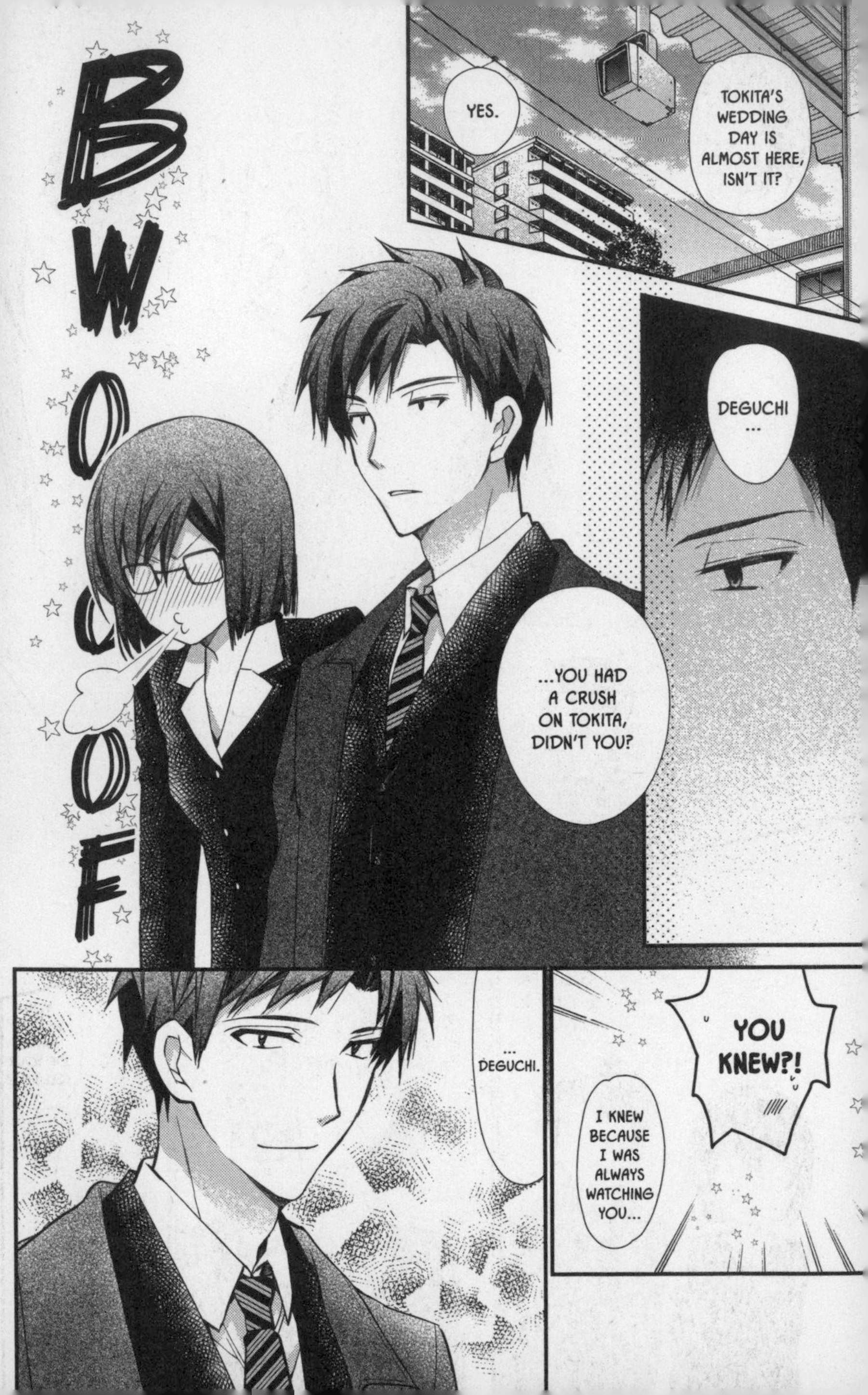
TOKITA'S WEDDING DAY IS ALMOST HERE, ISN'T IT?
YES.
DEGUCHI...
...YOU HAD A CRUSH ON TOKITA, DIDN'T YOU?
BWOOOOF
YOU KNEW?!
...DEGUCHI.
I KNEW BECAUSE I WAS ALWAYS WATCHING YOU...

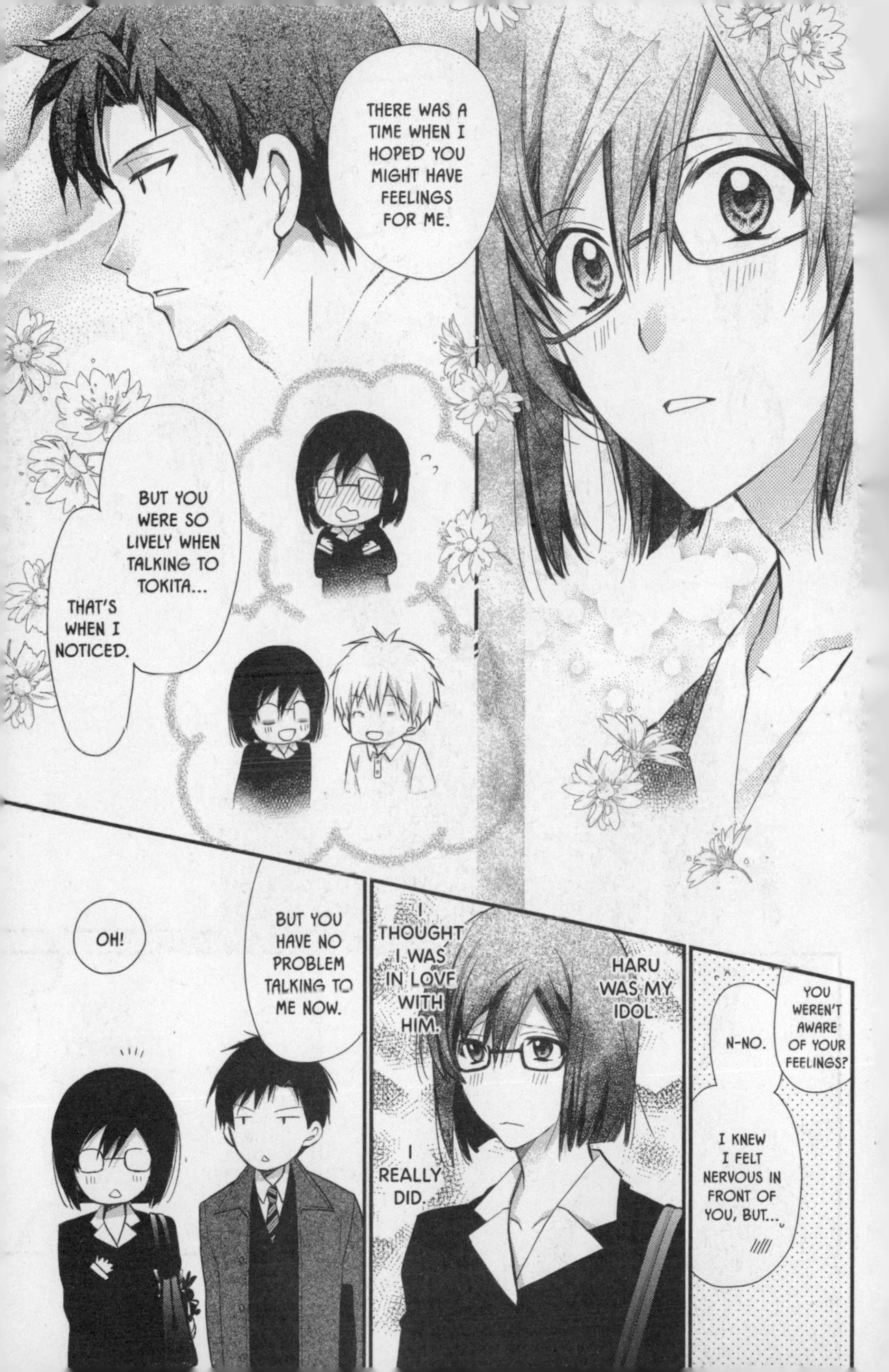
THERE WAS A TIME WHEN I HOPED YOU MIGHT HAVE FEELINGS FOR ME.
BUT YOU WERE SO LIVELY WHEN TALKING TO TOKITA...
THAT'S WHEN I NOTICED.
YOU WEREN'T AWARE OF YOUR FEELINGS?
N-NO.
I KNEW I FELT NERVOUS IN FRONT OF YOU, BUT...
HARU WAS MY IDOL.
I THOUGHT I WAS IN LOVE WITH HIM.
I REALLY DID.
BUT YOU HAVE NO PROBLEM TALKING TO ME NOW.
OH!

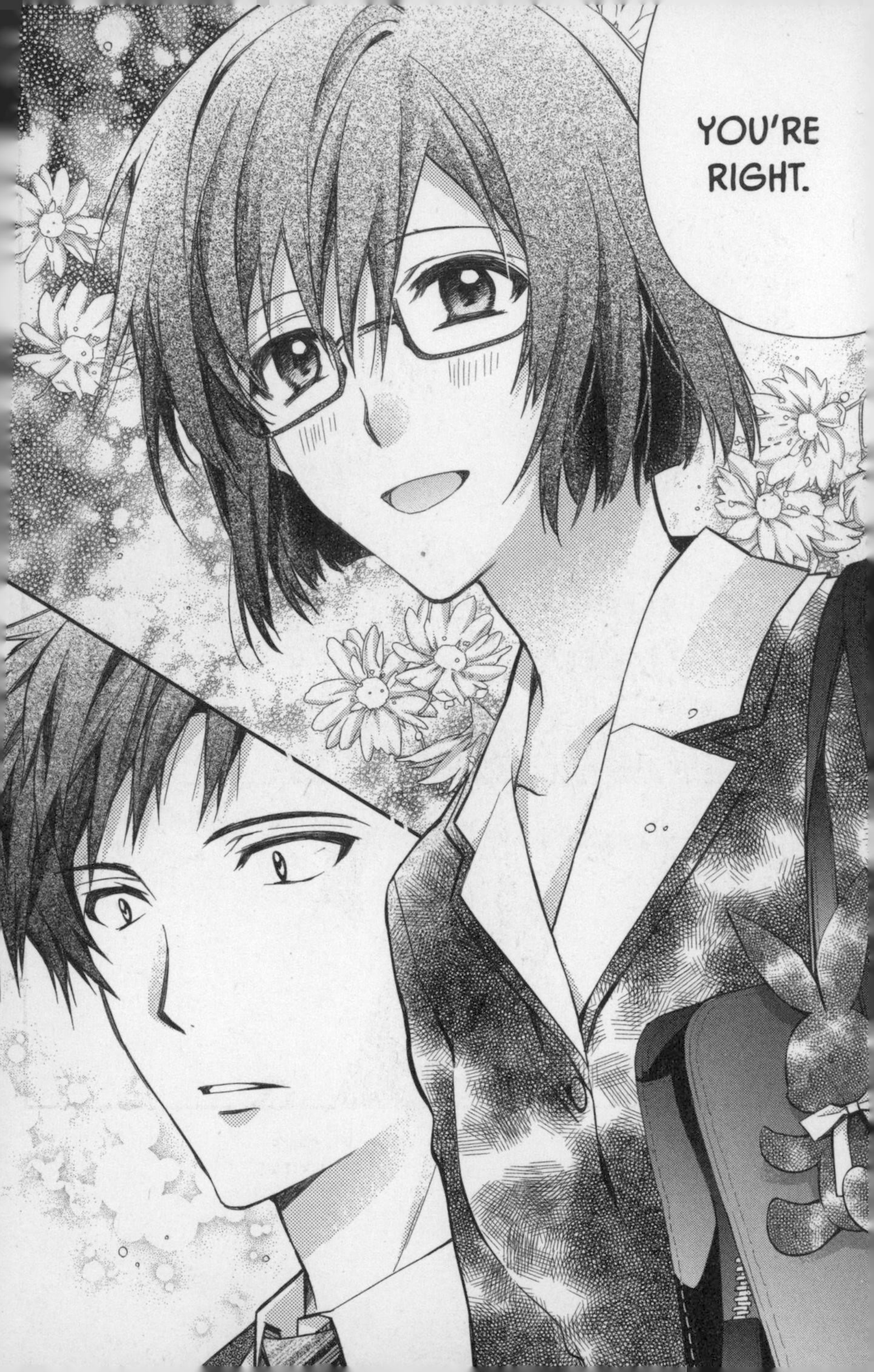
YOU'RE RIGHT.

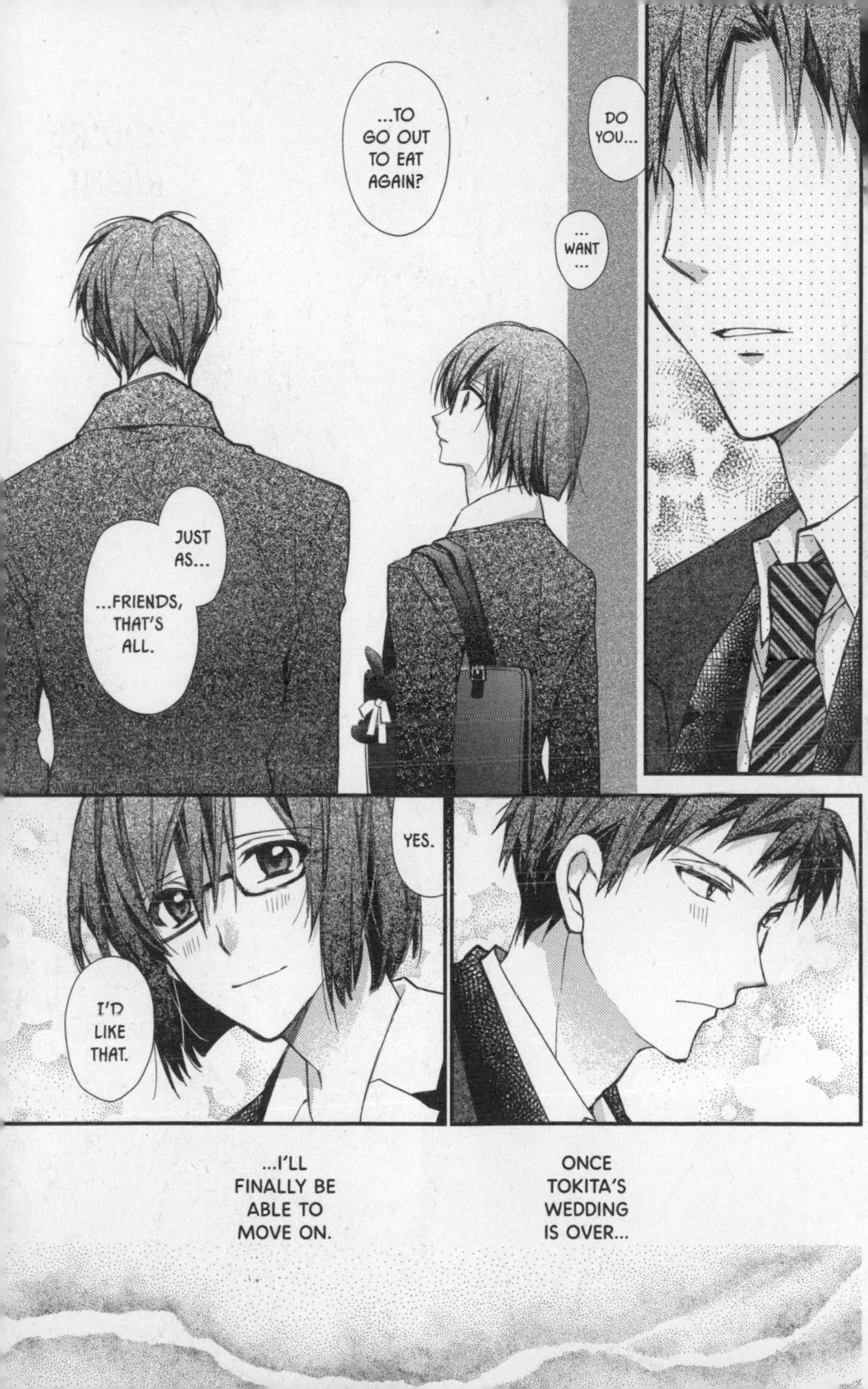
DO YOU...
...WANT...
...TO GO OUT TO EAT AGAIN?
JUST AS...
...FRIENDS, THAT'S ALL.
YES.
I'D LIKE THAT.
ONCE TOKITA'S WEDDING IS OVER...
...I'LL FINALLY BE ABLE TO MOVE ON.

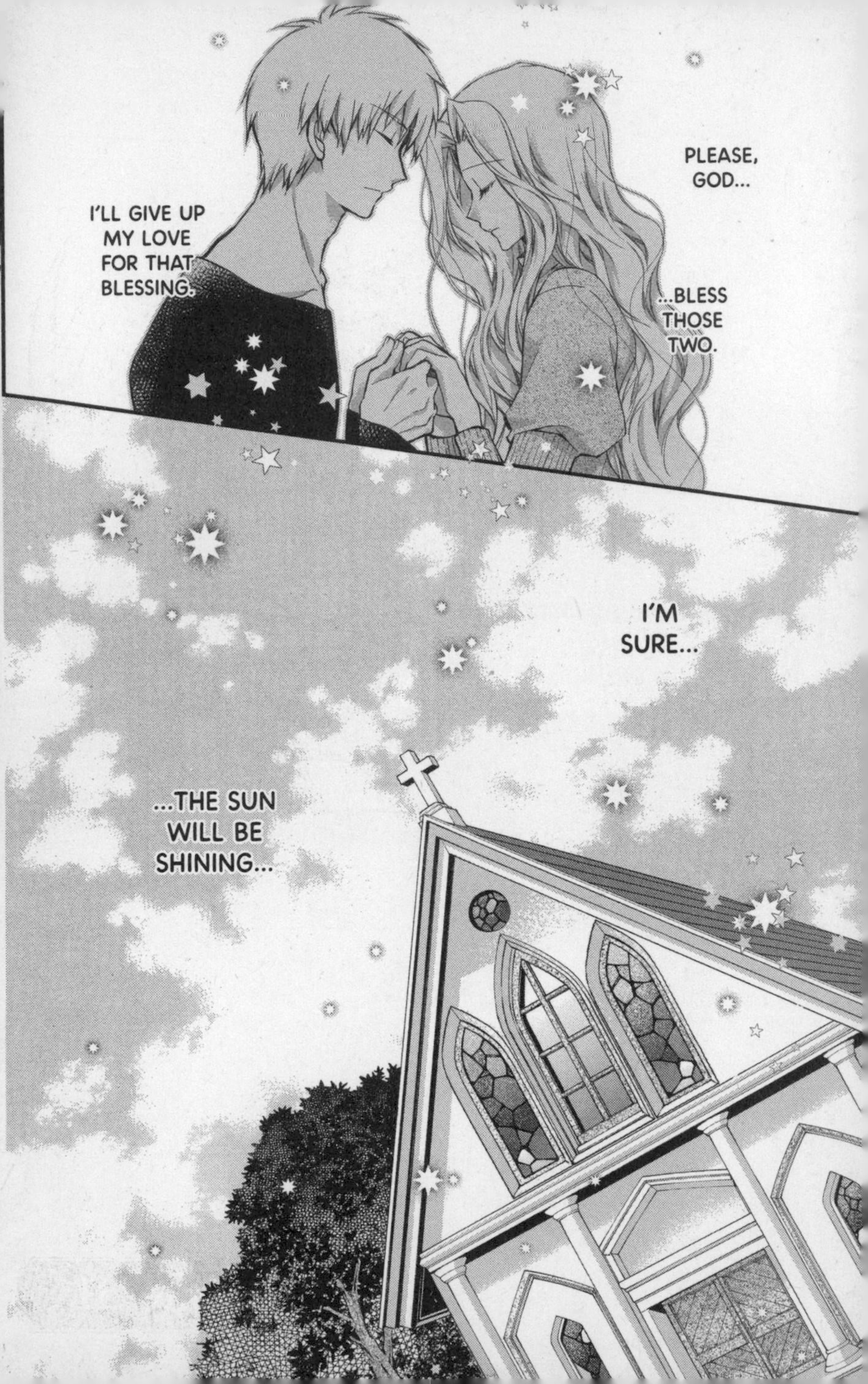
PLEASE, GOD...
...BLESS THOSE TWO.
I'LL GIVE UP MY LOVE FOR THAT BLESSING.
I'M SURE...
...THE SUN WILL BE SHINING...

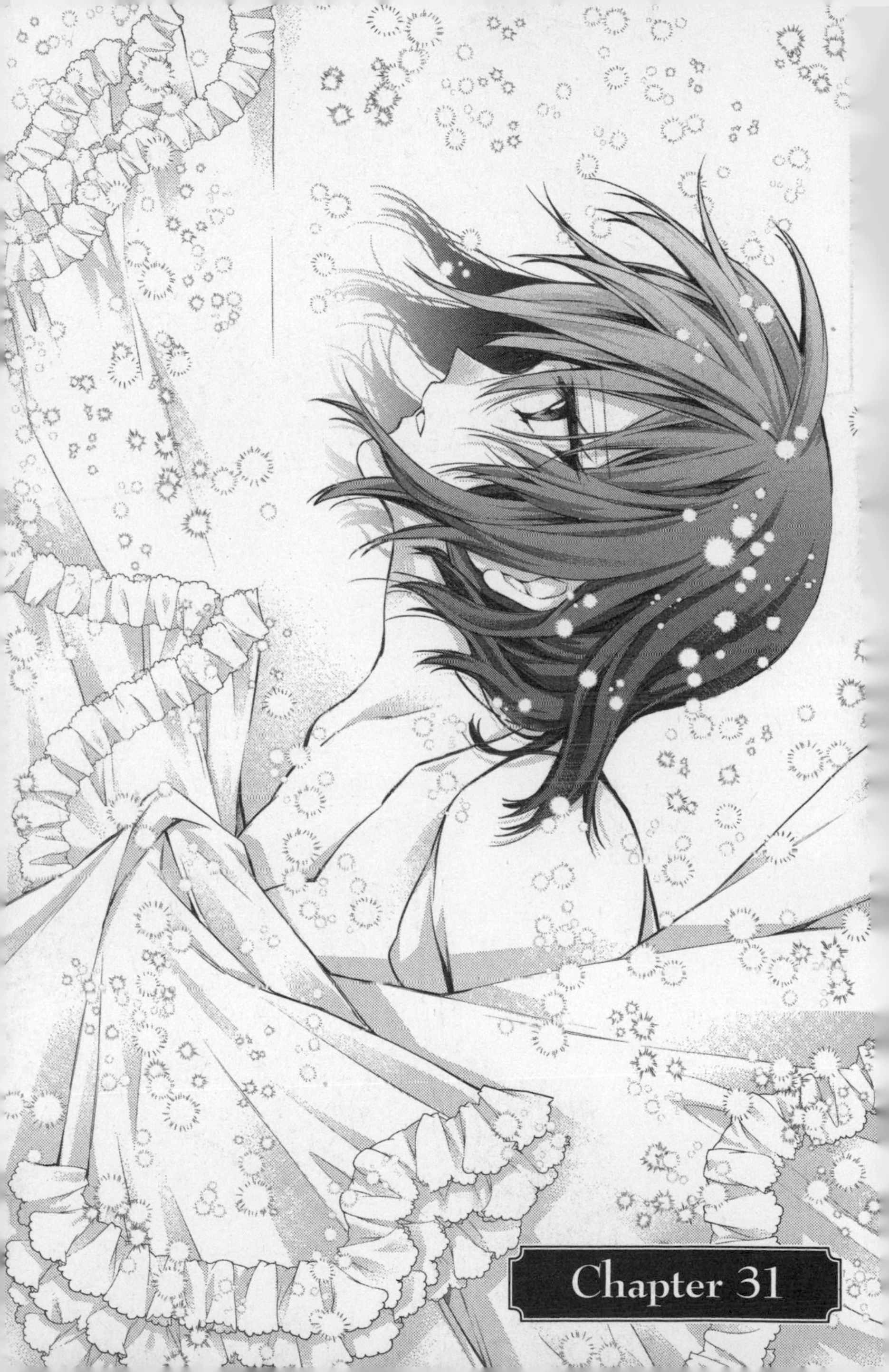
Chapter 31

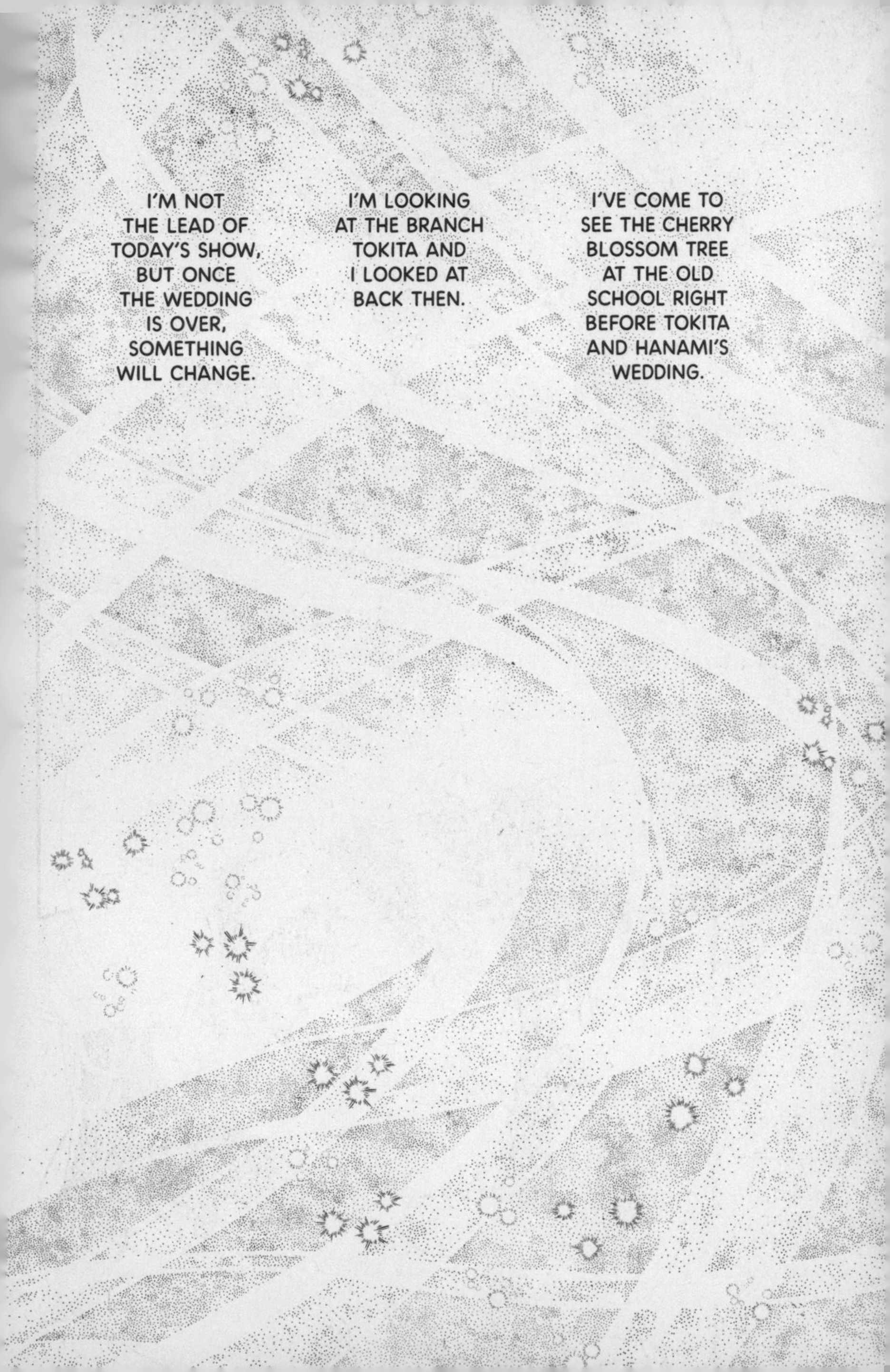
I'VE COME TO SEE THE CHERRY BLOSSOM TREE AT THE OLD SCHOOL RIGHT BEFORE TOKITA AND HANAMI'S WEDDING.
I'M LOOKING AT THE BRANCH TOKITA AND I LOOKED AT BACK THEN.
I'M NOT THE LEAD OF TODAY'S SHOW, BUT ONCE THE WEDDING IS OVER, SOMETHING WILL CHANGE.

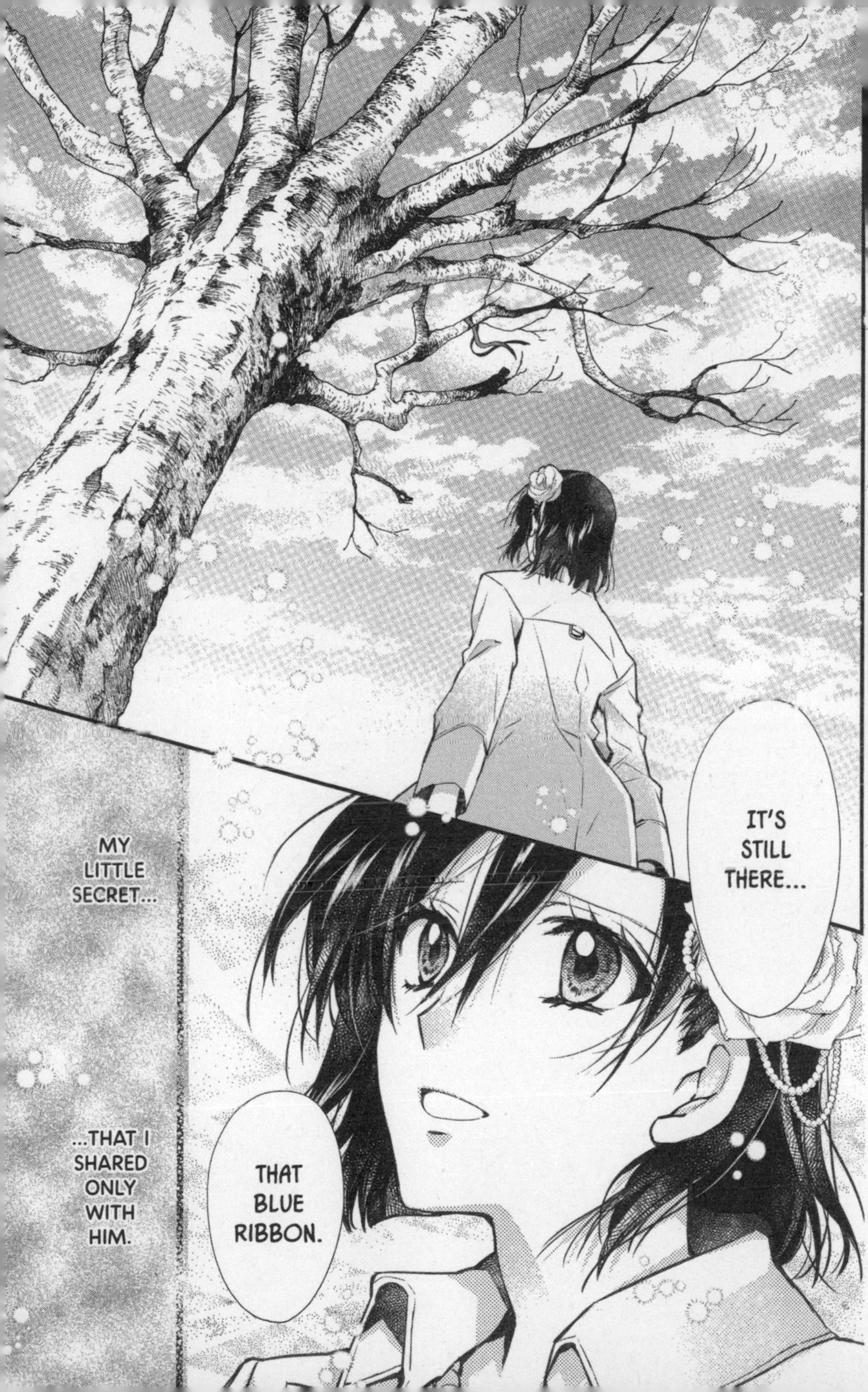
IT'S STILL THERE...
THAT BLUE RIBBON.
MY LITTLE SECRET...
...THAT I SHARED ONLY WITH HIM.

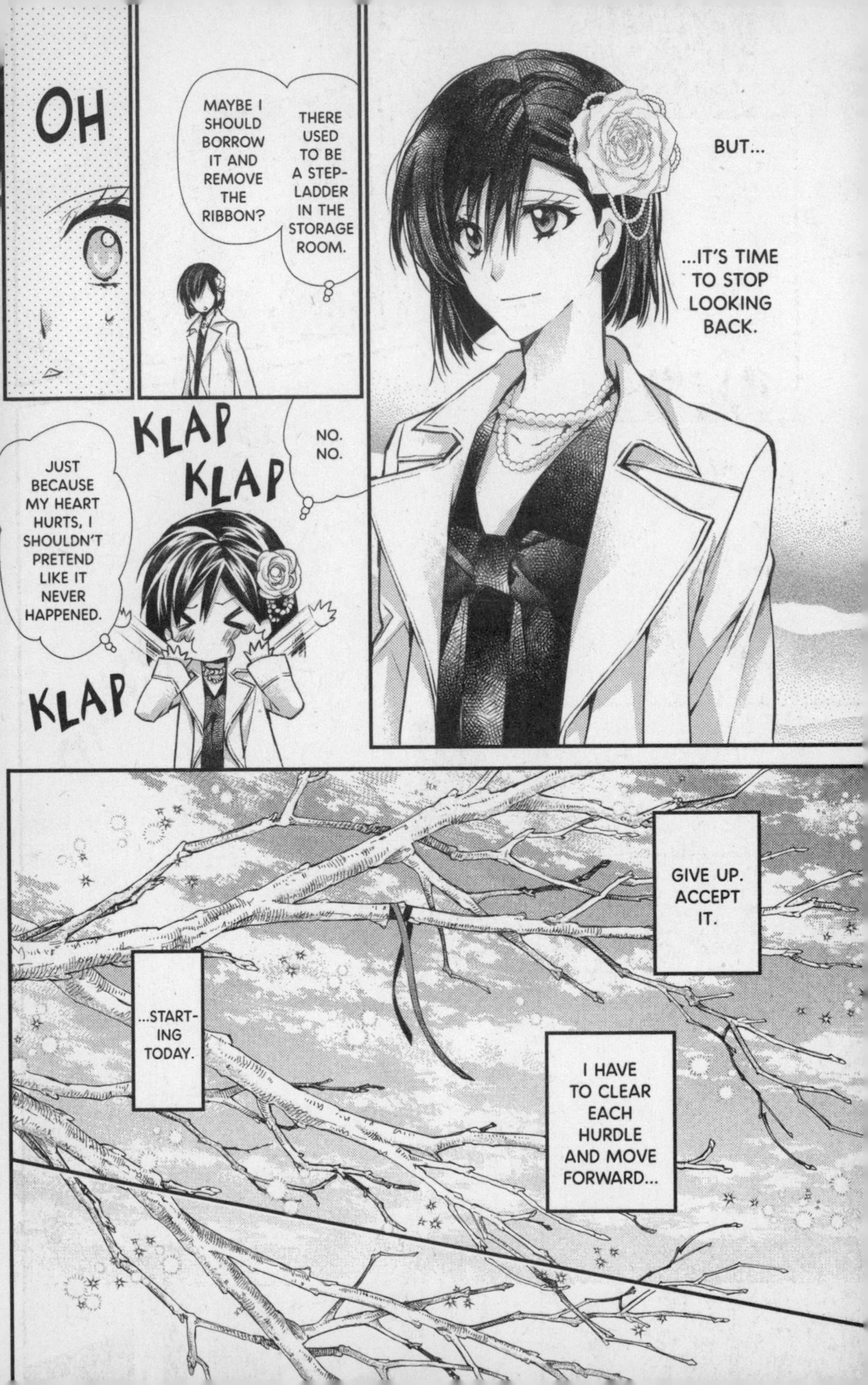
BUT...
...IT'S TIME TO STOP LOOKING BACK.
THERE USED TO BE A STEP-LADDER IN THE STORAGE ROOM.
MAYBE I SHOULD BORROW IT AND REMOVE THE RIBBON?
OH
NO. NO.
KLAP KLAP
JUST BECAUSE MY HEART HURTS, I SHOULDN'T PRETEND LIKE IT NEVER HAPPENED.
KLAP
GIVE UP. ACCEPT IT.
I HAVE TO CLEAR EACH HURDLE AND MOVE FORWARD...
...START-ING TODAY.

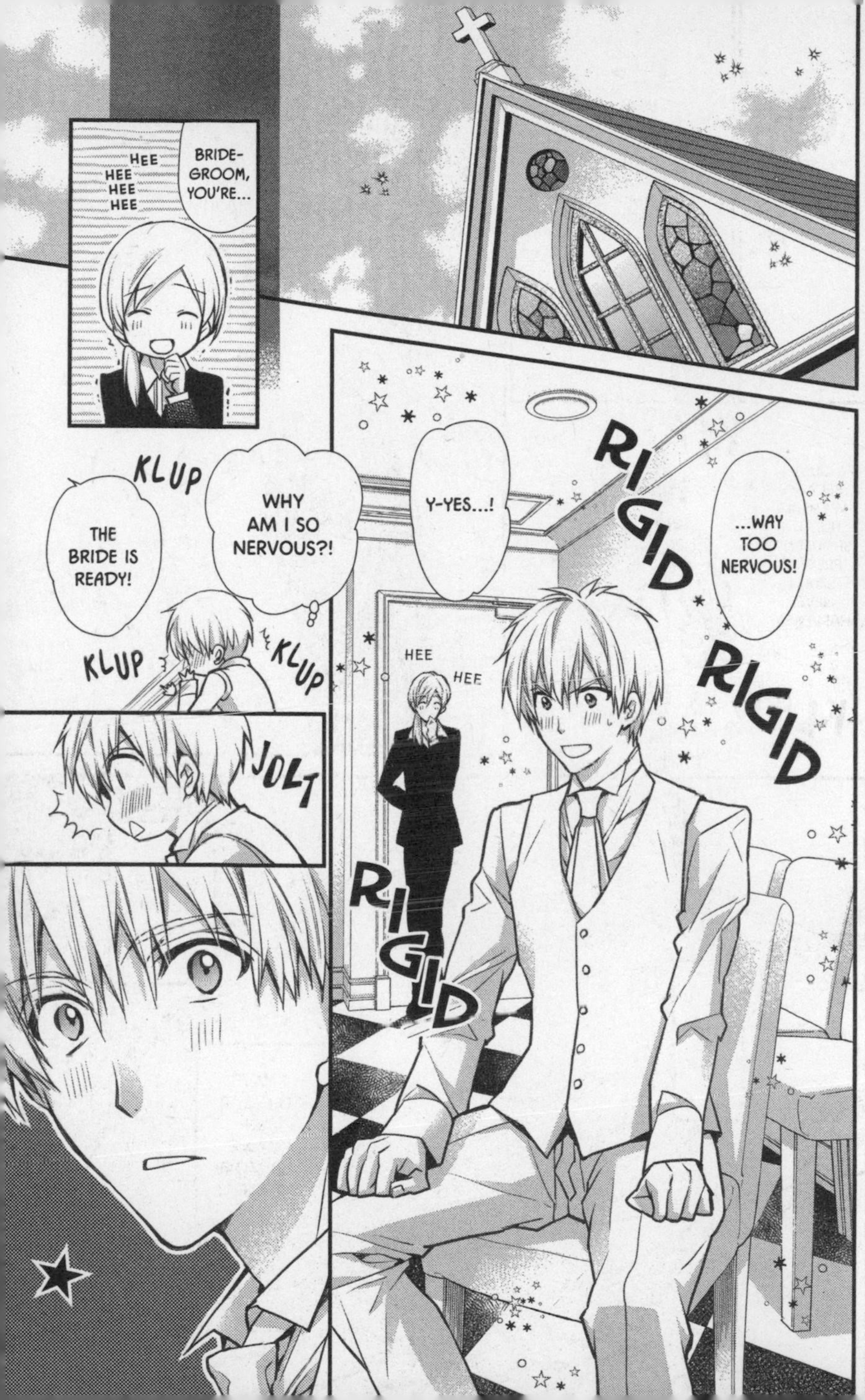
HEE HEE HEE HEE
BRIDE-GROOM, YOU'RE...
RIGID
...WAY TOO NERVOUS!
RIGID RIGID
Y-YES...!
HEE HEE
RIGID
WHY AM I SO NERVOUS?!
KLUP
THE BRIDE IS READY!
KLUP KLUP
JOLT

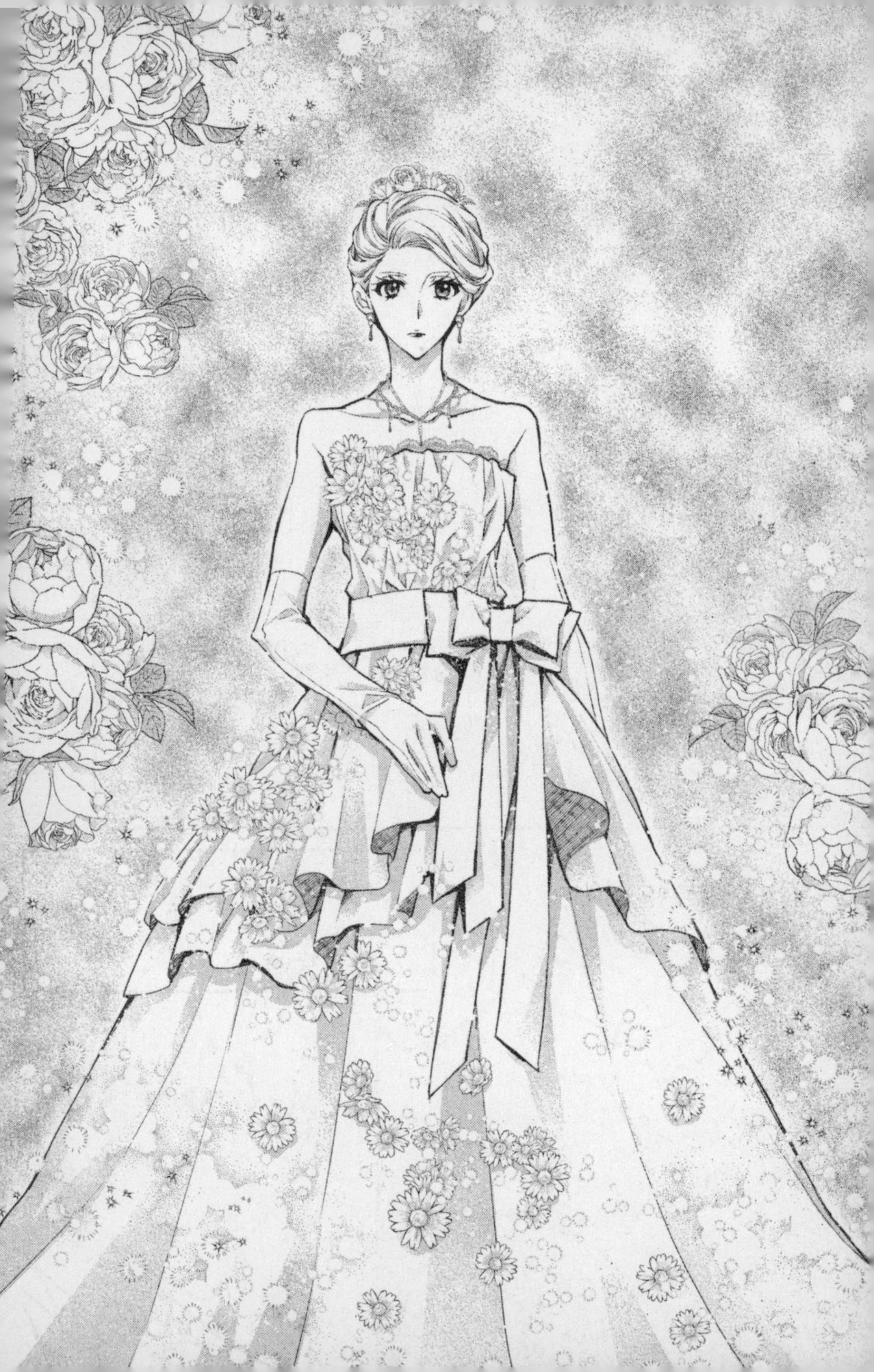

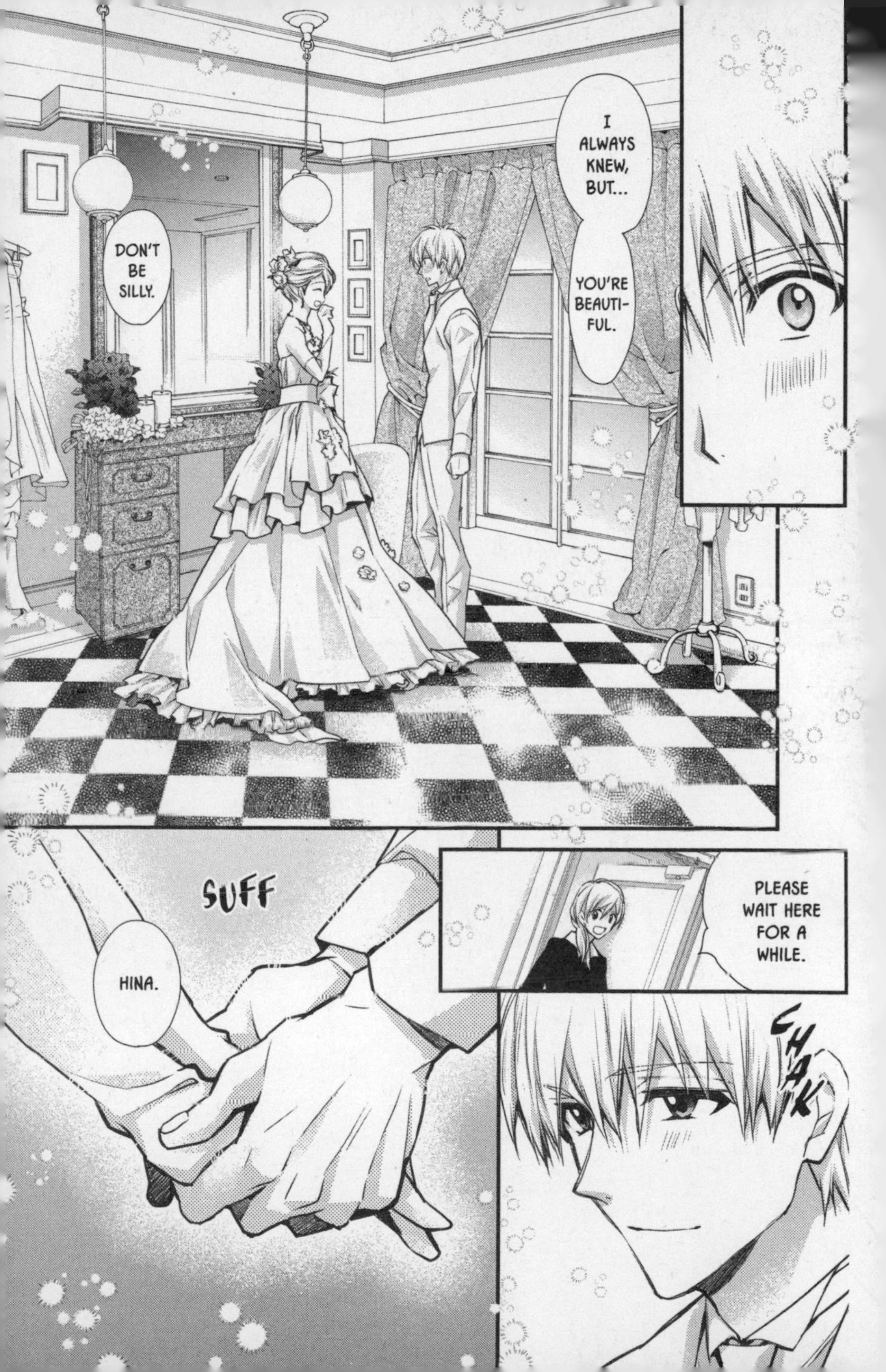
I ALWAYS KNEW, BUT...
YOU'RE BEAUTIFUL.
DON'T BE SILLY.
PLEASE WAIT HERE FOR A WHILE.
CHAK
SUFF
HINA.

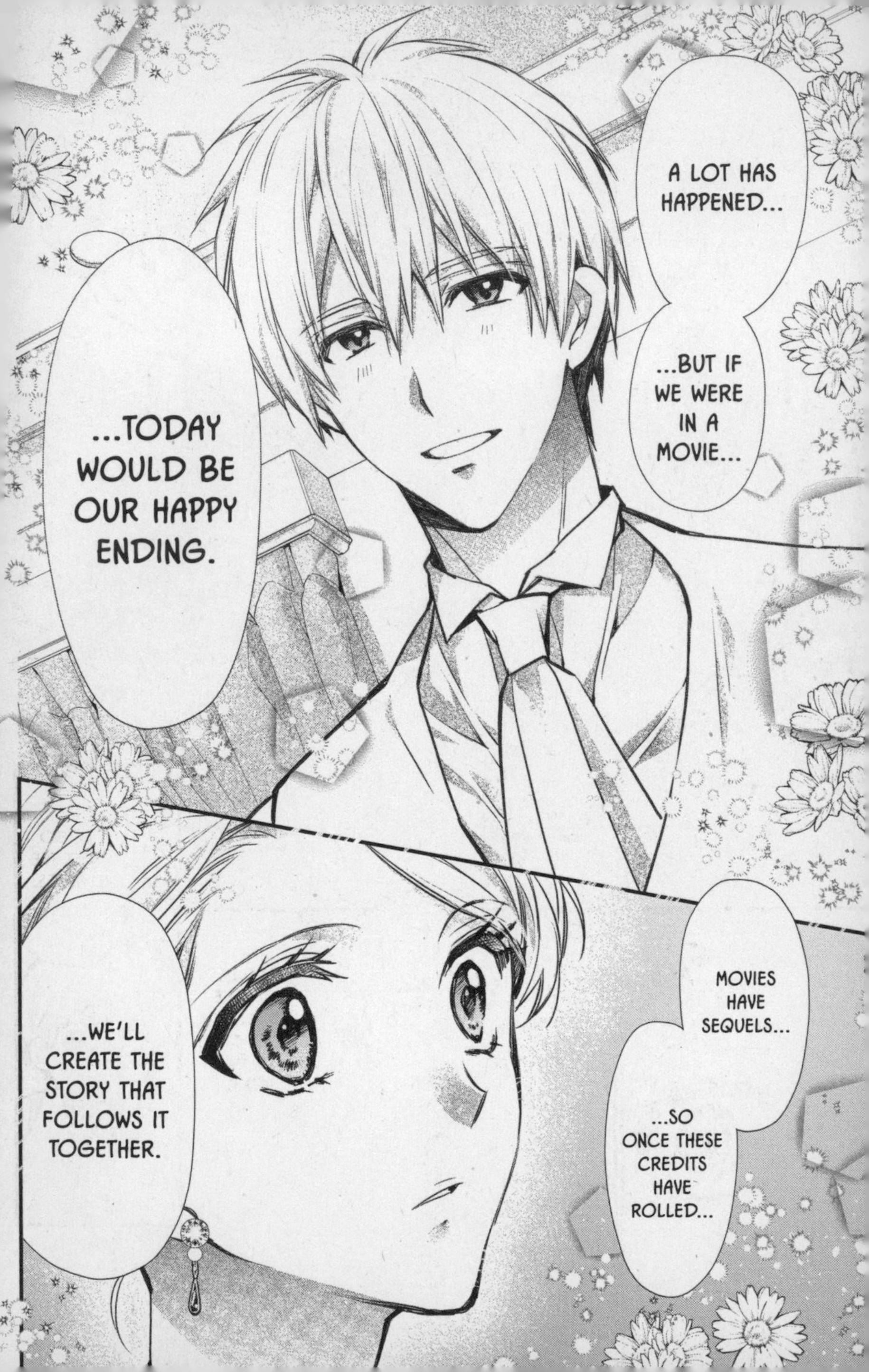
A LOT HAS HAPPENED...
...BUT IF WE WERE IN A MOVIE...
...TODAY WOULD BE OUR HAPPY ENDING.
MOVIES HAVE SEQUELS...
...SO ONCE THESE CREDITS HAVE ROLLED...
...WE'LL CREATE THE STORY THAT FOLLOWS IT TOGETHER.

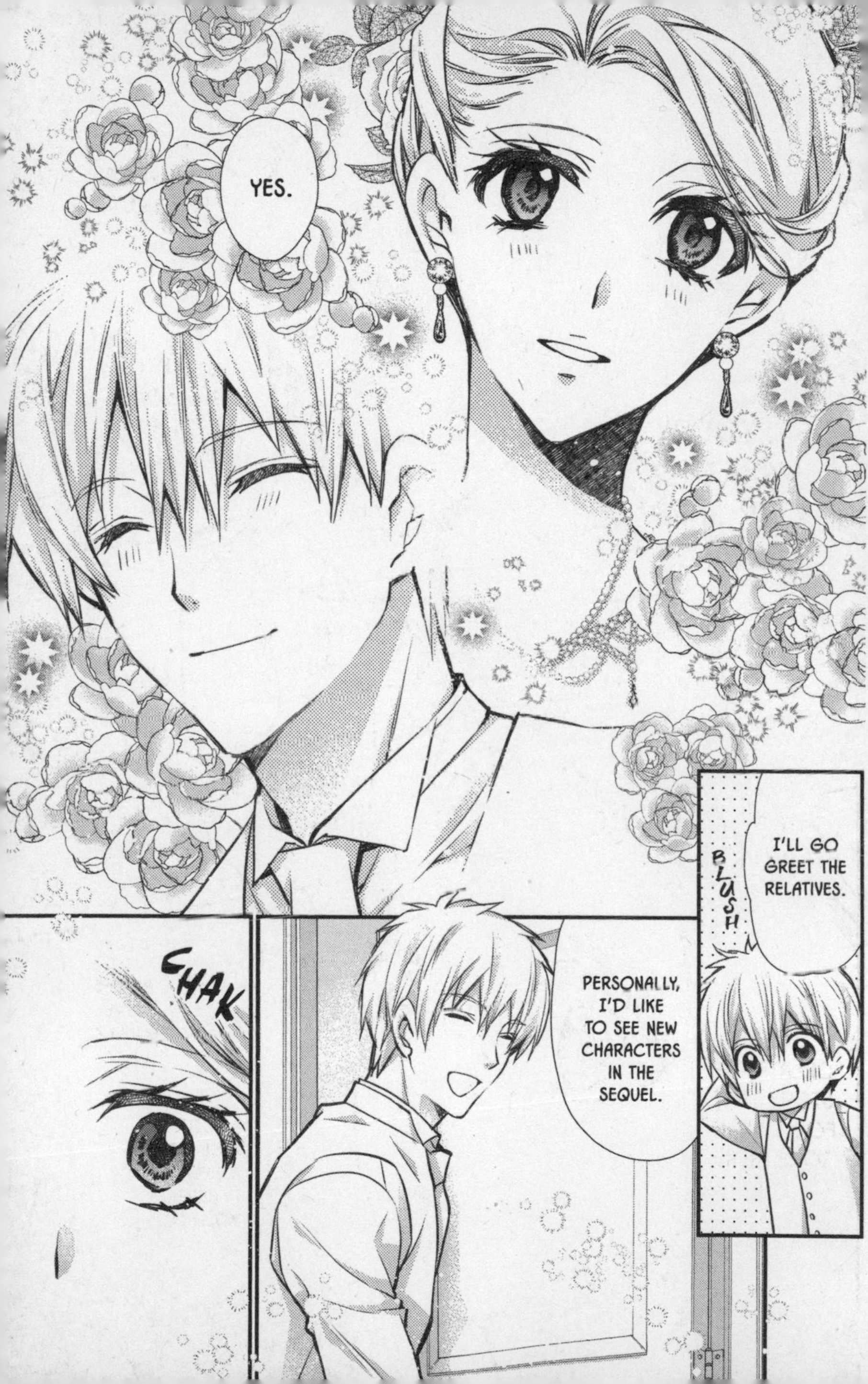
YES.
BLUSH
I'LL GO GREET THE RELATIVES.
PERSONALLY, I'D LIKE TO SEE NEW CHARACTERS IN THE SEQUEL.
CHAK

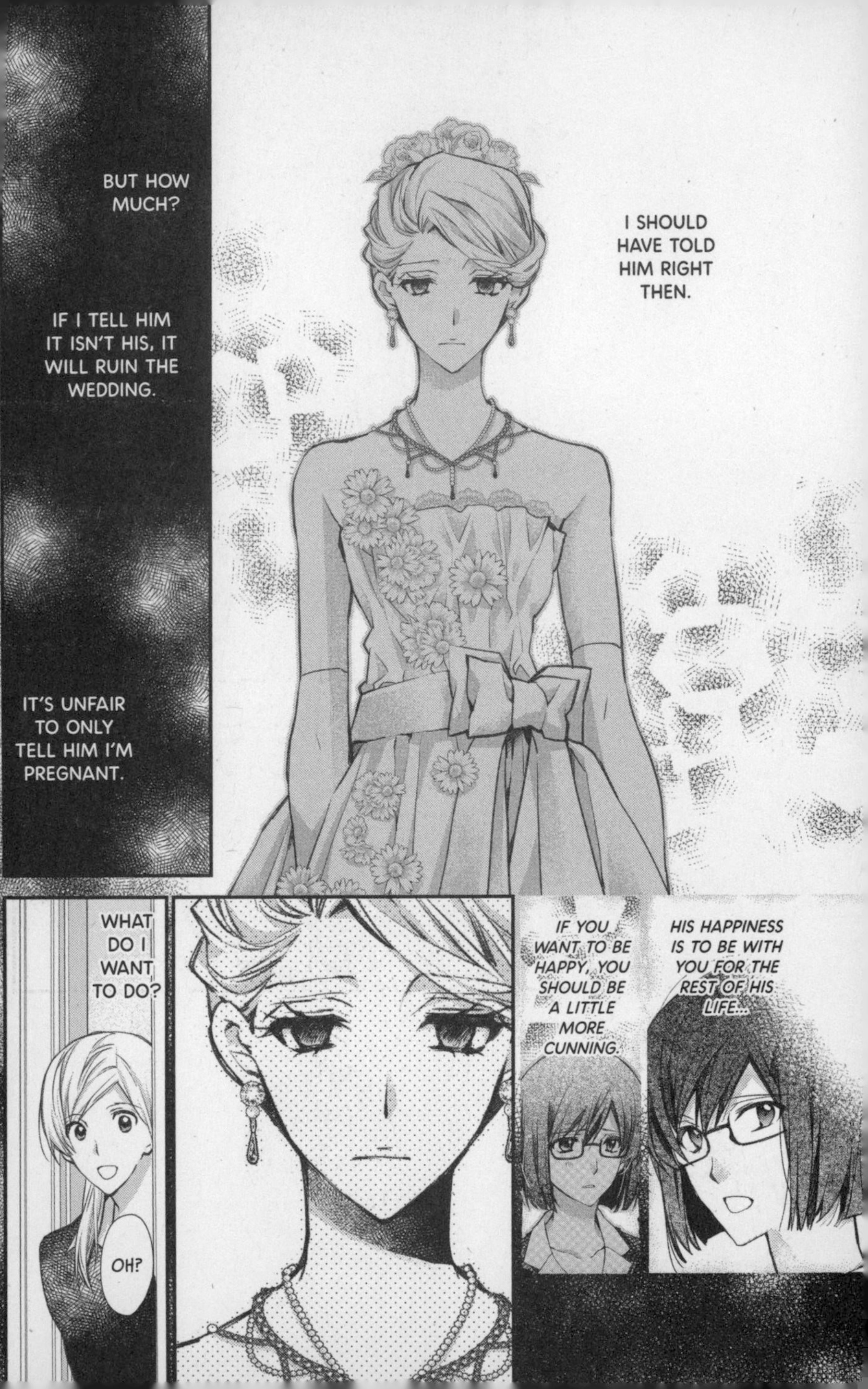
I SHOULD HAVE TOLD HIM RIGHT THEN.
BUT HOW MUCH?
IF I TELL HIM IT ISN'T HIS, IT WILL RUIN THE WEDDING.
IT'S UNFAIR TO ONLY TELL HIM I'M PREGNANT.
HIS HAPPINESS IS TO BE WITH YOU FOR THE REST OF HIS LIFE...
IF YOU WANT TO BE HAPPY, YOU SHOULD BE A LITTLE MORE CUNNING.
WHAT DO I WANT TO DO?
OH?

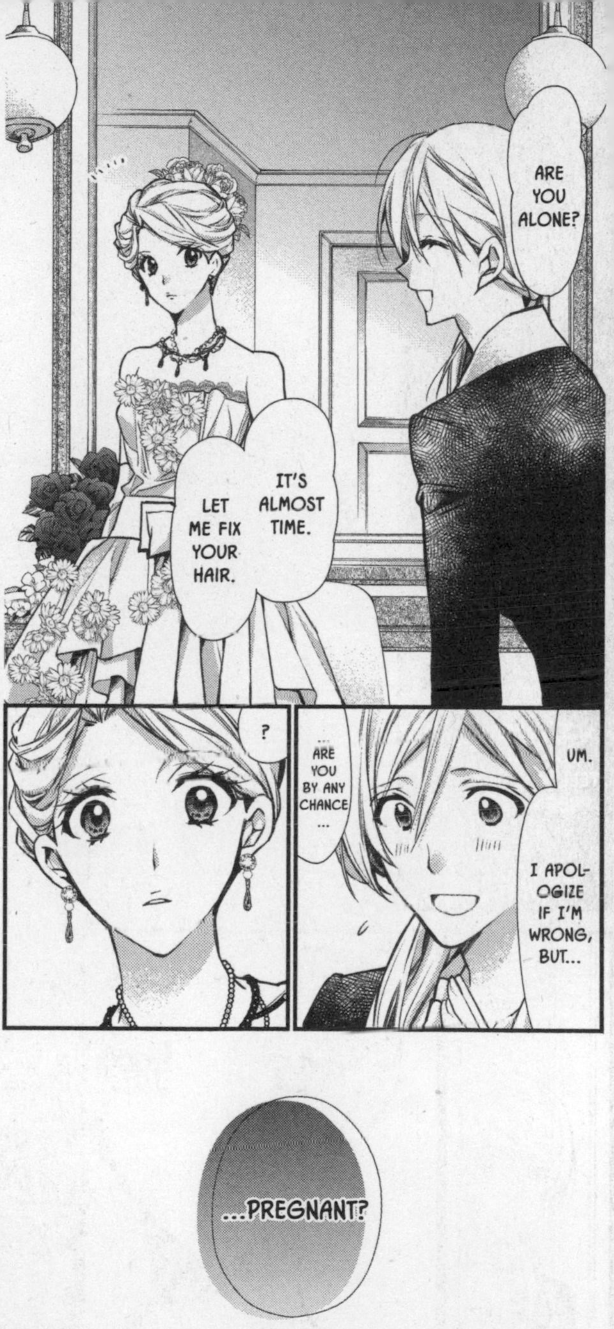
...
ARE YOU ALONE?
IT'S ALMOST TIME.
LET ME FIX YOUR HAIR.
UM.
I APOLOGIZE IF I'M WRONG, BUT...
...ARE YOU BY ANY CHANCE...
?
...PREGNANT?

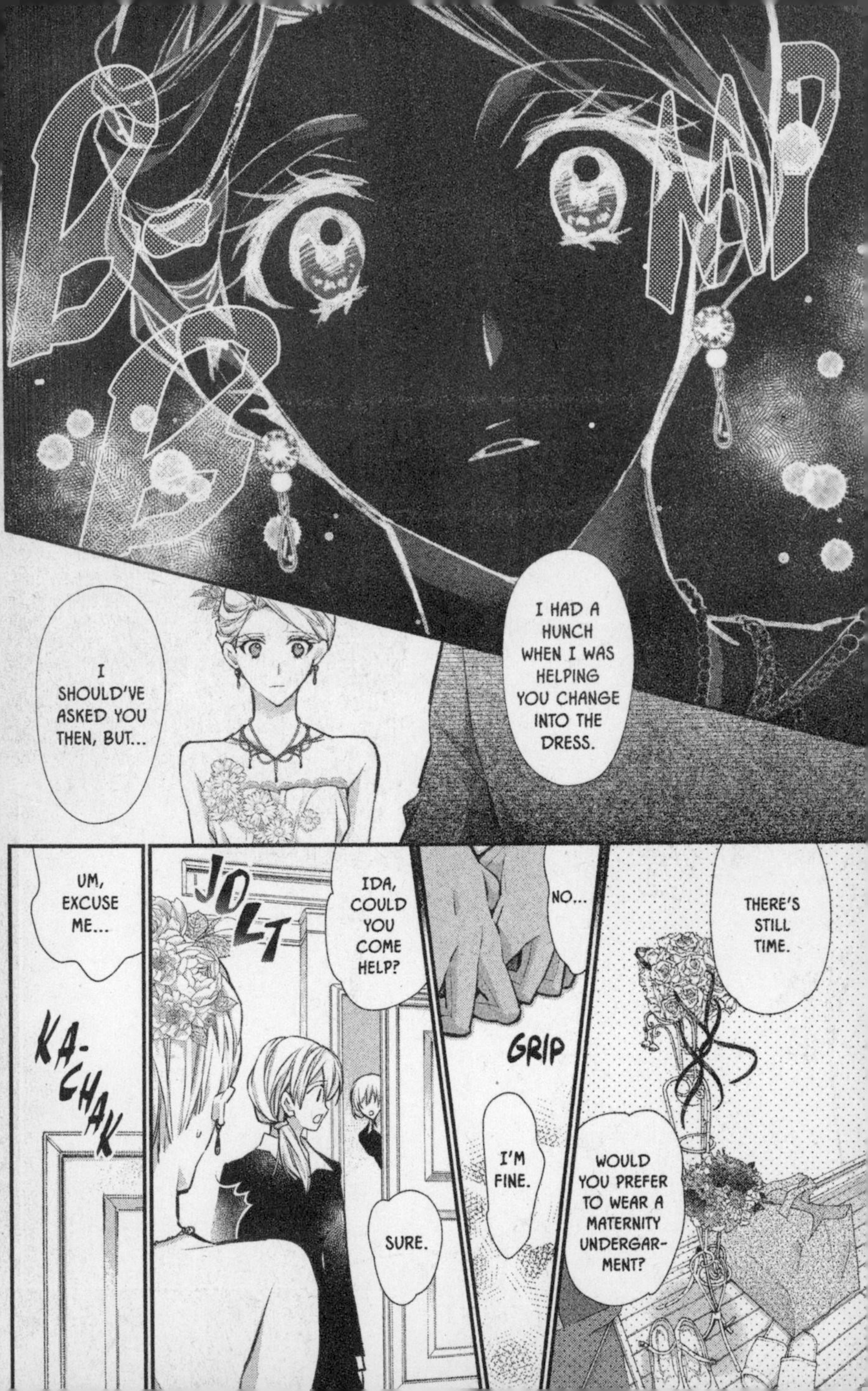
I HAD A HUNCH WHEN I WAS HELPING YOU CHANGE INTO THE DRESS.
I SHOULD'VE ASKED YOU THEN, BUT...
THERE'S STILL TIME.
WOULD YOU PREFER TO WEAR A MATERNITY UNDERGARMENT?
NO...
GRIP
I'M FINE.
IDA, COULD YOU COME HELP?
JOLT
SURE.
UM, EXCUSE ME...
KA-CHAK

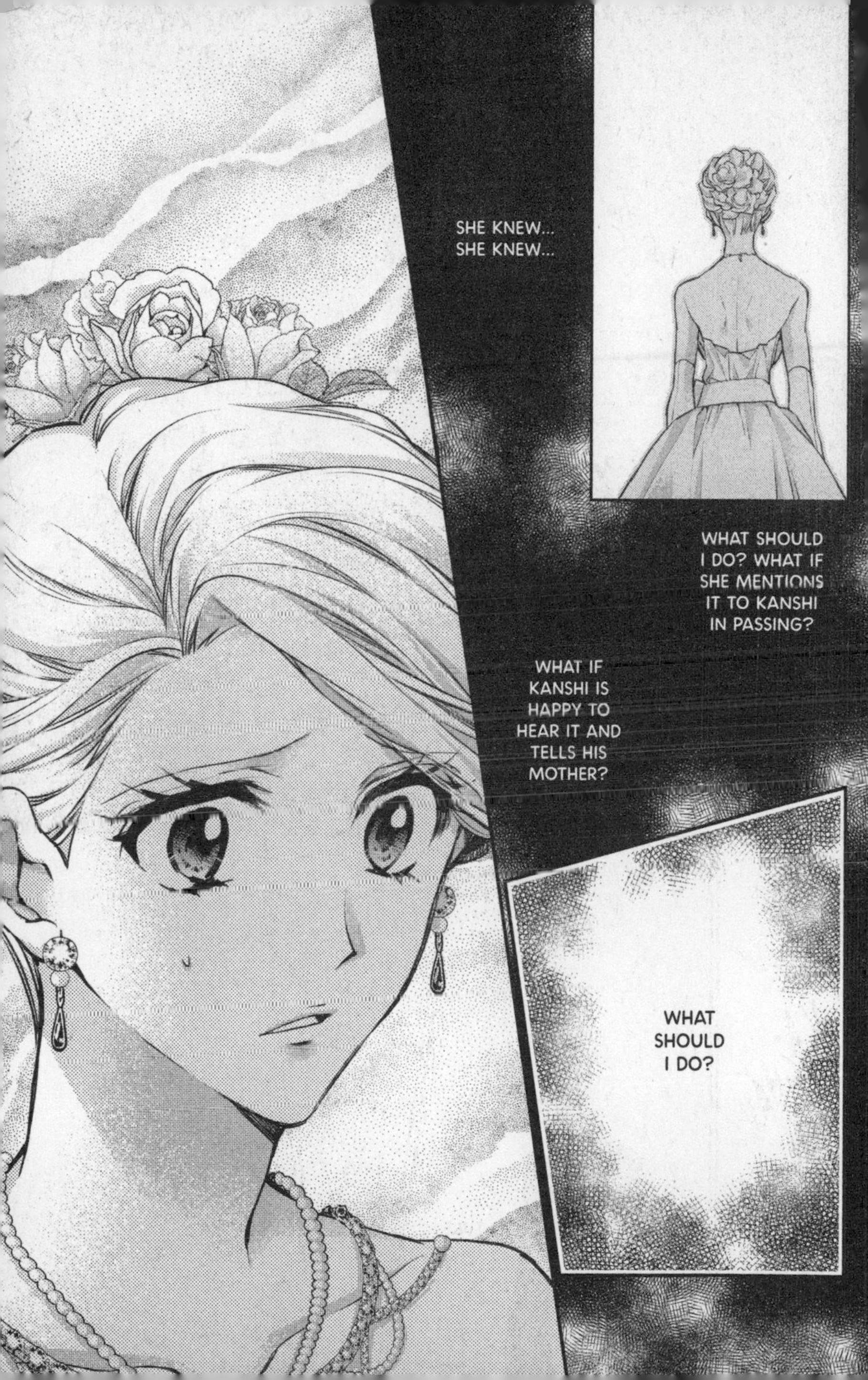
SHE KNEW... SHE KNEW...
WHAT SHOULD I DO? WHAT IF SHE MENTIONS IT TO KANSHI IN PASSING?
WHAT IF KANSHI IS HAPPY TO HEAR IT AND TELLS HIS MOTHER?
WHAT SHOULD I DO?

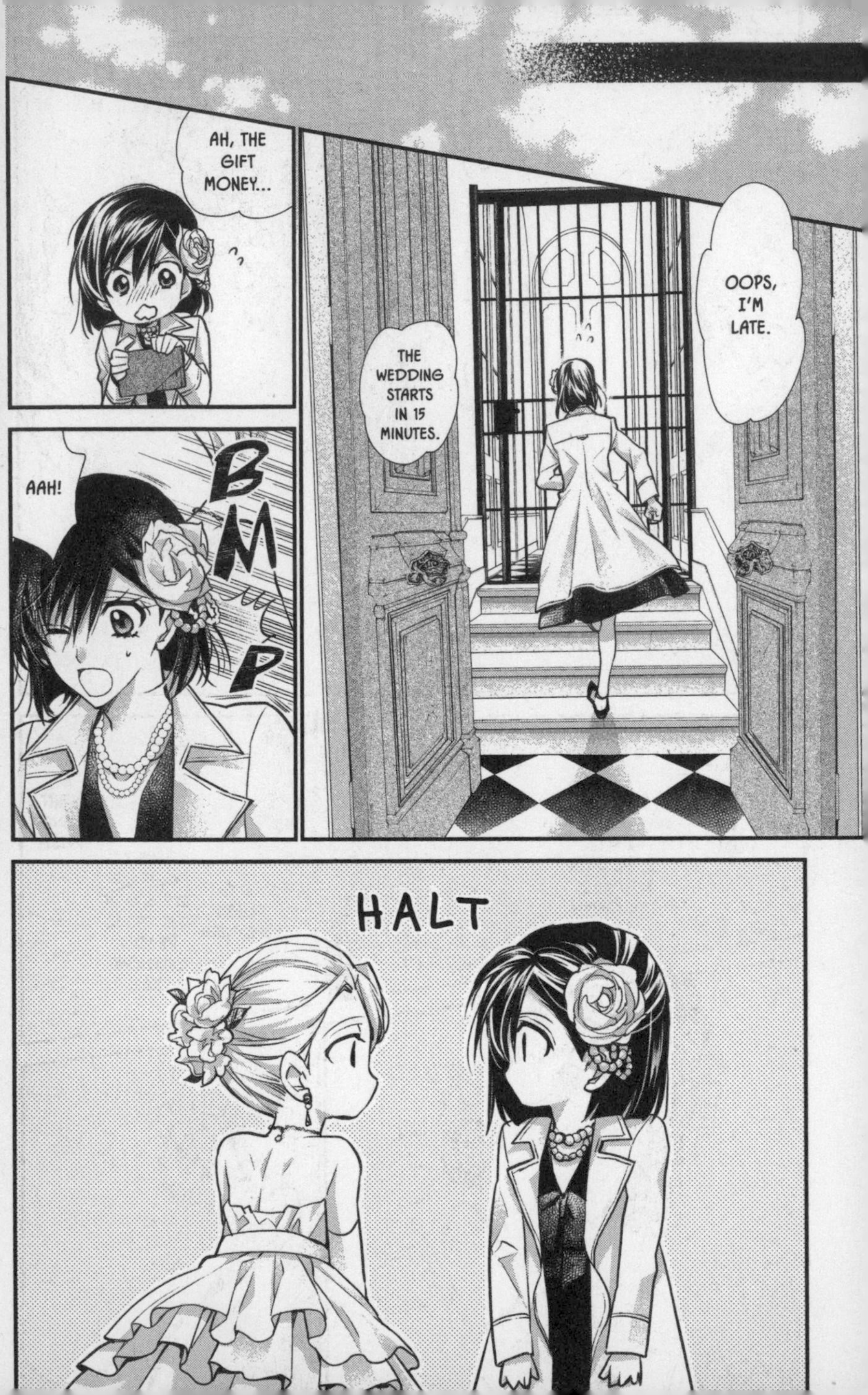
OOPS, I'M LATE.
THE WEDDING STARTS IN 15 MINUTES.
AH, THE GIFT MONEY...
AAH!
BUMP
HALT

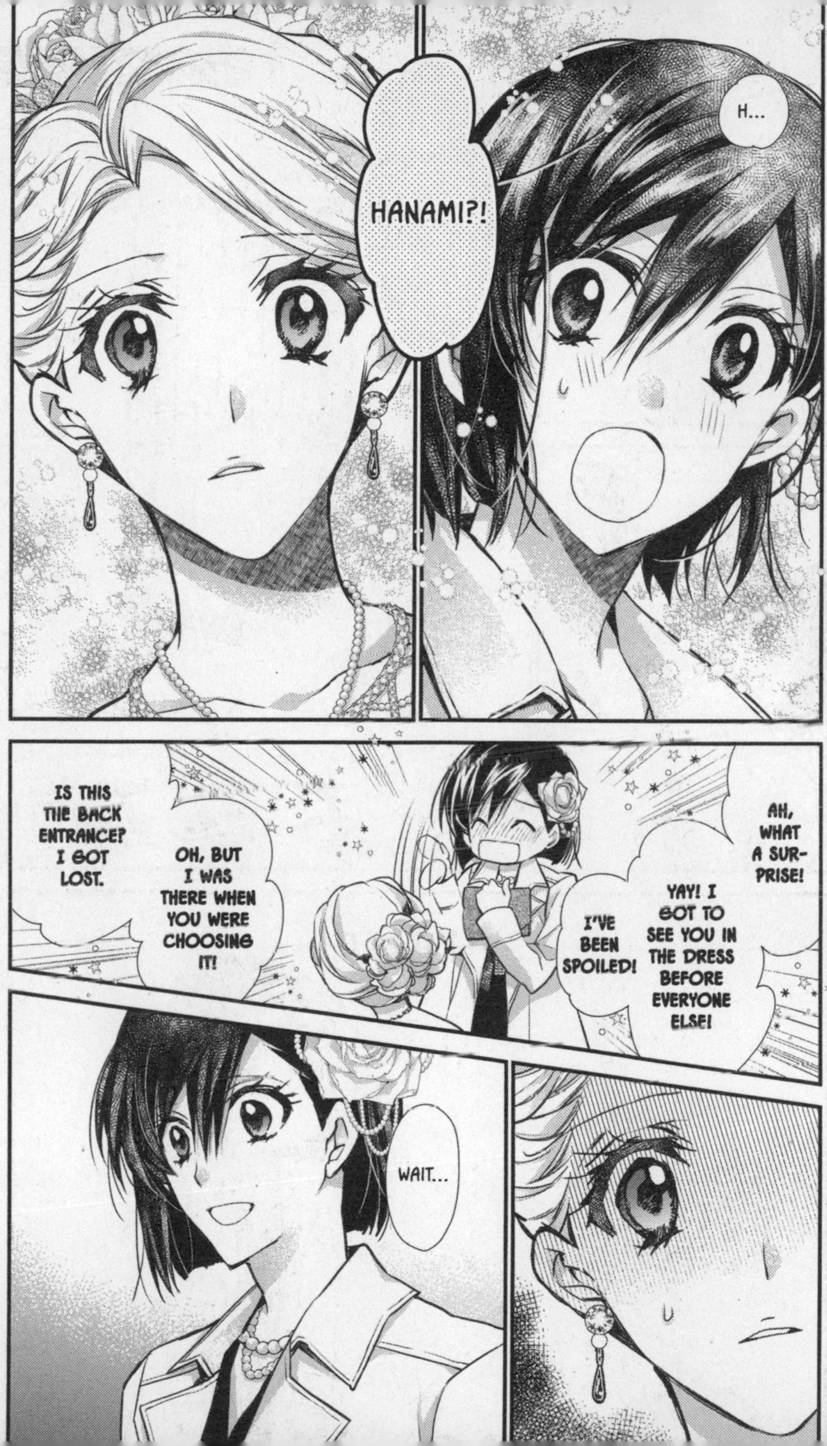
H...
HANAMI?!
AH, WHAT A SUR-PRISE!
YAY! I GOT TO SEE YOU IN THE DRESS BEFORE EVERYONE ELSE!
I'VE BEEN SPOILED!
OH, BUT I WAS THERE WHEN YOU WERE CHOOSING IT!
IS THIS THE BACK ENTRANCE? I GOT LOST.
WAIT...

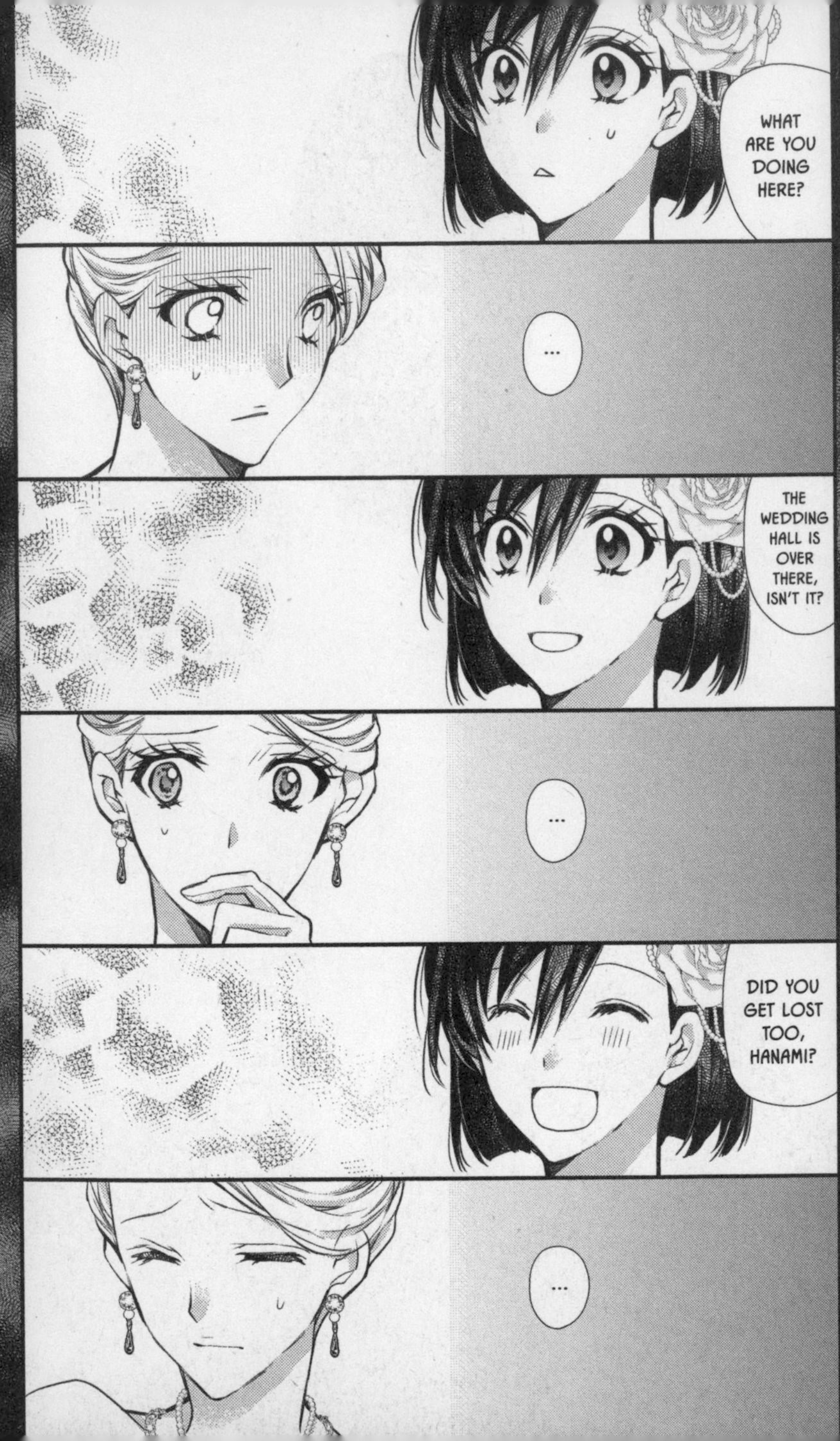
WHAT ARE YOU DOING HERE?
...
THE WEDDING HALL IS OVER THERE, ISN'T IT?
...
DID YOU GET LOST TOO, HANAMI?
...

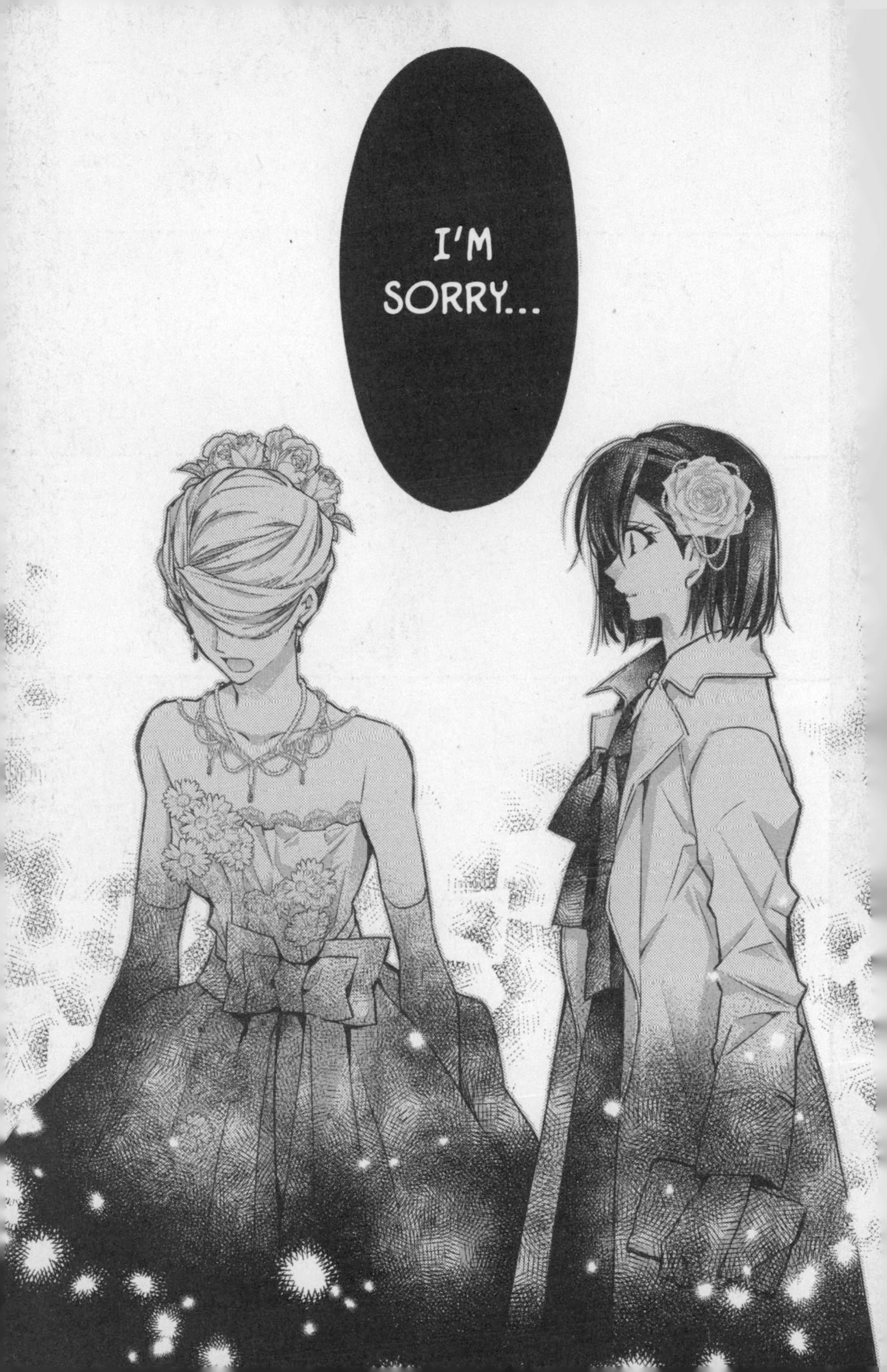
I'M SORRY...

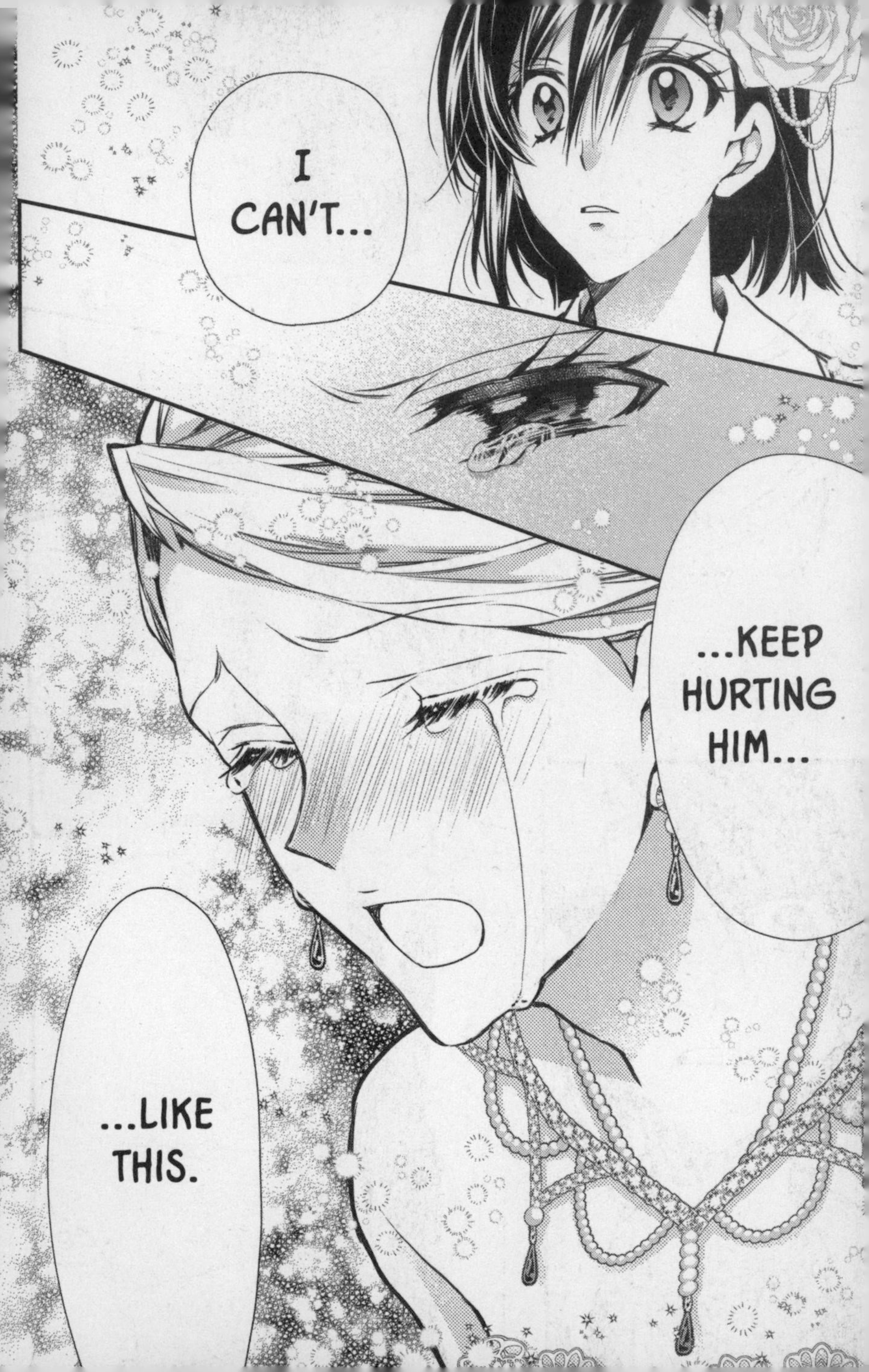
I CAN'T...
...KEEP HURTING HIM...
...LIKE THIS.

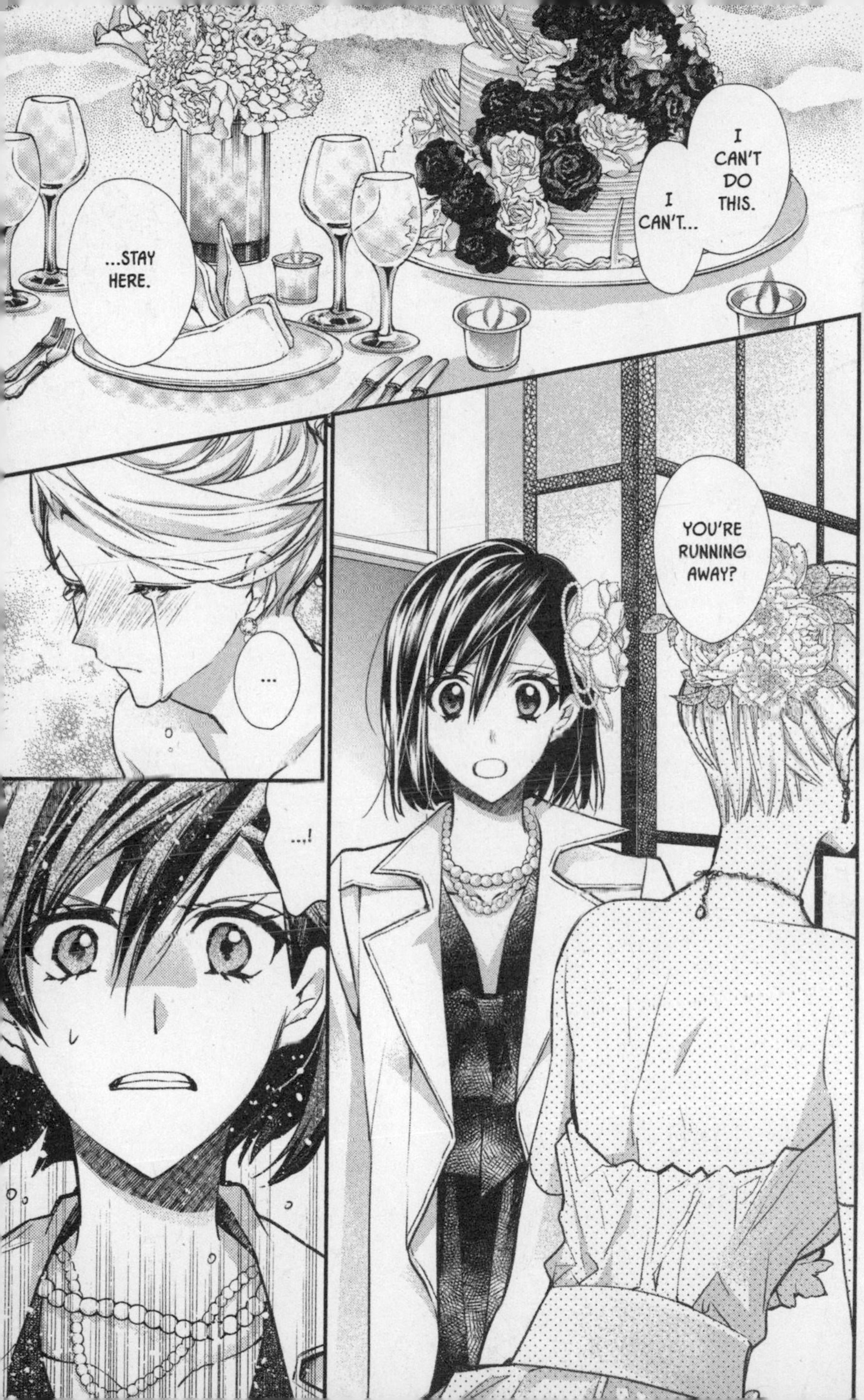
I CAN'T DO THIS.
I CAN'T...
...STAY HERE.
YOU'RE RUNNING AWAY?
...
...!

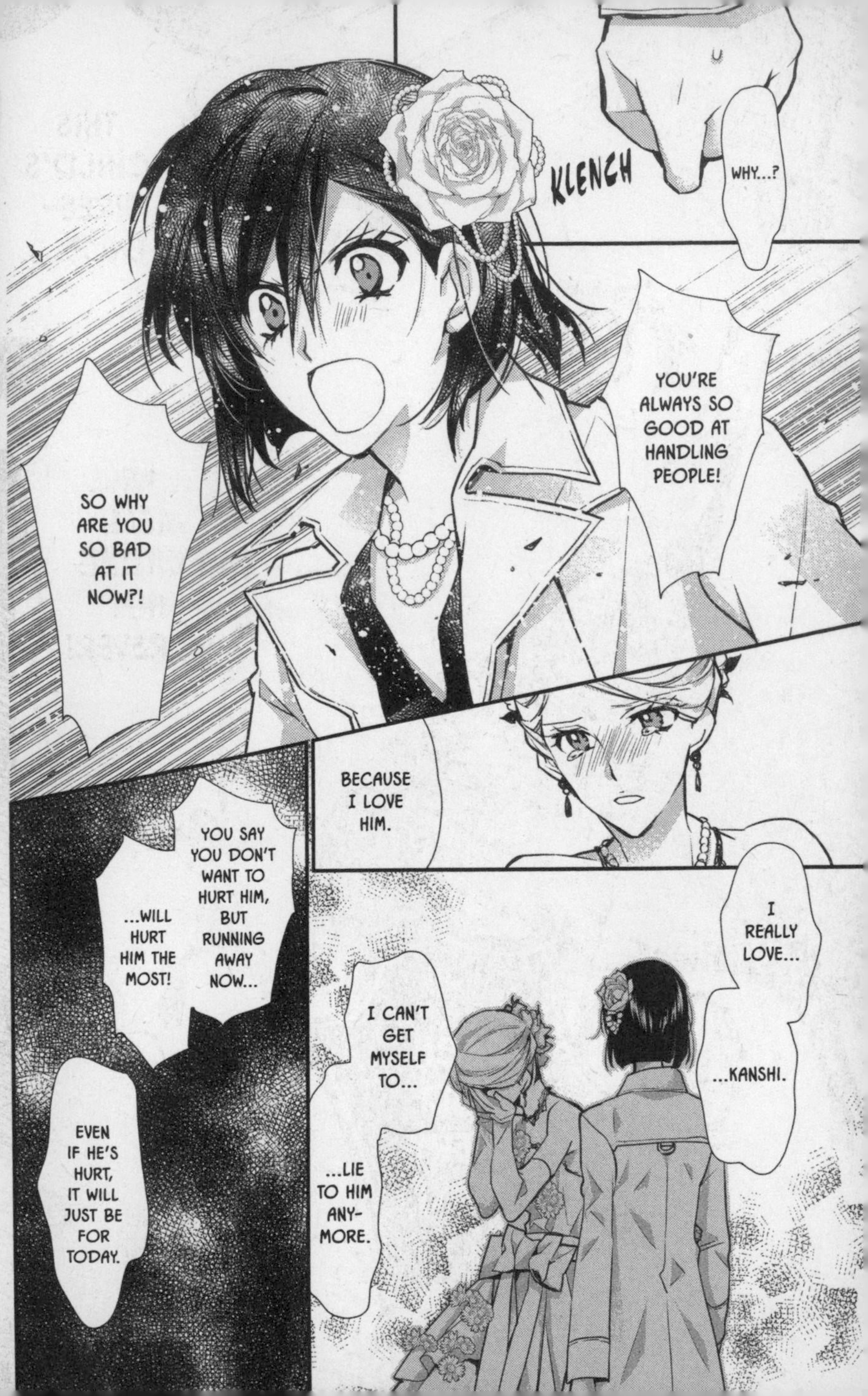
KLENCH
WHY...?
YOU'RE ALWAYS SO GOOD AT HANDLING PEOPLE!
SO WHY ARE YOU SO BAD AT IT NOW?!
BECAUSE I LOVE HIM.
I REALLY LOVE...
...KANSHI.
I CAN'T GET MYSELF TO...
...LIE TO HIM ANYMORE.
YOU SAY YOU DON'T WANT TO HURT HIM, BUT RUNNING AWAY NOW...
...WILL HURT HIM THE MOST!
EVEN IF HE'S HURT, IT WILL JUST BE FOR TODAY.

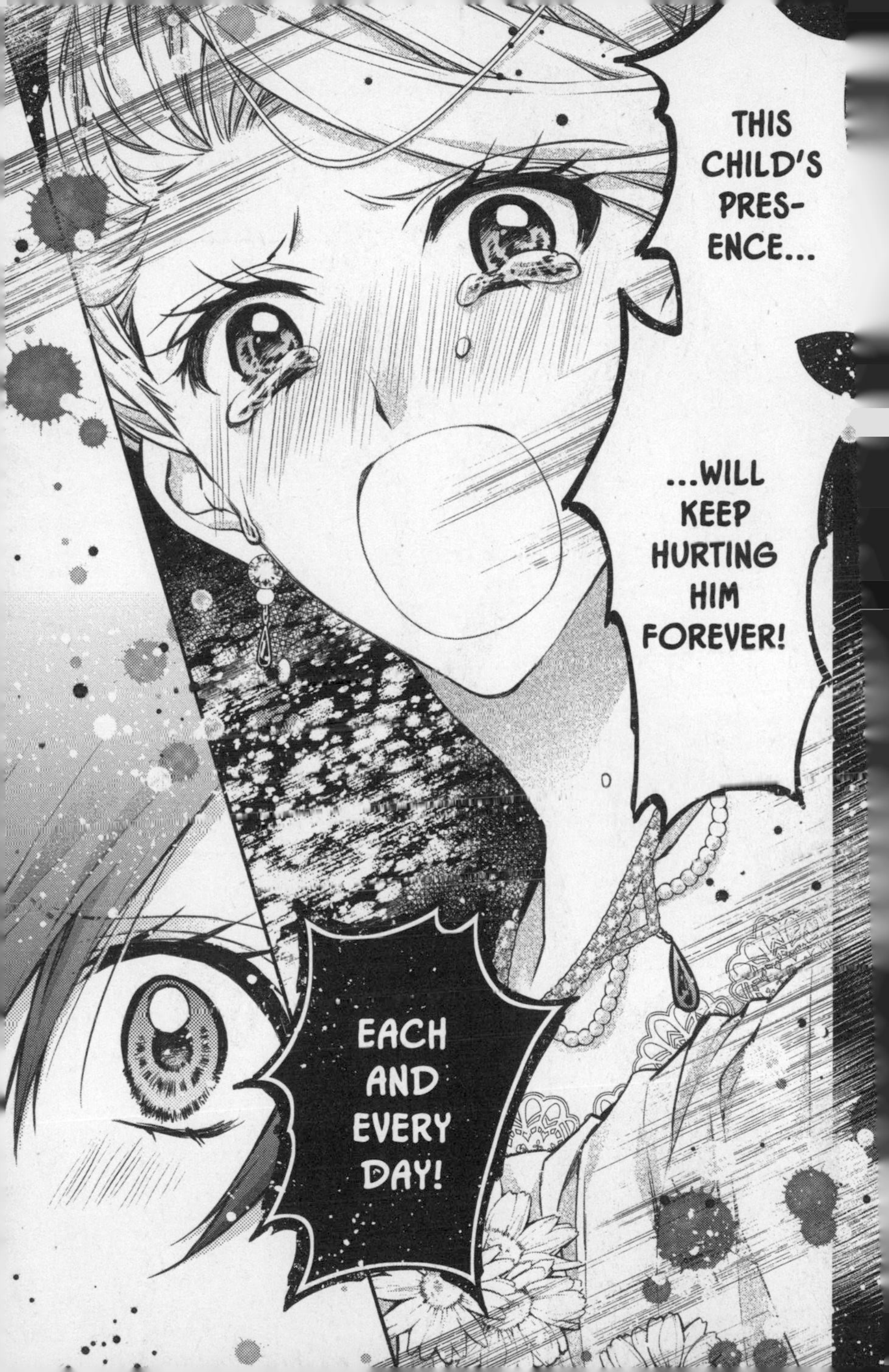
THIS CHILD'S PRES- ENCE...
...WILL KEEP HURTING HIM FOREVER!
EACH AND EVERY DAY!

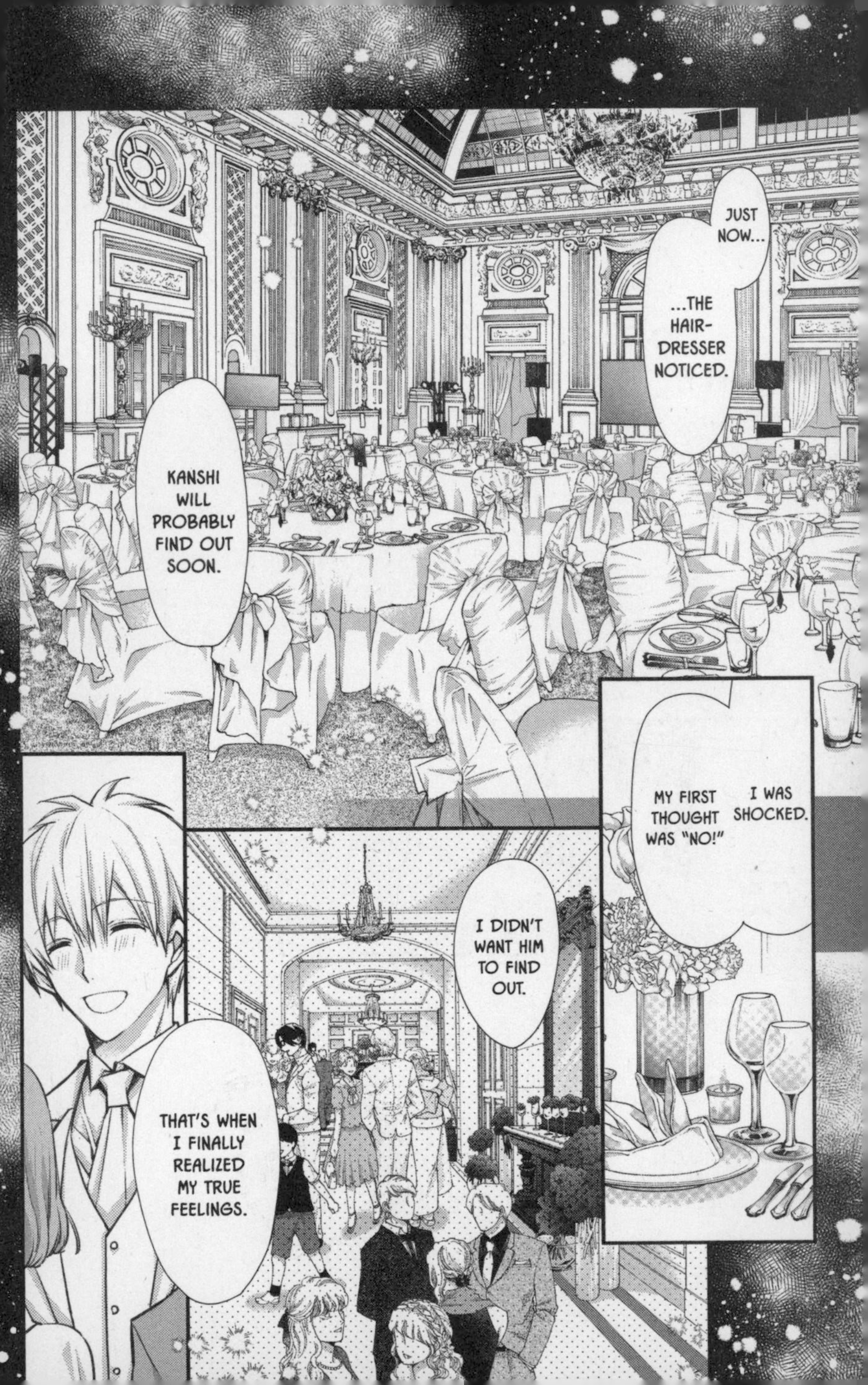
JUST NOW...
...THE HAIR-DRESSER NOTICED.
KANSHI WILL PROBABLY FIND OUT SOON.
I WAS SHOCKED.
MY FIRST THOUGHT WAS "NO!"
I DIDN'T WANT HIM TO FIND OUT.
THAT'S WHEN I FINALLY REALIZED MY TRUE FEELINGS.

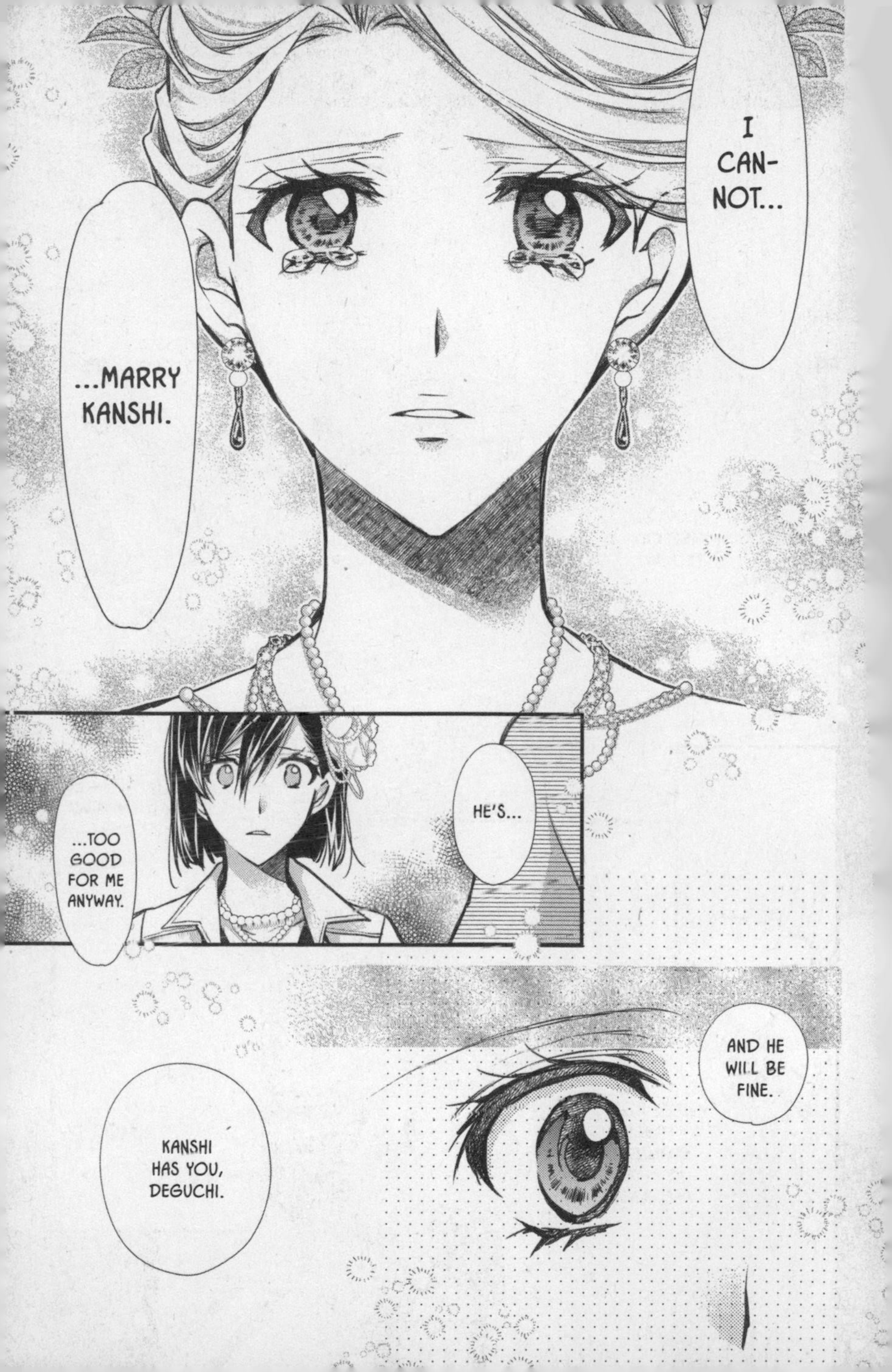
I CAN-NOT...
...MARRY KANSHI.
HE'S...
...TOO GOOD FOR ME ANYWAY.
AND HE WILL BE FINE.
KANSHI HAS YOU, DEGUCHI.

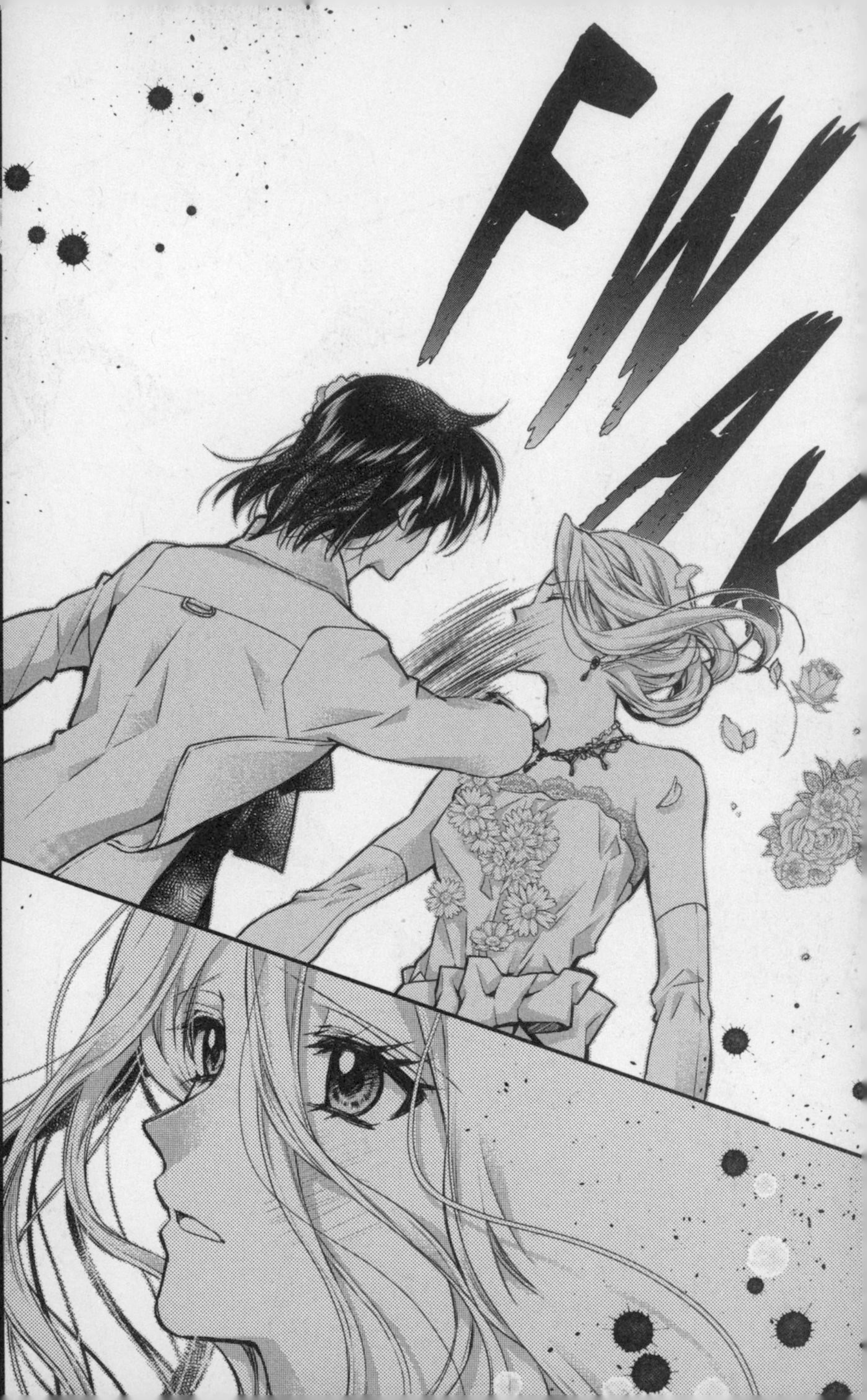
FWAK

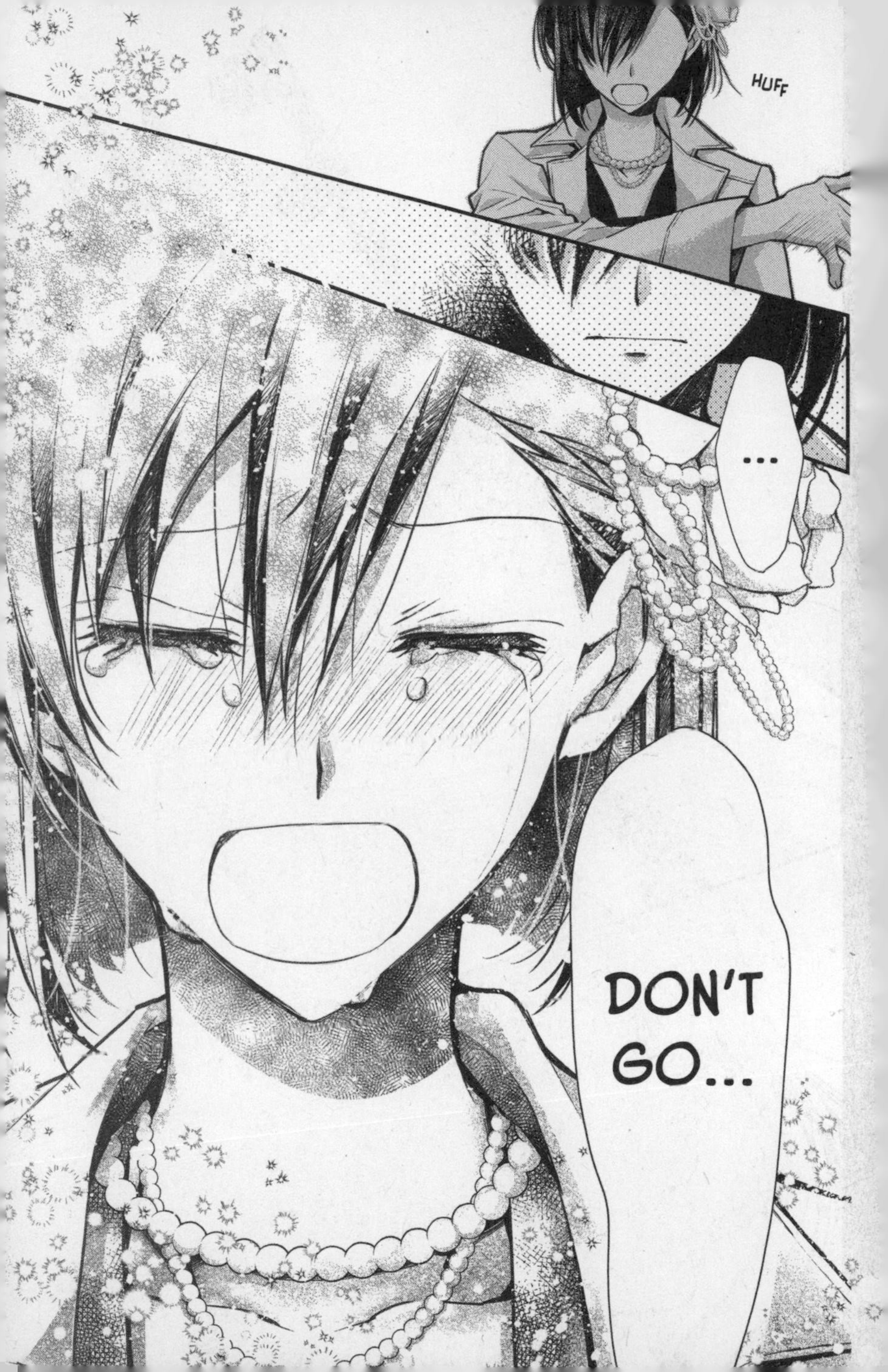
HUFF
...
DON'T GO...

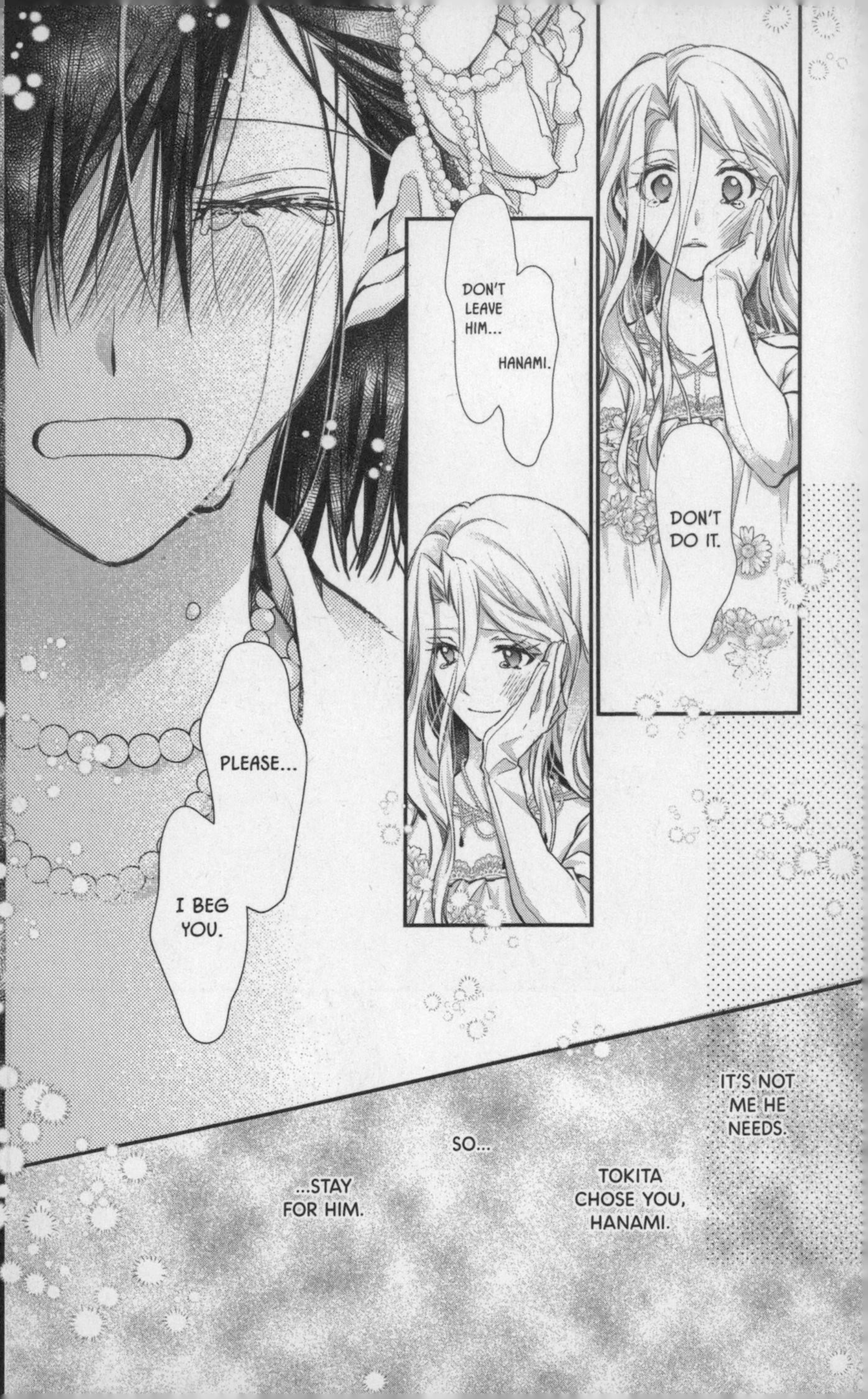
DON'T DO IT.
DON'T LEAVE HIM...
HANAMI.
PLEASE...
I BEG YOU.
IT'S NOT ME HE NEEDS.
TOKITA CHOSE YOU, HANAMI.
SO...
...STAY FOR HIM.

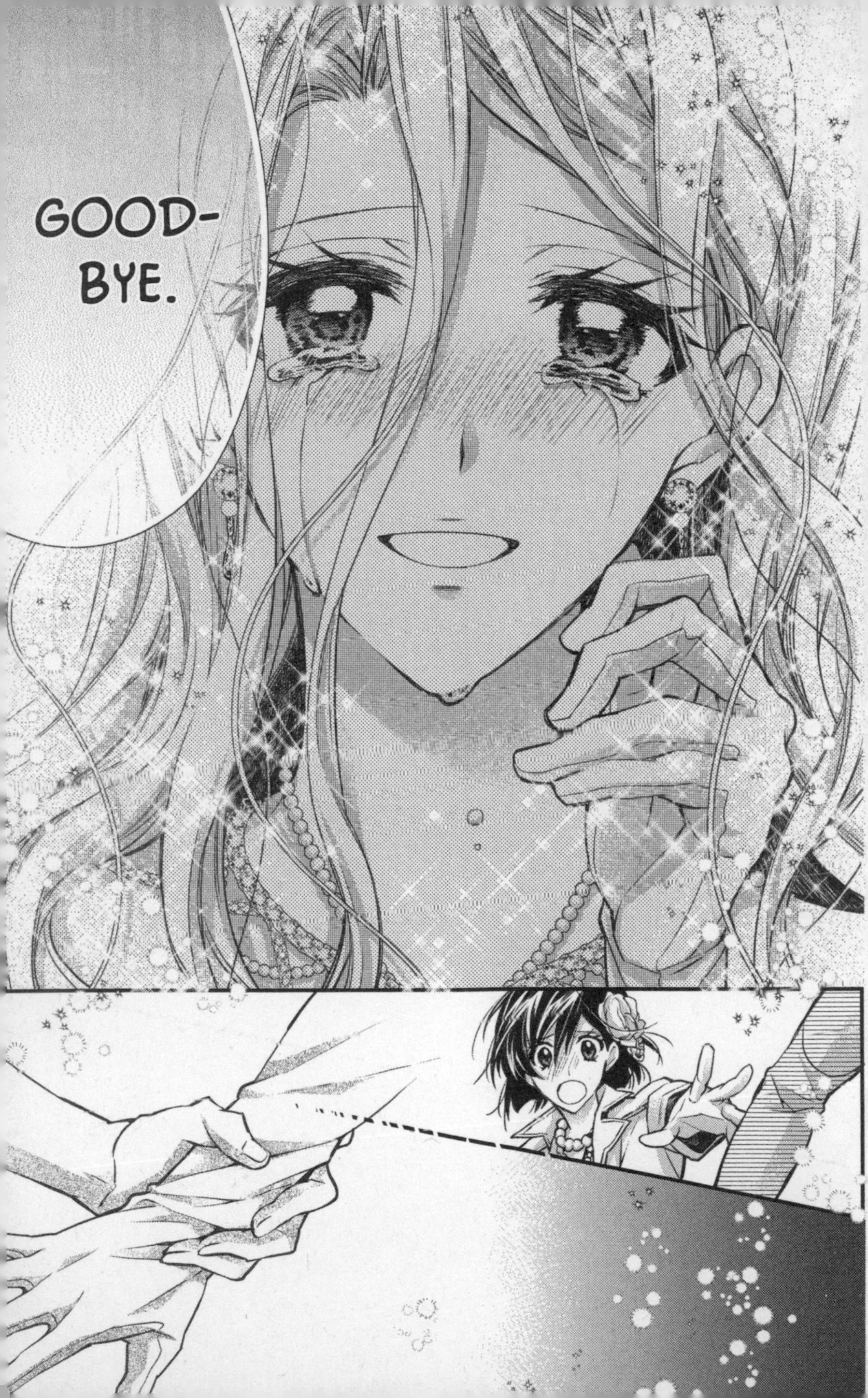
GOOD-
BYE.

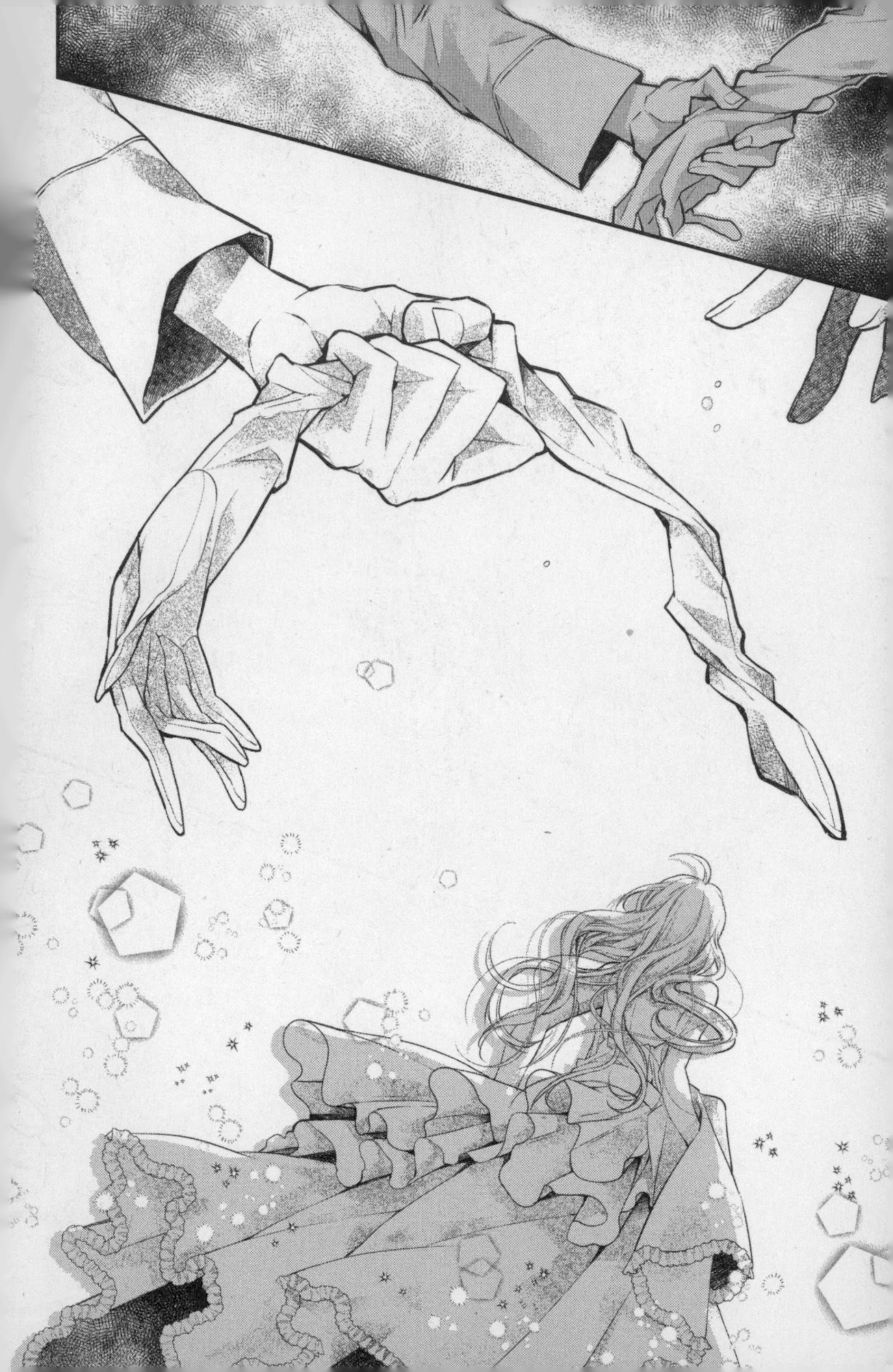

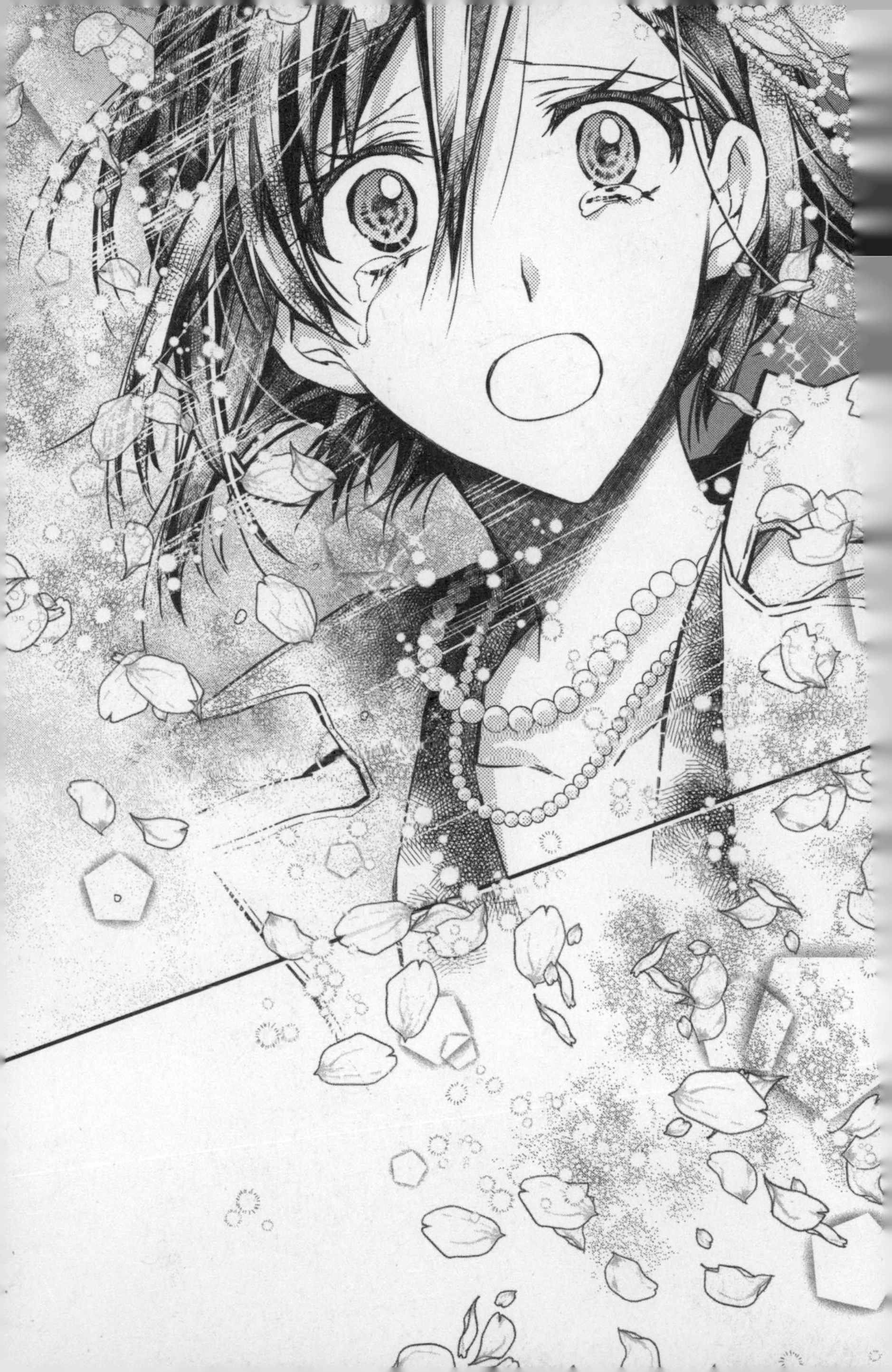

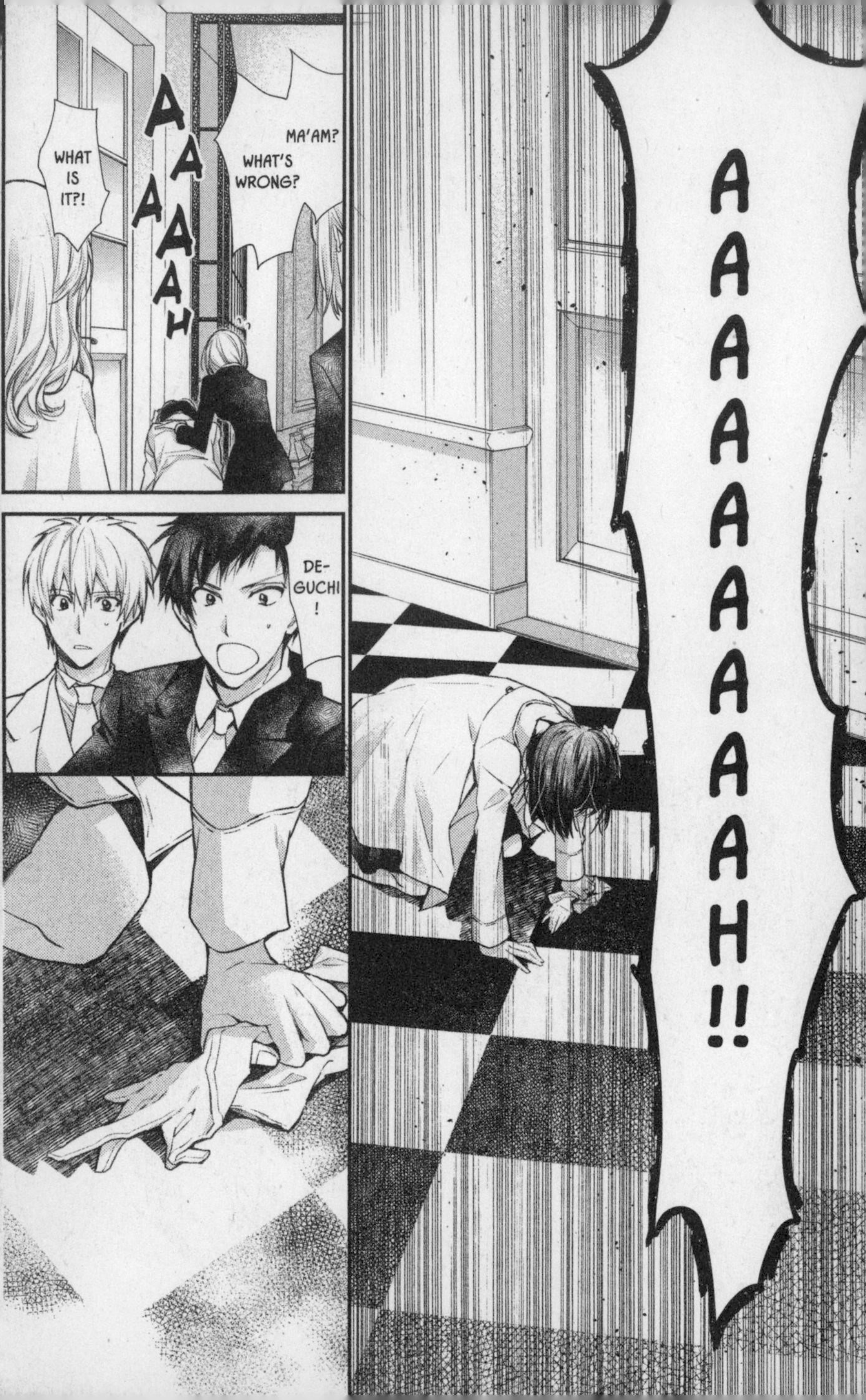
AAAAAAAAH!!
AAAAAH
MA'AM? WHAT'S WRONG?
WHAT IS IT?!
DE-GUCHI!

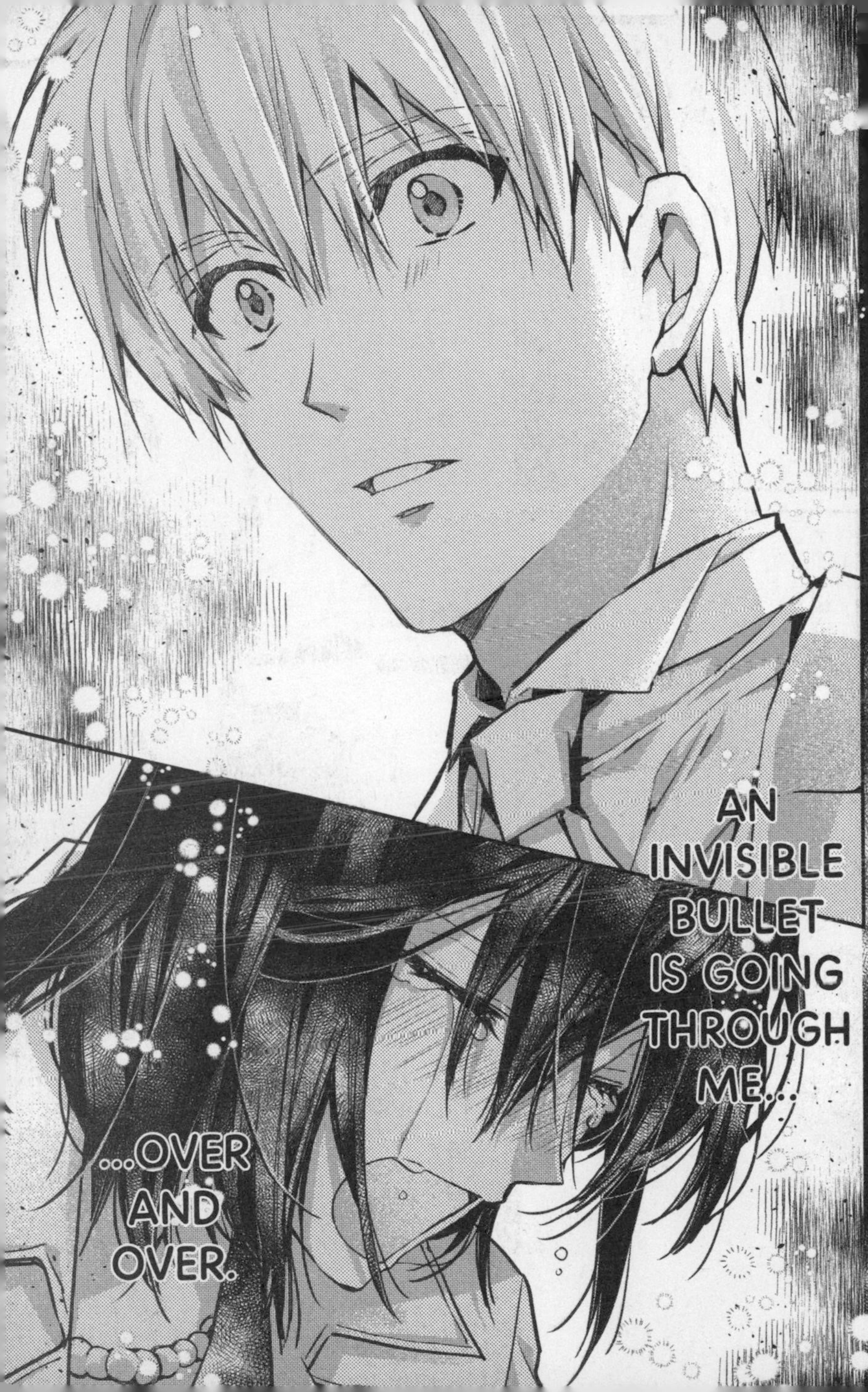
AN INVISIBLE BULLET IS GOING THROUGH ME...
...OVER AND OVER.

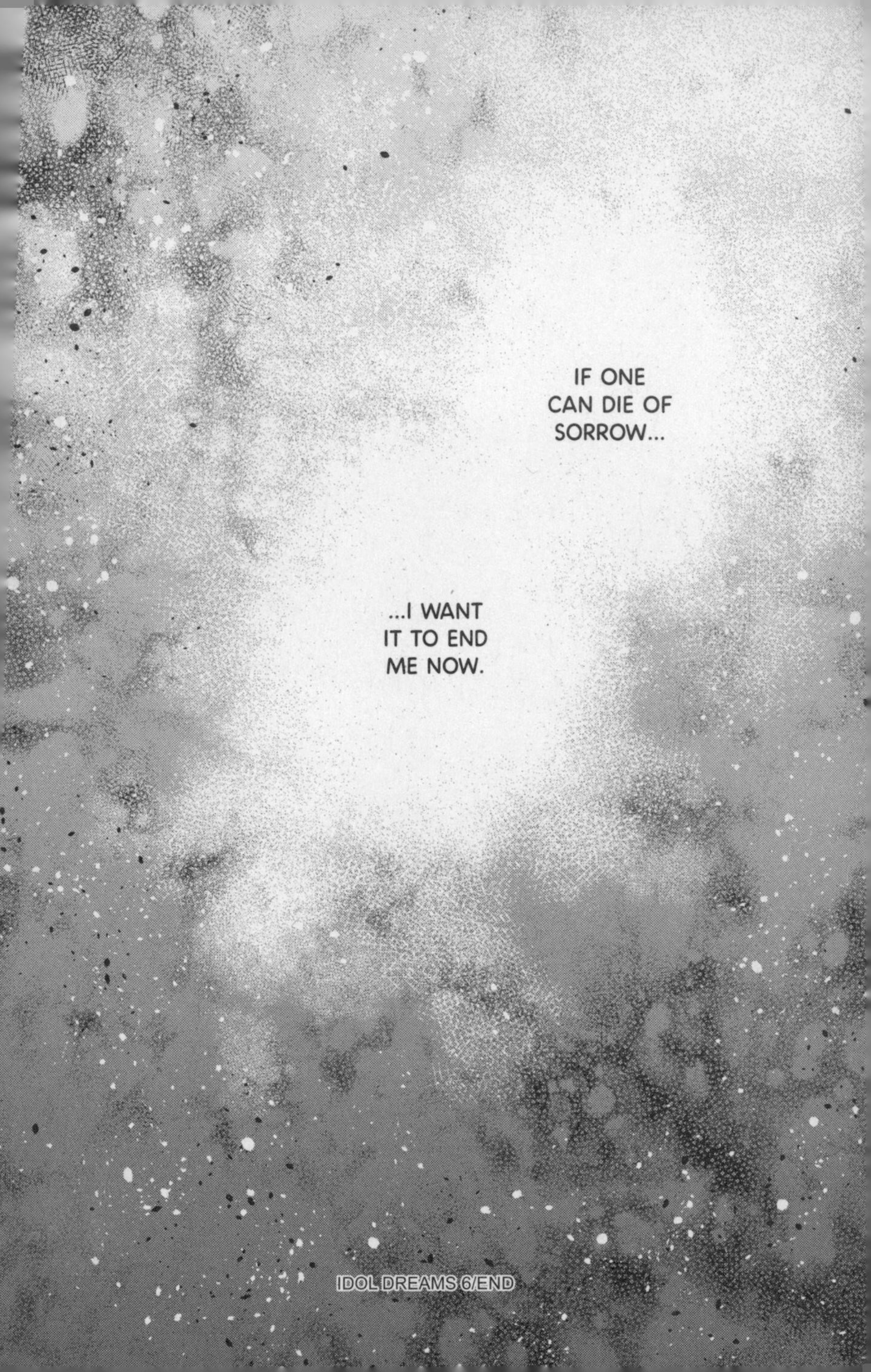
IF ONE CAN DIE OF SORROW...
...I WANT IT TO END ME NOW.
IDOL DREAMS 6/END

IDOL dreams

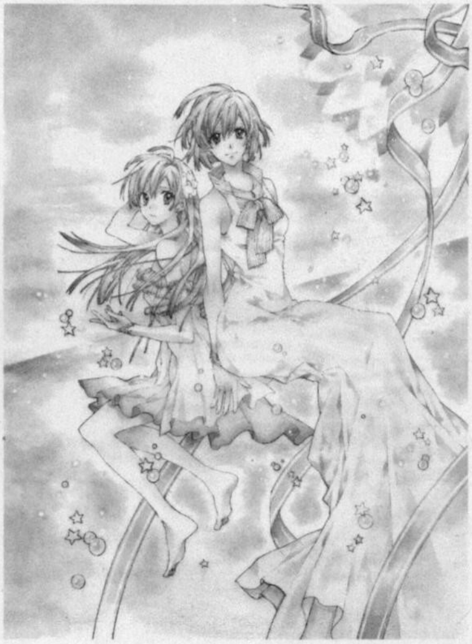

The chapters in this volume are very important to the story, and they've left a lasting impression on me. What are the emotions inside Chikage for her two friends who have lost something very important? What has disappeared from inside Chikage, and what has been born?

ARINA TANEMURA

Arina Tanemura began her manga career in 1996 when her short stories debuted in *Ribon Original* magazine. She gained fame with the 1997 publication of *I•O•N*, and ever since her debut Tanemura has been a major force in shojo manga with popular series *Phantom Thief Jeanne*, *Time Stranger Kyoko*, *Full Moon*, *The Gentlemen's Alliance †* and *Sakura Hime: The Legend of Princess Sakura*. Both *Phantom Thief Jeanne* and *Full Moon* have been adapted into animated TV series.

IDOL dreams 6

SHOJO BEAT EDITION

STORY & ART BY ARINA TANEMURA

TRANSLATION **Tetsuichiro Miyaki**
TOUCH-UP ART & LETTERING **Inori Fukuda Trant**
DESIGN **Natalie Chen**
EDITOR **Nancy Thistlethwaite**

Printed in Canada

Published by VIZ Media, LLC
P.O. Box 77010
San Francisco, CA 94107

10 9 8 7 6 5 4 3 2 1
First printing, August 2019

viz.com

shojobeat.com

STOP!
YOU MAY BE READING THE WRONG WAY!

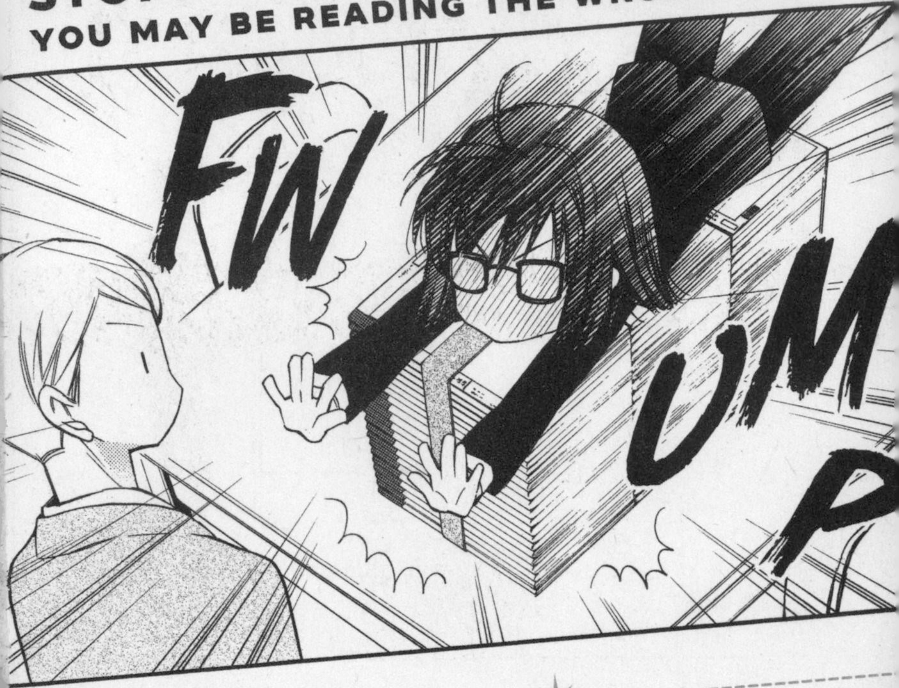
FWUMP

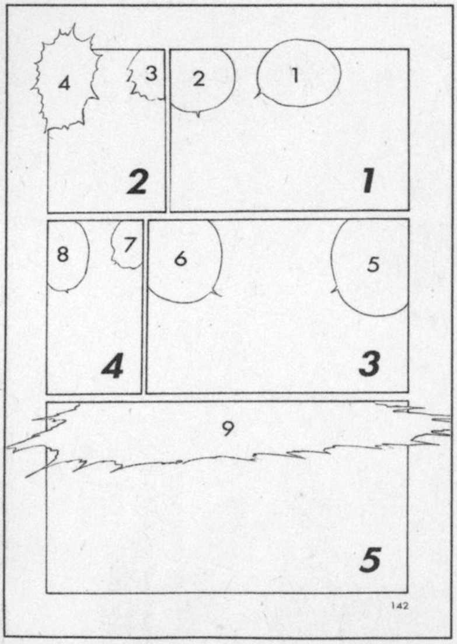
1
2
3
4
5
6
7
8
9
142

In keeping with the original Japanese comic format, this book reads from right to left—so action, sound effects and word balloons are completely reversed to preserve the orientation of the original artwork.

Check out the diagram shown here to get the hang of things, and then turn to the other side of the book to get started!